VBA For Dummi

D1298121

Displaying Windows

To Do This	Press
Display the Code window for the selected form or control	F7
Display the form corresponding to the active Code window	Shift+F7
Move to the next Code or UserForm window	Ctrl+Tab
Activate the Object Browser window	F2
Activate the Immediate window	Ctrl+G

VBA Data Types

Data Type	What It Stores	Range of Permitted Values
Boolean	Logical True or False	True (-1) or False (0)
Byte	Small whole number	0 to 255
Integer	Smallish whole number	-32,768 to 32,767
Long	Large whole number	-2,147,483,648 to 2,147,483,647
Single	Single-precision floating-point value	-3.402823E38 to -1.401298E-45 for negative values; 1.401298E-45 to 3.402823E38 for positive values
Double	Double-precision floating-point value	-1.79769313486232E308 to -4.94065645841247E-324 for negative values; 4.94065645841247E-324 to 1.79769313486232E308 for positive values
Currency	Large, precise number; 19 significant digits	-922,337,203,685,477.5808 to 922,337,203,685,477.5807 including four fixed decimal places
Decimal	Even larger, more precise numbers with 29 significant digits and up to 28 decimal places	+/-79,228,162,514,264,337,593,543,950,335 with no decimal point; +/-7.9228162514264337593543950335 with 28 places to the right of the decimal
Date	Dates and times	January 1, 100 to December 31, 9999
Object	VBA object	Any object reference
String	Sequence of text characters of variable length	0 to approximately 2 billion (variable length)
String	Sequence of specified number of text characters	1 to approximately 65,400 (fixed length)
Variant	Any valid data	Any numeric value up to the range of a Double; for strings, same range as for variable-length String
User-defined	Group of variables used together as a unit	The range of each variable (requires the Type statement) in the group corresponds to its data type, as shown in this table

For Dummies: Bestselling Book Series for Beginners

Working with Code Windows

To Do This	Press
Jump to the definition of the item at the insertion point	Shift+F2
Display the Find dialog box	Ctrl+F
Find Next (find the next occurrence of the Find text)	F3
Find Previous	Shift+F3
Replace	Ctrl+H
Jump to the previously edited line	Ctrl+Shift+F2
Undo	Ctrl+Z
List properties and methods	Ctrl+J
List constants	Ctrl+Shift+J
Display Quick Info about the variable or object at the insertion point	Ctrl+I
Display parameter information for the function at the insertion point	Ctrl+Shift+I
Automatically complete the word you're typing	Ctrl+spacebar
In the Property window, move to the next property in the list that begins with a particular letter	Ctrl+Shift+<letter>
Run the Sub procedure containing the insertion point or the UserForm in the active window	F5
Pause code execution and enter break mode	Ctrl+Break

Debugging

To Do This	Press
Execute code one line at a time (called *stepping* through code)	F8
Execute code one line at a time but without stepping into called procedures	Shift+F8
Jump out of a called procedure, returning to the code that had called it	Ctrl+Shift+F8
Run, stopping at the line containing the insertion point	Ctrl+F8
Specify (or *set*) the next statement to be executed	Ctrl+F9 (after placing the insertion point in the target statement)
Run the error handler code or return the error to the calling procedure	Alt+F5
Step into the error handler or return the error to the calling procedure	Alt+F8
Toggle a breakpoint on or off for the statement containing the insertion point	F9
Clear all breakpoints	Ctrl+Shift+F9

Hungry Minds™

For Dummies: Bestselling Book Series for Beginners

VBA

FOR

DUMMIES®

3RD EDITION

by Steve Cummings

Hungry Minds™

Best-Selling Books • Digital Downloads • e-Books • Answer Networks • e-Newsletters • Branded Web Sites • e-Learning

New York, NY ◆ Cleveland, OH ◆ Indianapolis, IN

VBA For Dummies, 3rd Edition

Published by
Hungry Minds, Inc.
909 Third Avenue
New York, NY 10022
www.hungryminds.com
www.dummies.com

Library of Congress Control Number: 2001086304

ISBN: 0-7645-0856-3

Printed in the United States of America

10 9 8 7 6 5 4 3

3B/RT/QW/QR/IN

Distributed in the United States by Hungry Minds, Inc.

Distributed by CDG Books Canada Inc. for Canada; by Transworld Publishers Limited in the United Kingdom; by IDG Norge Books for Norway; by IDG Sweden Books for Sweden; by IDG Books Australia Publishing Corporation Pty. Ltd. for Australia and New Zealand; by TransQuest Publishers Pte Ltd. for Singapore, Malaysia, Thailand, Indonesia, and Hong Kong; by Gotop Information Inc. for Taiwan; by ICG Muse, Inc. for Japan; by Intersoft for South Africa; by Eyrolles for France; by International Thomson Publishing for Germany, Austria and Switzerland; by Distribuidora Cuspide for Argentina; by LR International for Brazil; by Galileo Libros for Chile; by Ediciones ZETA S.C.R. Ltda. for Peru; by WS Computer Publishing Corporation, Inc., for the Philippines; by Contemporanea de Ediciones for Venezuela; by Express Computer Distributors for the Caribbean and West Indies; by Micronesia Media Distributor, Inc. for Micronesia; by Chips Computadoras S.A. de C.V. for Mexico; by Editorial Norma de Panama S.A. for Panama; by American Bookshops for Finland.

For general information on Hungry Minds' products and services please contact our Customer Care Department within the U.S. at 800-762-2974, outside the U.S. at 317-572-3993 or fax 317-572-4002.

For sales inquiries and reseller information, including discounts, premium and bulk quantity sales, and foreign-language translations, please contact our Customer Care Department at 800-434-3422, fax 317-572-4002, or write to Hungry Minds, Inc., Attn: Customer Care Department, 10475 Crosspoint Boulevard, Indianapolis, IN 46256.

For information on licensing foreign or domestic rights, please contact our Sub-Rights Customer Care Department at 212-884-5000.

For information on using Hungry Minds' products and services in the classroom or for ordering examination copies, please contact our Educational Sales Department at 800-434-2086 or fax 317-572-4005.

For press review copies, author interviews, or other publicity information, please contact our Public Relations Department at 317-572-3168 or fax 317-572-4168.

For authorization to photocopy items for corporate, personal, or educational use, please contact Copyright Clearance Center, 222 Rosewood Drive, Danvers, MA 01923, or fax 978-750-4470.

About the Author

Steve Cummings has been programming computers for over 20 years in languages as diverse as Assembler, Cobol, and C++, as well as VBA and Visual Basic. He is author or co-author of over ten computer books, including *Office 2000 Secrets* (published by Hungry Minds, Inc., then known as IDG Books Worldwide, Inc.). He has written hundreds of articles and columns — many on programming topics — for major computer magazines, including *PC World, Macworld, PC Magazine, PC/Computing,* and *PC Week*.

Dedication

For Grandmamoo on her 97th.

Acknowledgments

Thanks to everyone at Hungry Minds, especially my editors: James Russell, who has been a patient and skillful guide for this current edition of the book, and before him, Jade Williams and Kelly Oliver. I'm also indebted to V Communications (`www.v-com.com`) for providing me with their System Commander and Partition Commander software. These are great utilities for setting up separate operating systems on the same computer, something I needed to do to test the beta versions of Microsoft Office XP. Thanks also to Lisa Robbins of Waggener Edstrom, Microsoft's PR firm, for her help in tracking down technical info about the latest revision of VBA and in corralling review copies of the Microsoft products I needed.

Publisher's Acknowledgments

We're proud of this book; please send us your comments through our Hungry Minds Online Registration Form located at www.dummies.com.

Some of the people who helped bring this book to market include the following:

Acquisitions, Editorial, and Media Development

Project Editor: James H. Russell

Acquisitions Editor: Arlene Joy Pilkington

Copy Editor: Nicole A. Laux

Technical Editor: Namir Shammas

Editorial Manager: Kyle Looper

Senior Permissions Editor: Carmen Krikorian

Media Development Specialist:
Marisa Pearman

Media Development Manager:
Laura VanWinkle

Media Development Supervisor:
Richard Graves

Editorial Assistant: Jean Rogers

Production

Project Coordinator: Maridee Ennis

Layout and Graphics: Jackie Nicholas,
Jill Piscitelli, Julie Trippetti, Jeremey Unger

Proofreaders: Carl Pierce,
Dwight Ramsey, Charles Spencer,
TECHBOOKS Production Services

Indexer: TECHBOOKS Production Services

Special Help
Microsoft Corp.

General and Administrative

Hungry Minds, Inc.: John Kilcullen, CEO; Bill Barry, President and COO; John Ball, Executive VP, Operations & Administration; John Harris, CFO

Hungry Minds Technology Publishing Group: Richard Swadley, Senior Vice President and Publisher; Mary Bednarek, Vice President and Publisher, Networking and Certification; Walter R. Bruce III, Vice President and Publisher, General User and Design Professional; Joseph Wikert, Vice President and Publisher, Programming; Mary C. Corder, Editorial Director, Branded Technology Editorial; Andy Cummings, Publishing Director, General User and Design Professional; Barry Pruett, Publishing Director, Visual

Hungry Minds Manufacturing: Ivor Parker, Vice President, Manufacturing

Hungry Minds Marketing: John Helmus, Assistant Vice President, Director of Marketing

Hungry Minds Production for Branded Press: Debbie Stailey, Production Director

Hungry Minds Sales: Roland Elgey, Senior Vice President, Sales and Marketing; Michael Violano, Vice President, International Sales and Sub Rights

◆

The publisher would like to give special thanks to Patrick J. McGovern,
without whom this book would not have been possible.

◆

Contents at a Glance

Table of Contents

Introduction

· ·

*Y*es, this really is the book you need when you're starting out with VBA. With *VBA For Dummies,* 3rd Edition, you find out all the key concepts and skills you must have to write hot VBA (Visual Basic for Applications) programs that do genuinely useful things — and you discover all this stuff painlessly.

My approach in this book is casual and on the lighthearted side because goodness knows we have too many ponderous tomes in this world already. I explain everything in plain English, dumping the buzzword jargon overboard whenever possible. Now and then I throw in a bad joke, just to give you something to moan about.

On the other hand, I haven't dumbed-down or oversimplified the thornier topics. Jokes aside, this is a real reference book — it covers the essential VBA topics in enough depth that you'll actually want to refer to it later.

What the Book Covers

As you may know, VBA is the programming language built into many software applications, including everything from Microsoft Office, Microsoft Project, Visio, and AutoCAD to a host of specialized software in areas such as manufacturing, accounting, and help desk.

VBA For Dummies, 3rd Edition takes on all the essential aspects of VBA programming. You find complete information on the following topics:

- ✔ Taking charge of the VBA visual programming tools
- ✔ Recording and modifying macros
- ✔ Running VBA programs from within your applications
- ✔ Laying out lovely dialog boxes and other windows
- ✔ Working with objects, the key to tapping the power of VBA applications

This book covers VBA versions 6 through 6.3 (VBA 6.3 is the version of VBA included with Office XP applications). According to Microsoft, all sub-versions of VBA 6 up to and including version 6.3 are identical from the programmer's perspective. Microsoft has been fixing bugs and upgrading the performance of the VBA engine, but no changes have been made that affect the way you write code or create dialog boxes. So, when I refer to VBA 6, take that to mean VBA 6.0 and 6.3 and all versions in between.

I Shouldn't Make Any Assumptions . . .

But I have. I assume that you're not really a dummy at all — that instead, you already know how to use Windows quite comfortably. If you don't know how to work the mouse, make choices from menus, or click buttons on-screen, you should read one of the *Windows For Dummies* books (separate titles are available for all editions of Windows from Hungry Minds, Inc.) before you start on this book. To use VBA, you need at least one application that comes with the VBA software development environment built in. Again, applications that qualify include the mainstream Microsoft Office business software, along with a growing number of non-Microsoft products. Among many possibilities, any of the following Windows applications will do just fine:

- ✔ Any Microsoft Office application beginning with Office 97, including Word, Excel, PowerPoint, Access, Outlook, or FrontPage
- ✔ Microsoft Project
- ✔ Corel Draw version 9 or 10 and Corel WordPerfect Office 2000
- ✔ Micrografx iGrafx series of business graphics applications
- ✔ Visio 4.5, 5, or 2000
- ✔ AutoCAD Release 14, 2000, and 2000i for Windows
- ✔ Autodesk Map
- ✔ TurboCAD Professional
- ✔ M.Y.O.B Accounting Software
- ✔ Great Plains accounting software (certain products include VBA)
- ✔ OmniTrader, a securities trading analysis and management tool

Divide and Conquer

The skills and theoretical concepts you need to program with VBA form a seamless whole, an organic synthesis, an interdependent web like the circle of life. . . . Even so, I couldn't write about everything all at once, so I broke up the material into five parts, each of which contains two or more chapters.

Part 1: VBA Boot Camp

After just one chapter of dull theoretical stuff at the very beginning of the book, four quick chapters get you up and running with VBA. You find out how to record macros to avoid programming whenever possible and how to run your own VBA programs within your applications. You even get to write a complete working program. And you learn all about the VBA programming environment, officially called the Visual Basic Editor.

Part II: VBA Programming Essentials

Here is the heart of the book. In chapter after lovingly written chapter, I spread out before you the secrets of the VBA realm. The first chapter in the section catalogues the components of a VBA program and details their structures so that you know what to type where. This chapter also includes a practicum on the proper ways to name things in VBA and make your code presentable. A chapter on working with variables to skillfully manipulate information follows in turn. Other chapters explore techniques for controlling what happens while your program runs and for locating and correcting at least some of the bugs your program is bound to have. Part II closes with an introduction to laying out custom windows and dialog boxes — called *forms* in VBA — and the programming techniques required to get them to do your bidding.

Part III: Stretching Out

Several chapters with slightly more advanced topics comprise Part III. First, I take you on a tour of the abundant VBA built-in commands so that you won't have to reinvent the fission reactor. Next comes a chapter on programming with objects, a critical skill for realizing the full potential of VBA for customizing applications such as Word, Excel, or Corel Draw. The final chapter covers techniques for handling data in organized sets, especially arrays and collections.

Part IV: The Part of Tens

Two chapters on miscellaneous topics complete your tour of the VBA experience. First, I introduce a slew of advanced programming topics. The coverage isn't extremely deep, of course, but it's not overly shallow either — it's enough to get you started with actually using the capabilities. Next comes a catalogue of other VBA resources, including both information and software products. Turn here to enrich your knowledge of VBA programming and to fill your programmer's kit with software tools.

Bonus Part: Extras

Because this book just doesn't have enough pages to touch on a number of topics that are vital to the serious beginning VBA programmer, I've included this extra part on the CD-ROM. Lucky for you, this part is even indexed and listed in the book's Table of Contents, so you can see what's in those chapters without actually opening them first. In these chapters, you acquire programming tools that work across most of the Office applications, including techniques for customizing the user interface, programming the Office Assistant — which most often appears as that bouncy paperclip guy — and storing your program's data in the document that it pertains to. Further chapters hone in on programming details for Word and Excel, respectively — the most widely used VBA applications, and the later chapters are applicable to all VBA programmers, regardless of the application they're working in.

How to Use the Examples

Peppered throughout *VBA For Dummies,* 3rd Edition are examples of code that illustrate the concepts I try to get across. Code samples are indicated in monospaced type, either in a separate block, like this

```
WhatEverItIs.Color = "Chartreuse"
```

or, within ordinary paragraph text, like this: `Debug.Print`.

To minimize bulk, these samples are often just fragments that you can't run by themselves. VBA statements only run when they're inside a procedure, and many of the examples don't include the statements that define the procedure. The point is that if you want to really run the samples in your own copy of VBA, you're going to have to enclose them inside a procedure (and in some cases add additional code, as I explain in the text). On the CD-ROM, these source code examples do appear as complete procedures, so you can import them into a project and run them without any further work.

Because VBA statements (individual units of programming code) often run quite long, they tend not to fit within the book's margins. In general, I use the VBA line continuation character, the underscore (_), to indicate where a single statement is broken up over two lines.

Also, I use the following conventions in this book:

- ✔ When I want you to open an item in a menu, I write something like "choose File⇨Open." This means, "Pull down the File menu and choose the Open command."

- ✔ New terms are set off in italics, *like this.*

- ✔ Italic monofont, which looks `like_this`, shows parts of commands you need to change.
- ✔ Stuff you're supposed to type appears in bold type, **like this**.
- ✔ Sometimes an entire sentence is in bold, as you'll see when we present a numbered list of steps. **In those cases, we debold what you're supposed to type,** like this.

What's on the CD-ROM

I claim that typing code builds moral fiber, but I realize that argument may not impress some of you. Therefore, I've gallantly included the code for the longer examples in the text on the CD-ROM stuck to the back cover of this book. See the "About the CD-ROM" appendix for information on how to use this stuff.

In addition, I collected on the CD a variety of shareware, trial, and demonstration versions of various software products that you may find useful in VBA programming. I mention these, too, in more depth in the appendix.

Icons Used in This Book

By now, you've probably seen more than a few books that use icons in the margin to help you key in on important information. I settled on only four icons for this book, so the icons themselves won't need their own guidebook.

The Remember icon marks any kind of information that I think needs emphasis — either because it's an easier way to accomplish something or because the important stuff comes a few paragraphs after the last heading, and I was worried you might skip over it.

Finding out how to program in VBA is fun and easy, sure, if you're comparing it to physical chemistry or Sanskrit. But there's no question that VBA programming is more technically complex than working with Windows or ordinary software. In other words, the paragraphs I mark with the Technical Stuff icon aren't that much more technical than the other material. The icon does improve the book's design though, don't you think?

Ka-boom!

I mark the longer code examples with this icon just to reassure you that you won't have to retype them if you want to try them out in real life. If the icon is missing, don't worry — many of the shorter examples are on the disk, too, but I didn't want to crowd the book with icons.

The VBA For Dummies Web Site (s)

There are six chapters that are on both the CD-ROM and available for download at the book's home page at the following URL:

```
www.dummies.com/bonus/0764508563
```

Also, I'll put up my own Web page to accompany this book at the following address:

```
www.seldenhouse.com/vba
```

If all goes well, the latter site will include

- ✔ Updates and corrections to the text.
- ✔ Downloadable source code as I get my hands on it.
- ✔ Links to other VBA sites, including the relevant pages for specific VBA applications.

Don't expect fancy page layout or lots of entertaining graphics at this site — I'll concentrate on posting useful information instead. Please let me know if you come across any tips or solutions that other people should know about, or if you have suggestions for links to other sites.

Part I
VBA Boot Camp

The 5th Wave   By Rich Tennant

"Hey Philip! I think we're in. I'm gonna try linking directly to the screen, but gimme a disguise in case it works. I don't want all of New York to know Jerry DeMarco of 14 Queensberry, Bronx NY, hacked into the Times Square video screen."

In this part . . .

Chapter 1 introduces all the basic concepts that underlie the VBA programming experience. These ideas really are vital, I promise — until you understand them, serious work with VBA will be painful at best. But from then on, *VBA For Dummies,* 3rd Edition gets fiercely practical. Chapters 2 through 4 introduce the mechanics of recording macros, writing VBA code, and running your recorded macros and the programs you write. Chapter 5 takes you on a complete tour of the Visual Basic Editor, the software workshop for writing VBA programs. After acquainting yourself with the information in this part of the book, you'll own the fundamental skills for bringing VBA to life in your own programs. You still won't know what to put in those programs, but that's why this book has another ten chapters.

Chapter 1

Don't Sweat the Technical Stuff — and It's All Technical Stuff

● ●

In This Chapter

▶ What VBA programs are good for

▶ How VBA programs interact with your applications

▶ Planning, writing code, designing forms, and testing your work

▶ Why VBA isn't as standardized a standard as you might think

● ●

*T*hese days, software programs intended for professional use are overflowing with interesting, clever, and powerful features. But no matter how sophisticated the software, chances are that you can find something in it that needs improvement.

That's where VBA comes in. If the design of your software is too constricting, VBA can help you let out the waistline for a fit that's quite comfortable — and perfectly tailored to your curves and bulges.

Why Bother with VBA?

You should get up close and personal with VBA if you want to customize your software for yourself or other people.

After all, a computer is useless to you unless it does what you want. Visual Basic for Applications — that's what VBA stands for — is a set of programming tools for developing your own software. As the name suggests, VBA is designed for customizing existing *applications*. An *application*, of course, is a full-scale computer program that does practical work such as a word processor or database as opposed to a *utility*, which helps your computer system run smoothly.

With VBA, you can tweak the way an application looks and works, or even add entirely new features. The following are some situations in which VBA may be the right solution:

- ✔ A feature you rely on heavily is buried deep in a dialog box somewhere. Why not place that command on a toolbar button so you can activate it with one click of the mouse? And wouldn't it be slick to have the button appear only when you actually need that command?

- ✔ You often repeat the same series of commands. Wouldn't you like to have the program memorize those steps so that you can launch the whole sequence with one command?

- ✔ Your software just isn't equipped with a feature or two you really need. Why not add the missing commands yourself?

VBA enables you to make any of these modifications, and more — you can even build complete, custom programs of your own using VBA. See the section "More about What You Can Do with VBA," later in this chapter, to explore the possibilities.

Want another reason to get on board the VBA express? Try this one: VBA is now well established as a standard in the software industry. After you've figured out VBA, you can put it to use in any application that's equipped with VBA. (However, each VBA application you work with has its own special VBA jargon. For details, see the section "VBA is a standard — sort of," later in this chapter.)

If you know VBA, you automatically know a good deal of Visual Basic, a closely related programming tool. Also a Microsoft product, Visual Basic is one of the most popular software development tools on the planet and is used to create everything from simple shareware utilities to complex, major-league applications.

By the way, one other advantage of the VBA standard is that you need to install only one copy of the special support files that VBA requires for all the applications that use VBA. In a standard installation, the VBA *DLLs* (*Dynamic Link Libraries*) and related files are located in the folder \Program Files\ Common Files\Microsoft Shared\VBA.

VBA Is the Steering Wheel, but You Still Need the Car

Okay, so VBA is great for customizing applications. There's only one catch, however — VBA must be built into the application you're trying to modify. (In this book, I use the term *VBA applications* for applications that have VBA capability built in. I refer to the software you create with VBA as *VBA programs*.)

Microsoft created VBA and builds it into its flagship applications in the Office XP Suite (VBA is also included in Office 2000 and Office 97 applications). Word, Excel, Access, PowerPoint, and Outlook are all equipped with VBA. In Outlook, you use a simplified version of VBA called VBScript to add custom functionality to forms, whereas you use the full-fledged version of VBA to customize Outlook itself. VBA is also built into FrontPage, the Microsoft Web page authoring and Web site management tool (included with some versions of Office); Visio, the popular business graphics package; and Project, the Microsoft project management entry.

Non-Microsoft VBA applications

Microsoft also licenses its VBA technology to many other software developers. Here's a sampling of the non-Microsoft VBA applications now available:

- ✔ **Corel WordPerfect Office 2000:** A competitor to Microsoft Office, the Corel WordPerfect suite includes word processing, spreadsheet, database, and presentations applications.

- ✔ **Corel Draw:** The most popular PC graphics package, Corel Draw and its suite-mates enables you to create and edit both "draw"-style illustrations and "paint"-style graphics for use in print or Web page layouts.

- ✔ **AutoCAD:** A hugely successful Computer Aided Design application — several other programs from the same publisher are also VBA applications.

- ✔ **M.Y.O.B. Accounting:** A complete accounting package for small businesses.

- ✔ **Micrografx iGrafx series:** Business graphics applications for laying out flowcharts and organization charts and for modeling business operations graphically. A demo of iGrafx Professional is included on this book's CD-ROM.

- ✔ **OmniTrader:** A securities tracking and analysis application.

 You can buy applications that include programming tools similar to but different from VBA. Although you can customize these applications in much the same way as you can VBA applications, VBA programs don't run in these non-VBA applications.

The range of VBA applications

Applications of just about every type are more powerful when you can customize them easily. For this reason, you should see VBA popping up in all kinds of software, from the mainstream to the highly specialized.

With millions and millions of copies of Microsoft Office in circulation, the Office applications are about as mainstream as you can get. Non-Microsoft VBA applications with broad appeal include WordPerfect, Corel Draw, and AutoCAD. Many other VBA applications are designed for very narrow, highly specialized markets. One example is manufacturing control applications, the kind that run robotic production lines. Another example is help desk applications, which a company's technical support staff use to help customers or other employees solve problems. VBA has also found a home in software for sales force automation, civil engineering, telephony, data warehousing, document management, financial services, and the legal and healthcare industries.

VBA has also been licensed by a number of corporations that aren't in the business of selling software. These companies are developing their own in-house applications designed for the specific needs of each firm. Even so, they're building in VBA so that their applications can be further customized and extended with a minimum of hassle.

Programming with VBA

In essence, programming a computer means simply telling it what to do. For example, you may tell the computer to

- Display a window full of interesting buttons and menus.
- Summon a box asking you to type in your birth date.
- Click a Calculate Age button that figures your age based on the birth date you typed in.

Because computers don't understand human languages, programming traditionally required you to type program *code* — a list of instructions — using the terminology of a special programming language. VBA eliminates the need to type code to define the way your program looks on-screen. However, coding is still required in programs of any complexity. Part of VBA is a programming language. Here's an example of some VBA code:

```
Sub SelectNextQuestion()
  If SelectionStrategy = Randomly Then
  AskRandomQuestion
  Else If CurrentQuestion = TotalQuestions Then
  CurrentQuestion = 1
  Else
  CurrentQuestion = CurrentQuestion + 1
  End If
End Sub
```

If you read this code carefully, you may be able to guess what it's supposed to do because the VBA language has a lot in common with ordinary English — thankfully. But it's still a foreign language, so don't worry if it looks like gibberish. One of the major goals of this book is to make you comfortable writing VBA code.

What's so visual about Visual Basic for Applications?

Fortunately, VBA eliminates a lot of code-typing drudgery. For one thing, you can record the commands you use in your application as a starting point for a new program.

For another, VBA enables you to design the parts of your program that appear on-screen (dialog boxes, buttons, check boxes, and so on) by drawing them with the mouse or picking options from dialog boxes — a capability that makes VBA a visual programming tool. With VBA, you can slap together the on-screen structure of your program in no time flat. In contrast, you may take hours, days, maybe years if you have to type in the necessary program code to define and display these same elements.

Unfortunately, VBA can't guess what you want your program to do. You still have to type the code that defines the function of each button, check box, and so on in your program. Even if your program has no buttons or check boxes, you still have to write code for the steps it should follow when it runs.

The main events

In VBA, an *event* is something that happens while your program is running, in order to change what the program does. The obvious example is clicking the mouse button. When the user of your program clicks a button labeled Calculate Age, that action is an event. Likewise, each time the user presses a key on the keyboard, double-clicks the mouse button, or simply moves the mouse, an event occurs.

Of course, your program can't respond to these events by telepathy. Au contraire, you have to write an *event procedure,* a special snippet of VBA code, for each event that you want your program to recognize. You need one event procedure to respond to clicks on the Calculate Age button, but another if you want the program to do something when the mouse just points to the button without clicking. Of course, if you have another button labeled Lie about Age, you have to supply yet another event procedure for clicks on that button. In Chapter 10, I detail writing event procedures.

The programming cycle

No matter what programming tool you use, you can boil down the process of creating any new software program into the following five simple steps:

1. **Design.**

   Decide what the program is supposed to do, how it should look on-screen, and how it should interact with other software.

2. **Implement.**

   To get the results you planned for in Step 1, construct the windows and other elements the program will display on-screen, and then type the necessary code. This part is fun.

3. **Test.**

   Run the program to see whether it looks right and does what you want. It won't.

4. **Debug.**

   Hunt through the code until you find out what's wrong and then correct it (like all good programming tools, VBA gives you special features to help with the debugging process).

5. **Keep testing.**

   Repeat Steps 3 and 4 until you're too tired or hungry to go on.

Fortunately, you don't have to memorize these steps — they become second nature as soon as you start VBA programming in earnest.

More about What You Can Do with VBA

In the section "Why Bother with VBA?" earlier in this chapter, I mention the different ways you can customize your software using VBA. It's time to explore these in greater depth, just so you know what's possible with VBA.

Before you get carried away with your customization plans, remember that how much you can accomplish with VBA depends on the application with which you're working. Some programs let you redefine every element of the user interface and every built-in command, and they give you a wealth of building blocks with which you can construct your own new features. In other applications, you're much more limited.

Customizing the user interface

You can use VBA to change an application's user interface to match the user's work habits and personal style. (*User interface* means the way the program looks on-screen, how the mouse and keyboard work, and any other means the program provides for the user and the software to communicate.) In many applications, VBA permits you to alter the user interface elements as you see fit. With a few lines of code, you can add, delete, or rearrange the buttons on the toolbars, create new toolbars, redefine the keyboard layout, or modify the menu structure. Figure 1-1 shows Microsoft Word with a user interface modification courtesy of VBA.

Of course, you don't use a blowtorch when a match will do — and VBA is often overkill for simple user interface customizations. Many of today's applications allow you to customize the user interface without any programming at all, via drag-and-drop or dialog boxes.

Still, VBA can come in handy even with these applications. For one thing, even highly customizable applications may not let you change certain parts of the interface without VBA. Most importantly, VBA enables you to orchestrate automatic changes in the user interface — changes that occur while the application is running, based on what you're currently doing with the program.

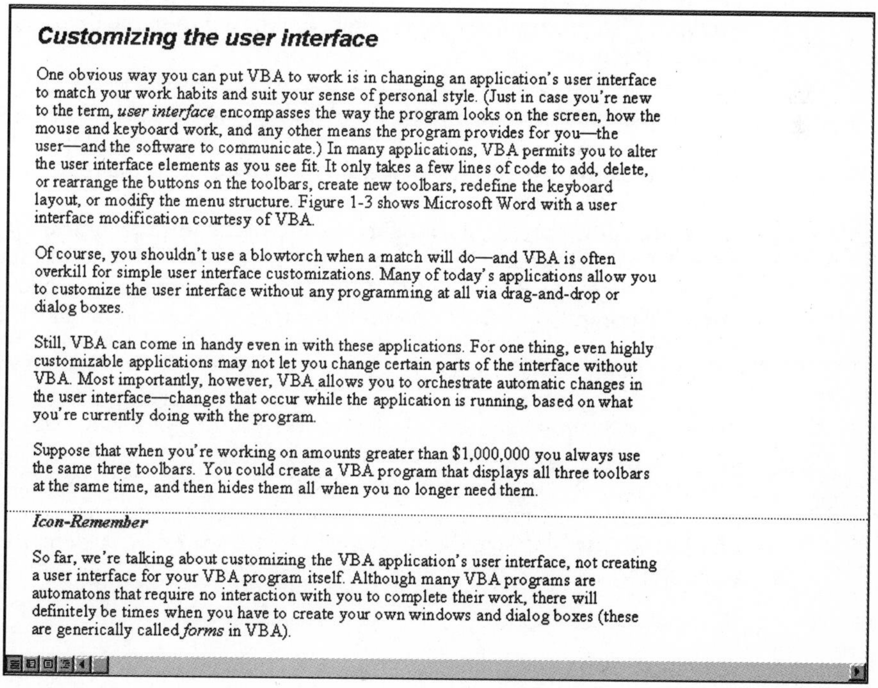

Figure 1-1:
You need
VBA to
work on
Microsoft
Word
documents
with a
completely
clean
screen —
that is, with
no toolbars
visible at all.

Customizing the user interface

One obvious way you can put VBA to work is in changing an application's user interface to match your work habits and suit your sense of personal style. (Just in case you're new to the term, *user interface* encompasses the way the program looks on the screen, how the mouse and keyboard work, and any other means the program provides for you—the user—and the software to communicate.) In many applications, VBA permits you to alter the user interface elements as you see fit. It only takes a few lines of code to add, delete, or rearrange the buttons on the toolbars, create new toolbars, redefine the keyboard layout, or modify the menu structure. Figure 1-3 shows Microsoft Word with a user interface modification courtesy of VBA.

Of course, you shouldn't use a blowtorch when a match will do—and VBA is often overkill for simple user interface customizations. Many of today's applications allow you to customize the user interface without any programming at all via drag-and-drop or dialog boxes.

Still, VBA can come in handy even in with these applications. For one thing, even highly customizable applications may not let you change certain parts of the interface without VBA. Most importantly, however, VBA allows you to orchestrate automatic changes in the user interface—changes that occur while the application is running, based on what you're currently doing with the program.

Suppose that when you're working on amounts greater than $1,000,000 you always use the same three toolbars. You could create a VBA program that displays all three toolbars at the same time, and then hides them all when you no longer need them.

Icon-Remember

So far, we're talking about customizing the VBA application's user interface, not creating a user interface for your VBA program itself. Although many VBA programs are automatons that require no interaction with you to complete their work, there will definitely be times when you have to create your own windows and dialog boxes (these are generically called *forms* in VBA).

Suppose that when you're working on amounts greater than $1,000,000 you always use the same three toolbars. You can create a VBA program that displays all three toolbars at the same time and then hides them all when you no longer need them.

So far, I'm talking about customizing a VBA application's user interface, not creating a user interface for your VBA program itself. Although many VBA programs are automatons that require no interaction with you to complete their work, you sometimes have to create your own windows and dialog boxes (generically called *forms* in VBA).

Adding new features

VBA really comes into its own when you use it to extend the functionality of your application. Suppose that you want red stars in the computer illustrations you draw on the first Monday of each month, but you want blue hearts every other Tuesday. Can you really expect the designer of your graphics program to anticipate your taste in graphical doodads? Using building-block functions provided by the application's designers, you could assemble little VBA programs that do special tricks like this.

At its simplest, a VBA program just triggers a series of commands in sequence, performing exactly the same steps each time you run it. Even at this level, however, the VBA program saves you time, compared to manually activating commands one by one.

As a simple example, Microsoft Word lacks a command for saving a selected block of text into a separate file. To accomplish this task, you must copy the selected text to the Clipboard, start a new document, paste in the Clipboard text, and finally save and close the new document. With VBA, however, you can write a little program that carries out all these steps automatically — providing Word users with a feature that most word processors have had since the days of CP/M (an operating system used in many of the earliest personal computers). The VBA code for this program looks like this:

```
Public Sub CopyBlockToFile()
Selection.Range.Copy ' copies the selection to
 ' the Clipboard
Documents.Add ' creates a new document
Selection.Range.Paste ' pastes the Clipboard into
 ' the new document
Dialogs(wdDialogFileSaveAs).Show ' displays the
 ' Save As dialog box
ActiveDocument.Close ' closes the new document
End Sub
```

However, a VBA program doesn't have to follow exactly the same steps in exactly the same order each time that it runs. Instead, your program can react to the conditions it finds at the time. Here are examples of how this feature can work:

- ✔ A VBA program can respond to what the application is doing or to current settings of the whole system at the time it runs. In the preceding Word example, for instance, you may decide that the program should save a new document only if some text is already selected — otherwise, it should scratch its head and pat its tummy simultaneously. Likewise, you may want your special program to do one thing in the morning but something else in the afternoon.

- ✔ A VBA program can take action depending on information contained in the current document, in another document created by the same application, or even in documents from other applications.

- ✔ A VBA program can respond to information supplied by the user when the program runs (see Figure 1-2). With VBA, you can easily build dialog boxes that allow the user to select from pre-fab options or to enter text or numbers from scratch.

- ✔ A VBA program can change its behavior based on the current sign of the zodiac or the phase of the moon. (Unfortunately, you must write the code needed to translate the date and time into the correct astrological sign or moon phase.)

Figure 1-2:
Create
dialog boxes
whenever
your
program
needs
information
from the
user.

Creating advanced custom programs

Creating VBA programs that add individual features to your existing applications is well within the reach of anyone who can recite the times tables or read cereal boxes while eating. You should know, though, that you're not limited to making minor additions and modifications to existing software. VBA gives you the tools to create complete and very sophisticated programs that rival the power of off-the-shelf applications.

Custom programs created with VBA usually take advantage of the features of the underlying VBA application (in fact, these custom programs can even access the functionality of multiple VBA applications). To the user, however, a custom program can appear as a distinct entity, with its own set of windows, buttons, and menus.

Creating a full-scale custom program is an ambitious project. This book gives you most of the skills you need, and even includes a scratch-the-surface introduction to accessing multiple VBA applications in a single program.

By the way, VBA doesn't force you to use the application's features. If you want, you can just ignore those capabilities and build an entirely unrelated program of your own. The trouble is that you would still need to run the VBA application each time you want to run your custom program, a step that wouldn't be necessary with Visual Basic. (You run into another catch, too — see the section "Why VBA is usually slower than Visual Basic," later in this chapter.)

Not Your Mama's BASIC

You could say that VBA is a direct descendant from the original BASIC programming language. Well, you could say so, but that would be like saying that people came from amoebas — a lot has happened since then.

The original version of the BASIC language (Beginner's All-purpose Symbolic Instruction Code) was created in the 1960s in hopes of making programming easier for ordinary folks. Compared to other programming languages, such as C++ or FORTRAN, the commands of the BASIC language are more like English; they're easier to understand and remember.

Many of the special-purpose "words" that the VBA programming language uses were part of the original BASIC language and had similar functions. Likewise for VBA "grammar" — some of the rules for which words go together, and in which order — originated with BASIC.

Still, the VBA language has evolved far beyond the early versions of BASIC. Many of the VBA commands, and the rules for fitting them together, just weren't part of the original BASIC. Simply put, the VBA language can do more than plain old BASIC — a whole lot more — especially when it comes to displaying interesting shapes on-screen and interacting with other software.

Besides, VBA isn't just a programming language. It includes a complete software *integrated development environment* (IDE) with all kinds of special-purpose windows that help you design and test your programs (see the following section).

Then, too, VBA has something BASIC never even dreamed of — it lets you design a sophisticated user interface without typing any program code. As you've seen, that feature is what makes VBA a visual software development tool.

The VBA integrated development environment

All your work with VBA takes place in an IDE (integrated development environment). This term may sound cold and intimidating, but don't let it scare you off — think of an IDE as a cozy home base where you can do all your programming chores in comfort.

The IDE that comes with VBA is called the Visual Basic Editor. The Visual Basic Editor constitutes a top-level application window with one menu and toolbar system, in which you have access to an assortment of subsidiary windows providing all the tools you need to create your programs. Figure 1-3 shows the Visio Word version of the Visual Basic Editor, but it looks the same in every VBA application.

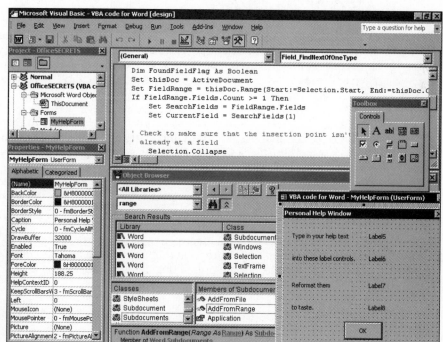

Figure 1-3: The Visual Basic Editor, opened in this case from Word.

Not all VBA applications come with the Visual Basic Editor (more on this in the section "Other VBA dialects," later in this chapter).

I delve deeply into the Visual Basic Editor in Chapter 5. For now, this partial list of its accouterments should give you a sense of the tools it gives you:

- ✔ A place for designing the forms (windows and dialog boxes) used in your programs

- ✔ A palette from which you can pick the buttons, check boxes, and other controls you want to add to your forms (see the section "Controls — ActiveX and otherwise," later in this chapter)

- ✔ A window for telling VBA how you want your forms and the controls on them to look and act

- ✔ Windows for typing and editing VBA code so that you can make your program do something useful

- ✔ Windows that display the current values of the program's variables — the numbers and text that it stores and changes — as the program runs (these are a big help when you're tracking down bugs)

Macros and VBA

One of the most common uses for VBA is consolidating a set of your application's commands. If you repeatedly use the same commands in the same sequence, storing this sequence as a VBA program makes sense. You can then activate the whole sequence with a single command — the one that fires up the VBA program you created for this purpose.

The easiest way to make this type of VBA program is simply to record the sequence of commands. Most VBA applications come with a macro recorder. It works something like a tape recorder. As soon as you start the macro recorder, it records all the commands you use in your application. After you stop the recorder, it converts those recorded commands into equivalent lines of VBA code. The resulting VBA program is called a macro. In Chapter 2, I cover the ins and outs of recording macros.

Aside from how you create a macro, no difference exists between a macro that you record and a VBA program that you type in as VBA code. You can edit the macro code, adding or deleting items at will, just as if you'd typed the code yourself.

Controls — ActiveX and otherwise

In any Windows program, the *controls* are the on-screen doohickeys that you can click or type into to get a certain action from the program. Familiar controls include push-button-type buttons on toolbars and in dialog boxes, radio buttons and check boxes for picking from predetermined options, and text boxes in which you can type or edit entries. Figure 1-4 shows a dialog box with lots of sample controls.

VBA comes with these and all the other standard types of Windows controls. They work like plug-in components: To add a control to one of your forms (a window or dialog box), you just click the control in the Toolbox, a special toolbar shown in Figure 1-5, and then plop the control down on the form.

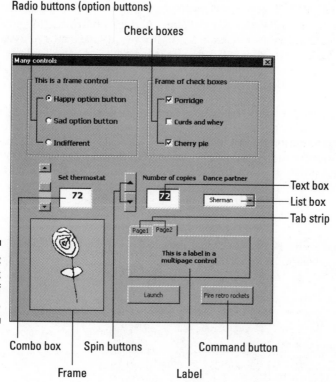

Figure 1-4:
A dialog box full of controls.

Figure 1-5:
The Visual Basic Editor's Toolbox offers a control palette for forms.

Because of something called ActiveX, you're not limited to the controls that come with VBA. Developed by Microsoft, ActiveX defines a standard by which software developers create interchangeable controls that you can plug into your programs as you see fit. The controls that come with VBA are ActiveX controls, but many others are available. ActiveX controls work in C++ and Java programs, too, as well as in VBA. Anyway, to use a new ActiveX control on your VBA forms, all you have to do is install it onto the Toolbox (see Chapter 14 for instructions). After it's there, it works just like the controls that come with VBA.

Folks who want to can create these special-purpose software widgets for their own uses — or for sale to programmers like you. With the huge market for Windows software, you can easily see why lots of ActiveX controls are available. You can find enhanced versions of the standard controls, as well as new types of controls, such as dials, meters, clocks, calendars, and many more. If VBA doesn't come with a control that you need, you can probably buy one that does the job. Figure 1-6 gives you an idea of the possibilities.

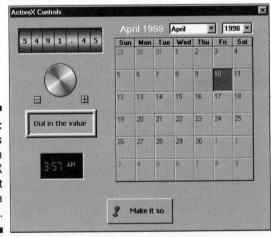

Figure 1-6:
This form is filled with ActiveX controls that don't come with VBA.

For some of these third-party ActiveX controls, the main selling point is looks. These controls more or less duplicate the functions of standard controls, but with a snazzier façade. Suppose that you're creating a space adventure game and you want to let players set the speed of their Astro-Cruisers. I know, I know, no one is going to use VBA to program a space adventure game. But just imagine — instead of a pair of drab spinner buttons, wouldn't you rather give them big, bright red rocket ship icons?

In many cases, though, add-on ActiveX controls do things the standard controls can't. For example, you can buy controls that create small spreadsheet grids on your forms. Chapter 14 reviews some of the most popular and useful third-party ActiveX controls.

If you're really ambitious you can create your own ActiveX controls. You need a copy of the Professional or Enterprise edition of Visual Basic (not VBA) version 5 or greater.

Object-oriented programming with VBA

Visual Basic has evolved into a (nearly) full-fledged object-oriented programming language. Although working with objects poses challenges for the VBA novice, the rewards are well worth your efforts. In Chapter 12, I take up the nuts and bolts of programming with objects, but you deserve a brief introduction here.

So what's an object?

Through objects — vital features of the VBA landscape — you have access to the functionality of the underlying VBA application you're working in. Eventually, you may go on to access objects from other compatible applications and even build your own objects.

From a practical standpoint, an object is simply a named item that has

- **Properties:** settings you can check and change
- **Methods:** actions the object can perform when your program asks it to
- **Events:** things that happen to the object, to which it can respond by automatically taking a predetermined action

Something is an object if it possesses both data and the code that acts on that data. An object encapsulates the data and the related code.

Objects as components of VBA applications

The easiest way to start thinking about objects is to see them as parts of your VBA application and its documents. A *shape* in a Visio drawing is an object, as is each *connect* (line) that joins two shapes. So is each *layer* to which shapes can be assigned, and so is each *page* where the layers reside. And so is the *document* itself, to which all the pages, layers, shapes, and connects belong.

Similarly, Excel objects include the cells in which you enter data or formulas, named ranges of cells, the charts that grace many worksheets, individual worksheets, and complete workbooks. And in most VBA applications, the toolbars and menus, and the buttons and menu choices they contain, are objects as well. VBA objects exist in a hierarchy in which one type of object contains objects of other types. These object hierarchies are called *object models*.

VBA is a standard — sort of

One of the big selling points of VBA is that it's a *standard* — it works the same in every VBA application. If you figure out how to build programs with VBA in, say, Microsoft Word, all those skills should transfer directly to Visio, AutoCAD, or any other VBA application. There is a lot of truth in this claim, but there's more to the story.

The Visual Basic Editor and all its parts are identical in all VBA applications (all that include the Visual Basic Editor, anyway). The way the Visual Basic Editor works is also the same. This fact holds, for example, for the visual process of creating forms (again, forms are the custom windows and dialog boxes you make for your programs). In fact, you can create a form in one VBA application and use it later in a different application. To be honest, though, form design is the easy part of VBA.

When it comes to the programming language at the core of VBA, things aren't quite so consistent. On the one hand, the core VBA language is identical in every VBA application (aside from the slight differences between VBA 5 and VBA 6). For example, you always use the special keyword `Dim` to define a new variable (remember, a *variable* is a parking place where the program stores a number, bit of text, or some other item that may change while the program runs). In any VBA application, the statement `Dim MyVariable as Integer` creates a variable called `MyVariable` and defines it as an integer — rather than text or a number with decimal points.

Likewise, you use the same techniques to set up the sub-units of your program that perform specific tasks (procedures and functions), regardless of which VBA application you're working in.

Apart from such essentials, however, many VBA programming commands are unique to the application you're using. The point is that you can have a lot of learning to do when you switch from programming in one VBA application to another — even though VBA is supposedly standardized.

If you think about it, this requirement makes sense — after all, a graphics application, such as Visio, logically has different commands from a word-processing application such as Word. Sometimes, however, different VBA applications use different commands even for features they have in common. Commands for customizing menus and toolbars are a good example of this discrepancy. Would you believe that, even Word, Excel, and PowerPoint — all kissing cousins in the Microsoft Office family — require different VBA commands for customizing certain elements? Oh, well, it ain't a perfect world.

Technically, the VBA language itself is the same in all VBA applications. It seems to vary because each application has its own unique set of objects, with their own *methods* (commands) and *properties* (characteristics). Check out Chapter 12 for the basics and more on objects, methods, and properties.

VBA 5 versus VBA 6

This book concentrates on VBA 6, the version used in the Office XP and Office 2000 applications — including FrontPage, Visio, and Project — and also available in Micrografx iGrafx products and in Corel WordPerfect 2000 and Corel Draw. However, you'll encounter only slight differences between VBA 6 and its predecessor, VBA 5, which came out with Microsoft Office 97 and is still included with some non-Microsoft applications. You can move back and forth between VBA 5 and VBA 6 without missing a beat. Still, you should know what the most important changes are, as follows:

- ✔ VBA 5 provides online Help using the older WinHelp program, while VBA 6 relies on Microsoft's new HTML Help technology for the same purpose (many people actually prefer WinHelp).

- ✔ VBA 6 enhances the core VBA language with 13 additional built-in functions, most of which are used for manipulating text or formatting values. Chapter 11 covers built-in VBA functions and identifies those that are available only in VBA 6.

- ✔ VBA 6 forms (custom dialog boxes) can be modeless or modal, whereas all forms in VBA 5 are modal. I won't try to define these terms now — they're covered fully in Chapter 10.

Several other enhancements in VBA 6 benefit advanced developers and are beyond the scope of this book.

If you use Office XP, you may have noticed that its version of VBA is numbered 6.3. According to Microsoft, the improvements in VBA 6.3 are all "under the hood" — they're bug fixes and performance enhancements, but features that affect the way you program haven't been added or changed.

Other VBA dialects

Most VBA applications come with all the bells and whistles — the macro recorder, the full version of the Visual Basic Editor, and the complete VBA programming language. Such Cadillac VBA applications include Visio, WordPerfect, AutoCAD, and, of course, the big guns from Microsoft — Word, Excel, Access, and PowerPoint.

 Microsoft Access diverges from mainstream VBA applications a bit. Access doesn't have a macro recorder — Access macros must be coded by hand, and for that matter, they aren't VBA macros. Access forms aren't interchangeable with those of other VBA applications. Access 97 doesn't even come with the Visual Basic Editor — instead, you get independent windows for typing VBA code, debugging, and designing forms.

VBScript is a pared-down version of VBA used in some applications, including Microsoft's Internet Explorer and Outlook. VBScript-based applications don't come with the Visual Basic Editor, and the programming language itself isn't as complete. Still, it's pretty powerful. Hungry Minds has a couple of whole books on VBScript programming; they're titled *VBScript and ActiveX* and *Web Scripting with VBScript.*

VBA versus Visual Basic

Besides the fact that you can't create separate, stand-alone applications in VBA, one other big difference exists between it and Visual Basic proper: VBA programs are slower, at least some of the time.

Why VBA is usually slower than Visual Basic

The reason for this difference is simple. A VBA program has to be compiled at least once during each session with the corresponding VBA application. *Compiling* is the process of converting the program code (that you can read) into machine code (the instructions that the computer actually executes when the program runs). A compiler is a software program that converts human-readable code into instructions the computer can follow.

After a standard Visual Basic program has been compiled, it is stored on the computer's hard drive in an executable form that can always run at the computer's full speed, as soon as the program has been loaded into memory. VBA programs, by contrast, are stored as VBA code. When you give the order to run a VBA program, the following steps occur:

1. **The program is compiled.**

    This step is the bottleneck. As the VBA compiler does its work, you hear your hard drive drumming, but nothing seems to be happening.

2. The compiled version is stored in the computer's memory.

3. Finally! The program runs.

Step 2 limits the damage. As long as the compiled version of a VBA program remains stored in memory, it can run at full speed as many times as you need it. After you exit the VBA application, however, the compiled program disappears into the ether. It has to be compiled again the next time you run the application. Unfortunately, a compiled VBA program may also lose its temporary home in memory even before you exit the application. This eviction can happen when the program is idle and when the memory is needed for some other purpose, such as running a bunch of other applications.

For the tasks that VBA specializes in — working with the objects of a VBA application — a program written in VBA actually runs faster than the same program written in Visual Basic.

Differences between VBA and Visual Basic

VBA shares a great deal with Visual Basic, its sister-programming tool for building standalone applications. Because the languages are so similar, you can transfer most of your programming skills from VBA directly to Visual Basic. However, keep in mind some important differences.

As of 2001, Visual Basic has been overhauled in its new incarnation as Visual Basic.NET. Although the changes further improve Visual Basic's power and ease of use, the core language has diverged somewhat from that of VBA. As a result, you'll have to modify some of your VBA programming techniques to work in Visual Basic.NET. Of course, you can stick with Visual Basic 5 or 6, tools that are going to be widely used for some years to come, and which share with VBA the identical core language. Even then, however, you'll have to cope with the fact that VBA and Visual Basic use a different system for creating and displaying forms (custom dialog boxes).

Chapter 2

Don't Program When You Can Record a Macro

In This Chapter

▶ Recording macros — sequences of commands — so you can use them again and again
▶ Starting the macro recorder
▶ Figuring out how to record macros so that they work the way they're supposed to work
▶ Viewing and modifying macro code in the Visual Basic Editor

*I*f you don't have to write program code, why bother? If all you want to do is automate a set of your application's commands, record them as a *macro*. Read on to find out how macros can help you minimize the amount of code you write.

Understanding How Macros Work

Some VBA applications include a *macro recorder,* which operates something like a tape recorder. Among the apps equipped with a macro recorder are Microsoft Word, Excel, PowerPoint, and Project (but not Access, Outlook, FrontPage, or Visio) and Corel Draw (but not Corel WordPerfect or Photo-Paint). Anyway, when you turn on the macro recorder, it records every command you use in your application from that point on, until you click the Stop button. After you've recorded the macro, you can play it back whenever you need to use that same sequence of commands again.

By the way, the word *macro* means big. The implication is that you're collecting a bunch of small commands into one bigger command. Actually, your macros can be as little and modest as you like — if you have too much time on your hands, you can record a useless macro that includes only one command.

Macros are not rows of Macintosh computers

A *macro* is actually just another term for a VBA program. While the macro recorder is running, it converts each command you use in the application into a corresponding line of VBA code. The finished macro is stored as a single VBA *procedure*. Procedures, as Chapter 6 makes plain, are units of VBA code that you can run by name. (To get squeaky-clean technically correct, a macro is a *Sub* procedure that takes no

arguments. Are you sure that you wanted to know that?)

One other technical point: Microsoft Access has macros and it has VBA, but Access macros *aren't* VBA programs. You construct an Access macro by selecting a series of commands in a special dialog box. To muddy the waters further, however, I must tell you that an Access macro can trigger an Access VBA procedure. Oh, dear.

In VBA applications that *don't* include the macro recorder, the term *macro* may refer to any VBA programs, the kind that you create by programming. In Visio 4.5 and 5.0, for example, creating a macro starts a new program in the Visual Basic Editor. On the other hand, in at least one major VBA application — Access — what are called "macros" have nothing directly to do with VBA. Although you can create macros in Access that trigger sequences of commands, Access macros aren't stored as VBA code. See the sidebar "Macros are not rows of Macintosh computers" elsewhere in this chapter. All versions of Access lack a macro recorder, so you have to select commands you want to store in a macro using a special dialog box.

When to record macros

Macros save time and make you less grumpy. Really. The computer can play back a command sequence much, much more quickly than you can click the corresponding buttons or menu choices. The computer doesn't make any mistakes, either. And your mood becomes better because people hate doing the same thing more than two or three times in a row.

So . . . train yourself to notice whenever you repeatedly use the same sequence of commands in your application, over and over again. As soon as you become aware that you're in a repeating pattern, record the commands as a macro right away. Better yet, when you know ahead of time that you're going to be reusing a series of commands, you can record the macro the first time you carry out the commands. From then on, use the macro instead.

Macros feel good, but they lead to the hard stuff

Although they are plenty useful in their own right, recorded macros are also a great way to ease into VBA programming. After you record a few macros, you soon start hankering after ways to make them more flexible. With just a little VBA programming, you can build rudimentary intelligence into a macro, allowing it to alter its behavior depending on what's going on at the time. See the section "Modifying Macros — the Easy Way to Write Code," later in this chapter.

Planning a Macro

After you've skipped this boring section and plunged right in to record a few macros, you may be ready to listen to some conservative advice. Here it is: To save yourself headaches, devote a few moments to planning your macros before you start recording them.

As soon as you have a vague sense of what you want a macro to accomplish, you are tempted to fire up the recorder and start piling on the commands. The trouble is that the recorder faithfully records every command you issue, including all your mistakes. Eight or nine times out of ten, you make some.

Of course, you can always delete a bungled macro and start from scratch. But you may as well save yourself that trouble and plan. Think through the steps the macro should perform, practice them to see that they do in fact get the job done, and *then* record the macro.

As you plan your macro, take into account any special conditions that must be in effect for the macro to work properly. Plan to include in the macro the commands needed to re-create these conditions.

As a simple example, imagine that you're working with Microsoft Word. Say that you want your macro to insert the date at the very beginning of a document. You could easily assume that the text insertion point (cursor) will already be at the top of the current document whenever you run the macro. Don't be so confident. Even if the insertion point is in the right place when you record the macro, the first command you record should be the one that moves to the top of the document. That way, the macro will work properly no matter where the insertion point happens to be.

Recording Macros

Fortunately, the mechanics of recording a macro are as easy as falling into bed. I detail the steps for you, anyway.

Starting the macro recorder

You can start the macro recorder with either of the following methods:

- ✔ Choose Tools⇨Macro⇨Record New Macro (in Corel Draw the command is Tools⇨Visual Basic⇨Record). If you're using recent versions of Office, the Macro menu item may not appear on the Tools menu until you click the down-arrow button at the bottom of the menu.

- ✔ Click the Record Macro toolbar button, if your application has one. In Microsoft Office applications, the Record Macro button is on the Visual Basic toolbar. To display the Visual Basic toolbar, choose View⇨ Toolbars⇨Visual Basic.

Either way, the Record Macro dialog box appears. Figure 2-1 shows the Record Macro dialog box from Microsoft Excel (it looks different in different applications).

Figure 2-1:
The Excel
Record
Macro
dialog box.

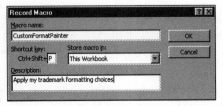

Naming the baby

Trying to be helpful, the Record Macro dialog box suggests a lovely and very distinctive name for your new macro, Macro1 (or Macro2, or Macro3). Offering polite thanks, you quickly erase the suggestion and type in a name of your own.

A macro's name should, of course, be descriptive of its function. However, you have to live within some rules. Class, repeat after me:

✔ **Macro names must start with a letter, not a number.** Numbers are okay after the first character, though.

✔ **A macro name can't contain spaces.** You have to use mixed-case capitalization to indicate separate words, as in

```
EraseEntireHardDrive
```

✔ **Punctuation marks are off limits, too.** Exceptions exist, but you can safely ignore punctuation marks. If you do use punctuation marks, VBA returns an Invalid procedure name dialog box.

Chapter 6 covers the VBA naming rules in detail.

Making other choices in the Record Macro dialog box

Other choices you can make in the Record Macro dialog box depend on the application. Here are some examples:

✔ You may be able to enter a lengthier description for the macro.

✔ You may be able to tell your application where to store the macro. Often, you can choose between placing it in the current document or in a document template.

✔ You may be able to assign the macro to a toolbar button or keyboard shortcut. If this option is available in your application, by all means, use it! See the next section for details.

Button, button, who's got the button?

Some VBA applications let you assign a new macro to a toolbar button or keyboard shortcut at the time you record the macro. Take advantage of this opportunity — the most convenient way to play back a macro is to trigger it using a button or the keyboard.

If your application permits this option, you should be able to see it on the Record Macro dialog box. In Excel, for example, the Record Macro dialog box has a Shortcut Key field. Here, you can type a key combination, such as Ctrl+M, that fires off the macro (refer to Figure 2-1). The Word version of the Record Macro dialog box (see Figure 2-2) has buttons that let you assign a new macro to a toolbar button or a keyboard shortcut. If you click one of these buttons, you're taken to another dialog box where you make the assignment.

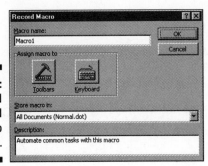

Figure 2-2:
The Word
Record
Macro
dialog box.

If you do assign the new macro to a keyboard shortcut, do yourself a favor and write down the shortcut now. Until you memorize the shortcut, stick a little note on your desk or computer screen as a reminder.

Starting the macro recorder

Clicking OK in the Record Macro dialog box starts the recorder. You know that it starts because the Stop Recording toolbar appears, as shown in Figure 2-3. The mouse pointer changes, too, becoming a little cassette tape graphic.

Figure 2-3:
The little
Stop
Recording
toolbar.

Recording commands

After you start the macro recorder, you don't have to do anything special to record commands into your new macro. Just use the application's commands as you would normally. Everything you do — whether picking commands from a toolbar or menu, formatting a graphic, or typing text — is stored in the macro.

Oh, yes, the macro recorder faithfully records all the mistakes you make, too. You can correct them by re-recording the macro, or by editing its VBA code in the Visual Basic Editor (see "Editing macro code in the Visual Basic Editor" later in this chapter).

Stopping and pausing the macro recorder

After you carry out all the commands you want to record, stop the macro recorder by clicking the Stop Recording button on the toolbar of the same name, as shown in Figure 2-3. The macro recorder finishes its business by storing all the recorded commands as a VBA program. (If you don't believe me, you can look at the resulting program code — see "Editing macro code in the Visual Basic Editor" later in this chapter.)

In Word, you can pause the recorder during the process of recording a macro. If you need to use a command that shouldn't be part of the macro, click the Pause Recording button (also on the Stop Recording toolbar). The recorder goes into hibernation, ignoring any commands you use for the time being.

When the macro recorder is paused, the Pause Recording button looks pressed in, as shown in Figure 2-4. Officially, the button is now known as the Resume Recorder button. When you're ready to pick up the macro where you left off, click it to continue recording your macro.

Figure 2-4:
The Pause
Recording
button in
use on
Word's Stop
Recording
toolbar.

Running macros

The whole point of recording a macro is so that you can play it back — or *run it,* if you prefer. Watching a long macro do a bunch of tedious work automatically for you is one of life's little pleasures. (For reasons I explain shortly, save your document before running any macro that makes significant modifications to its content.)

Because macros are VBA programs, all the techniques you can use to run the VBA programs you code yourself work with recorded macros. A method that always works is to open the Macros dialog box (Alt+F8), select the macro, and click Run — see Figure 2-5. I cover this and other techniques for running VBA programs fully in Chapter 4.

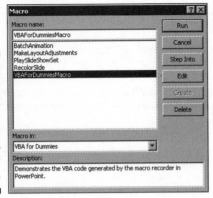

Figure 2-5:
The Macro
dialog box
(titled
Macros in
many VBA
applica-
tions).

A recorded macro has no intelligence — it can't modify its behavior to suit
current conditions. When you run a macro, it tries to execute the recorded
commands even if they aren't applicable to what's going on in your application at the time. For example, if your macro assumes that you're at the beginning of a document, but you run it when you're at the end of a document, the
macro probably won't do anything. If you trigger a text-related macro while
you're drawing graphics, it may destroy hours of painstaking artwork. My
advice: Save your document just before running a macro of any complexity,
and be ready with the Undo command (Ctrl+Z).

Modifying Macros — the Easy Way to Write Code

Don't think that the macro recorder will gather electronic dust after you
master writing VBA code. In fact, you may use it even more often. After all,
most fancy VBA programs rely heavily on the objects, methods, and properties found in your application. Instead of typing the corresponding commands yourself, why not record them as a macro?

Remember, the macro recorder converts the commands you record into corresponding statements in the VBA language. You can take the code from a
recorded macro as a starting point for your program, tacking on your own
VBA statements as required. At least for the recorded commands, you don't
have to worry about remembering the proper VBA statements or making
typing errors.

As a bonus, this technique also gives you the easiest way to assign your program to a toolbar button or keyboard shortcut. Of course, this only applies

if your application allows you to make such assignments when you record macros (see the section "Button, button, who's got the button?" earlier in this chapter).

Editing macro code in the Visual Basic Editor

After you've recorded a macro, you can easily enough edit the resulting VBA program (or just look at those lines of code). Here's how to proceed:

1. **Choose Tools⇨Macro⇨Macros or press Alt+F8 to display the Macro dialog box (see Figure 2-5).**

2. **From the list under Macro Name, select the macro you want to run.**

   The macro you just recorded is *not* selected automatically, so you may have to scroll through the list to find it.

3. **Click the Edit button.**

You're whisked to the Visual Basic Editor with the chosen macro's code available for editing. Figure 2-6 shows an example.

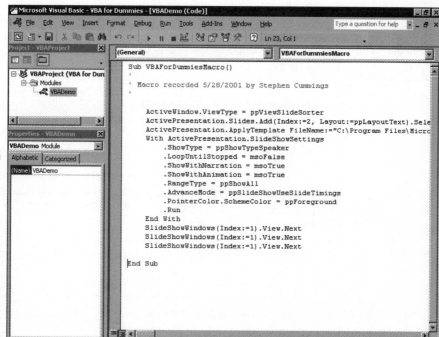

Figure 2-6: You just recorded a macro; here's the resulting code generated by the macro recorder.

Making easy macro modifications

This chapter isn't the place to lay out detailed techniques for modifying macros in the Visual Basic Editor. After all, the techniques are the same as the ones you use to create VBA programs from scratch, which is the subject of most of this book.

Still, I'm not jumping the gun to suggest a few simple and commonly useful modifications you can make to your macros. These ideas require a minimum of programming, but can make your macros a lot more powerful. Try the following:

- ✔ **Repeat the commands in the macro a set number of times.** You may know in advance that you'll want to run through the entire sequence — or one specific command — exactly 11 times. All you have to do is add a For...Next loop to the code. So what's a For...Next loop, you ask? It's one of the elements of the VBA programming language, and I discuss it in Chapter 8.

- ✔ **Repeat the macro commands, but determine the number of repetitions when you run the macro.** If you're a little more ambitious, you can add to your recorded macro both a For...Next loop and an InputBox. This is a little dialog box that asks for a typed response, in this case the number of repetitions you want. I cover the use of the InputBox in Chapter 11.

- ✔ **Choose the text used by the macro for a given step.** A macro that always inserts the same text into your documents isn't very flexible. By adding an InputBox to the recorded macro, you can tell it what text to insert each time you run the macro. Again, see Chapter 11 for details on the InputBox.

- ✔ **Check for a selection before starting the macro.** Your macro may not work right unless some text, a graphic, or another object is selected. You can use a VBA If...End If sequence to make sure that the proper type of item is selected, and if not, to cancel the macro. Chapter 8 has the skinny on the If...End If statement.

As soon as you realize how easily you can get dramatic gains in macro power by writing a little VBA code, you'll start looking forward to programming. When that happens, it's only a matter of time before you become a competent VBA programmer without any great effort.

Chapter 3

Basic VBA Programming

● ●

In This Chapter

▶ Starting the Visual Basic Editor

▶ Working with the VBA Help system

▶ Programming in VBA — a quick and dirty guide

● ●

Macros are fine, so far as they go, but you can accomplish much more with custom VBA programs. This chapter serves as your crash-course introduction to VBA programming proper. After introducing the Visual Basic Editor and the VBA Help system, I lead you through the process of building a simple VBA program. With these basics under your belt, you'll have a solid foundation for undertaking all the other complicated stuff in the rest of the book.

Starting the Visual Basic Editor

The Visual Basic Editor is command central for all your work in VBA. It's where you need to be whenever you're designing VBA forms, writing VBA code, or testing and debugging your VBA programs. Chapter 5 makes you an expert on the Visual Basic Editor. For now, you just need to know how to get the Editor onto your screen.

If you've done any nosing around in the code created by the macro recorder, you already know one way to start the Visual Basic Editor — by selecting a macro in the Macros dialog box and clicking Edit. You can, of course, start the Visual Basic Editor directly. In most VBA applications, either of the following methods works:

   ✔ Choose Tools⇨Macro⇨Visual Basic Editor.

   ✔ Press Alt+F11. After some chattering of the hard drive, the Visual Basic Editor appears on-screen. It should bear at least passing resemblance to the picture shown in Figure 3-1.

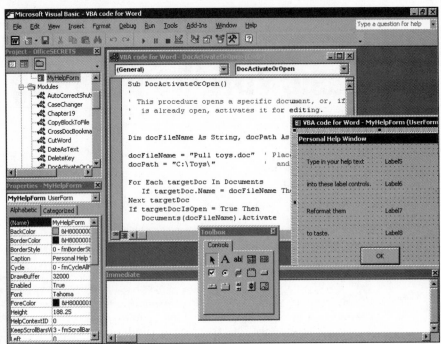

Figure 3-1:
The Visual
Basic Editor.

In a few VBA applications, you take a different route to get to the Visual Basic Editor. If the preceding techniques don't work, you can find the necessary command somewhere under the Tools menu.

One-click access to the Visual Basic Editor

If your application has a toolbar button for the Visual Basic Editor, you can also activate the Visual Basic Editor by clicking the button. In the Microsoft Office VBA applications (Word, Excel, and PowerPoint), this button is on the Visual Basic toolbar, shown in Figure 3-2. Display this toolbar by choosing View⇔Toolbars⇔Visual Basic. The collection of buttons is slightly different, depending on which application you're using.

Figure 3-2:
The Visual
Basic
toolbar as it
appears in
Word.

Here's what all the buttons on this toolbar are for, starting at the left side:

- The first two buttons are for running (blue triangle) and recording macros (blue dot), respectively.

- The middle button (in Figure 3-2, the fourth button from the right) activates the Visual Basic Editor. If you use the Visual Basic Editor frequently but don't need the other buttons, copy this button to another toolbar. To copy the button in Office applications, hold down Alt as you drag it into place.

- The button showing a hammer and a wrench displays the Control Toolbox, a palette of controls very similar to the VBA Toolbox. In Office, you can place VBA controls into documents themselves, not just on VBA forms.

- The button with the ruler, triangle, and pencil switches the document to Design Mode, in which you can edit VBA controls on the document.

A peek into the Visual Basic Editor

Your first few trips to the Visual Basic Editor can be confusing. The menus and toolbars at the top of the screen are familiar, of course, but what about all those windows? Keeping track of them is tough because they can be arranged and combined in infinite varieties (when you first start the Visual Basic Editor, the windows you see and their location can vary wildly, depending on how the Editor is set up). And if you're not already a programmer, the windows have unfamiliar names and functions.

I've designed Chapter 5 to give you a comfortable command of all the windows. For now, look to Table 3-1 for a quick summary of their names and functions.

Table 3-1	Names and Functions
Window Type	*What You Use It For*
Project Explorer window	Navigating and managing the components of a VBA project
Code window	Displaying, adding, and editing VBA code
UserForm window	Designing custom forms (windows and dialog boxes)
Toolbox	Adding controls, such as text boxes and buttons to your forms (and, in many VBA applications, to your documents)

(continued)

Table 3-1 *(continued)*

Window Type	What You Use It For
Properties window	Specifying individual attributes of the selected form or control
Watch window	Keeping track of the values of selected variables in your program
Locals window	Keeping track of the values of variables in the current procedure
Immediate window	Running individual lines of code for immediate results
Object Browser	Exploring the objects available to your programs window

At this point, focus your attention on the Code window, in which you write VBA code, and the UserForm window, in which you design your own windows and forms visually. You can see examples of Code and UserForm windows in Figures 3-3 and 3-4. Notice that the type of window appears in each window's title bar.

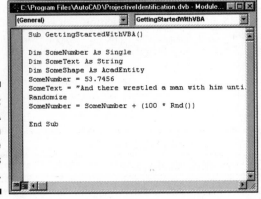

Figure 3-3:
Write VBA
code in
Code
windows
like this one.

```
C:\Program Files\AutoCAD\ProjectiveIdentification.dvb - Module...

(General)                    GettingStartedWithVBA

Sub GettingStartedWithVBA()

Dim SomeNumber As Single
Dim SomeText As String
Dim SomeShape As AcadEntity
SomeNumber = 53.7456
SomeText = "And there wrestled a man with him unti
Randomize
SomeNumber = SomeNumber + (100 * Rnd())

End Sub
```

Initially, you may see more than one Code or UserForm window — or none at all. It doesn't matter because, after a quick tour of the VBA Help system, you need new windows for the sample program that you're about to create.

Figure 3-4:
An example
of a
UserForm
window
with a
custom
dialog box
under con-
struction.

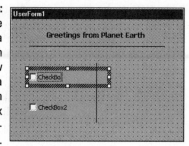

Figure 3-4:
An example
of a
UserForm
window
with a
custom
dialog box
under con-
struction.

1 Need Help!

These days, almost all software comes laden with self-explanatory menu choices, toolbar buttons with cute little icons that show you exactly what the buttons do, and pop-up tips that spell out the buttons' functions in writing. So who needs on-screen Help anymore? Well, you do, if you're trying to write VBA code.

To begin with, you need help with the Visual Basic Editor itself. Although the Editor's menus and toolbars work like those in any ordinary application, many of the specific commands they offer are unfamiliar at first. Likewise, the Editor barrages you with eight or nine different types of windows, and sorting them all out takes time.

Of course, you'll adapt to the Editor's user interface soon enough. Still, even the most seasoned programmer needs help when it comes to the details of the VBA language itself. With hundreds of objects, methods, properties, key-words, and whatnot to keep track of, you can expect to depend heavily on the VBA Help files.

Microsoft publishes a printed VBA reference manual, but it doesn't come with most VBA applications. The manual *is* included with the Developer's Edition of Office, however.

411 for VBA — or is it 911?

VBA Help screens look different depending on the VBA application you're working with. Most Microsoft applications display online assistance using HTML Help, the Microsoft standard introduced with Windows 98. The HTML

Help window looks and works much like a browser — it's based on Microsoft Internet Explorer. Unfortunately, HTML Help lacks some useful features, such as the ability to control whether the Help window remains on top when you're working in another application. Also, some implementations of HTML Help, including the Help system in Microsoft Office 2000, behave erratically (it functions better in Office XP).

Many other VBA applications are still using the tried-and-true WinHelp software engine, which dates back to Windows 3.1. Among the WinHelp faithful are AutoCAD 2000 and Corel Draw 10.

To display general help information on VBA, start from the Visual Basic Editor and choose Help⇨Microsoft Visual Basic Help (in VBA 6) or Help⇨ Contents and Index (in VBA 5). The resulting Help window describes VBA in general. Figure 3-5 shows an HTML Help window for a VBA 6 application. Unfortunately, though, the help information you get using these commands does *not* cover the VBA application you're working with.

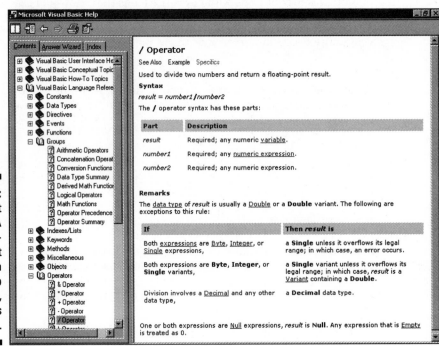

Figure 3-5: Microsoft Office VBA programmers get help in HTML Help windows, such as this one.

Getting Help for your VBA application

It's sad but true — the Visual Basic Editor doesn't provide a direct command for opening the Help files pertaining to your VBA application. Don't look for such a command because you won't find it. When you want to browse programming information about your application, not about VBA in general, the only sure-fire solution is a three-step process, as follows:

1. **Open the Object Browser by pressing F2 or choosing View⇨Object Browser (see Chapter 5 for the skinny on the Object Browser).**

2. **Use the drop-down list at the top left of the Object Browser to select your VBA application by name.**

3. **Highlight an item in the Classes pane at the left of the Object Browser — any item should do.**

4. **Press F1, or click the button with the question mark on it at the top of the Object Browser to open the Help system.**

   You should see the topic pertaining to the item you selected in the Object Browser, but you can now use the Contents tab to browse the entire Help system for your application.

Searching the Help haystack

The VBA Help system works according to the Windows standard. In both WinHelp and HTML Help, you can

✔ Use the Contents tab to see an outline of the available Help information arranged like chapters in a book.

✔ Use the Index tab to search for information in an alphabetical list of keywords assembled by the Help system's designers.

In the VBA Help system for Office, the tab labeled Answer Wizard is supposed to locate Help topics in response to complete questions you type. However, typing in just a word or two also works (unfortunately, the results often don't correspond very closely to what you're looking for). In WinHelp, the Find tab lets you search for almost any word that appears in the entire Help system.

Context-sensitive Help

In the Visual Basic Editor, F1 is *context-sensitive* — it brings up a Help topic specific to what you're doing at the moment. What you see depends on the type of window currently active in the Editor — and sometimes, on what's going on in the window.

This feature really comes in handy when you're writing code or designing a form. In the Code window, the F1 key responds to the term at the current location of the insertion point, or cursor (that blinking line that indicates where you can type or edit text). Don't fret if you've forgotten how to use a VBA statement, such as For...Next, or if you don't know which properties or methods are available for an object. Just place the insertion point in the relevant term and press F1. Figure 3-6 gives an example of what you may see.

F1 can likewise give you Help with the picayune details of form design. In the UserForm window, you can display a Help topic for any control on the form (at the risk of repeating myself, *controls* are items such as buttons, check boxes, and frames). Just click the control to select it, and then press F1. For Help on any specific *property* of a control, select the control, click the relevant line in the Properties window, and then press F1.

The F1 key works as follows in other windows:

✔ With the Project Explorer and UserForm windows, pressing F1 displays a Help topic briefly describing that window. This works in the UserForm window only if no control is selected.

✔ With the Watch, Locals, and Immediate windows, pressing F1 takes you to a Help screen containing a set of *jumps,* underlined text that you can click to take you to topics on each of these windows. I have no idea why the appropriate topic doesn't appear automatically with these windows.

✔ In the Object Browser window, when you select a class or one of its members and press F1, a Help topic on that item appears.

Understanding what's special about VBA Help topics

As you use VBA Help, watch closely for jumps or buttons that display other relevant items in the Help system. Train yourself to use them! The typical VBA Help topic, such as the one shown in Figure 3-7, offers a wealth of these hotspots. If the topic you're reading doesn't have the information you're looking for, you may find it in the related items. Besides, exploring the jumps is a great way to discover VBA programming sort of organically.

Figure 3-6:
Getting
context-
sensitive
Help for the
Add method
in Visio; if
you squint,
you can
probably
make out
that the
Code
window is
displaying
the Add
term.

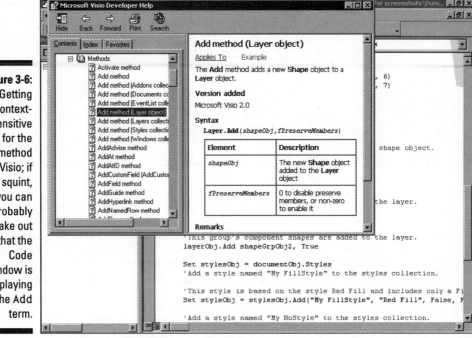

Figure 3-7:
Like most
VBA Help
topics, this
one from
Word offers
jumps to
other Help
topics.

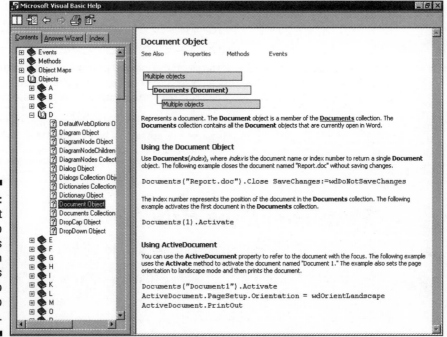

Steal that code! Scavenging from the VBA Help system

Be sure to take advantage of the many example code fragments scattered throughout the VBA Help system. You can often find pre-built code that will, with minor modifications, accomplish just the task you're working on. To use Help examples in your own code, select the relevant lines with the mouse, right-click the selection, and choose Copy. Then switch to the target Code window in the Visual Basic Editor and click the Paste toolbar button or press Ctrl+V.

Table 3-2 lists jumps you're likely to see.

Table 3-2	Jumping Buttons
Jump or Button	*How to Use It*
See also	Click these jumps to see information on related topics.
Example	If you see a button or jump labeled Example, by all means click it! The examples are vital to understanding muddy or incomplete explanations in the Help file proper. Also, you can copy the example to your own VBA program and modify it there to suit your own needs (see the sidebar "Steal that code! Scavenging from the VBA Help system," elsewhere in this section).
Methods, Properties, and Events	You see these jumps if the current Help topic covers an object. Click them to explore the methods, properties, and events you can use with that object.
Applies to	This jump is available when the current Help topic relates to a property, method, or event. Click to see which objects you can use the item with.

Installing all the Help files . . .

Depending on your application software and the way you installed it, you may or may not have a complete set of VBA Help files on your hard drive. Because the Help files are crucial for any serious work in VBA, be sure that you correct any deficiencies.

With Office, for example, the Setup program installs some, but not all, of the VBA Help files. Most people use the Typical option when they run the Setup program to install Office on their computers. True, this I-don't-want-to-get-my-hands-dirty approach is easy, but it omits many important VBA Help files. If you went this route, run Setup again and choose a Custom install. Go through each Office application in turn, selecting the Help and Sample Files item for each one. When you then click the Change Option button, a dialog box similar to the one shown in Figure 3-8 appears. Here, check the box labeled Online Help for Visual Basic.

Figure 3-8:
When installing Office, be sure that VBA Help files are copied to your hard disk — don't select the Installed on First Use option.

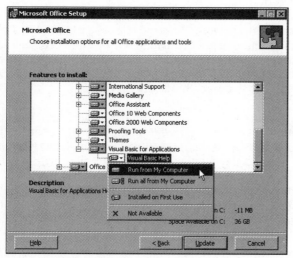

Creating a VBA Program

Now that you have a passing acquaintance with the Visual Basic Editor and the VBA Help system, you're ready for your first foray into the frontier of programming. In Chapter 1, I explain that the programming process consists of a few basic steps: design, implement, test, and debug (followed by test again, debug again, and so on). In this section, I take you through those steps in detail as you create a simple VBA program from scratch.

Step 1: Designing the sample program

Because I don't know which VBA application you're working with, I'm sticking with something quite generic but still potentially useful. The sample program opens a new window in which it displays a pithy quote and the date and time (I call this the *message*). The window stays on-screen until the user clicks OK.

Based on this description, you can list the elements that you must create to complete the program:

- ✔ Obviously, the program has one window, so you need one form (UserForm).
- ✔ The form requires two controls: a label control for the message, and a button control for the OK button.
- ✔ You must also write code for two procedures: one that displays the message in the label control, and another to exit the program when the user clicks the OK button.

One thing that this program does *not* need is a separate module for its VBA code (a *module* is a unit of code containing one or more procedures — Chapter 6 offers details on modules). You can write both procedures in the Code window associated with the form itself. After all, both procedures do their work in response to *events* that occur on the form.

Consider the procedure that displays the message and date: You don't need it until the moment that the program window appears on-screen. In this program, of course, that happens faster than you can blink, but the point is still valid — the event of displaying the form should trigger this procedure.

The exit procedure is also triggered by a form-related event — namely, the fact that the user has clicked OK. You can write this procedure on the form's Code window, too.

Note that many VBA programs don't display their own windows or other dialog boxes. If you're creating such a program, you definitely need to create one or more modules to hold its code.

Step 2: Implementing the design

With a clear plan in mind, you can begin programming in earnest. Take a little visual form design as your base, season it with a pinch of carefully typed code, and you can look forward to a tasty little VBA morsel.

Adding a new UserForm

To begin work in earnest, open the Visual Basic Editor. Do so in Microsoft VBA applications by pressing Alt+F11 or choosing Tools⇨Macro⇨Visual Basic Editor. The technique is different in other applications. In Corel Draw and WordPerfect, for example, you'd choose Tools⇨Visual Basic⇨Visual Basic Editor. If you don't see a likely entry on your application's Tools menu, consult the Help system for instructions.

Your first step is to create a new, blank form to serve as the sample program's window. From the Visual Basic Editor menu bar, choose Insert⇨UserForm to

place a new form on-screen. See how easy that was? In the bad old days of
Windows programming, you had to write out a long and very complex statement in code to add even something as simple as a blank window. As you can
see in Figure 3-9, a new UserForm is a featureless gray plane. Notice that you
can control the form's size by dragging those little white squares along the
right and bottom edges (they are the resize *handles*). The window for this
program should be a little wider (to fit all the text in the message on one line)
and much shorter (one line of text and a button take up very little room).

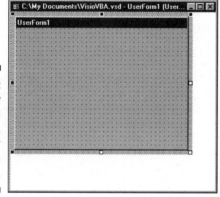

Figure 3-9:
A newly
inserted
UserForm,
looking for
a purpose
in life.

More interesting is the Toolbox — that palette of icons in its own little window
that pops up when you work with a form. Use the Toolbox, shown in Figure
3-10, to place controls onto a form.

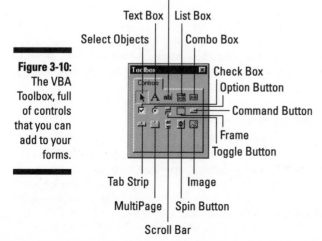

Figure 3-10:
The VBA
Toolbox, full
of controls
that you can
add to your
forms.

Label

Text Box | List Box

Select Objects | Combo Box

Check Box

Option Button

Command Button

Frame

Toggle Button

Tab Strip | Image

MultiPage | Spin Button

Scroll Bar

Adding a label control to the UserForm

Now you're ready to liven things up a bit by adding controls to the form. Start with a *label control,* which simply displays text — the label's *caption.* When a program is running, a label control is a look-but-don't-touch affair — although users can read the caption text, they can't change it.

However, your program can. The sample program needs this capability because it displays a different date and time each time that it runs.

To place a label control on your new UserForm, follow these instructions:

1. **Be sure the form window is active by clicking on it.**

   The Toolbox is only visible when a form window is active.

2. **Click the Toolbox icon that shows a bold letter A.**

3. **Move over to the form and, starting from the left side toward the top, drag a rectangle big enough to hold the message (see Figure 3-11 for guidance).**

Figure 3-11:
After plopping down a new label control, your form looks something like this.

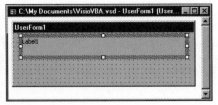

VBA gives every new label a caption automatically, so at this point you should see the magnificent text Label1 within the label control's rectangular outline. Obviously, that won't do. To erase the automatic caption, you need the Properties window.

Using the Properties window to tweak controls

Each control on a form has a lengthy list of *properties.* These specify how the control looks and how it should act when the program runs. One of VBA's great strengths is that you can control these properties without having to write any code.

The control panel for properties is the Properties window. As Figure 3-12 shows, it contains a list of all the properties of the control that's currently selected. To change a property, you just find the property in the left column and change its setting in the right column.

For the label control in the sample program, you need to change just two properties: Name and Caption. Change the control's name from Label1 to, say, lblNow (the first three letters identify the name as that of a label control). To do this, start by clicking on the label control to select it. Now find the Name property at the top of the property list where (Name) appears — it's the only property shown in parentheses. Double-click in the right column of that row so that the existing name becomes selected, and then type in the new name. You use a control's name to refer to the control when you're writing code, so try to select names that remind you of the control's purpose. Chapter 6 covers conventions you should use to identify the type of control in the names that you create.

Next, scroll down in the property list until you find the label control's Caption property. Here, simply delete the current entry for the property. Why? Because your program will supply the text for the label caption when it runs.

Now, you do have to write code if you want your program to change a control's property while the program runs. But because most properties stay the same, you usually need very little code to take care of such changes.

As long as you're changing properties, you may as well re-title the form itself. Select the form by clicking the title bar of the UserForm window. In the Properties window, scroll to the Caption property and type **Did You See Where I Put My Keys?** or **VBA For Dummies First Sample Program.** The new caption appears in the form's title bar.

Adding a command button

Unlike a label control, a *command button* control (better known as a button) interacts with the user of your program. When someone clicks the button, it looks pushed in, and the program does something.

The sample program needs just one button: the one that stops the program when a user clicks it. To place this button on the form, do the following:

1. **Click on the form's window to activate it once more.**

   The Toolbox, which vanished when you went to the Properties window, reappears.

2. **Click the little command button icon in the Toolbox (refer to Figure 3-11).**

3. **Starting just left of the midline and toward the bottom of the form, drag diagonally downward and to the right to create the button.**

At this point, the form should look like the example in Figure 3-13.

Figure 3-13:
Your form,
with an
added
command
button
control.

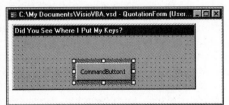

Now you can set the properties for the button. Make sure that the button is still selected — if necessary, click it to select it. Then, using the Properties window, follow these steps:

1. **Change the button's** (Name) **property to** OKButton.

   Again, you refer to the button in your code by name, so this title helps remind you what it does (it okays and closes the window).

2. **Change the button's** Caption **property to** OK.

   That's all the user of your program sees.

You've completed the form for the sample program. Even without any further work, you already have a functioning VBA program — one that displays the hugely fascinating form that you've just designed. To run it, press F5 or click the Run button on the Visual Basic Editor toolbar. It's the little blue arrow pointing toward the right.

When you run your new little half-baked program, the form appears on top of the document in your VBA application (not in the Visual Basic Editor). Check out Figure 3-14. The label control is blank and the OK button doesn't do anything — you haven't written any code yet, remember? To shut down your program, you have to click the Windows standard Close button (that X on the right end of the window's title bar).

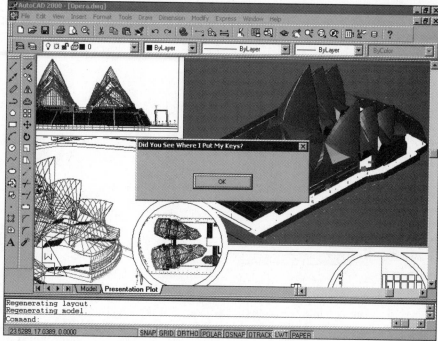

Figure 3-14:
Running the
custom
form as a
program
before you
add code.

Writing the code

Now comes the scariest, and the most exciting, part of VBA programming: writing the code that makes your program go. Recall that the sample program requires you to write two procedures, and that both are tied to events that occur while the program runs. The first procedure displays your message when the form appears on-screen, and the other terminates the program when someone clicks the OK button.

Opening the form's Code window

To write code *behind* (associated with) a form or one of its controls, you need to display the form's Code window instead of the form itself. To do so, start by selecting the form or control. The procedure for the OK button is easier, so why not start there? Click the OK button so that the selection handles appear around its border. You can then use any of the following methods to display the Code window:

- Choose View⇨Code.

- Press F7.

- Right-click the form and choose View Code from the shortcut menu.

When the Code window appears, it should already contain the skeleton of a procedure — see Figure 3-15. VBA automatically creates a procedure for the most common type of event, a simple mouse click on the button. Your program performs this procedure whenever someone clicks the OK button.

Figure 3-15:
VBA
creates this
procedure
skeleton as
soon as you
switch to
the form's
Code
window
with the OK
button
selected.

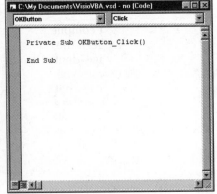

The two lines of code that you see in the procedure skeleton don't actually do anything; they simply provide the walls that tell VBA where the procedure begins and ends. The first line of code VBA generated for you is

```
Private Sub OKButton_Click()
```

In all VBA procedures, the first line of code defines the type of procedure (in this case, a private Sub procedure) and the procedure's name. Private and Sub are VBA *keywords,* words or symbols that are part of the VBA language. Keywords have fixed, special meanings in VBA, and you can't use them as the names of items such as procedures. And by the way, Chapter 6 covers the various types of procedures available in VBA. In this case, VBA chooses the name of the procedure, OKButton_Click, for you. The name is a combination of the button's name and the event type.

The last line of automatically generated code is

```
End Sub
```

All Sub procedures must end with this line. It tells VBA to stop running the procedure.

Adding your own code

The insertion point should be blinking between the two lines of code that VBA created. By typing just one line of your own, you can enable the button to shut down your program. Here it is:

```
Unload Me
```

The Unload statement removes a form from memory. If you're referring to the form whose code you're currently working with, you don't have to specify the form's name — you can simply call it Me, a special VBA term that refers to the current form and all its code.

Correcting errors as you write code

The VBA compiler (see Chapter 1 for more about compilers) watches over your shoulder, figuratively, as you write your code. If the compiler catches an obvious error, you see an immediate error message identifying the problem, at least in general terms. Suppose, for example, you type a stray character after the statement Unload Me. The compiler knows that Unload Me is a complete statement and nothing should follow it on the same line. When you move the insertion point to another line, the compiler displays the entire statement in red and highlights the extraneous character. You see the message Compile error. Expected: end of statement.

The compiler can only detect some types of errors as you write your code. It catches others when you try to run the program, as I discuss in the section "Running programs in the Visual Basic Editor" later in this chapter.

Creating a second procedure

The next procedure, the one that displays your message as the label control's caption, is only a bit more complicated. This procedure should activate when the form appears on-screen. With the form's Code window still active, proceed as follows:

1. **At the top of the Code window, click the arrow beside the text box at the left, which should still read** OKButton.

   This action drops down a list of the items that belong to the form (see Figure 3-16).

Figure 3-16: The Object drop-down list shows all the items belonging to the form that owns this Code window.

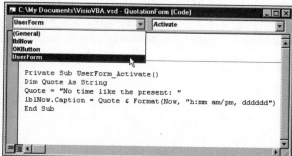

```
C:\My Documents\VisioVBA.vsd - QuotationForm (Code)
UserForm                    ▼    Activate                ▼
(General)
lblNow
OKButton
UserForm

   Private Sub UserForm_Activate()
   Dim Quote As String
   Quote = "No time like the present: "
   lblNow.Caption = Quote & Format(Now, "h:mm am/pm, dddddd")
   End Sub
```

2. **In the drop-down list, choose the UserForm item.**

   VBA creates a new procedure for the click event. In other words, a user clicking over any part of the form that doesn't have a control triggers this procedure. The sample program doesn't need this procedure, so leave it alone for the time being.

3. **Click the arrow at the top right of the Code window to drop down the Procedures list.**

   The list, which includes all the events that VBA can detect in connection with the UserForm, is long, which gives you some idea of how responsive you can make your programs (see Figure 3-17).

Figure 3-17:
The Procedure list displays every event available for the currently active object.

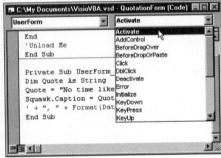

4. **Choose the very first item in the list, Activate.**

   You have to scroll up the list to find it. VBA dutifully creates a skeleton `UserForm1_Activate` procedure, which is triggered when the form gets loaded into memory.

5. **Now you can delete the** `UserForm1_Click` **procedure (if it bothers you) by selecting all the procedure's text and pressing the Del key.**

   This step is optional — the code does no harm. But because it does nothing at all except distract you, you may as well end its lonely life.

Writing code for the new procedure

With the skeleton for the correct event procedure in place, you can now go to work and flesh it out. Between the lines VBA has entered for you, type three new lines of code. The final procedure should look like this:

```
Private UserForm_Activate()
Dim Quote As String
Quote = "No time like the present: "
lblNow.Caption = Quote & Format(Now, "h:mm am/pm, dddddd")
End Sub
```

Here's what's going on:

1. The first line that you type, `Dim Quote As String`, creates a variable named `Quote` and defines it as a *string,* meaning a consecutive sequence of text characters.

2. The next line, `Quote = "No time like the present: "` stores the text "No time like the present: " in the `Quote` variable you just created. Just like in algebra class, you use the equal sign to assign a specific value to a variable. Notice also that a space occurs *before* the closing quotation mark to separate the proverbial statement from the next text.

3. The final line, `lblNow.Caption = Quote & Format(Now, "h:mm am/pm, ddddd")`, has the code that actually displays the complete message on the form.

   This line begins by identifying the label control named `lblNow` as the object with which you're working. Then comes a period, showing that what comes next is a property belonging to `lblNow` — in this case, its caption. A property is like a variable because you can change its value while the program runs. Therefore, you use the equal sign to change a property setting in code.

   The remainder of the line defines the message that should appear as the label's caption.

The first part of the message is the `Quote` variable. Then the plus sign tells VBA to add what follows to the text stored in `Quote`. Inside the parentheses, the `Now` *function* tells VBA to go fetch the current reading of the computer's clock, which keeps track of the date and time. The `Format` function then takes this raw information and converts it into a form you can read. Those letters inside the quotation marks define the particular format you see on the window, but I won't go into how they work in detail here — you can find more information in Chapter 11.

Step 3: Testing your program

This is only Step 3? Well, don't worry: The rest of the development cycle for the sample program doesn't take long.

Running programs in the Visual Basic Editor

You're ready to give the new program a trial run to see whether or not it works as you've planned. To run a VBA program from within the Visual Basic Editor, follow these steps:

1. **Click on either the UserForm window or the Code window for your program to be sure it's active.**

   Remember, you can tell which window is active by looking at the title bar — the active window's title bar is a different color than the title bars of inactive windows (which by default are drab gray).

2. **Then, to actually run the program, use any one of the following methods:**

   • Choose Run⇨Run Sub/UserForm.

   • Click the Run button on the Visual Basic Editor Standard toolbar. (The Standard toolbar is the only one visible in the Visual Basic Editor unless you customize the screen as described in Chapter 5.)

   • Press F5.

   After a brief pause, the program window appears over your VBA application (not over the Visual Basic Editor). If all goes well, what you see should look pretty much like Figure 3-18.

Figure 3-18:
The running version of the completed sample program.

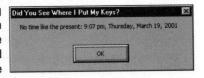

Be sure to include Step 1 (shown in the preceding step list) whenever you try to run a VBA program! If you don't activate the UserForm or Code window for the program first, nothing happens when you try to run the program (or a different program runs).

Compiling

A VBA program must be *compiled* before it can actually run the first time (see Chapter 1 for the definition of compiling). As the compiling process prepares your program for life in the fast lane, the code is checked line by line to be sure that it matches the conventions of the VBA language. The compiler stops at the first deviation and gives you a chance to correct the error. Even the slightest spelling error brings the compiling process to a screeching halt.

The compiler shows you an error message in a little window if it finds any mistakes. Among the suggested choices, the Debug button is usually your best course. Clicking Debug takes you straight to the Code window where the offending line is highlighted. The compiler keeps track of its work up to that point, so you can correct the error and continue compiling where you left off, using any of the techniques that I list earlier in this chapter (in the section "Running programs in the Visual Basic Editor") for running your program.

You can try your luck with the Help button if you want, but don't be surprised if the information it provides is too general to be of much use. The End button halts the compiler and your program, and returns you to the Visual Basic Editor.

Running clinical trials

The compiler may give your program a clean bill of health, but that doesn't mean the program works the way you want. Compiling a program without any errors is only a preliminary to real-life testing.

See, although the compiler never misses a VBA language error, it can't read your mind. It's perfectly content to pass lines that follow the VBA language conventions, even if they don't make sense in your program. Imagine a teacher who gives you an A for writing the following poem just because each line is a complete sentence:

```
Roses are red.
Violets are blue.
I have a bicycle.
Do you like fish?
```

The VBA compiler is that sort of grader.

After the compiler finishes its work, your program is running. You can now put it through its paces and see whether it works as you intended.

The sample program should be easy to test. If the window displays the intended message instead of `Inky Binky Bonky` and if clicking the OK button stops the program, congratulations. If not, you have bugs to eradicate.

Step 4: Debugging

As your programs get more complex, the likelihood for mistakes in the way they operate (*run-time errors*) grows exponentially. After you discover such an error, the task becomes identifying its cause and correcting the problem. In a word, that's *debugging*.

In smaller programs, this crude but reasonably effective debugging method sometimes works; simply read through your code line by line and see whether you can figure out what went wrong. After you understand the problem, it should be relatively easy to fix. (If something goes wrong with your sample program, all you have to do is compare your code against the printed version — if they don't match, change yours accordingly.)

Fortunately, VBA includes several debugging aids to complement the squint-and-scratch-your-head technique. Chapter 9 spells out the details.

Running a Form from Other VBA Code

Please keep in mind that the technique I gave in the previous section for running your first program works only inside the Visual Basic Editor. Selecting a form and pressing F5 is fine for testing a form as you work on it. However, after you've verified that the form functions properly, you need to put it into service in your VBA application. In other words, you want the form to pop up when it should, without having to switch to the Visual Basic Editor.

To trigger the display of a form from within a VBA application, you must first write a Sub procedure (a macro) that runs the form. You can then run *this* macro from the application.

For the little program you've been working on in this chapter, follow these steps:

1. **In the Visual Basic Editor, choose Insert⇨Module to create a module and open its Code window.**

2. **Type the following code:**

```
Sub ShowQuote()
   UserForm1.Show
End Sub
```

If your form is named something other than UserForm1, substitute that name for UserForm1.

After you save your work, you can run the ShowQuote program (macro) with the techniques that I describe in Chapter 4, which details running VBA programs. See Chapter 10 for further details on running form-based programs.

Returning to Your VBA Application

For my money, the best way to access a document in your VBA application while you're working with the Visual Basic Editor is to use the standard Windows technique for switching between applications. Press Alt+Tab until the application's icon is selected in the pop-up window and then release the keys.

Any of the following techniques also work:

- Choose View⇨AutoCAD (or whatever the application's name is).
- Click the View button at the far left of the Visual Basic Editor toolbar — it shows an icon representing the application's document.
- Press Alt+F11.
- Click the application's button in the Windows taskbar.

You can get back to the Visual Basic Editor with Alt+Tab, the taskbar, by again pressing Alt+F11, or by choosing Tools⇨Macro⇨Visual Basic Editor.

When you're ready to say goodnight to the Visual Basic Editor, either of the following options shuts down the Editor and takes you directly back to the VBA application you started from:

- Choose File⇨Close and Return to *<application>*.
- Press Alt+Q.

Chapter 4

Running VBA Programs

● ●

In This Chapter

▶ Running programs and macros from the Macros dialog box — reliable but not much fun

▶ Triggering macros from toolbar buttons and menu items

▶ Assigning macros to keyboard shortcuts

▶ Running programs automatically when something special happens

● ●

*N*o matter how much firepower a VBA program is packing, it doesn't do any blasting until you pull its trigger. For that matter, you have to *find* the trigger first. To put it more prosaically, until you find a way to run your VBA program, the program is worthless.

As you assemble a program in the Visual Basic Editor, you can always run it by pressing F5 or clicking the Run button on the Visual Basic Editor Standard toolbar. That's fine for testing purposes, but it doesn't help you in the real world. After the program is finished, you need to run it within your application.

In this chapter, I cover the options you can use to start your VBA programs and macros from a VBA application. (Remember, a macro is just a VBA program that you create by recording rather than coding the steps the program follows; see Chapter 2.) The Macros dialog box is the easy way to start most of your programs, but it's cumbersome. VBA programs become really useful when you hook them up to a menu command, toolbar button, or keyboard shortcut instead — or when you get them to run automatically.

To try out these techniques, use them with macros you record following the directions in Chapter 2, or with procedures you create in the Visual Basic Editor according to the outline in Chapter 6, or the detailed instructions in Parts II and III.

The Name Is Everything

You run VBA programs by name.

Sorry to hit you with the technicalities right at the outset, but I see no alternative. When you run a VBA program, you're running one specific VBA *procedure*. Your program may actually incorporate many different procedures, but only one of them contains the first line of code that you want the program to execute. This first procedure may run (*call*) other procedures, which in turn may call still others, and so on. Still, you have to run only the first procedure to get your program started — any called procedures run automatically as the program goes about its business.

So what's the point? Here it is: To run a VBA program, you have to know the name of the procedure that kicks off the program. In programs that do contain more than one procedure, the launch-pad procedure is usually named `Main`.

Hungry for something more substantial on the subject of procedures? Skip to Chapter 6 for a satisfying luncheon.

Running from the Macros Dialog Box

The surefire method for starting a VBA program is via the Macros dialog box. If you haven't gotten around to assigning the program to a toolbar button or keyboard shortcuts, or if you just plain forgot where you assigned it, the Macros dialog box is always there.

Displaying the Macros dialog box

To display the Macros dialog box in most VBA applications, do one of the following:

- ✔ Choose Tools➪Macro➪Macros.
- ✔ Press Alt+F8.

Some VBA applications may provide different methods for opening the Macros dialog box. In Corel Draw and WordPerfect, for example, you choose Tools➪Visual Basic➪Play. (And by the way, this dialog box is titled Macro instead of Macros in certain VBA applications, including Excel and PowerPoint — apparently inspired by Emerson, Microsoft eschews a foolish consistency.)

The Macros dialog box should look something like the dialog box shown in Figure 4-1. As usual, some of the details may vary, depending on the VBA application you're using. In any case, most of the dialog box is given over to a listing of the VBA programs currently available.

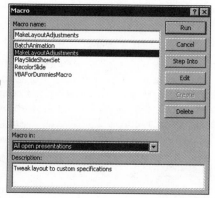

Figure 4-1:
The Macro dialog box as it appears in PowerPoint.

Technically speaking, all the procedures listed in the Macros dialog box are Sub procedures that take no arguments (this is the official definition of a macro; see Chapter 2). After you get such a procedure running, *it* can run other types of procedures, including Function procedures and Sub procedures that do take arguments. See Chapter 6 for more about these procedures.

Running a macro

Running a macro from the Macros dialog box is hardly a major challenge. The steps are:

1. **Select the macro in the list under Macro name.**
2. **Click the Run button.**

Pretty tough, huh? Alternatively, you can just double-click the program name in the list.

The only complication you may face is finding the program you want to run in the Macros dialog box. See the next section if you have trouble locating your program.

Finding your macro in the Macros dialog box

In the Macros dialog box, the VBA programs (macros) in the Macro Name list can sometimes be confusing. Depending on where a program is stored, it may be listed with an identifying preface.

Take the example of Excel, in which you can run VBA programs stored in the active workbook (the one you're currently using) as well as those in any other open workbooks. In the Macros dialog box, a macro stored in the active workbook appears under its own name. However, a macro that comes from another open workbook is listed as the workbook name followed by an exclamation point and then the macro name. Figure 4-2 shows an example.

Figure 4-2:
The Excel
Macro
dialog box
lists VBA
programs
(macros)
from non-
active
workbooks
by name.

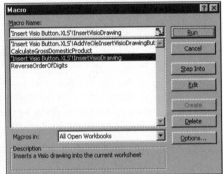

In Word, each program in the Macros dialog box is listed by the name of that procedure — *except* when two or more procedures have the same name. In that case, the duplicate procedures are listed under their module names, followed by a dot (period) and then the procedure name. I submit Figure 4-3 as evidence.

If the program you want to run doesn't appear at all, you may need to tell the Macros dialog box to display a different selection. To do so, use the drop-down list labeled Macros In. If the dialog box shows only programs associated with the current document, try a choice such as All Active Templates and Documents.

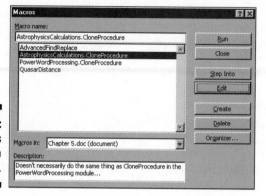

Figure 4-3:
The Macros
dialog box in
Word.

Launching Programs Quickly

The Macros dialog box may be foolproof, but it's ever so inefficient. When you want something done, you want it done *now*. Who wants to open up a dialog box, hunt through a long list of tiny names, and then click, click, oops, click, click, click.

There are better ways to fire up your VBA programs. Assign each one you use regularly to a toolbar button, menu item, or keyboard shortcut. Then one or two quick clicks or a single keystroke brings you immediate gratification.

As you may recall if you read Chapter 2, many VBA applications enable you to assign a macro to a toolbar button or keyboard shortcut at the time you record the macro. This capability is one good reason to start a new VBA program by recording a macro, which you can then edit with your own code. Refer to Chapter 2 if you need a refresher on how this process works.

But suppose you've already recorded your macro, without having hooked it up to a toolbar or keyboard shortcut at the time. Or say that you've written a VBA program from scratch, without using the macro recorder. In these situations, you can still assign your macro or program to a toolbar button, menu choice, or keyboard shortcut any time you like. Unfortunately, the techniques required vary somewhat among different VBA applications. I discuss some of the wrinkles in the remainder of this (fairly lengthy) section.

Push button programs

Nothing is quite like the thrill of clicking a cute little on-screen button and getting an immediate response from your computer. True, more thrilling thrills exist, but button pushing definitely has its appeal. And you get a little extra tingle when that button you click triggers your very own VBA program.

Some VBA applications make setting up custom buttons for running VBA programs easy — even if you didn't create the program initially by recording a macro. Most Office applications fall into this category. In other VBA apps, such as Visio, you may have to write VBA code to add custom buttons. Ouch! I thought VBA was supposed to be a visual interface designer.

Toolbar buttons versus menu items

When you think about it, you can see that an item on a menu is basically no different from a toolbar button: It triggers some command when you pick it. The typical menu choice looks different than a button because it displays text instead of, or in addition to, a picture. And you use a different technique with the mouse to trigger it. But the result is the same.

Office applications let you use the same drag-and-drop techniques to assign a VBA program to a custom toolbar button or menu choice.

Easy buttons and menu choices in Office

In Microsoft Word, Excel, PowerPoint, Outlook, or Project, assigning a VBA program to a new toolbar button is a simple matter of drag-and-drop with the mouse. After you have the button in place, you can dress it up with an appropriate picture.

Creating a button or menu item for a VBA program in Word

Here's how to create a button that triggers a VBA program in Word, PowerPoint, Outlook, or Project:

1. **Right-click any toolbar.**

   A shortcut menu pops up.

2. **Choose Customize at the bottom of the menu to display the Customize dialog box, which initially displays the Toolbars tab.**

   You can also display the Customize dialog box directly by choosing Tools⇨Customize.

3. **Click the Commands tab of the Customize dialog box, as shown in Figure 4-4.**

4. **Scroll down the list under Categories until you see the Macros item; click it to select it.**

   All the runnable VBA programs at your disposal then appear in the Commands list on the right. (If you look again closely at Figure 4-4, you can see that it shows the Customize dialog box set to display macros.)

5. **Locate your target macro in the list, scrolling to find it if necessary (again, this macro may be a VBA program that you've written from scratch).**

6. **If you're creating a toolbar button, drag the macro from the Commands list into position on any toolbar. If you're adding a custom menu item**

instead, drag the macro directly over the target menu, wait a moment until the menu drops down, and then position the macro where you want it on the list of menu items.

When you release the mouse button, a new button or menu item labeled with the name of your program appears. Don't worry if you don't like the button look — you can change that with the steps in the section "Putting on a pretty face," later in this chapter.

7. Close the Customize dialog box to complete the job.

Now, every time you click the new button, your VBA program runs. Miraculous!

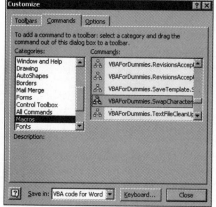

Figure 4-4:
The
Customize
dialog box
showing the
Commands
tab.

Making VBA buttons in FrontPage and Excel

In FrontPage and Excel, you use a slightly different procedure for creating custom toolbar buttons to fire your VBA programs. After recording a macro or writing a VBA program, follow Steps 1 through 4 in the previous step list, just as you would in Word, PowerPoint or Excel. At this point, instead of a list of the available macros, you see only two items in the Commands list on the right of the Customize dialog box: Custom Menu Item and Custom Button (see Figure 4-5). Proceed as follows:

1. Drag the relevant item, Custom Menu Item or Custom Button, to its place on any toolbar or menu (either item can be used on both toolbars and menus — they really are equivalent except for looks).

When you release the mouse button, the new button or menu item appears. If you're working with the Custom Button choice, you see a grinning yellow face on the target toolbar or menu. With the Custom Menu Item choice, you just see the macro's name.

2. Without closing the Customize dialog box, right-click your new toolbar button to pop up the shortcut menu that's shown in Figure 4-6.

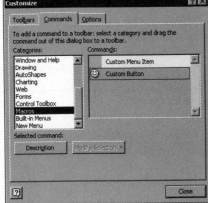

Figure 4-5:
The
Customize
dialog box in
Excel,
poised for
creating a
custom
toolbar
button or
menu item.

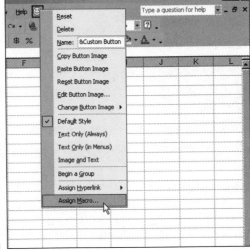

Figure 4-6:
Use this
shortcut
menu to
assign a
custom VBA
program to
a toolbar
button in
Excel or
FrontPage.

3. Choose Assign Macro on the shortcut menu.

A separate dialog box listing the available macros appears.

4. Make a selection from the list.

When you choose OK to return to the Customize dialog box your new button is ready for a facelift. See "Putting on a pretty face" later in this chapter for details.

5. Close the Customize dialog box.

Creating custom toolbar buttons in Access

Access diverges substantially from the other Office applications when it comes to assigning a VBA program to a custom toolbar button or menu choice. The most important difference is that Access requires your toolbar and menu programs to be written as `Function` procedures, not `Sub` procedures as in all other Office applications. See Chapter 6 for details about the differences between these two types of VBA procedures.

After you've written a Function procedure that you want to trigger from a toolbar button or menu choice, proceed as follows:

1. **Start by opening the Tools⇨Customize dialog box and switching to the Commands tab (just as you would in the other Office applications).**

   Refer to Figure 4-4 for a view of the Customize dialog box in Word.

2. **In the Categories list on the left side of the box, leave the top choice, File, selected.**

3. **Proceed by dragging the first item in the Commands list on the right to the destination toolbar or menu (as you would in the other Office applications).**

4. **When you drop it into place, right-click the new button or menu item to display the Access version of the shortcut menu for button or menu item customization.**

   To see a similar shortcut menu, refer to Figure 4-5.

5. **Choose Properties at the bottom of the shortcut menu to bring up the Database Control Properties dialog box.**

   The Database Control Properties dialog box is unique to Access.

6. **Here, use the On Action box to type the name of your custom VBA program (`Function` procedure).**

   You must precede the program name with an equal sign and follow it with parentheses as shown in the following example:

   ```
   =SomeFunction()
   ```

7. **Close the Database Control Properties dialog box.**

   You can customize the appearance of your new button or menu item by using the technique that I detail in the section "Putting on a pretty face."

Customizing toolbars in other VBA apps

Other VBA applications differ widely with regard to the techniques you must use to connect your VBA programs to custom toolbar buttons. In Visio, for example, you must write VBA code to do the job; if you need instructions, please consult this book's Web site at www.seldenhouse.com/vba. On the other hand, the Corel Draw custom button system is similar to that of Word, PowerPoint, and FrontPage, as follows:

1. **Start by choosing Tools⇨Options.**

   A dialog box appears.

2. **From the list in the left pane, select the Commands item under Customization.**

3. **Choose Macros from the bottom of the drop-down list at the top middle of the dialog box.**

   You can now drag any available macro to a toolbar.

Putting on a pretty face

Office programs assign a name automatically to each new VBA-based button. Of course, a super-wide button labeled something like the following is ugly as sin and wastes lots of space on your toolbar:

```
DummiesTemplate.GraphicsRoutines.MakeSalesGraph
```

You can, however, easily exchange that verbose text for a compact graphical image. Follow these steps:

1. **If the Customize dialog box is not already visible, open it and switch to the Commands tab.**

   See Steps 1 through 3 in the section "Creating custom toolbar buttons in Access."

2. **Right-click your new button on the toolbar.**

   A lengthy shortcut menu appears.

3. **About halfway down the menu, select the Change Button Image choice to display a graphical menu of stock button faces.**

   This procedure is illustrated in Figure 4-7.

Figure 4-7: With the Customize dialog box open, right-clicking an Office toolbar displays this shortcut menu.

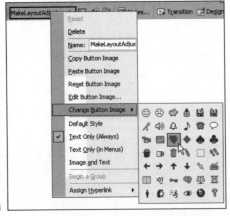

4. **If you like one of the supplied images, click it to select it and skip to Step 8; otherwise, continue with Step 5.**

5. **From the shortcut menu, choose Edit Button Image.**

   Figure 4-8 shows the Button Editor Window, a little art studio you get for painting the individual dots for your button.

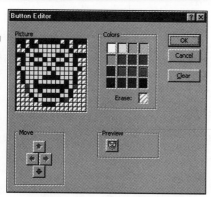

Figure 4-8:
Use the
Office
Button
Editor to
paint your
own custom
button
faces.

6. **Pick a color from the palette, and then click the blow-up of the button image to daub it on.**

   To get rid of color so that the toolbar background shows through, paint after clicking Erase. You can click the Move buttons to move the entire image in the direction of any edge that doesn't already have any colored dots.

   Now that you have a graphical face for your button, you can turn off that text.

7. **Reopen the shortcut menu (see Step 2).**

8. **Select the Default Style choice.**

   After you're finished, a pretty little button should be parked securely on the toolbar, ready to spring into action whenever you click it. The button shown in the margin is the button face that I designed in Figure 4-8.

Removing buttons

In Office, you can delete a toolbar button you no longer need by simply dragging it off the toolbar. The trick is to hold down the Alt key as you drag the button to any part of the screen that doesn't have a toolbar. When you see a boxed X beside the mouse pointer, you can release the mouse button to delete the button.

Custom buttons via VBA code

I feel for you if your VBA application doesn't provide an easy drag-and-drop route to custom buttons. Early on in your experience with VBA, the code required to create buttons looks daunting. Actually, however, it's not *too* hard to create buttons this way. The trick is figuring out which objects your VBA application uses to represent toolbars and buttons, and which properties or methods are required to change them.

And they call VBA a standard . . .

In Office, for example, buttons are called `CommandBarButtons` in VBA code, and they belong to `CommandBarControls` collections. A given CommandBar (the toolbar that contains a CommandBarControls collection) resides in a `CommandBars` collection, which can belong to the `Application` object or a `Document` object.

In Visio, on the other hand, the `ToolbarItem` object represents a single button in VBA code. To work with a particular `ToolbarItem` object, however, you have to access the `ToolbarItems` collection to which it belongs. That `ToolbarItems` collection itself belongs to a `Toolbars` collection, which in turn is a member of a `ToolbarSet` collection, which in turn belongs to a particular `UIObject` (user interface object).

If all that complication sounds terrifying, just remember that you probably don't have to write the code for the custom button from scratch. Hunt in the Help files for your VBA application on the subjects of customizing and toolbars, and you're likely to find an example that you can modify without much trouble. Again, I show you how all this works with some sample code on the Web site for this book (`www.seldenhouse.com/vba`).

Keyboard shortcuts in Word, Excel, and Access

If you're any good at all as a typist, the commands that you use most often cry out for keyboard shortcuts. In most applications, even those that are heavily oriented toward graphics, pressing keys is quicker than moving the mouse around and clicking it. The only drawback to keyboard shortcuts is that you have to memorize them.

At any rate, some VBA applications — including Word, Excel, and Access — give you direct access to the keyboard, allowing you to set up keyboard shortcuts for your VBA programs. If you're offered this kind of control, by all means take it.

Custom keyboard shortcuts in Word

When it comes to customizing the keyboard, Word is (hands down) the easiest and most versatile VBA application to manipulate. For example, if you want to assign a VBA program called `DoubleCurrentFontSize` to the keyboard shortcut Alt+Shift+> (that is, Alt+Shift+ the period key) in Word, follow these steps:

1. **Open the Customize dialog box by choosing Tools⇨Customize, or by right-clicking a toolbar and choosing Customize from the shortcut menu.**

   If you want another peek at this dialog box, refer to Figure 4-4.

2. **Click the Keyboard button at the bottom of the Options tab.**

   Up pops the Customize Keyboard dialog box, as shown in Figure 4-9.

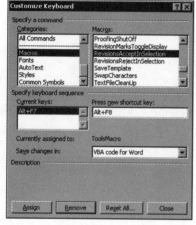

Figure 4-9: Assign your VBA programs keyboard shortcuts with this dialog box.

3. **Select Macros in the Categories list.**

4. **Locate and select your program in the list that appears in the Macros list box.**

   If the program has already been assigned to a shortcut, that shortcut appears in the Current Keys list box.

5. **Press the key combination for your shortcut.**

   If the shortcut you choose is already in use, the dialog box tells you which command it triggers so that you can decide whether to keep the existing shortcut or go ahead and replace it with the new one.

6. **Click Assign, and then click Close to leave the dialog box.**

Your shortcut is now in effect.

Look really cool: Put your programs on shortcut menus

With just a little work, you can give your humble VBA program a high-fashion home on the shortcut (right-click) menu of your choice.

In Office, you can customize any shortcut menu in the Customize dialog box. The trick is to display first the Shortcut Menus toolbar. After choosing Tools⇨Customize to open the dialog box, display the Toolbars tab (if it isn't already visible) by clicking the corresponding tab at the top of the dialog box. Scroll down the list of toolbars until you see the Shortcut Menus item, and click in the little box beside it.

The Shortcut Menus toolbar should now be visible on-screen. You can navigate through this toolbar's menu system to the particular shortcut menu you want to customize. After you've opened it, use the technique discussed at the beginning of the section "Launching Programs Quickly" to drag any macro from the Commands tab of the Customize dialog box.

Visio lets you place a macro on the shortcut menu for any shape. After selecting the shape, choose Window⇨Show ShapeSheet. In the ShapeSheet window, click in an Action cell. (If necessary, first insert an Actions section by choosing Insert⇨Section and checking Actions.)

Then choose Edit⇨Action. Now you can type in the text and other properties for the menu item and pick out which program you want it to run. After you're through, the shortcut menu that appears when you right-click the shape should include an item for your VBA program.

Keyboard shortcuts in Excel

Excel lets you assign VBA programs to keyboard shortcuts, but it restricts you to key combinations based on Ctrl with the type-able keys (letters, numbers, and punctuation marks). To assign a program to a shortcut, proceed as follows:

1. **Open the Macro dialog box. (Why not use the Alt+F8 keyboard shortcut?)**

2. **Locate and select your program in the list.**

3. **Click Options.**

4. **In the resulting dialog box (see Figure 4-10), type the key you want to combine with Ctrl for the shortcut.**

   Excel distinguishes between upper- and lowercase letters. (In other words, an alphabet key typed with the Shift key is different from an alphabet key typed without pressing Shift.)

5. **Click OK to return to the Macro dialog box.**

Keyboard shortcuts in Access

In custom Access database applications, you can easily create your own keyboard shortcuts. Access applications revolve around custom forms and their controls. All you have to do is create event procedures for these forms and controls, procedures that run when the user presses a key. Chapter 10 covers programming for event procedures in some detail. The events you're interested in are KeyPress, KeyDown, and KeyUp.

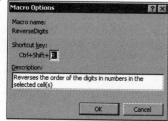

Figure 4-10:
Assigning
a VBA
program to
a keyboard
shortcut in
Excel.

Things are different if you're working with an Access database directly, using the stock menu commands and toolbar buttons. In this case, you create custom keyboard shortcuts that run VBA programs by assigning them to special Access macros. (Access macros, you may remember, are *not* VBA procedures.) Access lacks a macro recorder, so you have to handcraft your macros as follows:

1. **In the Database window, select the Macros button and then click the New button.**

   This action displays the Macro window (Figure 4-11).

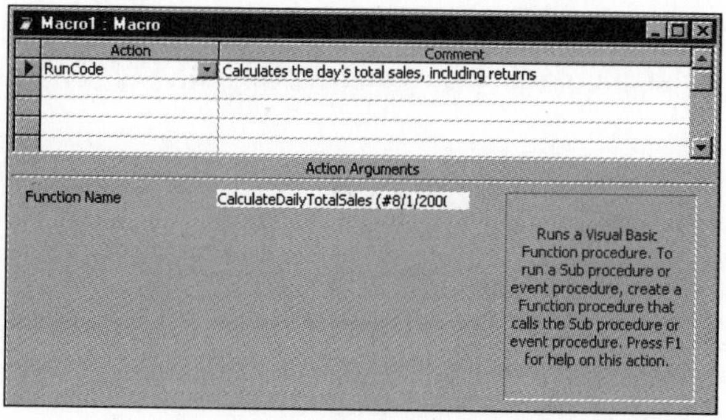

Figure 4-11:
Use this
window to
create
Access
macros.

2. **In the Action column, select the RunCode item, as shown in Figure 4-11.**

3. **Choose View⇨Macro Names to display in the window an extra column called Macro Name.**

4. **Enter the keyboard shortcut to which you want to assign your VBA program in the Macro Name column.**

Use the ^ (carat) symbol to indicate the Ctrl key and the + (plus sign) symbol to indicate the Shift key. You can type ordinary letters and numbers, but you must stick braces around function keys. For example, type **^k** to create a Ctrl+k shortcut, or **+{F8}** to create a Shift+F8 shortcut.

5. **Click the Function Name text box and type the name of the VBA procedure that the macro should run.**

   It has to be a Function procedure.

6. **Close the Macro window by clicking the x in the upper-right corner; when Access asks you to name the macro, type** AutoKeys.

Macros in Visio

Visio provides yet another way to run VBA programs — by double-clicking a shape that you've associated with your code. Here's how to set up a double-click shape:

1. **Click the shape to select it.**

2. **Choose Format⇨Behavior.**

   The Behavior dialog box materializes over the Visio workspace, as shown in Figure 4-12.

3. **Click the Double-Click tab to display the options shown in Figure 4-12.**

4. **Select the VBA procedure of your dreams from the Run Macro list.**

5. **Click OK.**

Now, whenever you double-click that shape, your VBA program runs.

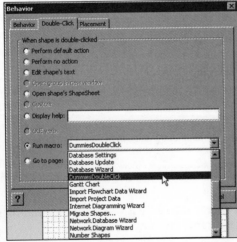

Figure 4-12: Use this dialog box to associate a Visio shape with a VBA procedure that runs when you double-click the shape.

Running VBA Programs Automatically

Suppose that you come up with a VBA program you like so much that you want to see it in action first thing, every time you start your application. If you love your program that much, even the slight delay of clicking a button may be too much to bear.

Fortunately for you, many applications let you run VBA code automatically when the application starts up or shuts down, when a document opens or closes, and when other events take place. Tables 4-1 through 4-3 survey the techniques that you can use in some popular VBA applications to run your VBA programs automatically.

Table 4-1	Automatically Running VBA Programs by Opening the Application's Shortcut	
Application	*Command to Type in the Target Box*	*Comments*
Microsoft Word	/m*procedure*	Type the name of your VBA procedure in place of *procedure*.
Microsoft Access	/x*macro*	Runs the Access macro you list. To run a VBA procedure, the Access macro should contain a RunCode action (see "Keyboard shortcuts in Access," earlier in this chapter).

Table 4-2	Automatically Running VBA Programs in Word by Giving the VBA Program a Special Name
Name for the VBA Program	*When It Runs Automatically*
`AutoExec`	When Word starts up
`AutoNew`	When each new document is created
`AutoOpen`	When any existing document is opened
`AutoClose`	When a document is closed
`AutoExit`	When Word exits

Note: The AutoExec macro must be stored in the Normal template (normal.dot).

Working with Windows shortcuts

Word and Access allow you to run VBA code by adding extra commands to the name of the application when you start it (see Table 4-1). Unless you want to type these commands at the DOS prompt, you need to modify or create a Windows shortcut to run the application.

In Windows, icons on the Start menu represent shortcuts. To create a shortcut to trigger your custom macro, make a copy of one of the shortcuts on the Start menu or create a new shortcut in Explorer or on the Desktop by right-clicking an empty area and choosing New⇨Shortcut. In the Create Shortcut dialog box, browse to the appropriate program file (Winword.exe or MSAccess.exe). Then, after you type in a name for your shortcut, it appears on your Desktop or in Explorer. Now right-click the shortcut and choose Properties

from the shortcut menu to display the Properties dialog box.

Next select the Shortcut tab. In the Target text box that appears, type the necessary command after the name of the application itself. The following examples make a VBA procedure run automatically when you start Word. The following shows how the complete Target entry might look if you're running a macro stored in the Normal template:

```
"C:\Microsoft
    Office\WINWORD.EXE"
    /mAutomaticNovel
```

This example runs a template stored in a particular document:

```
"C:\Microsoft
    Office\WINWORD.EXE" "C:\My
    documents\Hip.doc" /mHop
```

Table 4-3	Running VBA Programs by Writing Event Procedures in VBA Code (see Chapter 14 for details on event programming)		
Application	*When the Code Runs Automatically*	*Start with This Object*	*Write Code for This Event*
Word	When a document opens	Document	Open
Word	When a new document is created	Document	New
Word	When a document is closed	Document	Close
Excel	When any workbook opens	Application	WorkbookOpen
Excel	When a specific workbook opens	Workbook	Open

Application	When the Code Runs Automatically	Start with This Object	Write Code for This Event
Excel	When a new worksheet is created	Workbook	NewSheet
Visio	When a document is saved using another name	Document	DocumentSavedAs
Visio	When a new document is created	Document	DocumentOpened

Note: These are just a few of many available events pertaining to entire documents in Word, Excel, and Visio.

Chapter 5

The Visual Basic Editor at Your Command

In This Chapter

▶ Finding commands in the Visual Basic Editor menu system

▶ Displaying, moving, and customizing the Editor toolbars

▶ Understanding how docking works in toolbars and windows

▶ Grappling with the multitudes of Editor windows

▶ Discovering keyboard shortcuts available in the Visual Basic Editor

▶ A bird's eye view of your VBA projects with the Project Explorer

▶ Investigating project objects with the Object Browser

▶ Writing code — and having it written for you — in the Code window

*R*emember that scene in *Fantasia* where Mickey Mouse plays the Sorcerer's Apprentice? A magic broom to help with the chores seems like a great idea, but pretty soon he has an out-of-control bucket brigade — and he just about drowns.

Your early experiments with the Visual Basic Editor may leave you feeling equally inundated. You can quickly open up so many unfamiliar windows that your mind starts sinking. But don't panic — those windows don't let any water into your basement, and each can perform an important job for you. Armed with a little experience and the tips you get in this chapter, you can put the Editor and its windows completely under your power.

Specifically, I cover the Project Explorer, Object Browser, and Code windows in some detail — not just how they look and how their controls work, but how you put them to use during a programming session. Detailed coverage of the other windows — including the UserForm, Properties, and the four debugging windows — comes in Chapters 9 and 10, but you find basic information on them here.

Working with the Visual Basic Editor User Interface

The Visual Basic Editor user interface is standard Microsoft fare — the menus, toolbars, and keyboard shortcuts look and work much like those of Microsoft Office. You'll feel right at home if you're using VBA with an Office application.

On the other hand, you may notice a contrast between a non-Microsoft application's interface and that of the Visual Basic Editor. Remember, the other software publishers have licensed VBA from Microsoft and grafted it onto their own products, which in some cases took shape long before VBA arrived or the current Office interface emerged.

Out to lunch with Editor menus

I realize that you already know how to use menus. What you may be interested in, though, is where to find certain commands on the Visual Basic Editor menus.

For the most part, the Editor commands are organized logically. When you want to display a particular window, for example, you shouldn't have trouble locating the necessary command — it's on the View menu, of course. A few items aren't so obvious, however. The following little table clues you in to some of the Editor's hidden menu commands:

Task	Menu Cßommand	Comments
Control the settings for an entire project	Tools⇨Project Properties	This is an odd location for a command pertaining to the VBA project you're working with — I expected to find it on the File menu.
Customize the Visual Basic Editor itself	View⇨Toolbars⇨Customize and Tools⇨Options	
Turn on Design Mode	Run⇨Design Mode	The Design Mode command sounds like it's intended for laying out forms, so why is it on the Run menu? Because it stops any running program. It isn't a very useful command because you can design forms without it, and you don't need to leave Design Mode to run a program.

Tuning the toolbars

If you're familiar with Word, Excel, or PowerPoint, you're probably plenty comfortable with the way toolbars work in the Visual Basic Editor. If not, a few brief comments should suffice.

The Editor comes with four prefab toolbars:

- ✔ **Standard:** This is the only toolbar visible when you first run the Editor. It includes buttons for a broad range of functions, including saving your work, inserting new forms and modules, editing, and running your programs.

- ✔ **Edit:** The buttons on this toolbar are handy when you're editing code. They duplicate commands on the Edit menu.

- ✔ **Debug:** This toolbar contains buttons for commands that you're likely to need while tracking down errors in your programs.

- ✔ **UserForm:** Use this toolbar for form design. Most of the buttons duplicate commands on the Format menu for aligning, ordering, and grouping controls on forms.

You can use the stock toolbars in any combination. Just two quick clicks display a toolbar (if it's not currently visible) or hide it (if it's already on-screen). Here's the procedure:

1. **Start by right-clicking any toolbar.**

   A shortcut menu pops up (see Figure 5-1), listing the available toolbars. When a toolbar is visible, you see a check mark beside its name.

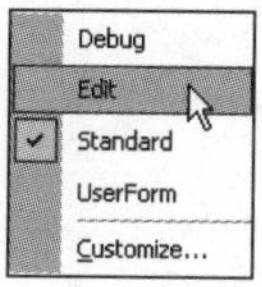

Figure 5-1:
A shortcut menu to display or hide toolbars.

2. **On the menu, select the toolbar you want to display or remove.**

   As soon as you release the mouse button, the change occurs.

The Editor toolbars can exist in one of three states, as shown here:

Toolbar Status	How tßhe Toolbar Appears On-screen
Hidden	Not visible on-screen.
Docked	Stuck up against any of the four edges of the main work area.
Floating	In a separate window with its own title bar and Close button. Floating toolbars can be positioned outside the Editor.

Figure 5-2 shows the Visual Basic Editor configured with two docked and two floating toolbars. Most of the main windows in the Visual Basic Editor can exist in docked, floating, or hidden form.

To make a docked toolbar float, just drag it away from its edge of the work area toward the center of the screen. The most convenient place to "grab" a docked toolbar is in the area of those two little bars at the left or top — this region is called the *move handle.* Alternatively, you can just double-click the move handle to float the toolbar.

Vice being versa, you can convert a floating toolbar to a docked one by dragging its title bar toward any edge of the work area. As soon as it gets close enough, the window's gravitational field pulls the toolbar in tight. This effect is cool, but you can dock a floating toolbar more quickly by double-clicking the title bar (it returns to its last docked position).

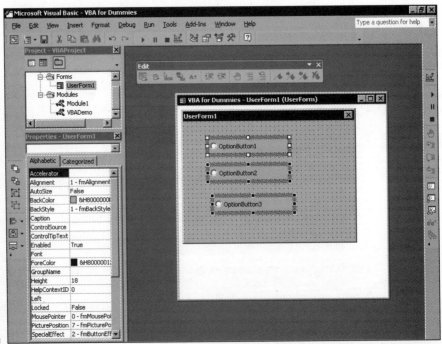

Figure 5-2: By default, Visual Basic Editor toolbars are docked below the menu bar; you can dock them along other edges or let them float freely on-screen.

Customizing your toolbars and menus

Suppose that you're not satisfied with the toolbars supplied with the Visual Basic Editor. Well, just make your own. You can add or remove buttons and menu items on the existing toolbars or menus, and if that's not radical enough for you, you can create your own toolbars from scratch (the process works just like it does in Office applications).

Moving and deleting toolbar buttons

If you only want to move or delete an existing button, all you have to do is hold down the Alt key while you drag the button to a new location. While holding down Alt, you can

- ✔ Drag a button to a new position on the same or a different toolbar. If you want to place a *copy* of the button at the new location, hold down both Alt and Ctrl as you drag.

- ✔ Add a separator line between a pair of buttons by dragging the button on the right just a little further to the right (go too far, and you move the button over one spot). To remove a separator line, drag the button on its right a bit to the left.

- ✔ Delete a button by dragging it to any location that isn't a toolbar. As soon as you see the X in the mouse pointer, you can let up on the mouse button — and that toolbar button is history.

Adding new toolbar buttons

For fancier modifications — for example, to create a new toolbar to hold your favorite buttons — you need to display the Customize dialog box. You use this dialog box to add new toolbar buttons, and it has to be open if you want to alter the menus.

Here are the steps for adding new toolbar buttons:

1. **Right-click any toolbar and then select Customize at the bottom of the shortcut menu.**

   This action brings up the Customize dialog box, shown in Figure 5-3.

2. **If the toolbar you want to customize isn't already visible, select the Toolbars tab of the Customize dialog box.**

   Check the box for the correct toolbar there. You can add a new toolbar by clicking the New button and typing a name.

3. **After you can see the toolbar you want to work with, switch to the Commands tab.**

   Now you can drag and drop items in the list to the toolbar or menu.

4. **Close the Customize dialog box when the toolbar is the way you want it.**

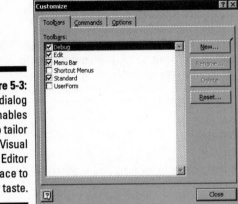

Note that with the Customize dialog box open, you can move or delete existing toolbar buttons without holding down the Alt key. However, you still must hold down Ctrl if you want to copy rather than move an item.

Monkeying with the menus

To customize the Visual Basic Editor menus, you must first display the Customize dialog box (see Step 1 in the previous section). This accomplished, you can click a menu to open it and then drag individual menu items to other positions or to other menus. Dragging a menu choice into the work area deletes it. You can add or remove a separator line between two items by dragging the lower item just a tad down or up.

To add new choices to a menu, drag them from the Commands tab of the Customize dialog box, just as you would for new toolbar buttons. Figures 5-3 and 5-4 give you the idea.

As if customizing the main menu system isn't enough, the Visual Basic Editor enables you to modify the shortcut (right-click) menus as well. You start by opening the Customize dialog box, switching to the Toolbars tab, and checking the box for the Shortcut Menus item.

This action brings up a special little toolbar just for customizing purposes. Here, locate and click the specific shortcut menu you want to work with. You can then drag items from the Commands tab to the shortcut menu, as shown in Figure 5-4.

Keyboard shortcuts

Table 5-1 lists the keyboard shortcuts available in the VBA Editor. You can also use the standard Windows keyboard commands for cursor control and text editing. Remember also that pressing Shift+F10 pops up the shortcut menu for the window or other item that's currently active — just as if you had right-clicked the item.

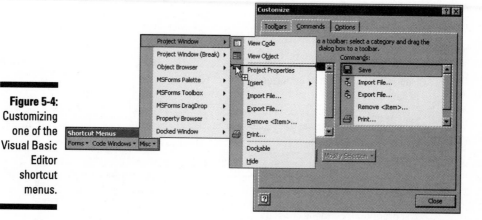

Figure 5-4:
Customizing one of the Visual Basic Editor shortcut menus.

Table 5-1   Keyboard Shortcuts in the Visual Basic Editor

Displaying Windows

To Do This	Press
Display the Code window for the selected form or control	F7
Display the form corresponding to the active Code window	Shift+F7
Move to the next Code or UserForm window	Ctrl+Tab
Activate the Object Browser window	F2
Activate the Properties window	F4
Activate the Immediate window	Ctrl+G
Activate the Call Stack window while a program is running	Ctrl+L

(continued)

Table 5-1 *(continued)*

Working with Code

To Do This	*Press*
Jump to the definition of the item at the insertion point	Shift+F2
Display the Find dialog box	Ctrl+F
Find Next (find the next occurrence of Find text)	F3
Find Previous	Shift+F3
Replace	Ctrl+H
Jump to the line previously edited	Ctrl+Shift+F2
Undo	Ctrl+Z
List properties/methods	Ctrl+J
List constants	Ctrl+Shift+J
Display Quick Info about the variable or object at the insertion point	Ctrl+I
Display parameter information for the function at the insertion point	Ctrl+Shift+I
Complete the word you're typing automatically	Ctrl+spacebar

Working with Properties

To Do This	*Press*
In the Property window, move to the next property in the list that begins with a particular letter	Ctrl+Shift+<letter>

Running Programs

To Do This	*Press*
Run the procedure or UserForm in the active window	F5
Pause code execution and enter Break mode	Ctrl+Break

Managing the Windows

Unless you have a really gargantuan monitor, plan to spend some time moving windows around in the Visual Basic Editor. Those windows aren't there just for looks — each has something very valuable to contribute to your programming effort. The problem is that keeping them all open at once is not practical — you won't have enough space left for your VBA code and forms.

Some windows are loners; some run in crowds

Here's One Basic Fact to understand about Visual Basic Editor windows: You can have as many Code and UserForm windows as you need — but only one each of the other window types. This restriction may make perfect sense to you already, but it took me a while to figure out how the system works.

You need multiple Code and UserForm windows because you're likely to create more than one form and one VBA module. With a window for each, you can keep all your forms and modules in memory and available for quick access.

Some of the remaining windows — the Properties and Locals windows, to name names — change their contents automatically when you switch to a different Code or UserForm window. It's like getting multiple windows for the price of one. Others, such as the Object Browser, the Project Explorer, and the Immediate window, apply to everything you do in the Editor, so only one of each is necessary.

Viewing and hiding windows

Most Editor windows have their own keyboard shortcuts, which means that you can pop up a window that isn't currently visible without taking your fingers off the keyboard. Table 5-1 lists the shortcuts you need. If you can't remember the shortcut, you can display any window via the View menu.

Perhaps unfortunately, the keyboard shortcuts *aren't* toggle switches. If a window is already open, pressing its key combination doesn't hide it. To put a window back to bed, you have to click the window's little Close button (the one with the X in it at the far right side of the title bar) or press Ctl+F4.

To display a specific window that's open but buried, you can choose it by name from the Window menu. Only non-dockable windows are listed there.

As in many Windows applications, two keyboard shortcuts are available for switching from one window to the next: Ctrl+Tab and Ctrl+F6. In the Visual Basic Editor, however, only non-dockable windows become active in sequence as you press the shortcut keys repeatedly.

By now you may be asking, "So what is a non-dockable window?" You find the answer just ahead in the following section.

Docking windows, or not

Like the toolbars, most of the Editor windows are *dockable* — you can attach them along any of the four edges of the main workspace where they can't cover up other windows. Of course, docking a window makes the workspace smaller. Figure 5-5 shows the Editor with most of its visible windows docked (the exception is the Toolbox toolbar). Those overlapping UserForm and Code windows in the center of the window occupy what's left of the workspace, but they could have been maximized to fill it.

Alternatively, you can let your windows float freely in the breeze. Floating windows leave you more room for writing code and designing forms, but they often cover up other windows. If you have a big monitor, you may prefer to display the Visual Basic Editor at less than maximum size and then move individual floating windows outside the Editor altogether.

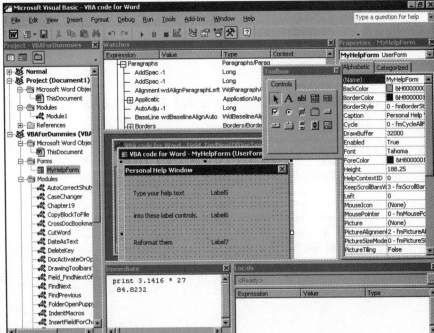

Figure 5-5:
As you dock windows along the edges of the Visual Basic Editor window, the space available for editing code and designing forms grows smaller.

No docking

Certain windows can't be docked. Docking is out for the Code and UserForm windows (however, you can maximize them to fill all the workspace that isn't occupied by docked windows). In addition, you can make any other window *non-dockable.* To check or set docking status for all window types (except Code and UserForm windows, of course), choose Tools⇨Options and click the Docking tab. The pedestrian dialog box shown in Figure 5-6 appears.

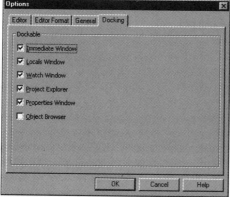

Figure 5-6: Set docking status for Visual Basic Editor windows in this dialog box.

You can also make a dockable window non-dockable (if the window is currently docked) by right-clicking its title bar and choosing Dockable from the shortcut menu. Unfortunately, this trick doesn't work in the reverse direction.

Docking factoids

Points to ponder while you're trying to figure out how window docking works:

- ✔ A Code, UserForm, or any other non-dockable window can be maximized, minimized, or *restored* (Microsoft jargon for windows of user-determined size). Non-dockable windows have the full complement of standard Windows buttons at the right side of the title bar: Minimize, Maximize (or Restore, if the window is already maximized), and Close.

- ✔ You can tell whether a window is currently dockable by looking at the title bar. Dockable windows have only a Close button; non-dockable windows have the Minimize and Maximize (or Restore) buttons.

- ✔ When you maximize any non-dockable window, it fills whatever space is left by any other windows currently docked in the work area.

- ✔ To move a floating window to the edge of the work area without docking it, you must first make the window non-dockable.

- ✔ All open, non-dockable windows are accessible in sequence via the Ctrl+Tab keyboard shortcut. They're also listed on the Window menu.

Saving the screen layout

The Visual Basic Editor automatically preserves the layout that's in effect at the time you exit. The locations of your windows, menus, and toolbars don't change from one Visual Basic Editor session to the next.

Managing Your Projects with Project Explorer

In VBA, a *project* is all the code and forms that belong to one document, along with the document itself. In the Visual Basic Editor, you use the Project Explorer window for a bird's eye view of all projects currently open in your application — and more importantly, to navigate quickly to the Code or UserForm window you want to work with.

To save the project you're currently working with — the one selected in the Project Explorer, as I describe later in this section — click the Save button on the Visual Basic Editor's Standard toolbar. You don't have to go back to your VBA application to save the document with its associated code.

Opening the Project Explorer window

The Project Explorer should already be visible when you first open the Visual Basic Editor. If it isn't, you can make it appear with any of the following techniques:

- ✔ Press Ctrl+R.
- ✔ Click the Project Explorer button on the Standard toolbar.
- ✔ Select View⇨Project Explorer.

Exploring the Explorer

If you've ever used the Windows Explorer to manage your disks and files (oops, documents), you're right at home in the Project Explorer. The Project Explorer gives you a branching, hierarchical look at your open projects. Figure 5-7 shows an example.

At the top of the hierarchy are the individual projects themselves. They're listed farthest to the left in the Project Explorer window.

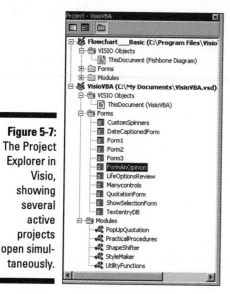

Figure 5-7:
The Project
Explorer in
Visio,
showing
several
active
projects
open simul-
taneously.

Each document that's open in your application automatically has a project, even if you haven't written any code or created any forms for its project so far. By default, a project takes on the name of its associated document, but you can change the name via the Project Properties dialog box or in the Properties window (see the section "Renaming a project or module in the Properties window," later in this chapter).

The next level in the hierarchy is formed by groups of related objects: forms, code modules, objects from the underlying application, and references to other object libraries. See Chapter 14 for instructions on adding such references to your project. Normally, the Project Explorer displays a folder for each of these groups. At the bottom of the hierarchy come the individual objects themselves.

Navigating the Project Explorer window

Fiddling around with the Project Explorer can be a way to avoid coding while still looking busy. Not only that, but it's also the fastest way to find and activate the modules, forms, and other objects you want to work with.

Just like the Windows Explorer, the Project Explorer displays a little box beside each item, or *node* — if the item contains subsidiary items in the hierarchy. When only the project itself is visible and its contents are hidden, this box, the *expand indicator,* contains a plus sign. If the nodes at lower levels of the hierarchy are visible, the expand indicator beside the project item displays a minus sign instead.

Here are the techniques you use to work with the Project Explorer:

✔ To expand a node, displaying items lower in the hierarchy, click the node's expand indicator when it contains a plus sign, or highlight the node and press the right arrow key.

✔ To collapse a node that is currently expanded, hiding its subsidiary items, click its expand indicator when it contains a minus sign, or highlight the node and press the left arrow key.

✔ To open the UserForm or Code window corresponding to a module, form, or class module item in the Project Explorer, double-click the item or highlight it in the list and press Enter.

✔ To activate a form's Code window, highlight the form in the list and press Shift+Enter.

If you can't remember the difference between Enter and Shift+Enter, you can fall back on those buttons at the top of the Project Explorer window, just below its title bar. They work like this:

✔ At the left, the View Code button displays the Code window for the highlighted item.

✔ The middle button, View Object, shows you the highlighted item itself. If the item is a form, you see it in its UserForm window. If the item is a document, you're switched back to the underlying VBA application with that document active.

✔ At the right, the Toggle Folders button turns on or off the middle level of the project hierarchy. Normally, the Project Explorer separates the forms, code modules, and document objects into separate folders. If you click this button, those folders disappear, and you see all the individual objects in each project in one alphabetical list. Click the button again to turn the folders back on.

Using the Project Explorer shortcut menu

The Project Explorer shortcut menu, shown in Figure 5-8, gives you yet more ways to get up close and personal with the elements of your project. These commands are all available via the menus, but the shortcut menu provides faster access when you're already working with the Project Explorer.

Setting project properties

The Project Properties dialog box lets you change the name of your project, add a brief description, attach a custom help file, and protect the project from unauthorized snooping or changes. Until you're a fairly advanced VBA developer, though, most of these options aren't terribly useful.

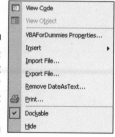

Figure 5-8:
The Project
Explorer
shortcut
menu.

But, anyway, at least now you know that this dialog box exists. To display it,
choose Tools⇨*Project name* Properties, where *Project name* is the name of
your project. Alternatively, right-click the Project Explorer window and select
Project name Properties from the shortcut menu. Figure 5-9 shows the
General tab of the Project Properties dialog box.

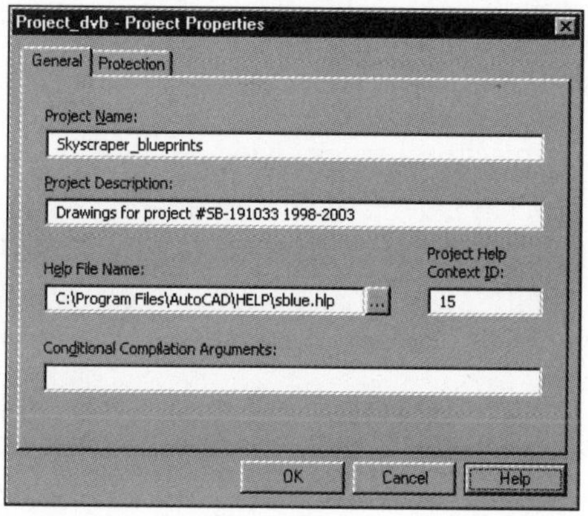

Figure 5-9:
The General
tab of the
Project
Properties
dialog box.

Renaming a project

The easiest way to change the VBA-supplied generic project name is in the
Properties window as detailed later in this chapter in the section "Renaming
a project or module in the Properties window." However, you can also change
the project's name on the General tab of the Project Properties dialog box, if
you have it open for other reasons.

Protecting your project

If there's any chance that someone else might get onto your computer and
mess around with your programs, consider protecting your VBA projects
with a password. To raise your security fence, display the Project Properties
dialog box and switch to the Protection tab, as shown in Figure 5-10.

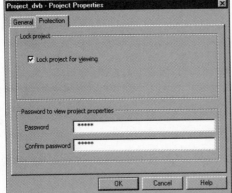

Figure 5-10:
The
Protection
tab of the
Project
Properties
dialog box.

Here's how the settings on this tab work:

- **Lock project for viewing:** Checking this box completely locks out anyone who doesn't have the password. They can't even view the project without the password. If you don't check this box, your password prevents anyone else from opening the Project Properties dialog box — and this prevents other users from locking *you* out of your own work.

- **Password:** Type the password you've chosen for your project.

- **Confirm Password:** Type it again to guarantee that you entered the password correctly the first time.

Unless your memory is infallible, write down the password and put it somewhere you can find it. VBA encrypts the project quite stoutly. If you forget the password, you will have to re-create the project from scratch.

Using the Object Browser

Although it looks different and has more bells and whistles, the Object Browser has a lot in common with the Project Explorer. Like the Project Explorer, it lets you navigate quickly through the hierarchy of objects available to your VBA programs.

Cosmetics aside, though, a fundamental difference is that the Object Browser displays only one project at a time — but lets you access *all* objects available to that project, not just the ones that belong to the project itself. In other words, besides your project's code modules and forms, you can also view the objects provided by your application, by VBA itself, and in other object libraries you may have opened for use by the project. See Chapter 14 for instructions on adding references to other object libraries.

Another great advantage of the Object Browser is that it can track down the procedures, methods, events, properties, and other such goodies from any of these object libraries.

Starting the Object Browser

The F2 key is your quick trigger command for displaying the Object Browser. Slower routes to the same destination include clicking the Object Browser button on the Standard toolbar, or choosing View⇨Object Browser. Figure 5-11 shows the Object Browser window.

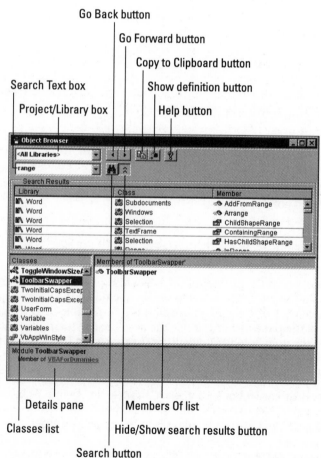

Figure 5-11: The Object Browser.

Browsing objects

Before you do any serious work with the Object Browser, be sure that you're browsing the right project. All you have to do is select the project you want to work with in the Project Explorer.

Clicking the Project/Library list box at the top-left of the Object Browser window displays the libraries available in the chosen project. (Your project should be there in the list — if it's not, go back to the Project Explorer and make sure that it's selected.) By choosing <All Libraries> in the Project/Library box, you can browse all the objects available to your project (that is, the objects of all libraries referenced in your project). To home in on a particular library, select it in the list.

Browsing panes

The Object Browser window is divided into several sections or panes (check out Figure 5-11 again). You can resize any of the panes by dragging the separator bars between them. The top pane contains the buttons with which you control the Object Browser. Below that comes the Search Results pane, which I discuss in the section "Searching for members," later in this chapter.

Below the Search Results pane are two side-by-side panes. On the left, the Classes list displays the objects, collections, modules, forms, and constants available in the selected library or project. Clicking any one of these items displays its members in the pane on the right, the Members Of list. The members may be procedures, methods, properties, events, or individual constants.

Want to know where your own VBA code lives? Just look for items displayed in bold in either the Classes list or the Members Of list.

The Details pane at the bottom of the Object Browser window displays information about the currently selected object, including the item's type and the object it belongs to. (If you can't see all this information, drag the separator at the top of the pane upward or use the scroll bar at the right.) Clicking the object that the item belongs to displays that object in the Object Browser.

Surfing the projects

The Object Browser works a lot like a Web browser. As in a Web browser, you can follow hyperlinks to related items — clicking the underlined object in the Details pane (at the bottom) displays it in the Object Browser.

And as in a Web browser, you can retrace your steps. To revisit objects you've previously examined, click the Go Back button at the top of the Object Browser window. Of course, you also have a Go Forward button, which reverses direction again, eventually returning you to the object you were looking at when you first clicked Go Back.

Instantly accessing your code

If the item you've selected in the Object Browser is a module or procedure from your own code, just press Enter to bring up its Code window. Mouse lovers can click the Show Definition button (shown in the margin) for the same service.

Getting help in the Object Browser

Pressing F1 or clicking the Help button at the top of the Object Browser window brings up a Help topic on the object, method, property, or event you've selected in the Object Browser. If your thinking style is more freeform than regimented, randomly nosing around with the Object Browser and displaying Help for any item that catches your eye is a great way to explore VBA painlessly. Just be aware that nothing may happen when you ask for help in the Object Browser — you get the information only if the creator of the library took the trouble to supply it.

Searching for members

Suppose you're not sure which of your code modules contains a particular procedure, or which object owns a particular method or event. Rather than comb through your modules in the Project Explorer or rummage through the Help system, you can get the Object Browser to locate the item for you. Here's how:

1. **Set the Library/Project drop-down list to <All Libraries> (if you need to search the entire project) or to a specific library.**

   If you select the wrong library, you may find something, but — because items in different libraries can have the same names — it won't be what you're looking for.

2. **Type the text you want to search for in the Search box.**

   You can repeat any of your last four searches by reusing it from the Search box's drop-down list of items.

3. **Press Enter or click the Search button (the one with binoculars).**

   After the obligatory hard-drive rattle, matching items appear in a new Search Results pane above the list panes. You can resize any column that's too small for the item displayed.

4. **To close the Search Results pane, click the double up-arrow button next to the Search button.**

   Click the same button (which now displays a double down arrow) to redisplay the Search Results pane.

Using browsed items in your code

The Object Browser does more than satisfy your curiosity about the objects in your project — it can be a modestly practical coding aid. After you locate an item that you actually want to use in your own code, you can press Ctrl+C or click the Copy to Clipboard button to place the term on the Clipboard. Then, after switching to the appropriate Code window, click in your code where you want the material to go and choose Edit⇨Paste to insert the Clipboard contents into your program. This technique ensures correct spelling — a little typo can make your code run amok (or prevent it from running in the first place).

Coding Secrets

Code windows are the heart of the Visual Basic Editor. Here you construct the VBA statements that actually perform useful work. In this chapter, I don't say anything about the content of those VBA statements — well, not much anyway. Instead, I focus on how to get the most out of the Code window when you're entering code. Three types of VBA items have associated Code windows: modules, class modules, and UserForms. Although each of these item types has a different function in VBA — which I cover in detail in later chapters — Code windows look and work the same for all three of them.

Opening Code windows

The VBA Editor gives you lots of different ways to open the Code window of an existing module, class module, or UserForm. First, you have to locate and select the item in the Project Explorer. After you have it in your sights, any of the following techniques brings up the corresponding Code window:

- Press F7.
- Click the View Code button at the top of the Project Explorer window.
- Right-click the object and select View Code from the shortcut menu.
- Choose View⇨Code.
- For modules, double-click the item or just press Enter (this doesn't work for UserForms).

If you're currently viewing a UserForm window, pressing F7 or choosing View⇨Code displays that form's Code window.

Creating new Code windows

Inserting a new module into your project automatically opens a new Code window for that module. Chapter 6 walks you through the process of starting new modules. When you create a new form, a Code window is automatically created for it (you don't see it until you use one of the techniques just listed).

Typing code

VBA Code windows are, in essence, simple text editors, but they include loads of special features designed for writing VBA code.

You type your VBA statements just as you would in a word processor, using the same cursor control and editing keys that are standard in Windows (you know, pressing Home takes you to the beginning of a line, while Ctrl+Home takes you to the top of the window — like *that*). You can select text with the mouse or by holding down the Shift key while you move the cursor.

Like every self-respecting text editor of the millennial era, the Code window supports drag-and-drop editing. After you select the text you want to work with, you can

- ✔ Move it, by dragging it into position and dropping it there.
- ✔ Copy it, by holding down the Ctrl key as you drag and drop.

You can drag text to another location in the same Code window, to a different Code window, or to the Immediate or Watch windows. If the destination is in a different Code window, you must arrange the two windows so that both the original text and the destination are visible before you start. (See the section "A First Look at the Debugging Windows," later in this chapter, for quick descriptions of the Immediate and Watch windows.)

The Code window also lets you undo previous changes you made to your code. Each time you press Ctrl+Z or choose Undo from the Edit menu, another change is reversed. The Edit menu does provide a Redo command as well — to undo the effects of the Undo command — but Redo has no keyboard shortcut in the Visual Basic Editor.

The ideal coach

Like that perfect servant you always wished for, the Visual Basic Editor is constantly (but unobtrusively) checking and correcting your work in the following ways:

- ✔ If you indent one line of code, the following lines are automatically indented to match (you can shut off this feature in the Tools⇨Options dialog box by removing the check from the Auto Indent box).

✔ If the editor recognizes a VBA *keyword,* it automatically capitalizes it according to VBA conventions (if you type an if...then...else statement, the Editor changes it to If...Then...Else). In addition, keywords are automatically colored (blue, by default) so that they stand out from the other items you type.

✔ In Code windows, you create a new procedure by typing Sub or Function followed by parentheses and an argument list, if required. When you then press Enter, the Visual Basic Editor automatically supplies the required closing statement for you — End Sub or End Function. Notice that a separator line appears between procedures.

✔ Finally, and most importantly, typing a VBA statement that's obviously incomplete or otherwise at odds with proper coding syntax provokes a warning message from the Editor (see Figure 5-12). With this immediate notification, you can correct the problem while you still remember what you were trying to accomplish with the statement in question. Even if you dismiss the warning for now, the Editor displays the statement in red to remind you that something serious is wrong.

Figure 5-12:
Incorrect
code syntax
warrants a
warning
message
like this one.

Navigating in a Code window

When you create a program of any complexity, a single Code window can contain pages and pages of code. Scrolling up and down randomly to find the section you're looking for would be much too primitive in such elegant surroundings. Instead, take advantage of those two drop-down list boxes at the top of the Code window, visible in both windows shown in Figure 5-13. They zoom you directly to the procedure you want to see or edit, as follows:

✔ The list box on the left is the *Object box.* In a module window, the only item in this list is (General), and you don't need to worry about it. But when you're working with the Code window for a form, this box lets you pick out a specific control on the form (or the form itself). When you do, the Code window displays the default procedure for that object.

✔ The list box on the right is the *Procedures/Events box.* Here, selecting the Declarations section or a specific procedure displays the code for the selected item. I describe the Declarations section in Chapter 6. If you're working in a form's Code window, this box lists only the events available for the item you chose in the Object box. When you select an event, the Code window displays the corresponding procedure for that event.

Bookmarking your code

It's 3:00 a.m. Your eyelids are so heavy that they're falling on your typing fingers, but the deadline looms and you keep on knocking out line after line of fairly routine code. Suddenly, inspiration strikes — you've just realized how to solve a major programming problem that you were working on yesterday morning.

Before you jump to that other module to implement your brilliant idea, drop a *bookmark* where you're now working. That way, when it's time to get back to this module, you can make like Hansel and Gretel and find your way home in a flash.

To place a bookmark on a line of code (well actually, alongside the code — see Figure 5-13), click the Toggle Bookmark button. All the bookmark-related buttons appear on the Edit toolbar, so you have to display this toolbar if you want access to them. Alternatively, you can use the corresponding menu command (Edit⇨Bookmarks⇨Toggle Bookmark), but this method takes longer. (Cruelly, Microsoft omitted keyboard shortcuts for the bookmark commands.) You can lay down as many bookmarks as you want.

Figure 5-13:
Those light ovals (which appear in light blue on a color monitor) along the left side of the Code windows represent bookmarks.

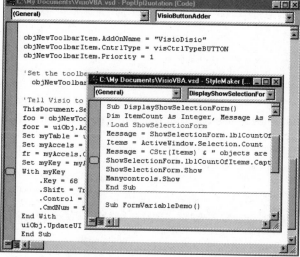

Of course, a bookmark does you no good by itself. Click the Next Bookmark or Previous Bookmark button to jump in sequence from one bookmark to the next until you arrive at your destination.

To remove a single bookmark, place the insertion point on the line containing the mark and again click the Toggle Bookmark button. If you've accumulated so many bookmarks that the Next and Previous Bookmark commands work like scroll bar buttons, you can wipe them all out by clicking the Clear All Bookmarks button.

Splitting a Code window

You can split any Code window into two separate panes (see Figure 5-14). These allow you to see code in different parts of the same module at the same time. They also give you an easy way to cut and paste between sections of your code.

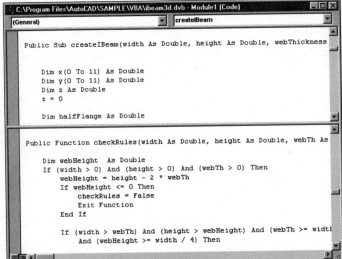

Figure 5-14:
I split this
Code
window —
both panes
are
displaying
code from
the same
module.

To split a Code window, use the split bar — it's that little gray bar just above the top-right scroll bar arrow. Drag the split bar downward until the panes are sized to suit you. To reunite them, remove the split bar by double-clicking it or by dragging it back to the top of the window.

More Code window creature comforts

Why write code when you can have someone else type it for you? The Visual Basic Editor pampers you by automatically entering those wacky VBA terms for you at just the right time. Not only does this minimize your typing, but it also guarantees accurate spelling.

Several related Editor features, which you can find on the Edit menu, provide these amenities. They are as follows:

✔ The List Properties and Methods feature

✔ The List Constants feature

✔ The Complete Word feature

Using the List Properties and Methods feature

Of these, the List Properties and Methods feature sees the most use. Here's how it works: To do anything useful with a VBA object, you change the setting of one of the object's properties or you activate one of its methods. To identify the property or method you want to work with, you type the object's name, a period (the *dot* operator), and then the property or method name, like this:

```
ActiveWindow.Selection.Group
```

See Chapter 12 for the full story on working in code with objects and their properties and methods.

With List Properties and Methods, all you have to type is the object name and the dot. As soon as you do, a little list of all the available properties and methods for that object pop up in the window. Figure 5-15 shows this list in action. To find the correct property or method, you can scroll the window (by using the arrow keys) or type the first letter or two of the item's name. After the correct item is highlighted, you can then press Tab to insert the item into your document.

Figure 5-15:
The List
Properties
and
Methods
feature
gives you
a power
assist when
entering —
what
else? —
properties
and
methods
in code.

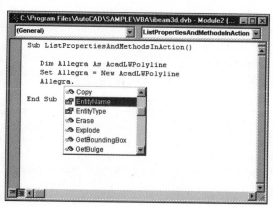

The List Properties and Methods feature performs a similar service when you're declaring a variable (defining its type). When you start typing a statement such as the following, a list of the available data and object types pops up just when you finish typing the word As:

```
Dim NumberOfLostKeys As Integer
```

Just as before, you pick from this list by scrolling or typing a letter or two and pressing Tab. By the way, Chapter 7 showers you with a gentle rain of information on declaring variables.

List Properties and Methods works not only with built-in VBA objects, but also with your own custom objects and user-defined variables.

Oh, one other point. The Properties and Methods list pops up automatically only if the proper setting is turned on in the Options dialog box. If you don't get the list, choose Tools➪Options and be sure that the box labeled Auto List Members is checked. You can pop up the list manually by using the appropriate command on the Edit menu or by using the keyboard shortcut Ctrl+J.

Listing constants automatically

The List Constants feature works just like the List Properties and Methods feature, except that it displays the names of the predefined constants for the property you're working with. This list pops up just after you type the = (equals sign) in a statement such as:

```
Oatmeal.Texture = Gluey
```

It's beyond me why this is considered a separate command rather than just another part of the List Properties and Methods. But because it is, it requires a slightly different keyboard shortcut: Ctrl+Shift+J. If you want to know how named constants work, see Chapter 7.

Completing words automatically

The Visual Basic Editor Complete Word feature enters just about any valid VBA term for you. To activate it, press Ctrl+spacebar. Doing so pops up a list that looks and works just like the one provided by the List Properties and Methods feature. The difference is that the Complete Word list includes just about everything you may want to type: objects, functions, procedures, constants, methods, properties, and your own variables. One exception is the keywords for built-in data types, such as Integer and Variant.

Typing a letter or two before you press Ctrl+spacebar limits the list to items starting with those characters. Better yet, if you've typed enough letters to match only one item, the Editor inserts it for you as soon as you press Ctrl+spacebar — the list itself never appears.

Getting into arguments

Many VBA procedures require you to specify one or more *arguments* when you execute the procedure. Such procedures base their calculations (or do whatever else they do) on the information supplied in these arguments. Many object methods require arguments just like procedures do.

Now, the Visual Basic Editor won't type the arguments for you — it can't, because it doesn't know which specific values you want the arguments to have. However, it does pop up a little bitty window containing a kind of cheat sheet — it tells you which arguments the function requires, which are optional, and the type of information each argument represents. You're looking at the Quick Info window, shown in action in Figure 5-16.

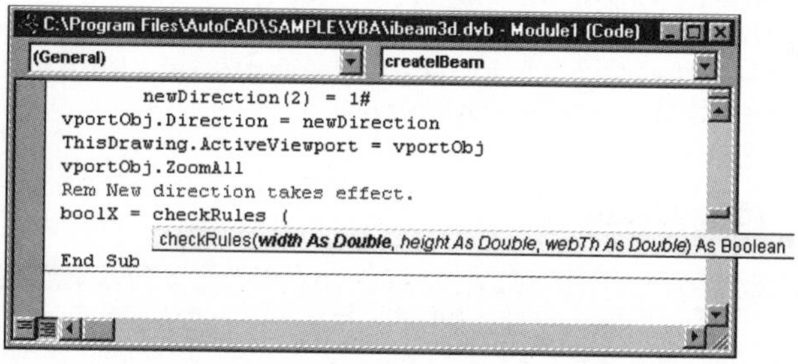

Figure 5-16:
The Quick
Info window
in action.

```
                  newDirection(2) = 1#
    vportObj.Direction = newDirection
    ThisDrawing.ActiveViewport = vportObj
    vportObj.ZoomAll
    Rem New direction takes effect.
    boolX = checkRules (
            checkRules(width As Double, height As Double, webTh As Double) As Boolean
    End Sub
```

If the Auto Quick Info box is checked in the Tools⇨Options dialog box, the Quick Info window appears automatically as soon as you type the name of a function, method, or procedure that requires arguments. If you shut off this automatic response, you can still display the Quick Info window by pressing Ctrl+I.

Many functions and procedures require multiple arguments. To help you keep track of where you are in the list of arguments, the Quick Info window displays the argument you're currently typing in bold. As soon as you type the comma that indicates the end of one argument, the next argument turns bold in the Quick Info window.

Quick Info versus Parameter Info

The Parameter Info feature complements Quick Info when you get into heavy VBA coding. Often, you want to use one function to determine the value of an argument required by another function, as in this simple example:

```
MsgBox(Str(AnIntegerVariable))
```

Here, the Str function converts the integer stored in the variable AnIntegerVariable into a text string. This string is then used as the argument to the MsgBox function (it becomes the prompt you see when VBA displays the message box on-screen).

But because you can *nest* functions within functions in this way, the Quick Info window isn't enough. It always shows you the argument list for the function containing the insertion point. An extra helper, the Parameter Info feature displays the argument list for the *outermost* function, the one within which all the other functions are nested. The keyboard shortcut for the Parameter Info feature is Ctrl+Shift+I.

Using the Properties Window

The Properties window enables you to view and edit the properties of whatever object (project, module, form, or control) is currently active in the Visual Basic Editor. (Don't confuse the crucial Properties window with the little Project Properties dialog box that I previously discuss and that's shown in Figure 5-9.) Look at Figure 5-17 to see the title bar of the Properties window showing the name of the active object, which also appears highlighted in the Project Explorer (if the selected object is an individual control on a form, only the form itself is listed in the Project Explorer).

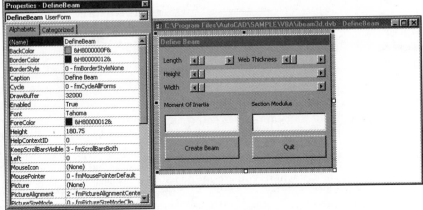

Figure 5-17:
The
Properties
window for
a form.

When a project or module is the selected object, the only property listed in the Properties window is the project name. With form and control objects, however, the Properties window gives you access to a myriad of properties governing the appearance and behavior of the selected object.

Because the Properties window is primarily useful for designing forms, I fully discuss how it works in Chapter 10. For now, I just show you how to display the window and use it to rename projects and modules.

Invoking the Properties window

You can do any of the following tricks to display the Properties window:

- Press F4.
- Click the Properties button on the Standard toolbar.
- Choose View➪Properties Window.

After the Properties window is visible, you can switch to a Code or UserForm window (or click an item in Project Explorer) to display that item's properties in the window.

Renaming a project or module in the Properties window

Projects and modules have only one property each: a name. Even so, you still use the Properties window if you want to change that one property. The Project Explorer and Object Browser list projects alphabetically by name; therefore you can move a project in either window by changing its name. (Of course, you may also want to change a project's name for purely artistic reasons.)

To rename a project or module, follow these steps:

1. **Select the project or module in the Project Explorer.**

2. **Activate the Properties window.**

   If you can't see it, display it by using any of the methods I list in the previous section "Invoking the Properties window." If the Properties window is visible, be sure it's active — click it or press F4.

3. **Type the new name.**

   Because this is the only property, you don't have to click the row for the (Name) property before you start typing.

A First Look at the Debugging Windows

Although Chapter 9 covers debugging in detail, this survey of the Visual Basic Editor windows wouldn't be complete without a quick look at the debugging windows. You have four of them:

- ✔ **The Immediate window** lets you execute individual VBA statements on the fly. You can also have your programs display messages in this window for debugging purposes. Figure 5-18 shows the Immediate window in action.

- ✔ **The Locals window** displays details about the objects and variables used in the procedure currently running.

- ✔ **The Watch window** (or Watches window, take your pick) shows the current values of objects or variables you choose to display in the window. They can come from any part of your program, not just the currently running procedure.

- ✔ **The Call Stack window** lists the procedures that have been executed by your program up to the time you display the window.

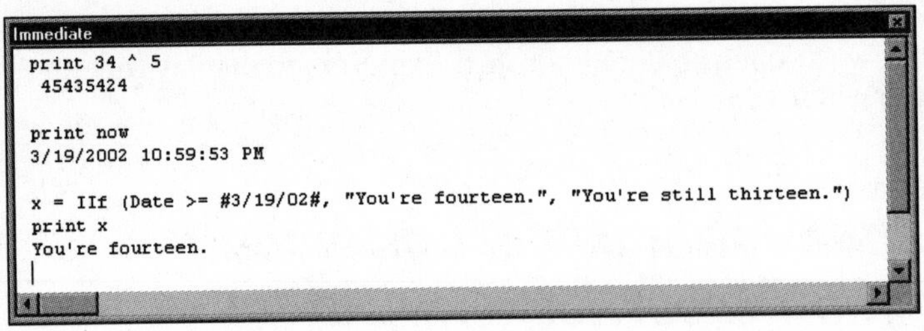

Figure 5-18:
Executing a
line of code
in the
Immediate
window.

```
Immediate
print 34 ^ 5
  45435424

print now
3/19/2002 10:59:53 PM

x = IIf (Date >= #3/19/02#, "You're fourteen.", "You're still thirteen.")
print x
You're fourteen.
|
```

Figure 5-18: Executing a line of code in the Immediate window.

You can display three of the windows at any time — the exception being the Call Stack window, which you can see only when code is executing in *break mode*. However, you also have to be in break mode to see anything useful in the Locals and Watch windows.

Part II
VBA Programming Essentials

The 5th Wave   By Rich Tennant

"You ever get the feeling this project could just up and die at any moment?"

In this part . . .

If you want to gorge yourself on VBA programming essentials, this part of the book is your meal ticket. Here's where you find satisfying staples of knowledge that fortify you for the day-to-day programming challenges you're bound to face. I foresee you returning to this part of the book for sustenance more often than any other.

Chapter 6 takes apart the structure of VBA programs, explaining every building block in detail. It goes on to lay out rules and conventions for naming things in VBA and suggests ways you can make your code prettier and easier to understand. In Chapter 7, you get an extensive tour of VBA variables and constants — named handles for the information you bandy about in your programs.

Chapter 8 explores the techniques you can use to direct the sequence in which your program does things — techniques that are critical for giving your programs a modicum of intelligence. Then, because nothing ever works the way that you plan for it to, Chapter 9 tells all about preventing, locating, and extinguishing errors in your programs.

Part II closes with a chapter on *forms*. In stand-alone versions of Visual Basic, the form is the only access point for interaction with a program while it runs. Forms tend to be less critical in VBA programming because you can tack your VBA programs onto the user interface of the underlying VBA application. Even so, plenty of situations in VBA programs call for custom dialog boxes, and Chapter 10 introduces the skills that you need to construct them.

Chapter 6

Anatomy of a Great VBA Program

● ●

● ●

*I*n previous chapters, I refer to the various components of code in VBA programs whenever they need mentioning, in an offhand, rather casual fashion. Now it's time to get at least semi-formal in my definitions of these elements. First, I offer a brief tour of each item in the VBA coding hierarchy. The first part of this chapter then covers these elements separately and in more detail, working from the top of the food chain down.

The focus then shifts to the service of readable, understandable, working code. You discover rules and conventions for naming variables, procedures, and other items. You also get tips on formatting your code for legibility, and on adding explanatory comments that keep you from forgetting why you wrote the dang procedure that way, anyway.

Program Building Blocks

A VBA program isn't just a random collection of instructions to the computer. *Au contraire,* it's a highly organized random collection of instructions. Lines of code are collected into procedures, which reside in modules, which in turn are housed within projects.

Programs defined

So what's a *program*? Conceptually, a program is a complete, functioning (or malfunctioning) software totality. A program consists of one or more statements that execute in the order defined by the programmer.

But a program isn't an official VBA entity. In VBA procedures, modules, and projects have names, but not programs as such. A VBA program requires at least one procedure — because VBA executes only statements within procedures — but it can encompass two or more procedures, within one or more modules, spanning one or more projects.

In this book, I stick mostly to programs that confine themselves to single projects at most. Chapter 14 briefly touches on cross-project programming.

A sample program

To make the discussion of this hierarchy of VBA elements a little less abstract, you can refer to the following module of code. It contains all the elements I mention (except a project because modules go inside projects rather than the other way around). After the sample come descriptions of each of these elements.

I guess you should know what the program does. It starts by creating a set (*array*) of six integers and filling them with random values between 1 and 1,000. After counting how many of those values exceed the cutoff value, 500, it displays the count in a little VBA message box.

```
Option Explicit
Const Maximum As Integer = 500
Const HowMany As Integer = 5
Dim ListOfNumbers() As Integer

Sub MAIN()
  Dim n As Integer, x As Integer
  Dim ItemsInList As Integer
  ReDim ListOfNumbers(HowMany)
  Randomize
  For x = 0 To 5
    ListOfNumbers(x) = Int((1000 * Rnd) + 1)
  Next x
  n = CountBigNumbers()
  MsgBox ("There were " & n & " values greater than " & _
            Maximum)
End Sub

Function CountBigNumbers()
  Dim Counter As Integer, y As Integer
  Counter = 0
```

```
For y = 0 To 5
If ListOfNumbers(y) > Maximum Then
Counter = Counter + 1
End If
Next y
CountBigNumbers = Counter
End Function
```

The entire block of sample code shown previously is a *module.* The module consists of a series of statements organized into three sections: the Declarations section, which starts with the Option Explicit statement, a Sub procedure, which starts with the Sub MAIN() statement, and the Function procedure, which starts with the Function CountBigNumbers() statement. Most of the module's statements occupy one line, but the statement that begins with MsgBox spills over onto a second line.

The VBA hierarchy

With the sample program in mind, you should be better able to understand the following definitions and descriptions of VBA code building blocks:

✔ A *statement* is the smallest unit of VBA code that can accomplish anything. A statement may be used to declare or define a variable, set an option of the VBA compiler, or carry out an action in your program. A valid statement is a lot like a complete sentence — it has to include the proper "parts of speech" or it isn't really a statement at all.

✔ A *procedure* is the smallest unit of code that you refer to by name. It's also the smallest unit of code that you can run independently. VBA recognizes two main types of procedures: *Sub* procedures and *Function* procedures. A procedure of either type consists of one or more statements sandwiched inside two special statements: the procedure's declaration at the top, and the End Sub or End Function statement at the end.

✔ A *module* is a named unit consisting of one or more procedures, plus declarations common to all procedures in the module. Although VBA allows you to place all your procedures in a single module, it makes sense to place related procedures into separate modules to make it easier to keep track of them.

Two types of modules are available in VBA. By far the most common is the *standard module,* the kind you use for the code you want to run. The other type, the *class module,* defines custom objects and their properties and methods. I discuss class modules briefly in Chapter 14.

✔ A *project* consists of all the modules, forms, and application-related objects associated with a particular document, plus the document itself.

Where Do Projects Come from, Mommy?

The stork brings them. Well, maybe not, but the point is that you never have to take special steps to create a project. Every document from a VBA application is a project automatically. Of course, a document's project doesn't contain any code or forms until you create them in the Visual Basic Editor or record macros in the application. Chapter 5 covers the techniques you need for working with projects.

Totally Modular

The module comes just below the project in the hierarchy of VBA code elements. A module stores one or more VBA procedures, along with a Declarations section containing statements that apply to the entire module.

Planning your modules

Deciding how to organize your modules doesn't have to be a big deal. It does make sense to think about how many modules you should create and which procedures each one should contain. The basic points to remember are these:

- ✔ Your procedures can *call,* or run, procedures stored in other modules. One module can use variables declared in another module, too.

- ✔ However, using procedures and variables from other modules can introduce slight complications. For example, you can call a procedure in another module by entering the procedure's name alone. If the procedure you're calling has the same name as a procedure in the current module, however, you must enter the procedure name preceded by the module's name, as in `OtherModule.DoSomethingNow`. (I recommend using this `Module.Procedure` technique even when you don't have to, so you always know which module contains the procedure you're calling.)

In general, you should place related procedures together in a single module. Typically, a module contains all the procedures for one complete VBA program — and no extraneous procedures. That setup simplifies your programming because you don't have to deal with the little complications involved in accessing procedures or variables in other modules.

However, if you create procedures that you plan to use in more than one program, you can organize them in modules according to type, as in `MyMathProcedures` or `TextHandlingRoutines`. You might also create modules called something like `BrandNewProcedures` or `OldProceduresIMight NeedSomeday`. See the section "Naming Your Babies," later in this chapter, for details on what's legal and what's not when it comes to procedure names.

Adding a new module to a VBA project

To create a new module in the Visual Basic Editor, start by making sure that you're working with the correct project. In the Project Explorer, select the project itself or any of the objects it already contains (this can be a form, an application object, or an existing module — it doesn't matter). You can then use any of the following techniques to insert the new module:

- Click the Insert button on the Standard toolbar. This is a split (multi-function) button for inserting various items. If the icon for inserting a module isn't visible on the main part of the button, click the narrow vertical bar with the arrow just to the right of the main part of the button, and choose Module from the drop-down menu.

- Right-click the Project Explorer window — make sure that you do it over the correct project — and choose Insert Module from the shortcut menu.

- Choose Insert➪Module.

The Visual Basic Editor automatically opens the new module's Code window. It also christens the module with a generic name. To change it, type a new name in the Properties window (see Chapter 5).

What goes where in a new module

The Code window for a brand-new module has only one section, the Declarations section. You can tell which section you're in by looking at the list box at the top right of the Code window.

You can enter the following two types of statements in a module's Declarations section:

- Declarations of variables, constants, and user-defined data types. These tell the compiler the name and type of each item (but not its value). Variables and constants declared in a module's Declarations section can be used in any procedure in that module.

- Compiler options that control the way the VBA compiler operates.

What you can't place in the Declarations section are assignment or executable statements — statements that actually do something when the code runs. You must place all assignment and executable statements within a procedure. For example, you can't specify the *value* of a variable in the Declarations section. That requires an assignment statement, which must go inside a procedure elsewhere in the module. (I discuss the differences between executable statements, assignment statements, declarations, and compiler options in the section "Making Statements" later in this chapter.)

The term *module-level code* refers to all statements in the Declarations section.

Each procedure you add is considered a separate section of the module. After you add a procedure, its name appears in the list box at the top right of the Code window, enabling you to jump directly to that procedure by selecting its name in the list.

Standard modules and modules with class

The garden-variety VBA module is a *standard module*. Standard modules were known as *code modules* in older versions of VBA and Visual Basic. They contain statements that declare variables and constants, define custom (user-defined) data types, and set compiler options, as well as executable statements that actually get things done. You can create and use objects of any accessible object type in a standard module, but you can't create new object types in this type of module.

Procedure types

The bulk of the VBA code you write lives within two types of procedures, Sub procedures and Function procedures. Event procedures, which VBA executes when an event such as a mouse click occurs, are specialized Sub procedures. VBA also has another type of procedure, the Property procedure.

Here's a summary of the various procedure types:

- A Sub *procedure* is a general-purpose procedure for getting things done in VBA. Sub procedures are the only type you can run independently with the techniques that I cover in Chapter 4. However, one Sub procedure can also run, or *call,* another.

- A Function *procedure* can execute any VBA statements you like. However, it differs from a Sub procedure in that it calculates a value and then *returns* that value to the procedure that activated the Function procedure in the first place.

- An event *procedure* is a special type of Sub procedure. I know, I already said so. What I didn't say is that Chapter 14 covers the particulars on event procedures.

- A Property *procedure* determines or assigns the value of a custom object's property. I cover Property procedures in Chapter 14, but I mention them here because you see them listed in the Add Procedure dialog box.

A VBA macro is, technically speaking, a Sub procedure that *takes* (requires) no arguments. Macros are the only kind of Sub procedures that you can run directly, by name, in the Visual Basic Editor or your VBA application. To run a Sub procedure that does take arguments, you must call it from another procedure. I discuss arguments in the section "Winning arguments" later in this chapter.

You use *class modules,* by contrast, to define your own custom types, or *classes,* of objects. As I explain further in Chapter 12, a class is the pattern on which objects are based. After creating a class module for the custom object, you fill it with the code for the class's properties and methods. Code in other modules can then create and use objects based on the class — just as if they were built-in VBA objects. See Chapter 14 for information on creating your own object classes.

Writing Procedures

Procedures are critical functional units of your VBA code because code must be stored within a procedure or it won't run. There are two everyday types of VBA procedures: Sub procedures and Function procedures (see the sidebar "Procedure types," elsewhere in this chapter).

Procedure skeletons

Here are two simple procedures, one of each type (Sub and Function):

```
Public Sub SubMarine()
    MsgBox "Up Periscope!"
End Sub
```

```
Public Function FunkShun (Birthdate As Date)
    FunkShun = DateDiff("yyyy", Birthdate, Date)
End Function
```

As you can see, each procedure comprises an opening declaration statement, one or more lines of code, and a terminating End statement. I go into these elements in the sections "Sub procedures in detail" and "Function procedures in detail" later in this chapter.

Creating a new procedure

Before you can start a new procedure, you have to first open the Code window for the module in which you're going to store the procedure. Create a new module with the steps in the section "Adding a new module to a VBA project," earlier in this chapter, or open an existing module by double-clicking it in the Project Explorer.

After the module's Code window is open and active, you're ready to begin the new procedure. Your initial task is simply to insert into the module the procedure's declaration statement, and its complement, the End statement that signals the end of the procedure. You can accomplish this by

✔ Filling in the Add Procedure dialog box. To display it, choose Insert⇨ Procedure or click the narrow vertical bar with the arrow on the Insert button (Standard toolbar) and select Procedure from the drop-down menu that appears.

✔ Typing the statements yourself.

Typing versus the dialog box

I recommend typing in the procedure's "shell" yourself, simply because the dialog box method doesn't save any time unless you're a *really* slow typist. The do-it-yourself approach also lets you control where in the module to place the procedure, which you can't accomplish with the dialog box. Just do the following:

1. **Click where you want the procedure to go.**

2. **Type the procedure's declaration statement.**

3. **Press Enter.**

You don't have to type the closing End Sub or End Function statement — the Visual Basic Editor puts the correct one in for you.

However, when you're getting started in VBA, you may feel more secure using the dialog box. To use the latter technique, follow these steps:

1. **Choose Insert⇨Procedure.**

   The Add Procedure dialog box appears.

2. **Type the procedure name in the Name box.**

3. **Choose the Type of procedure and its Scope using the radio buttons, and check the box for static local variables, if that applies.**

   I know, I haven't said anything about the terms *scope* and *static* so far, but you can find answers to all your questions in the section "Scoping Out the Scope" later in this chapter.

4. **Click OK.**

   The Visual Basic Editor inserts paired procedure declaration and End statements at the end of the module, regardless of where the insertion point was when you started.

Completing the procedure

Entering the declaration and End statements is definitely the easy part of creating a new procedure. Your real work consists of typing in the filling — a series of VBA statements — between those pieces of bread. I devote much of the rest of this book to details on what to type. For now, suffice it to say that the statements within a procedure are executed in the order in which they appear, except when your code instructs VBA to jump to another location.

Sub procedures in detail

The term *Sub procedure* still looks odd to me, but that's the proper usage in VBA. In some programming languages, "subprocedures" or "subroutines" are those that are called by main procedures. In VBA, while a Sub procedure can be called by another procedure, the main procedure of a program is itself *always* a Sub procedure. Weird.

Enough of my grousing — on to the facts. The following is a sample Sub procedure, with the declaration at the top, the terminating End statement at the bottom, and a few statements in between:

```
Public Sub ASweetProcedure()

Dim ANiceMessage As String
ANiceMessage = "Have a nice day!"
Msgbox ANiceMessage
(more statements)
...

End Sub
```

The first line, the Sub procedure declaration, performs two vital duties. First, it tells where the procedure starts, so that VBA knows where to start executing code when you run the procedure. Second, it declares the procedure's characteristics, as I discuss in the following sections.

Every Sub procedure must be terminated with an End Sub statement. This line lets VBA know that it's time to stop executing code.

Items in a Sub procedure declaration

In the procedure's declaration statement, the first term, `Public`, specifies the procedure's scope. This can be `Public` or `Private`. `Public` is the default, so you don't need to include this keyword. However, doing so makes the scope obvious so you don't have to wonder. Again, I leave a full discussion of scope to the section "Scoping Out the Scope," later in this chapter.

Next comes the Sub keyword, which simply indicates that you're declaring a Sub procedure. After that comes the procedure's name, which can be anything you like, as long as it conforms to the naming rules described in "Naming Your Babies," later in this chapter.

Forgoing arguments

Closing out the declaration is a pair of parentheses. Why are they there when nothing is inside them? Those parentheses would hold *arguments,* if the procedure had any. Arguments are elements of data that the procedure expects to receive when it is launched. In this case, the procedure has no arguments, so not only is it quite friendly, it has nothing inside the parentheses (however, the parentheses are still required — but if you omit them, VBA types them in for you). I further discuss arguments in the section "Winning arguments," later in this chapter.

To repeat a point I make elsewhere, a VBA macro is by definition a Sub procedure that requires no arguments. To run a Sub procedure that does take arguments, you must call it from another procedure.

Calling Sub procedures

You can run, or call, any Sub procedure — whether or not it takes arguments — from another procedure. To call a Sub procedure, just include a statement consisting of the name of the Sub procedure you want to call (if the procedure you're calling takes arguments, you must type these after the procedure's name).

In the following code fragment, the line that reads WashMyOldCar calls the Sub procedure by that name, which takes no arguments.

```
...
MyOldCar = "Valiant"
WashMyOldCar
NumberOfCarwashTrips = NumberOfCarwashTrips + 1
...
```

Function procedures in detail

A Function procedure can conduct general business just like a Sub procedure, but its main *raison d'être* is to calculate a value. When the Function completes its work, it returns that value to the calling procedure, which can use the value in further computations.

Here's a sample Function procedure:

```
Public Function DeFunct (x As Integer, y As Integer) _
          As Integer
 Dim z As Integer
 z = x + y
 DeFunct = x ^ z
End Function
```

Obviously, the basic form of a Function procedure is much like that of a Sub procedure. The declaration begins with an optional keyword defining the procedure's scope (in this case, Public). Next comes the Function keyword, specifying the type of procedure, then the procedure's name. After the name come the procedure's arguments, enclosed in parentheses. I explain arguments in "Winning arguments," but you can see how they work by reading the code.

Declaring a Function procedure's return type

The final element in the Function procedure's declaration — an element that is never found in a Sub procedure — specifies the procedure's *return type*. The return type specifies the type of data — Integer, String, Date, Object, or what have you — that the Function procedure will return to the procedure that called it.

The return type can be any valid VBA data or object type. You specify it in exactly the same way you do for variables, as I detail in Chapter 7. In the example, the keywords As Integer at the end of the procedure declaration specifies that the DeFunct procedure returns an Integer value. If you don't declare a return type explicitly, your Function procedure returns its value as a Variant, a generic data type that I discuss also in Chapter 7.

Completing the Function procedure

After the declaration comes the code for your Function procedure. This is the code that actually does the work of the procedure, but it's not our focus just now. A Function procedure always ends with a terminating statement, End Function.

I must pause here to point out that VBA comes with numerous built-in *functions*. Like a Function procedure, a VBA function returns a value to a calling procedure. Also, you use the same technique to call both functions and Function procedures. The only difference between Function procedures and functions (besides the name) is that you don't have to write code for functions! Chapter 11 offers an overview of the functions available in VBA.

Coding the Function procedure's return value

One critical difference separates Sub and Function procedures: Somewhere in the Function procedure, at least one statement specifies the value that the procedure is to return. It does so by assigning that value to the name of the procedure itself, as if that name was a variable. In the previous example, this occurs in the line DeFunct = x ^ z. After this line executes, DeFunct holds the value that will be returned to the calling procedure and used there.

Calling Function procedures

You can only run Function procedures by calling them from within other procedures. Typically, you do so by setting a variable equal to the name of the function. In the following example, the variable called ZPower receives the value returned by the DeFunct procedure:

```
...
ZPower = DeFunct(3, 4)
...
```

After this statement runs, the ZPower variable would contain the value calculated by DeFunct, a Function procedure; the value equals 37. Note that this statement passes the arguments required by the DeFunct procedure in parentheses following the procedure name.

Winning arguments

Arguments represent values that VBA is to transfer, or *pass,* from one procedure to another. The procedure on the receiving end is said to *take* the arguments. You build arguments into a procedure when you want the procedure to modify its behavior based on values you supply at the time you call the procedure. Both Sub and Function procedures can take arguments.

Here again is the Function procedure DeFunct:

```
Public Function DeFunct (x As Integer, y As Integer) _
          As Integer
 Dim z As Integer
 z = x + y
 DeFunct = x ^ z
End Function
```

The procedure takes two arguments, x and y. As the code illustrates, a procedure's arguments are declared as part of the declaration of the procedure itself. They always appear in parentheses following the name of the procedure. In this *argument list,* you declare individual arguments by listing each argument's name and its data type (see "Writing procedures that take arguments," later in this chapter, for further details).

A procedure that takes arguments requires those arguments to do its job. Within the procedure, arguments serve exactly the same role as variables that you declare in the usual way — for details on variables, see Chapter 7.

Look carefully at the code for the DeFunct procedure. After declaring a variable z, the procedure calculates z's value as the sum of the two arguments, x and y. Then, to calculate the procedure's own return value, the next line of code raises the x argument to the power of z. As you can see, x, y, and z all have similar roles. If you want, you can raise z to the power of x instead of the other way around.

Productive arguments

So if arguments are so much like variables, why use arguments at all? Actually, you don't have to — you can use ordinary variables to accomplish everything you can do with arguments. But arguments make your procedures easier to use and your code easier to read.

It's time for a couple of comparative examples. This first pair of procedures uses the arguments Model and Year to communicate values:

```
Public Sub CallingProcedure()
 ProceedsFromOldCar = SellOldCar ("Rambler Classic",1962)
End Sub
```

```
Public Function SellOldCar(Model As String, _
 Year As Integer)
Dim AgeFactor As Integer
Dim PriceFactor As Single
 AgeFactor = Year - 1900
 If Model = "Rambler Classic" Then
 PriceFactor = .001
 Else If Model = "Dodge Dart" Then
 PriceFactor = .005
 Else If ...
 (more statements)
 End If
 SellOldCar = AgeFactor * PriceFactor * 1000
End Function
```

To summarize what's going on here in English, the procedure named CallingProcedure uses SellOldCar, a Function procedure, to calculate a result called ProceedsFromOldCar. Because the Function procedure takes arguments, you can tell right away which car you're selling and how old it is.

Now, here are two comparable procedures that conduct the same sort of business without arguments. Note that you must declare two variables at the module level, outside either procedure, so that both procedures have access to the variables.

```
Dim Model As String
Dim Year As Integer

Public Sub CallingProcedure2()
 Model = "Dodge Dart"
 Year = 1963
 ProceedsFromOldCar = SellOldCar2()
End Sub

Public Function SellOldCar2()
Dim AgeFactor As Integer
Dim PriceFactor As Single
AgeFactor = Year - 1900
If Model = "Rambler Classic" Then
 PriceFactor = .001
 Else If Model = "Dodge Dart" Then
 PriceFactor = .005
 Else If ...
 (more statements)
 End If
SellOldCar2 = AgeFactor * PriceFactor * 1000
End Function
```

So why argue?

With the preceding examples fresh in your mind, I can list the advantages of using arguments when sharing information between two procedures. Here you go:

- ✔ Again, when you're reading through a procedure's code, arguments make clear which values the procedure requires from elsewhere in the program to do its job.

- ✔ When you're writing code, arguments help you minimize the number of variables you need to create (in the Declarations section of the module, outside any procedures).

   One obvious problem with such module-level variables is that you can't see their declarations when you're writing code for a procedure that uses them.

- ✔ When you call a procedure that takes arguments, VBA *forces* you to state values for those arguments. This requirement helps ensure that the procedure gets the correct values it needs.

Writing procedures that take arguments

To write a procedure that takes arguments, enclose the arguments in parentheses immediately after the name of the procedure in the procedure's declaration. Here's an example:

```
Sub Novelizer(Title As String, Pages As Integer, Deadline As
              Date)
```

As the example illustrates, you designate the data type for each argument by following the argument name with *As type,* where type can be any VBA data type or object class. If you list only the argument name, omitting *As type,* VBA assigns the argument the Variant data type. (I know, I know, I haven't discussed data types and object classes in this chapter, but you can find out all about them in Chapters 7 and 12, respectively.)

Calling procedures that take arguments

To call a procedure that takes arguments from your code, you simply list each argument's value following the name of the procedure you're calling. You must list the values in the same order the corresponding arguments appear in the procedure declaration. The values you supply must match the respective data types of the arguments specified in the declaration of the called procedure.

The only complication you face is whether or not to place the arguments in parentheses. The rules are as follows:

- When you use a Function procedure to return a value, you surround the arguments in parentheses, as shown in the previous line of code.
- *Omit* the parentheses when calling a Function procedure without using its return value in the calling code.
- When you call a Sub procedure that takes arguments or when you call a Function procedure but you don't want to use its return value, omit the parentheses.

Organizing your procedures

An entire VBA program, no matter how large, can fit in a single procedure. Then why go to the trouble of writing separate procedures? The main reason is to keep track of your work more easily.

As a program grows in size, the likelihood that you'll get lost in all that code grows even more quickly. By dividing the program into a series of procedures, each named for what it does, you can jump to the part of your program you want to concentrate on. Remember that you can use the list box at the top right of the Code window to select the procedure from an alphabetical list and get beamed directly to that procedure, wherever it happens to be in the module.

Another good reason to place a block of code into a separate procedure is to eliminate redundant code. If your program repeatedly uses the same sequence of code statements in various places, you can minimize its size and complexity by placing those statements into a separate procedure. You can then call that procedure from anywhere in the program.

As a bonus, creating a separate procedure for the repeated statements minimizes drudgery and the mistakes that you otherwise may make (*will* make, truth be told) if you have to revise a bunch of identical series of statements. When you consolidate the repeated statements into a single procedure, you need to change only that one procedure.

Scoping Out the Scope

Each VBA procedure has a defined *scope,* which determines the parts of your program from which you can call that procedure. If you have a visual imagination, think of it this way: A procedure's scope decides which parts of your program can "see" the procedure.

Procedures can have the following three different scopes:

- ✔ By default, VBA procedures (except event procedures) are *public* in scope. That means that you can call them from any part of your program — from the same module, from another module, or even (if your program includes multiple projects as I discuss in Chapter 14) from a different project.

- ✔ When it suits your programming needs, you can create procedures that are *private* in scope. Private procedures are visible, if you will, only within the same module. In other words, you can call a private procedure from another procedure in the same module, but not from procedures in any other modules.

- ✔ In a VBA program that includes more than one project, you can create procedures that are accessible to all the modules within a given project but off-limits to other projects.

Variables have scope, too, and scope works in a similar way for them. See Chapter 7.

Specifying a procedure's scope

To specify the scope of a procedure, all you have to do is place the Public or Private keyword at the beginning of the procedure's declaration. Look at these examples:

```
Public Sub IKneadYou()
... (procedure statements)
End Sub
Private Function IKneedYou()
... (procedure statements)
End Function
```

Because procedures are public by default, you don't have to include the Public keyword to give a procedure public scope. If a program contains any private procedures, however, I recommend that you explicitly declare the public procedures so you can tell at a glance which is which.

To restrict the scope of a public procedure to its project only, so that it is inaccessible to other projects, place the statement Option Private Module in the Declarations section of the module in which you declare the procedure. See the section "Declarations" and "Compiler options," later in this chapter, for details on working with such statements.

Using private procedures

Making a procedure private helps prevent errors. Because you can only call the procedure from within the same module, you can more easily control the conditions in effect at the time the procedure gets called (conditions such as the values of variables that the procedure uses).

Making a procedure private in scope is easy enough, but why bother? After all, VBA doesn't *demand* that you call a procedure from another module just because that procedure is public.

Well, the reason is self-protection. You may forget that you designed a procedure so that it should only be called from within the same module. If the procedure is private, VBA doesn't let you call it from another module even if you try to. As a bonus, in programs of substantial size and complexity, limiting the number of access points to a given procedure helps you better keep track of the program's organization.

Making Statements

Procedures are made up of *statements,* the smallest viable units of code. Most statements occupy only one line of code, and a line of code usually has only one statement — but not always, as I discuss later in this section. VBA distinguishes four different statement types: *declarations, assignment statements, executable statements,* and *compiler options.*

Declarations

A *declaration* is a statement that announces to the VBA compiler your intention to use a named item — a variable, constant, user-defined data type, or procedure — in your program. The declaration goes further, specifying which type of item it is and providing any additional information the compiler needs to make use of the item. After you've declared an item, you can use it elsewhere in your program.

The first example declares a *variable,* a named value that can change as a program runs — see Chapter 7 for full details. The following statement declares the variable named MyLittleNumber and specifies that it always contains an integer:

```
Dim MyLittleNumber As Integer
```

Also in Chapter 7, I discuss *constants,* named values that never change. The following statement creates a *string* (text) constant named `UnchangingText`, consisting of the characters `Eternity`:

```
Constant UnchangingText = "Eternity"
```

You can place a declaration for a variable or constant in the Declarations section of a module or within an individual procedure. Your choice of location determines where the item will be accessible — I refer you to Chapter 7 for details.

You can find more examples of procedure declarations in the section "Writing Procedures," earlier in this chapter.

Assignment statements

Assignment statements set a variable or a property of an object to some specific value. These statements always have three parts: the name of the variable or property, an equal sign, and an *expression* that specifies the new value.

I define the term expression in a moment. First, though, some examples of assignment statements are in order. This statement sets the value of the `MyLittleNumber` variable to the sum of the `SomeOtherNumber` variable plus 12:

```
MyLittleNumber = SomeOtherNumber + 12
```

The following statement sets the `Color` property of the `AGraphicShape` object to `Blue` (presumably, `Blue` is a named constant representing the numeric value of a particular color):

```
AGraphicShape.Color = Blue
```

To assign a value to the `SquareRoot` variable, the next example statement calls the `Sqr` function — a built-in VBA function for calculating square roots — with the current value of the `MyLittleNumber` variable:

```
SquareRoot = Sqr(MyLittleNumber)
```

Just before the examples I used the term expression. In VBA, an expression is any snippet of code that specifies a particular numeric value, string of text, or object. It can contain any combination of actual numbers or characters, defined constants, variables, object properties, built-in functions, and Function procedures, all combined with any of the operators (such as + or *) that act on these items. The following are examples of expressions:

Expression	Value
3.14	3.14
AGraphicShape.Sides	5 (assuming the AGraphicShape object represents a pentagon)
(12 - Sqr(x))/5	2 (assuming the x variable = 4)
"Roses are red," & " violets are blue"	Roses are red, violets are blue

Executable statements

Executable statements do the program's work. You use statements of this type to do the following:

- ✔ Call another procedure in your own code.
- ✔ Activate a method belonging to an object.
- ✔ Control the order in which other statements get executed, by defining loops or by choosing which section of code (of several alternatives) to execute.
- ✔ Execute one of the VBA built-in statements or functions.

Gaze upon the following examples. The following statement executes the Rotate method of the AGraphicShape object:

```
AGraphicShape.Rotate(90)
```

The following small block of code contains two executable statements: The If...Then statement checks to see if the current value of the AudibleThreshold variable is greater than 3. If so, it directs the program to execute the next executable statement, the one that calls the PlayLoudSound procedure:

```
If AudibleThreshold > 3 Then
  PlayLoudSound
End If
```

Compiler options

Instructions that control the VBA compiler's behavior constitute the last class of statements. The following compiler option statements are available:

Statement	What It Does
Option Base *number*	This statement sets the default numbering system for array variables to begin with 0 or 1 — see Chapter 13 for details.
Option Compare method	This statement determines the method VBA uses for comparing string (text) variables. The *method* term can be *Binary,* for comparisons based on each character's numeric code; *Text,* in which upper- and lowercase characters are considered equivalent; or *Database,* which is available only in Access and which uses the database's sort order.
Option Private Module	When you include this statement in a module's Declarations section, other projects can't access the module's procedures, variables, or constants, even if those items are declared as public in scope. See "Scoping Out the Scope" in this chapter for more on the topic of scope.
Option Explicit	The Option Explicit statement is one compiler option you need to know and use. When you place it in a module, VBA doesn't allow you to use variables without declaring them first. See Chapter 7 for details.

Naming Your Babies

Within limits, you're free to choose your own names for your variables, procedures, and what have you. The following rules apply to all the named elements in a VBA program, including variables, constants, data types, procedures, modules, forms, controls, and projects:

✔ Names must begin with a letter, not a numeral. After the first character, however, you can use numerals and the underscore character, as in `Hidden_Variable3`

✔ Aside from the underscore character, punctuation marks are off limits altogether in VBA names. *Verboten* characters include the following:

```
! @ & ' $ # ? , * . (period) { } ( ) [ ] = + - ^ % / ~ < >
: ;
```

✔ Names can't include spaces.

✔ You're limited to a maximum of 255 characters (40 characters, for forms and controls).

✔ A name can't duplicate a VBA keyword, function, or statement.

✔ You can't use the same name more than once in the same scope. For example, all procedures in the same module must have different names. For that matter, a procedure and a module-level variable — one declared in the Declarations section of a module — can't share the same name. However, you can use duplicate names for variables declared inside different procedures. (I clarify the muddy issue of scope earlier in this chapter and also in Chapter 7.)

If you enter a name that violates any of these rules, the Visual Basic Editor warns you as soon as you move the insertion point off that line of code. The line appears in red characters, and the Editor displays a quasi-explanatory error message, as shown in Figure 6-1. The exception: You aren't notified of duplicate procedure names until you run the program.

Figure 6-1:
The Visual Basic Editor lets you know when you enter an invalid name.

Here are some examples of law-abiding and illegal VBA names:

Valid	*Unacceptable*
a	AReallyLongNameOfMoreThan255CharactersThatWon'tAllFit...
Go4It	4ScoreAnd7
You_Did_It	WhoDunIt?
IrishEyes	Spanish Eyes

One naming detail about which VBA is completely flexible is capitalization. VBA ignores the case of names, so you can type a variable name in all capitals in one place, all lowercase letters in another, and in some strange coMBinAtION in a third. VBA treats all these versions as identical. As a courtesy, however, VBA preserves the capitalization pattern you use when declaring the variable. The Editor automatically corrects any mismatched capitalization as soon as you move the insertion point to another line.

VBA naming conventions

As long as you live by the rules that I list earlier in this section, you can give any name you like to any item in your program. Nevertheless, you can make your programming life a lot easier by sticking to a logical naming scheme. As your programs get longer, remembering the purpose and type of your variables gets harder — much harder. So drop yourself hints by designing names that make some sense.

Ideally, adopt and stick to a systematic naming practice. One method that many people use is to start each name with a short prefix that indicates the type of item, and follow that with a capitalized brief descriptive name. For an obvious example, say that you're writing a program that tracks inventory. If the program needs an integer variable to store part numbers, you may call it `intPartNo`.

Table 6-1 lists suggested prefixes for the most commonly used VBA items. You can make up your own, or use them as suffixes, if you prefer. The important thing is to use them consistently.

I don't use this convention in this book in Chapters 1 through 6 because the convention requires this explanation first. But from here on out I try to practice what I preach.

Table 6-1	Suggested Prefixes for Naming VBA Items	
Use This Prefix	*To Name This Type of Item*	*Example*
Variables		
byte	Byte	byteDaysInMonth
bool	Boolean	boolClearedStatus
int	Integer	intWeeksOnChart
lng	Long integer	lngPopulation

Use This Prefix	To Name This Type of Item	Example
Variables		
sng	Single	sngRadius
dbl	Double	dblParsecs
cur	Currency	curUnitPrice
str	String	strLastName
date	Date/Time	dateBirthdate
var	Variant	varSerialNumber
obj	Object	objStampCollection
Controls		
txt	Text box	txtEnterName
lbl	Label	lblAnswerMessage
cmd	Command button	cmdCalculateInterestRate
mnu	Menu	mnuTools
cmb	Combo box	cmbToyCategory
fra	Frame	fraHabitat
opt	Option button	optGasolineGrade
chk	Check box	chkCaseSensitive
Other Items		
bas	Module	basTextFormatFunctions
frm	UserForm	frmOptionsDialog

Making Your Code Pretty

Okay, your code doesn't really need to be good-looking — just easy to read. This section offers a few simple suggestions for writing code that you can decipher when you come back to it tomorrow, next week, or next year.

Judicious indenting helps organize your code

The Eleventh Commandment: Develop and practice a consistent indenting style. The VBA compiler ignores blank space at the beginning of a line, so you're free to use indentation to set off related lines of code. Compare these two sample code fragments and tell me which one is easier to understand:

```
If intA = 27 Then
If txtChooseColor.Text = "Beige" Then
intA = 33
intB = 0
End If
For Each objCbar in CommandBars
If objCbar.Name = "Big Toolbar" Then
If objCbar.Visible = False Then
objCbar.Visible = True
End If
End If
Next objCbar
End If
```

```
If intA = 27 Then

    If txtChooseColor.Text = "Beige" Then
        intA = 33
        intB = 0
    End If

    For Each objCbar in CommandBars
        If objCbar.Name = "Big Toolbar" Then
            If objCbar.Visible = False Then
                objCbar.Visible = True
            End If
        End If
    Next objCbar

End If
```

Although both fragments produce identical results, the indenting in the second one makes it (reasonably) easy to tell which End If statement belongs to which If...Then statement above it. As a result, you can readily trace the flow of program execution, depending on the conditions in effect when you run it.

Indenting customs

So which lines of code should you indent, and by how much? Your goal is to indent related statements by the same amount, so that the relationship between them is visually obvious. More specifically, statements that are executed only when some condition is in effect should all be indented together.

For example, VBA executes the statements within an If...Then...Else construction or inside Do...Loop and For...Next loops as a group; so they should have the same indentation. Here's another example:

```
Do While intC <> 20
   intA = intA + 1
   If intA = intB Then
      intA = 5
      intB = 10
   Else
      intA = intB
      intC = 20
   End If
Loop
```

VBA executes the statement intA = intA + 1 and the If...Then...Else structure with every pass of the Do...Loop structure. For this reason, I used the same indentation for the intA = intA + 1 statement and the three statements that define the If...Then...Else structure (If intA = intB Then, Else, and End If). The two statements immediately following the If ... Then statement are only executed if intA equals intB, so they receive additional indenting, as do the two statements following Else.

Note that *control structures* like Do...Loop and If...Then...Else always consist of at least two statements — one that starts the structure, the other that terminates it. For Do...Loop, the terminating statement is Loop; for If...Then...Else, it's End If. Statements that are part of a given control structure should all be indented by the same amount. This format allows you to see clearly the outline of the structure, and which other statements fall inside it. Control structures are one of the major topics that I cover in Chapter 8.

How to indent

To indent a line of code, you can simply press the spacebar or the Tab key to move the insertion point over. You can control how far the Tab key moves each time you press it by choosing Tools⇨Options. The Editor tab of the Options dialog box has a box labeled Tab Width where you type the number of spaces you want. Because space in the Visual Basic Editor is so dear, I decreased my Tab Width setting to 3, but you can enter any value from 1 to 32.

If pressing Tab or the spacebar is beneath you, you can always use the VBA Indent and Outdent buttons on the Edit toolbar to move the beginning of your lines of code to the right or left, respectively. These buttons work on selections, not just single lines, so you can indent or outdent an entire block with one click. Note that they ignore the location of the insertion point — they always indent or outdent the entire line, no matter where the insertion point rests.

Automatic indenting

To cut your workload to a minimum, the Visual Basic Editor automatically indents each new line of code to match the previous one. When you get to a line that requires a smaller indentation, just press the Backspace key to back up. If you don't like the assistance, you can shut off automatic indenting in the Editor tab of the Tools⇨Options dialog box.

Space-iousness is good

Placing a blank line between groups of related statements clues you in to meaningful units of code. Besides, it makes your program a little less dense and easier on your visual cortex. To see this practice, peek up ahead at Figure 6-2.

Don't scroll if you don't have to!

A single line of the Code window can hold over 300 characters (would you believe that 308 is the maximum?), so you can certainly write some very long one-line statements if you like. Obviously, however, each line is much easier to read if it all fits into the visible portion of the Code window so you don't have to scroll sideways.

Using the line-continuation character

To continue a statement onto another line, place an underscore (_) at the end of the line. For example, the following three lines together constitute one statement:

```
sngWackyNumber = Cos(12 * 57.5 / Sqr(intMyTinyNumber + _
intMyBigNumber) + CustomDataMassage(sngrawinfo, 12) + _
(bytFirstTuesdayInAugust * curLastPayCheck) + 1)
```

Be sure that you remember to type a space before the underscore (also called the *line-continuation character*) on every line where you use it. Otherwise, VBA gives you an `invalid character` error message.

One more caution about breaking up statements over multiple lines: Don't place the underscore within a pair of quotation marks that enclose a string of text — not unless you want to include the underscore character as part of the string. Chapter 7 contains details about how to split strings across two or more lines.

Not using multiple-line statements

Although multiple-line statements are better than long single-line statements that trail off the edge of the Code window, they're not at all ideal. VBA may have no trouble interpreting statements that continue over two or more lines, but most human beings find them confusing.

Unless you've made the Code window very skinny, you can usually break up a long statement into several separate statements that get the same job done. You may need to create additional variables for temporary storage of some intermediate calculations, but this is a fair price to pay for improved clarity in your code.

For instance, you may rewrite the previous sample code as follows:

```
sngTemp1 = Sqr(intMyTinyNumber + intMyBigNumber)
sngTemp2 = 12 * 57.5 / sngTemp1
sngTemp3 = CustomDataMassage(sngrawinfo, 12)
sngTemp4 = bytFirstTuesdayInAugust * curLastPayCheck
sngWackyNumber = Cos(sngTemp2 + sngTemp3 + sngTemp4 + 1)
```

This code is longer and it does involve extra variables, but it makes the calculation you're performing easier to follow. Also, if you get the wrong final results, you can follow each part of the computation individually as the program runs to see whether you can catch the error — this *stepping* isn't possible when one long statement performs the entire calculation. Chapter 9 covers the process of stepping through your code.

Remarks About Comments

Like all serious programming languages, VBA lets you add explanations to your code. *Comments* allow you to translate the code into understandable English and to record the purpose of each statement or group of statements. For that matter, you can use them to embed phone numbers, recipes, and positive affirmations in your code.

The comments you type are totally ignored by the VBA compiler. They live only in the text file representing the contents of the Code window, not in the compiled program. They don't make the compiled program any longer, nor do they slow it down in any way. Comments cost you nothing except a minuscule amount of disk space, so use them freely.

How to make comments

A comment begins when you type an apostrophe. Everything you type to the right of the apostrophe on that line of code is part of the comment. You can place comments on lines all by themselves, or add comments after a line of active code. Figure 6-2 shows a Code window with lots of comments interspersed among the active code statements.

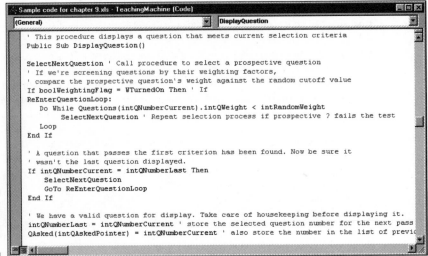

Figure 6-2:
Comments,
please?

One place you can't put a comment is on a line that ends with the line-continuation character, the underscore. In other words, you get an error message if you enter code like this:

```
a = b _ ' No comments on the 1st line of a multi-line
        statement
  + c
```

To comment a multiple-line statement, you must place the comment on a line of its own before the statement starts, or on the last line of the statement, like this:

```
' Here is a properly commented multi-line statement
z = x - _
  y ' The last line CAN take a comment.
```

When to use comments

Be lavish with comments. Train yourself to add at least a brief clarification to every line of code, and/or to record in detail the function of each group of three or four statements. When you declare a variable, add a comment about what it's for and where it will be used. When you declare a procedure, write down what it does, which arguments and variables it uses and why, and which other procedures it calls. Train yourself to type comments whenever you experience a lull in your creative coding process.

Excuse my preachiness, but this point is really important! When you're actively working on a particular project, the logic behind your coding choices may seem transparently obvious. However, that lovely sense of clarity soon fades. If you turn your attention elsewhere, even for a few days, only your comments save you from laboriously translating the work you've already done back into terms your mind can understand. Comments are critical when you're working on a project with other people — you can explain your program's goals and choice of programming techniques in context by using comments.

Commenting out one or more lines of code is a good way to take real code statements off active duty without deleting them for good. This can come in handy when you want to try two alternative approaches to the same coding problem, or to shut off code that you know contains an error while you test another part of the same module. You can type apostrophes at the beginning of each line you want to temporarily deactivate, and then delete the apostrophes when it's time to bring the code back on line. Alternatively, you can use the Comment Block and Uncomment Block buttons that I describe in the following section to quickly deactivate and reactivate continuous blocks of code of any length.

Long-winded comments

To include a long comment spanning two or more lines in your code, you still have to place an apostrophe at the beginning of each line. But fortunately, VBA provides a one-button command for commenting blocks of lines in bulk.

To insert a multiple-line comment in your code, type the comment as you would in a word processor, dismissing any error messages you get when you press Enter to start each new line. After you're through, select the entire block that you intend for comment-hood, and click the Comment Block button on the Edit toolbar. The Visual Basic Editor adds the required apostrophe at the beginning of every line in the selected block.

You can also "uncomment" a block of lines that currently begin with apostrophes. Select the block and click the Uncomment Block button, also on the Edit toolbar.

One little note about the way these buttons work is in order. If a line in the block is already a comment — if it already starts with an apostrophe — the Comment Block button adds a second apostrophe to it. If there are two leading apostrophes, you get three, and so on. Likewise, each time you click the Uncomment Block button, only one apostrophe is removed. This means that when you comment and then uncomment a block of active code, you don't lose any real comments that it contained.

Chapter 7

Storing and Modifying Information

- -

In This Chapter

▶ Using variables as named storage bins for whatever data you want to store

▶ Declaring variables in your code for fast, error-free programs

▶ Lightening your programming workload by defining named constants

▶ Expressing your values in VBA code as expressions

▶ Calculating and computing with VBA operators

▶ Understanding practical details on the different data types for variables and constants

- -

*T*o tap the full potential of VBA, programs require variables to store information that can change. Variables are the key to writing programs that alter their own behavior based on up-to-date information or other changes in prevailing conditions. This chapter surveys the topic in some depth, explaining how variables work and how to use them in your programs. The various types of data that you can store in variables receive special attention, as do related topics such as constants, which represent unchanging values, and operators, the symbols and keywords you use to calculate a new value from two or more existing ones.

Although fairly hefty, the material here isn't the last word in this book on variables. Chapter 12 shows you how to use variables to work with objects and Chapter 13 discusses variables in relation to arrays and user-defined data types.

The sample code in this chapter is available on the CD in complete modules that you can run and modify.

Working with Variables

In essence, a *variable* is an ID tag for a chunk of information stored by your program.

It's like when you go to the theater and leave your hat at the hatcheck. The attendant puts your hat away somewhere in a back room — you couldn't care less where, as long as it's safe. In return, you get a slip with a number on it. When you leave, you give the attendant the number and you get your hat back. At the next performance, the staff uses that same number for somebody else's hat.

What, you say you don't have a hat? Well, until now, you haven't had any variables, either.

A variable lets you access a whole chunk of information all at once via the variable's name, instead of working with each individual digit, character, or what have you. What's more, you don't need to know the details of where your program stores the data, or in what form — all you need is the variable's name. Finally, you can change the information represented by the variable any time you like.

This last characteristic is the key to creating programs that can respond automatically to changing conditions. Whenever appropriate, your program can examine the information the variable stands for, comparing it to criteria that you specify. If the information matches the criteria, the program can execute one set of statements; if not, it executes a different set.

Technically, a difference exists between the variable (which is a named information container) and the information it contains. However, people don't go around saying things like "the information represented by variable x" very often. You can refer to the information itself by the variable name, as long as you keep in mind that the information can vary.

Declaring variables: The overview

Chapter 6 introduces the concept of declarations, VBA statements that notify the compiler that you plan to use a named item and that describe exactly the type of item it is. One of the most common uses of declaration statements is to declare variables. Variable declarations look like this:

```
Dim varAnyOldVariable
Private intIntegerVariable As Integer
Static strNewYearsResolution As String
```

Most variable declarations are `Dim` statements. The `Dim` keyword is short for dimension, used as a verb. The idea is that the `Dim` statement gives VBA the dimensions for the storage area that the variable refers to. You can also use the `Private`, `Public`, and `Static` keywords to declare variables and at the same time specify their scope. (See the section "Specifying a variable's scope," later in this chapter.)

After you declare a variable, you can then use it in other statements in your program. Typically, the first time a variable sees action is when you place specific information in it using an assignment statement (see the section "Giving variables their values," later in this chapter). You can then go on to use that information (via the variable's name) anywhere else you like in your code.

Where to declare variables

You can declare a variable in either of the following two places in your program:

- ✔ The Declarations section of the module (at the module level)
- ✔ Anywhere within a procedure (at the procedure level)

The location you choose helps determine which procedures can access the variable — in other words, that location determines the variable's scope. In general, if you declare the variable at the module level, any procedure in the module can use the variable. If you declare it in a particular procedure, it can be used only in that procedure. You can also use the `Public`, `Private`, and `Static` keywords to specify a variable's scope. (I introduce scope in Chapter 6 and offer further detail in the section "Specifying a variable's scope," later in this chapter.)

Although VBA won't object if you interleave variable declarations with executable statements within a procedure, your code will be clearer if you declare all the procedure's variables at the very beginning. Note how the following procedure follows this practice:

```
Public Sub VariableProcedures ()
 Dim strChildsName As String
 Dim intToyCount As Integer
 Dim curAllowance As Currency
 strChildsName = InputBox ("Enter the child's name:")
' in the next two lines, CountToys and NewAllowance
' represent Function procedures that are presumably
' defined elsewhere in your code
 intToyCount = CountToys(strChildsName)
 curAllowance = NewAllowance(strChildsName, intToyCount)
End Sub
```

When to declare variables

All the experts agree that declaring variables ahead of time, before you use them in your program, is the best practice. One simple reason for doing so is to make your code easier to understand. Other advantages come into play when you use the `Option Explicit` compiler directive, which I cover in the section "Explicit declarations are good," later in this chapter.

By default, however, VBA permits you to use variables without declaring them first. If you type **A = 7** anywhere in your code, VBA dutifully creates a variable named A and stores the value 7 in that variable. Variables you create without declaring them are automatically defined as variant variables, which I discuss in the next section.

Choosing and using data types

When you write a variable declaration, you can simply name the variable. The following statement tells VBA to set aside storage space for a variable named varIable but does not say what sort of information that variable should hold:

```
Dim varIable
```

Alternatively, you can declare the variable's data type explicitly. The following statement declares the variable sngMyOldSocks an *As Single* data type:

```
Dim sngMyOldSocks As Single
```

An As Single data type holds a relatively small floating-point number. Floating-point numbers are the kind written in scientific notation — you know, with a decimal point and an exponent, as in 6.02×10^{23}.

VBA recognizes a variety of other distinct data types for your variables, including helpful types like Date and Currency. Familiarize yourself with the available types because collectively they are an important key to writing code that works right. Table 7-1 summarizes key facts about the data types. The section "Details on Data Types," later in this chapter, offers tips on working with many of the specific types.

Table 7-1		VBA Data Types
Data Type	*Explanation*	*Range of Permitted Values*
Boolean	Logical True or False	True (–1) or False (0)
Byte	Small whole number	0 to 255
Integer	Smallish whole number	–32,768 to 32,767
Long	Large whole number	–2,147,483,648 to 2,147,483,647
Single	Single-precision floating-point value	–3.402823E38 to –1.401298E-45 for negative values; 1.401298E-45 to 3.402823E38 for positive values

Data Type	Explanation	Range of Permitted Values
Double	Double-precision floating-point value	−1.79769313486232E308 to −4.94065645841247E-324 for negative values; 4.94065645841247E-324 to 1.79769313486232E308 for positive values
Currency	Large, precise number; 19 significant digits	922,337,203,685,477.5808 to 922,337,203,685,477.5807 including four fixed decimal places
Decimal	Even larger, more precise numbers with 29 significant digits and up to 28 decimal places	+/−79,228,162,514,264,337,593,543,950,335 with no decimal point; +/−7.9228162514264337593543950335 with 28 places to the right of the decimal
Date	Dates and times	January 1, 100 to December 31, 9999
Object	VBA object	Any object reference
String (variable-length)	Sequence of text	0 to approximately 2 billion characters of variable length
String (fixed-length)	Sequence of specified number of text characters	1 to approximately 65,400 (see "Fixing your strings" later in this chapter for details on fixed-length strings)
Variant	Anything goes	Any numeric value up to the range of a Double; for strings, same range as for variable-length String
User-defined	Group of variables used together as a unit	The range of each variable (requires the Type statement) in the group corresponds to its data type, as shown in this table.

Pros and cons of using specific data types versus variants

Depending on whom you talk to, declaring a variable as a specific data type — that is, as a type other than Variant — is either a great idea or a bad one. The practice helps prevent some errors, but fosters others. It definitely makes for smaller and faster programs — but in most real-world scenarios, these improvements probably aren't significant.

Here's some background on error prevention: When you specify a particular data type when declaring a variable, VBA bars you from placing other types of data in that variable. Suppose you declare a variable as in this example:

```
Dim dateAnniversary As Date
```

VBA displays an error message if you try to assign text to the variable with a statement such as

```
dateAnniversary = "Trip to Fiji" ' Causes error
```

An error message may be a nuisance, but it's better than allowing your program to keep running with erroneous information.

You wouldn't get that error message if you had declared `dateAnniversary` as a *variant,* a catchall type that can hold any kind of data. You can declare variants just as you do variables of other types, as in this example:

```
Dim varTootSuite As Variant
```

However, because `Variant` is the default data type, you automatically get a variant variable if you omit the data type. Just listing the variable name in your declaration will do, as shown here:

```
Dim TootSuite
```

Now, how about the performance question? Declaring a variable with a specific data type lets you select the type that requires the least storage space to hold the information you plan to keep there. Variants consume more memory than variables of other types, and accessing their information slows down your program. However, these effects are trivial unless you work with very large numbers of variables. And by declaring all variables as variants, you can make your code easier to write, more flexible, and less complicated to modify. I don't have room to explore this issue in detail, but you should be aware that some very good programmers recommend coding exclusively with variants.

Decide on one of these strategies — declaring the specific data type of every variable, or using variants for all your variables — and resolve to stick to it, at least within a given program.

Explicit declarations are good

Whether or not you decide to use a particular data type for each variable, it's always a good idea to declare each variable before you use it. As a Serious Programmer, you can set VBA so that it forces you to do so. When you place the following statement in the Declarations section of a module, VBA displays an error message every time you try to use a variable that you haven't declared:

```
Option Explicit
```

Duly reminded, you can go back and add the necessary declaration. Requiring explicit declarations in this way produces an even more important benefit: It prevents spelling errors or typos from introducing major problems into your code.

Imagine this scenario: You decide to wing it without the Option Explicit statement in your module. Somewhere in the body of a procedure, however, a random finger spasm strikes while you're typing one of your variables' names. When the VBA compiler encounters the line with this misspelling, it thinks that you've just designated a new variable and cheerfully creates it for you. Your program may still run, but don't be surprised if it turns all your text purple or tells you that the world's population just hit 12.

By now, maybe you're convinced that the Option Explicit statement should be a part of every module you create. If that's the case, why should you have to type it each time? You don't have to, of course. Go to the Options dialog box by choosing Tools⇨Options. On the Editor tab, check the Require Variable Declaration check box. From now on, the Visual Basic Editor automatically inserts an Option Explicit statement in every new module. You still have to type the statement yourself in old modules that don't have it.

Specifying a variable's scope

A variable's *scope* — that is, where in your program the variable is accessible — depends on two interacting factors:

- The location where you declare the variable (either inside a procedure or in the Declarations section of a module — see the section "Where to declare variables," earlier in this chapter)
- The keyword you use to declare the variable (Dim, Public, Private, or Static)

If you declare a variable inside a procedure using Dim, you can only use that variable inside that procedure. Elsewhere in your program, VBA won't recognize the variable. Variables declared with Dim in the module's Declarations section are accessible throughout the module — but not from other modules.

Private variables — the default

The Private keyword works exactly like Dim. The two declaration statements shown here function identically:

```
Private strLouie As String
```

```
Dim strLouie As String
```

Because Private and Dim work the same way, you can forget about Private if you like. You may want to use Private instead of Dim, however, to remind yourself when you read the code that the variable is accessible only in the current module or procedure.

Public knowledge

Declaring a variable with `Public` makes the variable accessible, or public, throughout your entire project. Here's an example:

```
Public intUnclassified As Integer
```

You can only declare variables with `Public` in the Declarations section of a module.

The Static advantage

Use `Static` to declare a variable within a procedure when you want the variable to remain in memory and even more importantly, to retain its value — even when the procedure isn't running. In the following example, the variable `intLastingVariable` acts as a counter, recording the number of times the procedure runs:

```
Sub TransientProcedure()
 Dim strTransientVariable As String
 Static intLastingVariable As Integer
 strTransientVariable = Format(Now(), "Medium Time")
 intLastingVariable = intLastingVariable + 1
 MsgBox "The time is " & strTransientVariable & ". " & _
   "You have executed this procedure " & _
 intLastingVariable & " times."
End Sub
```

In the previous example, the statement `intLastingVariable = intLastingVariable + 1` adds 1 to the value of the variable each time the procedure runs. If you declare `intLastingVariable` with `Dim` instead of `Static`, the variable always starts with the same value (zero) with every pass through the procedure, which makes the procedure essentially worthless.

You can only declare `Static` variables within a procedure. If you want all the variables in a procedure to remain intact — even when the procedure isn't running — declare the whole procedure as `Static`. In the procedure declaration, place the keyword `Static` immediately before the `Sub` or `Function` keyword that defines the type of procedure you're declaring. Here are a couple of examples of this technique:

```
Private Static Sub DoItAll ()
```

```
Static Function DontDoVeryMuch(intTimeToWaste as Integer)
```

Note that Static comes after `Private` or `Public` in the procedure declaration, if you include either of these optional scope-related keywords.

Declaring a variable or procedure `Static` preserves its value only while the program as a whole is running, *not* between different sessions of running the program. To retain a value for use the next time that you run the program, you must store it on disk or in the Windows registry (see Chapter 14 for the techniques required).

Declaring multiple variables on the same line

To conserve space, you're free to declare more than one variable on the same line of code. You have to type the `Dim` keyword only once per line. A comma should separate each variable. Just remember to specify the data type for each variable that you declare — even if all the variables on the line are of the same type. Here's an example of the right way to do it:

```
Dim intA As Integer, intD As Integer, intL As Integer
```

Mixing data types on the same line works, too:

```
Dim curNetWorth As Currency, datSecondTuesday as Date
```

Declaring multiple variables on the same line increases the likelihood that you'll accidentally fail to specify a data type. Any variables on the line for which you don't supply a data type are automatically registered as variants. If your declaration reads as follows, `strX` and `strY` are treated as variants, not string variables:

```
Dim strX, strY, strZ As String
```

Giving variables their values

After you've declared a variable, the next thing you do with it, usually, is fill it with information (putting known information into a variable for the first time is called *initializing the variable*). To place information in a variable, you assign the value of the information to the variable. Whenever it suits your purposes, you can store different data in the variable by assigning a different value to it.

Giving assignments

To assign a value to a variable, all it takes is one little equal sign. For example, to store the number 3 in a variable named `intC`, just type **intC = 3**.

In VBA, an assignment statement consists of an equal sign between a variable on the left and an expression specifying the variable's value on the right. In the example, the expression is simply the number value, 3. Values you specify directly like this are called *literal values*. (I discuss expression in the section "Expression-ism" later in this chapter.)

Take a look at another assignment statement:

```
strQuote = "Ask not what your country can do for you, " & _
    "ask what you can do for your country."
```

In this case, the statement assigns all the text to the right of the equal sign to the variable strQuote. As before, the information in this statement's expression consists entirely of literal values — the actual text you want to place in the variable. However, the statement is broken up over two lines, so the text expression has to be divided into two separate strings. That & (ampersand) sign tells VBA to join them together.

The point I'm trying to illustrate here is that expressions very often have two or more components. No matter how many parts an expression has, VBA computes its overall value and then assigns that value to the variable.

Understand that until an assignment statement actually executes, it isn't a statement of fact. In math, when you write an equation — such as 2 + 2 = 4 — you're proclaiming that the values on either side of the equal sign are actually equal. By contrast, a VBA assignment statement compels the variable to become equal to the expression's value. Another assignment statement can change the variable's value at any time.

Using variables in assignment statements

You can base a variable's assigned value on other variables, as well as on literal values. The following statement multiplies the curCost and sngMargin variables together and assigns that result to the curSalePrice variable:

```
curSalePrice = curCost * sngMargin
```

Note that in this statement, the expression consists of other variables, not literal values. VBA makes the necessary calculation based on the current values stored in those variables. (By the way, following the naming convention that I recommend in Chapter 6, curSalePrice and curCost are variables of the Currency data type.)

Using functions in assignment statements

Functions and Function procedures can also be used in assignment statements, as in this example:

```
strFavorite = InputBox("What's your favorite flavor?")
```

VBA functions and the `Function` procedures you write can be used in an assignment statement because each returns a value. The `InputBox` function used in the previous line of code displays a little dialog box with the specified message and provides space for the user of your program to type a response. That response is the value returned by the function, in the form of a string (more on the `InputBox` function in Chapter 11).

Expression-ism

An *expression* is a portion of a VBA statement that can be evaluated to give a value, such as a number, a text string, or a reference to an object. It can consist of one or more of the following, in any combination:

- ✔ Variables, such as `bytMonth` or `boolWinter`
- ✔ Literal values, such as `1234` or `This is only a test`
- ✔ Constants, which stand in for literal values and which I cover in the section "Working with Values Constant-ly" later in this chapter
- ✔ VBA functions, such as `InputBox()` or `Sqr()`
- ✔ Function procedures in your code

If the expression has more than one of these elements, they are joined with operators such as the + sign, or in some cases, by nesting functions and `Function` procedures inside other functions and `Function` procedures.

Note that if an expression has more than one component, each component is itself an expression — it has a value.

Working with Values Constant-ly

When your program uses a value that will never change, you don't need a variable to represent that value. Although you can always assign literal values to variables or use them directly in other expressions, declaring constants to represent these values is usually better. The reasons why follow after a discussion of how to declare constants.

Declaring constants

Use a `Const` statement to declare constants:

```
Const cstrPetsName As String = "Foo-foo"
Const cdateTargetDate As Date = #5/26/2000#
Const cboolUp As Boolean = True
```

Note that this technique is quite similar to the way you declare variables. The difference is that *you specify the value of the constant when you declare it.* You can declare constants as any of the same data types you use for variables, except object, user-defined, and decimal (refer to Table 7-1).

Notice also that I declared the name of each example constant with an initial lowercase *c* (which stands for "constant"). This method is the simplest way to indicate that a declared name is a constant rather than a variable. However, you can choose another meaningful prefix if you prefer.

You may follow the example of VBA and Visual Basic and choose a prefix based on your name or on the name of your VBA project. VBA and Visual Basic identify constants with the prefix vb, as in vbBlue (representing the code number for the color blue, 16711680) or vbKeyTab (representing the code for the Tab key, 9). VBA applications often name the constants they define using an application-specific prefix, as in xlBarStacked (representing the code for an Excel stacked bar chart, 58).

By the way, you're free to use the constants defined by VBA or your VBA application in your own programs. You can use the Help system or the Object Browser to locate information on these predefined constants (see Chapter 5 for a discussion of the Object Browser).

Reaping the benefits of a constant approach

After you declare a constant, you can use it by name in your program wherever you would have entered the corresponding literal values. For instance, let's say that you write a program that determines an employee's salary based on his shoe size. One way to code a part of the program would be:

```
If bytShoeSize > 12 Then
  curJoesSalary = 75000
End If
```

One problem with this approach is that it *hard-codes* the exact salary amount in your program. If a rising cost of living increases salaries across the board, you have to dig through your code to find the amount that needs to be changed. And if you use the same value more than once in the program, you have to change each occurrence — and you run a bigger risk that typing errors will creep in and gum up the works.

Here's the same code written with a constant:

```
Const ccurTopSalaryStep As Currency = 75000
...
If bytShoeSize > 12 Then
            curJoesSalary = ccurTopSalaryStep
End If
```

With this solution, you can easily locate the constant declaration at the top of the module or procedure. Change the constant's value there, and you instantly alter your code to match at every place the constant appears. As a bonus, the code is much easier to understand. Instead of asking, "What does this number 75,000 represent?" you know at a glance that Joe is due the top step of the salary scale if he wears size 12 shoes.

You could use a variable to gain the advantages of a constant. However, variables take up more space in memory, and more importantly, you run the risk of accidentally changing the variable's constant value in your program.

Using constants to represent attributes

Constants are handy for working with a group of named elements or characteristics, such as days of the week (Monday, Tuesday, and so on) or tastes (sweet, salty, sour, and bitter). Instead of manipulating the names of these items as text strings in your program, an easier approach is to pick a number to represent each item and then declare a constant equal to that number based on the item's name. From then on, you can refer to the items by name rather than number. Here's a little bit o' code that uses this technique:

```
Const cbytSweet = 1, cbytSalty = 2
Const cbytSour = 3, cbytBitter = 4
Do While intTaste = cbytSour
 AddSweetener
 intTaste = CheckTaste()
Loop
```

Hello, Operators

In VBA, an *operator* is a special symbol or keyword in an expression that combines two values (sub-expressions, if you will) to give a new result. The two values are listed on either side of the operator.

In the following expression, the + (addition) operator adds 3 to the value of the intA variable.

```
intA + 3
```

The result of this addition is the expression's value. (Remember, an expression is only a part of a VBA statement and you can't run it by itself — you must include it in a complete statement such as `intB = intA + 3`. For information on expressions, see "Expression-ism," earlier in this chapter.)

VBA includes operators in three main categories — arithmetic, comparison, and logical — plus a few miscellaneous operators such as the ones for string concatenation (that is, glomming two or more strings together to make one). I review each category separately later in this section.

When used with text strings, the + operator performs concatenation, not addition — it joins the two strings together. But it's better to use the "real" concatenation operator — the & symbol — because it clarifies your intention to combine the strings. VBA interprets the following expression as "My name is Ellie.":

```
"My name is " & "Ellie."
```

By the way, if a text string consists exclusively of numeric characters, you can use the + operator to add the string's numeric value to another number. After running the following statement, you get 579 as the value of variable `intC`:

```
intC = 123 + "456"
```

In VBA forms, numbers typed in by the user in are stored as strings. VBA lets you use such numeric strings as numbers without explicitly converting them first, as in the above example.

Here's a comparison operator at work:

```
Tan(sngAngleA) <> 1.4
```

The <> symbol is the "not equal to" operator. It tests to see whether the two values in the expression are unequal, returning a result of `True` or `False`. If the tangent of `sngAngleA` is not equal to 1.4, the result of this expression is `True`. Otherwise, the result is `False`.

Taking precedence

In fancier expressions that include more than one operator, VBA has to figure out which operation to perform first, second, and third. The following expression contains two operators — + (the addition operator) and * (the multiplication operator):

```
intA + intB * intC
```

In English, you would read the entire thing as "`intA` plus `intB` times `intC`."

Although the * symbol is the second operator in the expression, it has precedence over the addition operator. VBA multiplies `intB` by `intC` first, and then adds this result to `intA`. As this example illustrates, VBA follows a fixed sequence in evaluating the parts of an expression when it contains more than one operator.

You can use parentheses to override the predetermined precedence order by which operators are processed. If you type the following, VBA adds the first two variables first, and then multiplies the value of `intC` by that number:

```
(intA + intB) * intC
```

Without parentheses to guide it, what are the rules VBA follows when deciding which operator to process first? If the expression includes two or more categories of operators, VBA evaluates all the operators in each category in the following order:

1. Arithmetic and concatenation operators come first.

2. Comparison operators follow.

3. Logical operators are processed last.

Within a category, VBA applies preset rules to determine which operator comes first. Arithmetic, comparison, and logical operators are processed according to the order shown in Table 7-2. VBA takes comparison operators as they come, working from left to right. If two or more operators at the same level of precedence appear in an expression, VBA processes them from left to right as well.

Table 7-2	Precedence Order for VBA Operators (Within Each Category, Operators Are Processed in the Order Listed)
Operator	*Operation Performed*
Arithmetic	
^	Exponentiation
–	Negation
* or /	Multiplication or division
\	Integer division
Mod	Modulus arithmetic
+ or –	Addition or subtraction

(continued)

Table 7-2 *(continued)*

Operator	*Operation Performed*
Concatenation	
&	String concatenation
Comparison	
=	Equality
<>	Inequality (not equal to)
<	Less than
>	Greater than
<=	Less than or equal to
>=	Greater than or equal to
Like	String comparison to pattern
Is	Test whether two items refer to the same object
Logical	
Not	Logical not
And	Logical and
Or	Logical or
Xor	Logical exclusive or
Eqv	Logical equivalence
Imp	Logical implication

Performing calculations with arithmetic operators

VBA has seven arithmetic operators (refer to Table 7-2). You can tell what four of these do — that would be the +, –, *, and / operators — just by looking at the symbols. For example, the expression 6/2 gives 3 as the result, of course.

The other three arithmetic operators are less self-evident, however. Here's how they work:

✔ The ^ operator raises the first value in the expression to the power of the second value. The expression

```
2 ^ 3
```

equals 8 (2^3 or $2 \times 2 \times 2$).

✔ The \ operator performs integer division, giving an integer result. VBA simply discards any fractional part of the answer rather than rounding it up or down. (***Note:*** This operator is the *backslash* character, whereas the operator for ordinary division is an ordinary *forward* slash.) Try this example:

```
244 \ 7
```

The answer, 34, tells you how many full weeks occur in 244 days.

✔ The Mod operator divides the first value by the second but returns only the remainder as the result. Continuing with the last example, if you want to know how many days were left over after all 34 complete weeks have been accounted for, the expression you need is as follows:

```
244 Mod 7
```

The result is 6. Note that the result given by the Mod operator is always a whole number. If for some reason you want to know the fractional part of a division result expressed in decimal form, use an expression like this:

```
(244 Mod 7)/7
```

This is the same as 6/7, which works out to .857 or so.

Comparing values

VBA has six all-around comparison operators for comparing numeric and string values, plus two special-purpose comparison operators, Like (for strings) and Is (for objects). I summarize the comparison operators in Table 7-2.

The result of an expression based on any of these operators is always either *True* or False. For example, here's an expression based on the <= (less than or equal to) operator:

```
intX <= 11
```

If the value of intX is 12, the result of the expression is False because 12 is not less than 11. Most often, you use comparison operators in conditional statements such as `If...Then` statements. I discuss conditional statements in detail in Chapter 8, but a simple sample is in order here:

```
If intX = 2000 Then
  MakeWhoopee
End If
```

Here, the = operator tests to see whether the values on either side of it are the same. The expression's result is `True` if they are the same and `False` otherwise. The English translation of this code is, "If `intX`'s value equals 2000, run the `MakeWhoopee Sub` procedure."

Note that VBA uses the equals sign, =, in two different ways. In declarations, it serves to assign values to variables, as I discuss in the section "Giving variables their values," earlier in this chapter. But the equals sign also functions as a comparison operator to determine whether two values are the same.

Comparing strings

You can use the comparison operators to compare strings of text as well as numbers. The following expression gives `False` as a result:

```
"Sweetpea" = "Daffodil"
```

Obviously, these two strings aren't equal.

But in other cases, the results of a string comparison aren't so easy to predict. To get the results you want when comparing strings, you have to understand the rules VBA uses to decide whether one string is "greater than" another one.

Unless you specify otherwise, VBA uses a binary comparison method. The two strings are compared on the basis of the numeric codes in which the characters are actually stored in your program. In this coding system, common punctuation marks have the lowest numbers, followed by numerals, uppercase letters, lowercase letters, and then accented characters. Because the code numbers for lowercase letters are larger than those for uppercase letters, the expressions `"a" > "A"` and `"a" > "Z"` both give `True` results.

To use a different, more intuitive method for comparing strings, include the statement `Option Compare Text` in your module's Declarations section. With `Option Compare Text` in force, the strings are compared alphabetically, ignoring case (accented letters are still treated as higher in value than the corresponding unaccented versions). Under these conditions, the following are all `True` expressions:

```
"a" = "A"
"a" < "Z"
"Aunt Hill" < "Äunt Hill"
```

When comparing two strings, VBA starts by comparing the first characters in each string. If these characters differ, the greater string is the one with the greater character code number. If the first characters in each string are the same, VBA then compares the next, and so on.

Comparing strings of unequal length

What happens when you compare strings that aren't the same length? If the strings are identical except that one is shorter than the other, the longer string is greater than the shorter one. For example, the following is a True expression:

```
"In a canyon, in a cavern" > "In a canyon"
```

However, if the two strings differ in content as well as length, the usual comparison criteria apply. The following expression is True because the w in two is greater than the h in three (even though the first part of the expression is shorter than the second):

```
"I'll take two" > "I'll take three"
```

What's not to Like?

The Like operator compares a string to a wildcard pattern rather than to a specific set of characters. Use it to see whether a string falls within, or outside, a given range. For example, the value of the following expression is True in VBA.

```
"Yreka Bakery" Like "y*y" ' that palindrome is a real place
```

I don't have room to explain the many details involved in using the Like operator, but you should know that it exists — it's a powerful tool for handling text.

Using comparison operators in code

The results of a comparison operation can be stored in a variable, typically one of the Boolean data type, using a standard assignment statement:

```
boolTheAnswerIs = 5 > 4
```

Because 5 is greater than 4, the result of the greater than operation is True, and in turn VBA assigns True as the value of the boolTheAnswerIs variable.

The True and False keywords are actually built-in VBA numeric constants, representing the values –1 and 0, respectively. You can assign the result of a comparison to any numeric variable.

Comparison operators are frequently used in conditional statements to decide whether to execute a particular branch of code:

```
If intP <= intQ Then
  SomethingWentWrong 'call error-handling procedure
End If
```

Stringing text together

The concatenation operator, & (ampersand), joins strings together. You can use it with literal strings, string variables, or any function that returns a string value. You can use it repeatedly to construct a long string from multiple string values, as in this example:

```
strA = "You answered " & InputBox("Type an answer:") & _
  " . The correct answer was " & strAnswer & "."
```

After this statement executes, strA might contain "You answered Portugal. The correct answer was Spain." Or some similar string.

When assembling large strings from smaller ones, don't forget to build in the spaces and punctuation marks the final string needs.

You need the concatenation operator to break up a string over two or more lines of code, even if you're not combining the string with variables or functions. Here's an example:

```
strB = "I gave my love a cherry " _
  & "that had no stone."
```

You can place the & operator at the end of the first line (before the underscore) or at the beginning of the next one. Compare the previous lines of code to this fragment:

```
strB = "I gave my love a chicken " & _
    "that had no bone."
```

Details on Data Types

This section offers tips on when and how to use the various VBA data types, with an exception or two. The object data type is crucial but quite complex, so it rates special treatment in Chapter 12. I don't cover user-defined data types in this book.

Converting between data types

Data types are a convenience for human beings — VBA actually stores all information in numeric form. That being the case, conversions between different data types aren't a big challenge for VBA.

VBA comes with many functions for converting one data type to another under your control. See Chapter 11 for a review of these functions. Realize, however, that whenever possible, VBA automatically converts between different types of data as the context suggests. For example, the + operator adds the number in a string to a numeric value, as long as the string contains only numerals. Similarly, if you assign a decimal value to an Integer variable, VBA automatically rounds off the value for you.

Sometimes these automatic conversions are just what you want. But the real point is that even if you take pains to declare your variables precisely, errors are still possible because of VBA's efforts to anticipate your needs.

Understanding variants

The Variant data type provides a one-size-fits-all container for your data storage needs. Variants can hold any kind of data you can use in VBA, including numeric values, strings, dates and times, and objects. What's more, the same variable can store different types of data at different times within a single program. The following code is perfectly acceptable, though hardly very productive:

```
Dim varAnythingGoes as Variant
varAnythingGoes = 3
varAnythingGoes = "I suppose."
varAnythingGoes = #12/31/99 11:59:59 PM#
```

Not only does VBA permit such statements, but it also figures out and keeps track of the type of data you're placing in the variant. After that last statement in the series above, for example, varAnythingGoes is cataloged as a Variant/Date variable. You can find out which type of data VBA is currently storing in a variant, using the TypeName function. Suppose the previous code fragment continues with the following statement:

```
strVariantType = TypeName(varAnythingGoes)
```

After this statement executes, the value of strVariantType is Date — because that's the data type it currently stores.

Because they're so flexible, `Variant` variables are very convenient. Instead of worrying about which data types to use, all your variables can be variants, and you can stash any type of data in them as the need arises. But there are potential drawbacks to this approach, as discussed in the "Pros and cons of using specific data types versus variants" section earlier in this chapter.

Even if you declare most variables using specific data types, variants can still have a role as temporary scratch variables for simple computations in short procedures. Also, you must use variants for variables of the Decimal type, used to maximize the precision of calculations (see the bulleted points in the next section).

Choosing a numeric data type

If you declare variables as specific data types rather than variants and choose the smallest possible data type, your programs will be faster, smaller, and more likely to work properly. Of course, the variable should have enough storage capacity to accommodate the range of values that it may contain — any extra room is just wasted space.

For example, suppose that your program requires one variable for the day of the week (possible values 1 – 7) and one for the month (1 – 31). You can get away with using the `Byte` data type, which holds values between 0 and 255. To work with the 365 days of the year, you would need an `Integer` variable.

Table 7-1 summarizes the value ranges for each type of numeric data type. Here are some tips on specific data types:

- ✔ Use the `Boolean`, `Byte`, `Integer`, or `Long` data types to hold whole numbers (the kind without decimals).

- ✔ Use the `Single` and `Double` data types to store floating-point numbers of up to 15 significant digits and their exponents. Though the range of values is huge, be aware that rounding may introduce errors — and these may be significant in operations on values of very different sizes. To assign a floating-point value such as $4.72 \times 10{-}22$ to a `Single` or `Double` variable, use the following format (VBA assumes the exponent is positive if you leave out a + or – sign after the letter E):

  ```
  sngFloating = 4.72E-22
  ```

- ✔ If you need more precise calculations, the `Currency` data type gives you up to 19 significant digits, and with the `Decimal` type you can have as many as 29 (neither type provides exponents). In the current version of VBA, however, `Decimal` isn't a standalone data type — in other words, you can't declare a `Decimal` variable. Instead, `Decimal` is available only as a subtype of the `Variant` data type. To ensure that a number is stored as a `Decimal` variant rather than one of the floating-point types, use the `CDec` function in the assignment statement.

Here's an example of how to do this (notice that within the `CDec` function you must enter long numbers as strings):

```
Dim decvarPi As Variant
decvarPi=CDec("3.141592653589793238846426433833")
```

If your program does calculations with the numbers in a variable, you may need to choose a data type large enough to hold the result of those calculations, even if you don't assign the calculation results to the variable itself. Peruse this example:

```
Dim bytByte1 As Byte
Dim bytByte2 As Byte
Dim intInteger As Integer
bytByte1 = 255 ' maximum permitted byte value
bytByte2 = 1
intInteger = bytByte1 + bytByte2 ' error!
```

Here, even though `intVariable` has enough storage capacity to hold the results of the calculation, VBA gives an overflow error on the last line because VBA first stores the result in those byte-sized variables. To make the calculation work, you must change at least one of those byte variables to integers.

When to use Boolean variables

Variables of the `Boolean` data type can hold only one of two values: `True` (stored as –1) or `False` (0). Declare a `Boolean` variable whenever you need to know which of two alternative conditions currently prevails. For example, you may have a variable called `boolIsOn`, whose value would be `True` if whatever it is, is on, and `False` if it's off.

Another way to use `Boolean` variables is to define other constants with the same values as `True` and `False`. Your variable names can then be neutral, while the constants explicitly refer to the two alternative conditions. This technique is definitely easier to show than to explain, so look here:

```
Dim boolBellyButtonStyle as Boolean
Const Innie As Boolean = True
Const Outie As Boolean = False
If boolBellyButtonStyle = Outie Then
  TickleLightly
End If
```

This is a great tip! To toggle the value of a Boolean variable or object property to its opposite, use the Not operator. In Word, for example, you can turn on the document map if it's off, or turn it off if it's on, with this line of code:

```
ActiveWindow.DocumentMap = Not ActiveWindow.DocumentMap
```

Working with currency values

The main reason to use the Currency data type is to ensure accurate results. True, the floating-point data types Single and Double can store numbers with decimal points — which is basically what currency values are. However, calculations involving floating-point values often produce small errors, and these drive the bean counters crazy.

Adapting to local money formats

One of VBA's many strengths is its capability to adapt automatically to the local customs regarding formatting of items such as dates and currency values. If you write your program properly, you don't need to build currency symbols such as $, ¥, or £ into your code — VBA adds the right one for you, based on the language and country selections in the Regional Settings applet of the Windows Control Panel.

For example, consider the following code:

```
Const ccurMoneyTalks As Currency = 5463.72
MsgBox Format(ccurMoneyTalks, "Currency")
```

In the U.S., the message box displays $5,463.72. When exactly the same program runs in France, you see 5463,72F in the message box. See Chapter 11 for an in-depth discussion of the Format function.

But you don't need to declare a variable as Currency to display it as a properly formatted money amount. Used with the "Currency" named format, the Format function dresses up any numeric value as dollars, francs, or whatever is appropriate locally.

Other uses for the Currency data type

Regardless of whether you're working with money, however, you can use variables of the Currency type any time that:

- ✔ You need to store larger numbers than will fit in a Long integer variable.
- ✔ You need to make calculations on large numbers with more precision than you could get from the floating-point data types.

Currency values can have up to 19 significant digits, 15 to the left of the decimal point and 4 to the right (the decimal point is fixed).

Working with dates

Use the `Date` data type to work conveniently with dates, times, or both. Behind the scenes, VBA encodes a date or time as a number such as 35692.9201273148 — apparently meaningless to mere mortals. But you can ignore this detail and work with dates and times in your programming as you would on paper or in a word processor.

The one trick you have to remember is that you must always type date and time values — called *date* and *time literals* in VBA — between paired number sign characters. For example, the following statements declare two `Date` variables and assign them values:

```
Dim dateWeddingDay As Date, dateTimeOfCeremony As Date
dateWeddingDay = #4/20/99#
dateTimeOfCeremony = #3:15:00 PM#
```

As with currency, VBA automatically outputs dates according to local formatting customs. The expression `Format (#10/24/89#, "Long date")` gives the string "Tuesday, October 24, 1989" in the U.S., but "Terça-feira, 24 de Outubro de 1989" in Brazil.

Entering date values

You can type date literals in just about any format that appeals to you. The following are all acceptable:

```
#09/1/2003#
#Sep 25, 93#
#Janua 9 1905#
```

If the Visual Basic Editor recognizes your entry as a valid date, it converts it into the "short form" date format specified in the Windows Control Panel. If you omit the year, VBA adds the current year for you. The conversion happens as soon as you move the insertion point off the line of code, before you run your program.

Time has value

Enter time literals in the format `#hours:minutes:seconds symbol#`, where *symbol* is AM or PM. Examples include:

```
#10:45:00 PM#
#2:3:30 AM#
```

You don't have to type in leading zeros, as in `#01:02:03 PM#`, but VBA adds them for you when you move the cursor to another line of code. Similarly, you can omit portions of the time value you don't need, but VBA fills in the blanks. For example, you can enter seconds alone by typing something like

#0:0:23#, but VBA changes such an entry into a complete time value — in this case — #12:00:23 AM#.

Date and time math

Adding or subtracting dates with the standard VBA arithmetic operators is possible, but unfortunately it doesn't work the way you would expect. For example, #3/19/2005# - #3/19/2004# doesn't equal "1 year," but #12/30/1900#. The explanation has to do with the way VBA stores date data, which I won't trouble you with here. All you really need to know is that VBA has two functions (DateAdd() and DateDiff()) that handle your needs for date math. Chapter 11 reviews their use.

In contrast, you can do time calculations fairly easily with the standard arithmetic operators. Take a gander at the expressions in the following code:

```
Dim dateThen As Date
dateThen = #07:15 AM# + #12:00# ' = #07:15:00 PM#
dateThen = #07:15:00 AM# - #0:15 AM# ' = #07:00:00 AM#
dateThen = #07:15:15 AM# + #0:0:30 AM# ' = #07:15:45 AM#
```

The examples show the minimum entries you can type. As always, VBA converts your entries into complete time literals — #0:0:30 AM# becomes #12:00:30 AM#, for example. One other point: As shown in the sample code, you must explicitly declare variables using the Date data type to get the expected results when you subtract times.

Stringing you along

Because VBA so freely converts between different data types, you need string variables less often than you might think. If all you need to do is display a non-string value in a form that humans can read, you don't need to convert it into a string first. Instead, you can use a number or date — or a variable containing one — as the argument to a function or as the value of an object property that by rights should be a string.

This example is based on the ever-popular MsgBox function, used for displaying string data in little dialog boxes (see Chapter 11 for more on this function). The following statements produce the message that you see in Figure 7-1:

```
Dim dateThisIsADateNotAString As Date
dateThisIsADateNotAString = #17:23:16#
MsgBox dateThisIsADateNotAString
```

Or how about this heresy:

```
Dim intSmall As Integer, sngTall As Single
Dim varYouAll As Variant
intSmall = 3
sngTall = 9.99E+33
varYouAll = intSmall & sngTall
```

Following this sequence, `varYouAll` contains "39.99E+33". The presence of &, the concatenation operator, causes VBA to convert both numeric variables into strings so it can concatenate, by golly.

What you really need string variables for is to work with non-numeric characters, that is, letters and punctuation marks. You can't get these out of number values, not no way, not no how.

Careful programming practice dictates that you explicitly convert numeric values into strings before manipulating them as such. If you follow this advice, you're likely to make fewer errors and produce code that's more understandable. Still, it's nice to know that you can output variables with so little work.

Using quotes in string declarations: Optional?

Along the same lines, you don't really have to use those quote marks when you assign numeric, date, or currency values to a string variable (one that you've declared using the string data type). Ever the pampering parent, VBA makes its best effort to convert such values into strings, with never a mutter of complaint. If your program executes the following code, the `strGString` variable contains the string "7/22/1904" until some other statement changes it:

```
Dim strGString As String
strGString = #July 22, 1904#
```

But humor me — use the quotation marks to make sure that the variable contains exactly what you intend.

Fixing your strings

VBA lets you declare string variables in two ways. A standard string declaration, such as `Dim strMessage As String`, sets up a variable that can hold a string of any length. You can change the size of the variable at will, too, simply by assigning it a string of different length.

In some circumstances, presetting the size of a string variable is handy. This is primarily of value when you read and write records in a random-access file, a technique that I discuss in the chapter "Working with disk files" on the *VBA For Dummies* 3rd Edition, CD. For now, showing you how to declare a fixed-length string is enough. Here's an example:

```
Dim strFixed As String * 5
```

Declared this way, the variable always contains exactly 5 characters. If you assign a shorter string to it, VBA adds spaces in after the characters. If you assign it a longer string, VBA stuffs the first 5 characters of the string into the variable, summarily discarding the remainder:

```
strFixed = "abc" ' strFixed now contains "abc "
strFixed = "Fourscore and seven years" ' now, "Fours"
```

Chapter 8

Controlling the Flow

· ·

In This Chapter

▶ Using control structures to control what happens

▶ Testing criteria with conditional expressions

▶ Making decisions with `If...Then` and `Select Case` statements

▶ Repeating code blocks with `For...Next`, `For Each...Next,` and `Do...Loop` statements

▶ Branching at will with `GoTo` statements

· ·

*C*ontrol structures are code statements that determine what the procedure will do next, based on some condition that is in effect at the time the code runs. VBA offers a healthy assortment of powerful control structures. This chapter takes these structures apart and demonstrates their use in practical examples (well, at least quasipractical examples).

Many of the examples in this chapter are available on the CD.

Controlling Wild Programs with Control Structures

Control structures fall into three main groups: conditional statements, loops, and the `With` statement. They work as follows:

✔ A *conditional statement* determines which branch of code to execute based on whether a condition is `True` or `False`. VBA conditional statements include `If...Then` (in several permutations) and `Select Case`.

✔ A *loop* repeatedly executes a block of code a fixed number of times or until some condition becomes `True` or `False`. When you know in advance how many times to execute a loop, use a `For...Next` loop. If your code needs to test some condition to see whether to continue running the loop, use the `Do...Loop` statement, which is available in multiple flavors. To repeat actions on the objects in a collection, use a `For Each...Next` loop, which I discuss in Chapter 12.

✔ The `With` statement allows you to perform multiple actions by using the same object without having to name the object in each action. I cover the `With` statement in Chapter 12.

Control structures lend clarity, organization, and . . . well, structure to your program, making it relatively easy to trace the branches of the path that your program may follow as it runs.

Control structure anatomy

What makes a control structure a "structure" is the fact that it's not just a single statement, but a whole block of them. Your basic `If...Then` statement serves as a model for all control structures:

```
If a < b Then ' "If a is less than b, then"
 b = a ' "set the value of b equal to a"
 a = c ' "and then set the value of a equal to c."
End If ' "That's all--proceed with the program."
```

The skeleton of this structure is an opening statement that identifies its type and sets up a condition and a statement that tells VBA where the structure ends. Sandwiched in between is the meat of the structure — the statements that actually *do* something.

All control structures have this general outline, but in some of them, the structure's condition comes in the last statement rather than the first.

Nested control structures

When you're talking about control structures, *nesting* means placing one structure inside another, above the statement that marks the end of the first structure. VBA enters the second structure before it finishes executing the first. Nesting is a necessity for solving many complex, real-life programming problems. You can nest control structures to as many levels as you think necessary.

In the following example, a `Do While...Loop` structure is nested inside an `If...Then` structure, and another `If...Then` structure is nested inside the `Do While...Loop`:

```
If a < b Then ' Start of outer If...Then
 Do While b > c ' Start of nested Do While...Loop
 b = b - 1
 If c > d Then ' Start of nested (inner) If...Then
 d = a
 End If ' End of inner If...Then
 Loop ' End of Do While...Loop
End If ' End of outer If...Then
```

Use indents!

Consistent indenting is vital to writing understandable code. In the example in the preceding section, each pair of statements that defines a structure is indented by the same amount. Indentation makes it easy to see which End If statement belongs to which If...Then structure, for example. The statements that execute within a given structure are all indented by the same amount, so you can see that they are under the jurisdiction of that structure.

The Road Taken: Using Condition Expressions

Making choices is fundamental in software, as it is in life. Although they are simple in concept, decision-making control structures are among the most powerful programming tools at your disposal. "All" that these structures do is choose which of two or more different blocks of code to execute. But after one block executes and the other does not, you can say with Frost, "And that has made all the difference."

To decide whether to execute a block of code, three of VBA's control structures evaluate a *condition expression* that you write. These three include the Do...Loop looping structure, If...Then, and Select Case. I devote the rest of this section to the condition expressions used in all three of these structures. Two other decision-making control structures, For...Next and For Each...Next, don't use condition expressions.

How condition expressions work

If...Then, Select Case, and Do...Loop structures all decide what to do based on one simple test: Is the condition True, or is it False? The condition in question can be any VBA expression. (Remember that 0 is equal to False in VBA. All other values are considered True.)

Most often, condition expressions are built around a comparison operator that compares the values of two subexpressions. In Chapter 7, I list and discuss in some detail the VBA set of comparison operators. You can get the basic idea, however, by looking at the sample expressions in the following table. Are the expressions in the table `True` or `False`? Only the control structure knows.

Expression	Translation into English
`a < b`	a is less than b.
`b = c`	b is equal to c.
`colTBears("Henry")` `Is objCurrentBear`	The object stored in the `colTBears` collection under the name "Henry" is the same one now referred to by the `objCurrentBear` variable.
`sqr (1/x * 29.3234) >=` `CDbl (strNumber) + 12`	The square root of the quantity 1 divided by x times 29.3234 is greater than or equal to the numeric value of the string variable `strNumber` plus 12.

Condition expressions without comparison operators

Although most condition expressions contain comparison operators, you're free to create conditions without them. Before I explain how this works, though, some background is in order.

I discuss this topic not to encourage you to write condition expressions without comparison operators, but because many programmers do. You commonly see such condition expressions in the code published in programming magazines and posted on the Internet. Until you live and breathe VBA, however, I suggest that you include comparison operators in your condition expressions for clarity's sake, even when they're not strictly necessary.

Now for the details. As you know, the value of a Boolean variable is always equal to either `True` or `False`. So the expression

```
boolUnder18 ' value can be only True or False
```

obviously works fine as a condition in a conditional statement, such as

```
If boolUnder18 Then
  GiveDiscount
End If
```

But because `True` and `False` have numeric values, you can use any numeric expression as a condition. The following expressions are all valid conditions:

```
1234 ' Always True
0 ' Always False
True ' Always True
False ' Always False
intHowManyPets ' False if intHowManyPets = 0
lngA + lngB + lngC ' False if sum = 0
```

Object properties often represent Boolean (`True`/`False`) values, so expressions such as `frmHelpWindow.Enabled` are often tested as conditions, without comparison operators.

You can't use strings or objects as conditions by themselves; however, they work fine as components in expressions constructed with appropriate comparison operators.

Using logical operators in conditions

Introduced and listed in Chapter 7, logical operators evaluate two subexpressions separately as `True` or `False` and then combine them according to a set of rules to produce a final value — also `True` or `False` — based on a set of rules.

The most important logical operators — or at least the ones that are easiest to figure out how to use — are `And`, `Or`, and `Xor`. The following table shows how these operators work.

Operator	Returns True	Examples	Result
And	Only if *both* subexpressions are `True`	3*2 = 6 And 12 > 11	True
		2+2 = 4 And 4–2 + 1	False
Or	If *either* or *both* subexpressions are `True`	10 > 20 And 20 > 10	True
		5 < 4 And 6 < 5	False
Xor	If only one subexpression is `True` (`False` if both subexpressions are `True` or both are `False`)	5 + 5 < 9 Xor 5 + 5 = 10	True
		5 + 5 > 9 Xor 5 + 5 = 10	False

If you're so inclined, you can combine multiple logical operations in a single condition expression. Feast your eyes on this expression:

```
(a + b > 20 And c = 10) Or (objDoor.Open)
```

In English, this example can translate to "This expression is true if either:

a + b is greater than 20, and also c = 10; or

the Open property of the objDoor object is False."

Unless you're so smart that you really don't need a computer, don't go overboard with logical operators in a single expression. Above all, use parentheses to clarify what the operators are comparing. In the preceding example, the parentheses around the objDoor.Open subexpression clarify that it is being "Or'd" with the first subexpression.

Using If...Then Statements

By far the most commonly used conditional statements are If...Then and its variations, If...Then...Else and If...ElseIf. You can see lots of examples of If...Then statements in other chapters, but in this section they occupy center stage.

The basic form: If...Then

At its most basic, an If...Then statement executes a special block of code if the condition that you feed it is True, but simply does nothing if the condition is False. The syntax is:

```
If condition Then
(statements to execute if condition is True)
End If
```

For a simple example of a complete If...Then statement, refer to the section "Control structure anatomy" at the beginning of this chapter.

Heed these few points concerning If...Then statements:

✔ Condition is a condition expression of the type that I describe earlier in this chapter in the section "The road taken: Using condition expressions." If *condition* is True, VBA executes the statements between If... and End If. If *condition* is False, VBA skips these statements, continuing with the next statement in your program following End If.

✔ Notice that the `Then` keyword goes on the same line as the `If` and the `condition` expression. VBA won't know what to think if you drop `Then` to the following line, and an error results (unless you use the underscore line-continuation character).

✔ Be sure to include the `End If` statement. Otherwise, VBA displays an error, because it can't identify which statement is the last in the block.

One-liners with If...Then

When an `If...Then` structure needs to execute a single statement only if the condition is `True`, you can put the entire thing on one line. In that case, an `End If` statement isn't required — in fact, it's illegal. The statement

```
If curPrice > 20 Then MsgBox "Warning! Price too high!"
```

functions identically to this structure, which requires the `End If` statement:

```
If curPrice > 20 Then
 MsgBox "Warning! Price too high!"
End If
```

If...Then...Else statements

If you want your program to choose between two alternative blocks of code based on a condition, you need an `If...Then...Else` statement. In this case, one block is executed if the condition is `True`, and a completely different block is executed if the condition is `False`. Here's the syntax:

```
If condition Then
(statements to execute if condition is True)
Else
(statements to execute if condition is False)
End If
```

If `condition` is `True`, VBA executes the first block of statements and then skips the rest of the structure to the line of code following the `End If` statement. If `condition` is `False`, on the other hand, only the statements in the block following `Else` get executed.

Consider the following example:

```
If TypeOf ctlCurrentControl Is CommandButton Then
 ctlCurrentControl.BackColor = &HFF& 'Red
Else
 ctlCurrentControl.BackColor = &HFFFF00 'Cyan
End If
```

Indexer: Please, please index "TypeOf"

Here, the `condition` expression is `TypeOf ctlCurrentControl Is CommandButton`. You can assume that the `ctlCurrentControl` variable already holds an object reference to a particular control on a `UserForm`. The `TypeOf` keyword allows you to check whether the object referred to by a variable or other object reference is of a specific type — in this case, a `CommandButton` object.

The `If` statement on the first line of code uses this expression to check if the control is a command button. If so, the expression paints the button's background color red. All other controls are painted cyan (sky blue).

If...Then complexities: The introduction

Frequently, you need to test two or more conditions before you know what path your program should take. It's just like in real life. If you were writing a book about VBA, you may be thinking something like "If I finish by the deadline, and if I don't run out of money before then, and if the dollar holds its value against the peso, I can go to Mexico for two weeks in October. But if the dollar falls, I'll have to settle for Turlock."

Depending on the specific tests involved, you may need to include `ElseIf` clauses in your `If...Then` structure or to nest one or more levels of `If...Then` statements.

Complexities, Part 1: Using If...ElseIf statements

Use the `ElseIf` keyword to test a new condition when you want to execute certain statements only if the first condition *isn't* `True`. The syntax is as follows:

```
If condition1 Then
(statements to execute if condition1 is True)
ElseIf condition2
(statements to execute if condition1 is False but
                     condition2 is True)
ElseIf condition3
(statements to execute if condition1 and condition2 are
                     both False but condition3 is True)
... (additional ElseIf clauses)
Else ' optional clause
(statements to execute if all the conditions are False)
End If
```

Only one ElseIf clause is required, but you can have as many ElseIf clauses as you like. The Else clause is optional, but if it is included, it must be the last one in the structure.

To put this monstrosity into action, imagine a program that helps you inventory your camera store's stock of film. A roll of film that has already expired shouldn't be counted. But if the film is still good, the program should add it to the inventory count for the correct type of film.

The following code fragment performs this job. The code assumes that you have an object that represents a roll of film and that the object has properties for expiration date, type of film, and color (versus black and white).

```
If objRollOfFilm.ExpDate < Date Then
  MsgBox "This film is no good."
ElseIf objRollOfFilm.Type = "Slide" Then
  intCountSlide = intCountSlide + 1
ElseIf objRollOfFilm.Color Then
  intCountColorPrint = intCountColorPrint + 1
Else
  intCountBWPrint = intCountBWPrint + 1
End If
```

The initial statement checks the ExpDate property of the object against the current date. If the date has already passed, the program displays a message box to that effect, and that's it. Only if the film is still good — in other words, if the first condition is False — is the first ElseIf clause executed. This clause looks at the film object's Type property. If this property is "Slide", the count of slide rolls is incremented by the next statement.

If the film is some other type, however, the program skips to the next ElseIf clause, where the object's Color property is tested without a comparison operator (you can assume that this property is Boolean and can take only True or False as its value). If the value is True, the roll is counted as color print film. If the value is False, the Else statement near the end is the only place left to go — and the roll is counted in the black-and-white print category.

In an If...ElseIf structure, only the statements associated with the first True condition are executed. After those statements run, any remaining ElseIf and Else clauses are skipped.

Complexities, Part II: Nesting If...Then statements

Nested If...Then statements are sort of the opposite of If...ElseIf statements. Use these statements when you want to test a second condition to decide whether to execute a block of code, but only if the first condition is True. Nesting two If...Then statements is like saying, "If X is True *and* Y is True, I'm going to do A, B, and C."

You can nest `If...Then` statements of any variety — `If...Then...Else`, `If...ElseIf`, or garden-variety `If...Then` — in any combination. In schematic form, here's a pair of nested `If...Then` statements:

```
If condition1 Then
 If condition2 Then
 (statements that execute if both condition1 and
                     condition2 are True)
 ElseIf condition3 Then
 (statements that execute if condition1 and condition3 are
                     True but condition2 is False)
 End If ' Ends the inner If...Then block
 (other statements that execute if condition1 is True,
                     regardless of condition2)
Else
(statements that execute only if condition1 is False)
End If
```

The following simple example of nested `If...Then` statements displays a congratulatory message box for high grades achieved with a minimum "full-time" class load:

```
If sngGPA > 3.5 Then
 If sngUnits > 10 Then
 MsgBox "You're on the Dean's List!"
 End If
End If
```

Complexities, Part III: Using logical operators in conditions

Using logical operators in condition expressions can be a more elegant alternative to `ElseIf` clauses and nested `If...Then` structures — but only when just one branch of a multiple-condition path has the statements that you want to execute.

Look at the code fragment at the end of the preceding section. You can accomplish exactly the same goal with a single `If...Then` statement, as follows:

```
If sngGPA > 3.5 And sngUnits > 10 Then
 MsgBox "You're on the Dean's List!"
End If
```

Conditional expressions constructed with logical operators have little value when you want to execute statements on more than one branch of the decision path. Try to consolidate this variation of the earlier example by using logical operators:

```
If sngGPA > 3.5 Then
 If sngUnits > 10 Then
 MsgBox "You're on the Dean's List!"
 Else
 MsgBox "You did well, part-timer!"
 End If
End If
```

The only solution I can come up with still requires two If...Then statements, which are just not nested:

```
If sngGPA > 3.5 And sngUnits > 10 Then
 MsgBox "You're on the Dean's List!"
End If
If sngGPA > 3.5 And sngUnits <= 10 Then
 MsgBox "You did well, part-timer!"
End If
```

Using Select Case Statements

If...ElseIf and nested If...Then statements are ideal for testing different expressions before deciding which block of code to execute. If, however, you need to test the *same* value against different conditions, a Select Case statement usually is the way to go. The syntax is as follows:

```
Select Case value
 Case test1
 (statements to be executed if value meets test1
                     criteria)
 Case test2
 (statements to be executed if value meets test2
                     criteria)
 ... ' additional Case clauses
 Case Else ' optional
 (statements to be executed if value meets none of the
                     above criteria)
End Select
```

Testing conditions in Select Case statements

The Select Case structure doesn't directly use complete condition expressions of the type that I outline earlier (see "The road taken: Using condition expressions"). Instead, you have to break up each condition into two parts. In the previous section, the first part of the condition is represented by value, while each test (test1, test2, and so on) makes up the second part of one expression. If the equivalent condition expression is

```
a + b = c
```

you can think of value as being the part to the left of the comparison operator (a + b) and testn as being everything to the right, including the operator (= c).

A sample Select Case statement

I definitely need to use an example to illustrate how a "real" Select Case structure may look. Here comes one now:

```
Select Case objRollOfFilm.Type
  Case cintSlide
  intCountSlide = intCountSlide + 1
  Case cintColorPrint
  intCountColorPrint = intCountColorPrint + 1
  Case cintBWPrint
  intCountBWPrint = intCountBWPrint + 1
  Case Else
  MsgBox "Not a known type."
End Select
```

This code performs essentially the same job as the example that I use in the section on If...ElseIf statements earlier in this chapter (omitting the check for expired film). Since then, however, the hypothetical roll-of-film VBA object seems to have been modified — the black-and-white versus color information is now represented in the Type property, not in a separate Color property, and named constants are used to represent the property's possible values.

That being so, the program needs to work with only one value — the one returned by the Type property — but it must be compared with several possible alternatives. The Select Case statement is just what Dr. Dobbs ordered in this situation.

The example's first Case clause is equivalent to writing If objRollOfFilm.Type = cintSlide Then. That is, if the object's Type property is cintSlide, the program executes the next statement; if not, it moves on to Case clause number 2.

Notice, though, that the operator that you'd expect is missing from the tests in all three Case clauses. That's because in Select Case statements, equality is assumed to be the comparison that you're making.

The Case Else clause

If the value of the `Type` property isn't equal to the tests in any of the `Case` clauses, control falls to the `Case Else` clause, which is always the last one in a `Select Case` structure. In the previous example, the result is the error message "Not a known type." A `Case Else` clause is optional because you may not want anything to happen if none of the criteria are satisfied. As in the example, though, it's often wise to include the `Case Else` clause, if only to alert you to unexpected values stored by your program.

More about Case clause tests . . . a lot more

The tests performed by the `Case` clauses in the previous example are sweet, simple tests of a single equality, as in "Is the `Type` property equal to such and so?" But you can do much more sophisticated testing with each `Case` clause.

This is easiest to illustrate with a numeric example. Suppose that your `Select Case` statement opens with the following line of code:

```
Select Case intPatientAge
```

In this example, the value being tested is an integer variable called `intPatientAge` that represents the age of a patient at a family-practice medical clinic. This value is the one to be tested in the `Case` clauses that follow. In the following list, I describe the kinds of tests you can make in `Case` clauses, and illustrate them with example clauses:

- ✔ You can test the value against a range, as follows:

```
Case 18 To 35
  Messages("YoungAdult").Print
```

  Notice that you place the `To` keyword between the values that define the boundaries of the range. The range includes values and everything in between.

- ✔ You can test the value by using a comparison operator other than =, as follows:

```
Case Is > 65
  Messages("OlderAdult").Print
```

  In this example, you're supposed to use the `Is` keyword before the comparison operator. Actually, you don't have to type `Is` — VBA puts it in for you if you omit it.

✔ You can perform multiple tests in the same `Case` clause, as follows:

```
Case 0 To 5. 15. Is > 55
  Messages("ImmunizationReminder").Print
```

Be sure to separate the tests with commas. By the way, a `Case` clause with multiple tests is equivalent to an expression built on a series of `Or` expressions — if the value passes *any* of the tests, the following statements get executed.

Repeating Yourself with Loops

Use a loop control structure to execute the same block of code more than once. Repeating one or more statements is a fundamental chore when you perform many mathematical computations, extract smaller data items from larger ones, and repeat an action on multiple items in a group.

VBA offers three main types of loop structures:

Loop Type	How It Loops
`Do...Loop`	While or until a condition is `True`
`For...Next`	A specified number of times
`For Each...Next`	For each object in a collection

When working with nested loops, remember this simple truth: The inner loop finishes looping before the outer loop.

Do-ing loops

The various versions of the `Do...Loop` statement all are designed to repeat a block of code indefinitely, until a condition is met. To determine whether to continue looping, a `Do...Loop` statement evaluates a condition expression of the type that I describe in the section "The road taken: Using condition expressions" earlier in this chapter and that you use in `If...Then` statements.

Uses for `Do...Loop` structures are legion. These include:

✔ Displaying an error message repeatedly until the user makes a valid entry in a dialog box

✔ Reading data from a disk file until the end of the file is reached

✔ Searching for and counting the number of times a shorter string occurs within a longer one

▶ Idling your program for a set period

▶ Performing actions on all items in an array

▶ With If...Then statements, performing actions with multiple items that meet criteria in an array or collection — see Chapter 13 for details on arrays and collections

Types of Do...Loop statements

VBA offers the Do...Loop in five flavors, all of which work very much alike. Here they are:

Statement	What It Does
Do While...Loop	Begin and repeat the block only if the condition is True
Do...Loop While	Execute the block once and then repeat it as long as the condition is True
Do Until...Loop	Begin and repeat the block only if the condition is False
Do...Loop Until	Execute the block once and then repeat it as long as the condition is False
Do...Loop	Repeat the block indefinitely, exiting when a conditional statement within the loop executes an End Do statement

The Do While...Loop statement

The prototypical Do structure is Do While...Loop. The syntax is as follows:

```
Do While condition
(statements that execute while condition is True)
Loop
```

When it encounters a Do While statement, VBA begins by evaluating the condition. If this expression turns out to be False, VBA ignores the rest of the loop, skipping to the program statement following Loop. But if the condition is True, VBA executes the statements in the block. When VBA reaches the Loop statement, it jumps back up to the Do While statement to test the condition again.

Typically, one or more statements in the body of the loop can change the value of the condition, so it may now be False. If so, VBA terminates the loop, skipping over it to the statement immediately following the Loop statement. But if the condition is still True, the loop statements again get executed.

The whole process repeats until at some point, the condition becomes False. In other words, no set limit restricts how many times the block of statements in the loop are executed. Assuming an infinite power supply and a computer that never breaks down, the loop repeats forever if the condition never becomes False.

A Do While...Loop example (two examples, actually)

The following example relies on two Do While...Loop statements to reverse the digits in a number selected by the user. It probably has no practical value — but it's cute, it runs in any VBA application, and it's short enough to illustrate how Do loops work.

```
Sub ReverseTheDigits()
Dim intOriginalNumber As Integer
Dim intOneDigit As Integer, strBackwardsNumber As String
Do While intOriginalNumber < 10
  intOriginalNumber = _
  InputBox("Type in an integer greater than 9.")
Loop
Do While intOriginalNumber
  intOneDigit = intOriginalNumber Mod 10
  strBackwardsNumber = strBackwardsNumber & intOneDigit
  intOriginalNumber = Int(intOriginalNumber / 10)
Loop
MsgBox strBackwardsNumber
End Sub
```

The example explained

The first Do loop checks the value of the number typed in by the user of the program to make sure that it's not a negative number and that it has at least two digits — otherwise, why bother reversing them? The first time the program encounters this loop, the value of the intOriginalNumber variable is zero because nothing has been assigned to it so far. Zero is less than 10, so the condition is True, and VBA enters the loop.

The loop contains one statement: an input box asking the user to type a suitable number. After the user types the number, the Loop statement sends VBA back to the top of the loop, where the number entered is checked. Only after a valid number has been entered does the loop terminate. (Notice that this example omits important validity checks, such as whether the number is an integer and whether it's not larger than the maximum value for an Integer variable.)

When VBA confirms a valid entry, it moves on to the next loop. The condition for executing this loop is that the variable containing the number must be greater than zero. Because a nonzero value is True, you can simply write Do While intOriginalNumber instead of Do While intOriginalNumber > 0 — both versions work identically.

In the loop proper, a simple three-step procedure takes apart the digits of the original number, working from right to left, using the digits in reverse order to build a new string. You don't have to understand how this code works to figure out the loop, but it won't hurt you to know that:

- ✔ The first line uses the Mod operator to divide the number by 10 and assign only the remainder to the intOneDigit variable. Because you're dividing by 10, the remainder is the last (rightmost) digit of the original number.

- ✔ The second line takes the digit obtained by the first line and adds it to the end of the string under construction.

- ✔ The third line again divides the number by 10, this time keeping the result of the division in the original variable. The division effectively lops off the rightmost digit. Notice, however, that before the result is assigned to the variable, it is processed by the Int function. The Int function is necessary because, otherwise, VBA would round off the result — which could change the digits that were originally entered.

- ✔ As the loop loops, intOriginalNumber becomes 0 after all its digits have been processed (any digit divided by 10 is less than 1, and the Int function drops the fractional part of the result). In VBA-land, zero is False, so the loop ends, and the program displays the reversed number.

Other Do statements

Variations on the Do While...Loop are easy to understand once you get the basic form. This section discusses three of the alternative Do loops; see "When to use Do without While or Until" later in this chapter for the fourth.

Do...Loop While

The difference between the Do While...Loop and Do...Loop While statements is simple: Do While...Loop has the condition at the top of the loop, whereas in Do...Loop While, the condition comes at the end.

In a Do While...Loop structure, the loop is entered only if the condition is True the first time that the program reaches it. If the condition is False to start with, the statements in the loop never execute.

In a Do...Loop While structure, by contrast, the loop always executes at least once: the first time the program runs through the code. Only then is the condition tested, the loop repeating as long as the condition remains True. Use a Do...Loop While structure when the loop block contains a statement that sets a value in the condition before the condition gets tested.

Another situation that calls for a Do...Loop While structure is when you're performing an action on an item (such as a string or an array) that may have more than one element. If you already know that the item has at least one element, you want the loop statements to execute at least once and then repeat as many times as needed for the remaining components.

Do Until loops

The Do While...Loop and Do Until...Loop statements are functionally equivalent — that is, you can execute exactly the same statements with either one by modifying the condition expression to perform the opposite test. The Do...Loop While and Do...Loop Until pair are similarly complementary.

Pretend that you're Julia Child talking her audience through a recipe. You may say, "Keep whipping the batter as long as you see even the slightest little lump" or "Keep whipping the batter until it is perfectly smooth." Either way, you mean the same thing.

Do While and Do Until are similarly complementary. If the condition for a Do While statement is A = B, a Do Until statement with A <> B functions identically.

To Do or not to Do

At their most elegant, Do loops provide all the information that VBA needs to decide whether to execute the loop in the condition expression. Unfortunately, things aren't always so tidy in real-world programming. Sometimes, a change in a different condition occurring in the body of the loop demands a hasty exit, which is why VBA has an Exit Do statement.

Valid only in a Do structure, Exit Do summarily terminates the loop, passing program execution to the statement that comes after the loop. The following example concatenates a string variable to an existing string, but if the variable contains more than one character, the loop terminates:

```
Do While strA < "Z"
  If Len(strA) > 1 Then
  Exit Do
  End If
  strB = strB & strA
  strA = GetNextCharacter
Loop
```

Normally, the Exit Do statement should appear in an If...Then or Select Case statement nested in the loop. That way, the loop runs normally unless some special or aberrant value occurs. You can also use Exit Do as a debugging device to bypass the loop temporarily, without having to comment out the code by placing a ' in front of each line.

When to use Do without While or Until

With standard Do...While/Until...Loop statements, you can test a condition at the beginning or end of a loop. But what if you want to test the condition somewhere *within* the loop?

In this situation, use a Do...Loop statement — without While or Until. This technique requires an If or Select Case statement nested inside the loop. One or more branches of the nested conditional statement include an Exit Do statement, allowing the program to terminate the loop when a specified condition is met.

Here's how a Do...Loop statement looks in schematic form:

```
Do
(statements to be executed with each pass of the loop)
If condition Then
 Exit Do
 End If
(more statements to be executed only if loop continues)
Loop
```

As you can see, this technique is appropriate when you want to execute some of the loop statements regardless of whether the condition is met. It's also useful if the loop should terminate under several different conditions.

Frequently, for example, you must validate a user entry based on several criteria. In the following example, a Do...Loop structure repeats the loop until the user enters a valid letter answer:

```
Sub GetAnAnswer()
strAnswer = InputBox("Enter your answer (A-E)")
Do
 If strAnswer = "" Then
 strAnswer = InputBox("You didn't enter anything." _
& " Please type a letter between A and E.")
 ElseIf Len(strAnswer) > 1 Then
 strAnswer = InputBox("Your answer should be" _
& " only one letter long. Please try again.")
 ElseIf strAnswer < "A" Or strAnswer > "E" Then
 strAnswer = InputBox("You typed an invalid" _
& " character. Type a letter from A to E.")
 Else
 Exit Do
 End If
Loop
End Sub
```

The program executes the Exit Do statement only after all three validation criteria — expressed in the If and ElseIf clauses — have been met.

An alternative syntax that does exactly the same thing uses Do While True as the first line of the loop structure. Because True (the constant) is always a True value, the condition is always met, and VBA always enters the loop. Again, you need an Exit Do statement in the body of the loop to terminate the loop.

Repeating on count with For...Next loops

When you know how many times a loop should execute before the loop runs, use a `For...Next` loop. You specify how many passes VBA should make through the loop by supplying `start` and `end` values, which can be literal integers, variables, or even complex expressions. As the loop executes, a `counter` variable keeps track of the number of completed cycles. When the counter's value equals that of `end`, the loop is finished.

Simplified, the syntax of a `For...Next` structure is as follows:

```
For counter = start To end
(statements to be executed during each pass of the loop)
Next counter
```

Keeping it simple for starters, the following example procedure uses the Immediate window to display a message for each repetition of the loop (in the Visual Basic Editor, open the Immediate window by pressing Ctrl+G):

```
Sub CountToTen ()
Dim j As Integer
  For j = 1 To 10
  Debug.Print "This is pass " & j
  Next j
End Sub
```

In the preceding example, the `start` and `end` values are both literal numbers. When the loop begins, `j` is set to 1 — in other words, the value of `start` is assigned to the `counter` variable. Each time a loop cycle completes, the statement `Next j` increments `j` (raises its value by 1), and control shifts back to the beginning of the loop. When `j` finally equals 10, the loop terminates.

Important tips about For...Next loops

Keep your code easy to understand. Use 1 as the start value for a `For...Next` loop unless you have good reasons to choose another number.

Such good reasons do exist. One is when the value of the counter is used in the loop itself (not changed in the loop, mind you). If the loop takes some action based on consecutively numbered items, such as part numbers, you can use the actual values of the items as the `start` and `end` values. More commonly, you set `start` to 0 when you're working with arrays, as I show in the next section.

In the `Next counter` statement that ends a `For...Next` loop, the counter variable's name isn't actually required — the keyword `Next` by itself automatically calculates the next `counter` value and sends VBA back to the top of the structure. However, you should definitely train yourself to include counter in the `Next` statement. That way, when you nest two or more `For...Next` loops, you can see at a glance to which loop a given `Next` statement belongs.

Do not change the value of the counter variable within a For...Next loop. Because counter is just another variable, it's possible — and sometimes tempting — to write code that changes the counter value. Resist the urge. Fool with the counter, and the loop is likely to skip important steps or to go on infinitely.

Although you can specify the end value for a For...Next loop with a variable, changing the variable value after the loop starts doesn't affect execution of the loop. The loop still executes the number of times dictated by the original end value.

For...Next loops and arrays

For...Next loops are perhaps most useful for working with *arrays*, which are named storage bins for sets of data items. I cover arrays in detail in Chapter 13; still, my discussion of For...Next loops would be incomplete without mentioning the use of these loops with these important data baskets.

You can use a For...Next loop to fill an array with a set of calculated values, as in the following example:

```
Dim intArrayOfSquares (14) As Integer
For a = 0 to 14
  intArrayOfSquares (a) = a * a
Next a
```

The example code begins by declaring an array of 15 integer values (15, not 14, because VBA normally numbers the first item in an array 0). The code then uses a For...Next loop to assign a value to each item in the array, counting from 0 to 14. Notice that the variable a is used not only as the loop counter, but also as the array *index,* pointing to a numbered slot in the array.

Nested For...Next loops

Like other VBA control structures, For...Next loops can be nested within one another — or within other control structures — as deeply as you need to nest them. The following perfectly useless bit of code illustrates the concept:

```
Dim sngR ' R probably stands for random number
Randomize ' initialize the random number generator
For A = 1 To 5
  sngR = Rnd ()
  For B = 1 To 5
  Debug.Print sngR * Rnd ( )
  Next B
Next A
```

If you're observant, you can trace the steps that VBA follows to execute this code. Here they are:

1. **Preliminaries first.**

   The code starts by declaring a variable and initializing VBA's random-number generator.

2. **The outer** For...Next **loop starts.**

   The program calls the Rnd function to assign a random number to the sngR variable.

3. **Then comes the inner** For...Next **loop.**

   This loop calculates five other numbers by repeatedly multiplying sngR by a new random value during each pass. The results appear in the Immediate window.

4. **The inner loop terminates after it completes all five calculations.**

   Now the outer loop takes over again. Obeying the Next A statement, VBA jumps back to the top of the outer loop.

5. **Steps 2 and 3 are repeated for four more passes of the outer loop.**

This example may be a trivial one, but it could be extended to perform Genuinely Useful Work. Suppose that you want to write a jukebox program that selects five playlists at random, playing five random selections from each one. Assuming that you know how to write the code that selects playlists and plays MP3 files, the preceding example should get you started.

Nested For...Next loops are also the key to working systematically with multidimensional arrays, which I discuss in Chapter 13. Each loop corresponds to one dimension of the array.

Get out now with an Exit For

The Exit For statement provides a quick way to terminate a For...Next loop before the end of the loop has actually been reached. This statement is typically used within a conditional statement (If...Then or Select Case) nested within the main For...Next loop.

One use of the Exit For escape hatch is to test an array for invalid data, halting whatever process is underway if an aberrant value is detected.

Suppose that you learn that a malevolent genius inserted an array containing false information into your pricelist data. You happen to know that this evil-doer left his trademark behind. As you update the price information to reflect inflationary price hikes in each array, you want to be sure that the price data hasn't been tampered with. This code does both jobs at once:

```
For p = 1 To varArraySize
 If varPriceArray(p) = "Kilroy was here!" Then
 MsgBox "Infested data in this array!"
 Exit For
 End If
 VarPriceArray(p) = varPriceArray(p) * sngCOLA
Next p
```

Interrupting the Flow with GoTo

If your program is behaving in an unruly fashion, tell it where to go — by transferring execution to another location in the procedure. A GoTo statement, combined with a special label statement at the destination, allows you to hop at will from place to place within a procedure. A label is a statement that simply marks a location in your code. To enter a label, type its name (VBA naming rules apply) followed by a colon.

A GoTo example

In this example, a GoTo statement redirects program flow out of the main part of the function to the SpecialValue label when an unusual value is encountered:

```
Function GoToExample (ItemNumber As Integer)
Dim intR As Integer
Select Case ItemNumber
  Case 2412
    GoTo SpecialValue
  Case Is < CutOffValue
    DoSomething
  Case >= CutOffValue
    DoHardlyAnything
End Select
(statements that execute no matter what)
GoToExample = intR
Exit Function
SpecialValue:
  DoSomethingSpecial
  GoToExample = -intR
End Function
```

Notice the format of the SpecialValue label, which sits on a line by itself, followed by a colon. The colon is crucial — VBA gets indigestion and displays an error message if you leave it out.

GoTo caveats

Use of the GoTo statement is considered to be inferior programming form. The problem is that it creates *spaghetti code,* with the path of execution wandering all over the place. Spaghetti is hard to unravei, and code containing more than an occasional GoTo quickly becomes impossible to read. Whenever possible, use control structures to direct program execution.

Occasionally, however, a GoTo statement is the most practical way to get your program to do what you want it to. Your brain may be just too tired to come up with the intricate set of nested loops and conditionals required to implement a complex set of criteria. At such times, GoTo may cut through the maze. Just don't use it too often.

Chapter 9

Unbreakable Code: Debugging and Error Trapping

*W*riting VBA code is the easy part. Getting that code to run — and then to produce the expected results — is what takes real work. Hunting down and stamping out bugs is a crucial part of the coding process, and I tell you how it's done in VBA in this chapter. I also discuss error trapping, which enables a program to respond gracefully if something goes wrong while it's running.

What Can Go Wrong Does Go Wrong

Three main kinds of problems can beset the programs that you write in VBA or most any language. They are as follows:

✔ **Compile errors:** Syntax and other errors that prevent the program from running in the first place.

✔ **Logic errors:** Flaws in the program's design that cause it to do something you *don't* want it to do or not to do something you *do* want it to do. The program runs, but it doesn't run correctly.

✔ **Run-time errors:** These bring the program to a halt while it is running. Run-time errors can result from logic errors or can occur if the program encounters unexpected conditions. (See "Where run-time errors come from," later in this chapter.)

Of the three types, syntax errors are definitely the easiest to uncover and correct. I mention these errors only briefly, spending most of my time in this chapter on detecting and eliminating the other two types, which are the true bugs.

Fixing Syntax Errors

If you make the first type of mistake — a syntax error — the Visual Basic Editor helps you figure out what you did wrong before you try to run the program. As soon as you type something that the Editor can't figure out, it displays the line in red. Then, if the Auto Syntax Check feature is on (which it is by default), you get a message clarifying the problem as soon as you move the insertion point off the line. For example, if you type **If x = 3**, for example, but forget to type **Then**, the message is `Compile error: Expected: Then or GoTo`. (To turn Auto Syntax Check on or off, choose Tools⇨Options, switch to the Editor tab of the Options dialog box, and check or clear the appropriate box.)

VBA doesn't catch some syntax errors until you try to run the program. In particular, VBA doesn't initially protest if you try to `GoTo` a nonexistent label or call a nonexistent procedure; you get a compiler error message only after you give the Run command.

When you know you made the mistake, correcting syntax errors is relatively easy. If you have any doubt about the correct way to call or declare a procedure or function, name or declare a variable, create a new instance of an object, or use a control structure, consult the relevant chapters of this book or look up the item in the VBA Help system.

Entomology for VBA Programmers

After you get past all the compile errors and your program starts running, feeling an immediate wave of pride and relief is natural. But if the program reports that `2 + 2 = 22` or if all the text in your document turns chartreuse, you know that you have a mistake somewhere in your code.

These types of errors are examples of errors in program logic. The program is running and, in fact, is doing exactly what you told it to do; the problem is that what you *told* it to do with the code you wrote isn't what you actually *wanted* it to do. Your job is to track down exactly which statements led to the wrong outcome. This process is called *debugging* your program. In this section, I've cataloged all the tools and techniques that you can use in your debugging campaigns.

Of course, the same debugging techniques that you use to stamp out logic errors are vital in preventing the many run-time errors that result from logic errors. But because no program can anticipate every possible circumstance that it may face, you should still incorporate code for handling run-time errors in any program destined for other people to use.

Test, test, test

It's handy when errors announce themselves by displaying obviously wrong answers, turning things on-screen weird colors, or causing error messages to pop up. Unfortunately, many logic errors are more subtle, and many run-time errors occur only intermittently. Instead of assuming that your program is going to work properly after it's freshly hatched, budget plenty of time for testing it under different conditions.

Here are some testing suggestions:

- ✔ If the program is supposed to work with different documents, test it by running it with different documents. Try running the program while two or three documents are open in your VBA application — and while no document at all is open.

- ✔ See what happens if you run the program while the document window is in different states (minimized, maximized, or restored).

- ✔ Start the program while different items or groups of items are selected in the document window.

- ✔ If the program requires input from the user via an input box or custom form, make all kinds of typical and outlandish test entries to see what happens. If the required value is supposed to be an integer, try floating-point, date, and string entries to see how the program responds.

- ✔ If the program works with date or time values, see what it does with different dates (including February 29) and different times of day (including midnight). Feed various date or time values to the variables but also try running the program on different dates or at different times. You don't need to stay up late or wait for a leap year; just set the system clock to the test time or date temporarily.

As you test-run the program, look closely for evidence that something has gone wrong. Examine your document to ensure that it reflects all the changes that you wanted the program to make — and no others. Scrutinize for accuracy and correct format of any results that the program displays in dialog boxes or pastes into your document. Ideally, you should also check your variables while the program runs to make sure that no aberrant values occur. (I show you how to check your variables in the following section.) Obviously, if VBA reports a run-time error, you have a problem.

If you do find any mistakes, you need to start debugging in earnest. But if not, don't assume that mistakes aren't there. Remember — bugs are the most widespread and numerous animals on earth.

Keyboard shortcuts for debugging

Table 9-1 lists the keyboard commands at your disposal while you're debugging your programs. I cover most of these commands separately and in some detail throughout this chapter.

Table 9-1	Debugging
To Do This	*Press This*
Execute code one line at a time (step)	F8
Execute statements one line at a time without stepping into procedure calls	Shift+F8
Run, stopping at the line containing the insertion point	Ctrl+F8
Toggle a breakpoint in the code line with the insertion point	F9
Clear all breakpoints	Ctrl+Shift+F9
Specify (set) the next statement to be executed	Ctrl+F9
Add a watch for the item at the insertion point	Shift+F9
Run the error-handler code or return the error to the calling procedure	Alt+F5
Step into the error handler or return the error to the calling procedure	Alt+F8

Take a break

The key to debugging a program is using VBA's break mode. In *break mode*, your program has begun running but is suspended at a particular statement in the code. Because the program is still live, you can inspect the current values of all the variables. Beginning from that point, you can use the Step commands to run the program one statement at a time, watching the variables change to see whether you're getting the expected results at each step in the process. Later sections of this chapter provide details on working with variables and the Step commands.

Figure 9-1 shows a VBA procedure in break mode. With the exception of a yellow highlight and arrow marking the next statement to be executed, the Visual Basic Editor looks almost exactly as it does while you're writing or editing code.

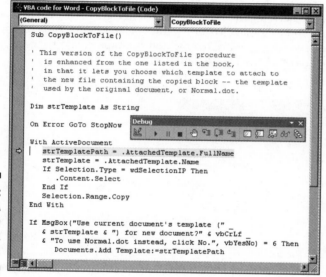

```
VBA code for Word - CopyBlockToFile (Code)

(General)                                    CopyBlockToFile

Sub CopyBlockToFile()

' This version of the CopyBlockToFile procedure
'   is enhanced from the one listed in the book,
'   in that it lets you choose which template to attach to
'   the new file containing the copied block -- the template
'   used by the original document, or Normal.dot.

Dim strTemplate As String

On Error GoTo StopNow       Debug

With ActiveDocument
⇒   │   strTemplatePath = .AttachedTemplate.FullName
        strTemplate = .AttachedTemplate.Name
        If Selection.Type = wdSelectionIP Then
            .Content.Select
        End If
        Selection.Range.Copy
End With

If MsgBox("Use current document's template (" _
    & strTemplate & ") for new document?" & vbCrLf _
    & "To use Normal.dot instead, click No.", vbYesNo) = 6 Then
        Documents.Add Template:=strTemplatePath
```

Figure 9-1: A VBA procedure in break mode.

In break mode, in fact, you can actually edit the code while your program is running, making changes or adding brand-new lines as whim or necessity dictates. This feature isn't at all a frill but a key debugging feature that you should train yourself to take advantage of — more on this topic in the section "Adding and editing code in break mode" later in this chapter.

Entering break mode

You can use a variety of techniques to put a program into the break-mode state of suspended animation. Here's the full list:

✔ Start the program in break mode from the outset by using the Step Into command. (See "Steppin' through code," later in this chapter.)

✔ Set a *breakpoint* on a line of code. After a running program reaches the statement at the breakpoint, it suspends execution and enters break mode.

✔ Place a Stop statement in your code. As the program runs, it enters break mode, ready to execute the statement following the Stop statement.

✔ Click the Break button, choose Run⇨Break, or press Ctrl+Break while the program is running. Use this technique to get back control of a runaway program that doesn't stop on its own. Where you end up when the program enters break mode is anyone's guess, but at least you can see what's going on after you get there.

✔ Create a Break When True or Break When Changed *watch*. The program enters break mode if the value of the watch expression becomes True or undergoes any change.

A program can also enter break mode if a run-time error occurs. VBA displays a dialog box describing the error, as shown in Figure 9-2. Clicking the End button stops the program altogether, but clicking Debug puts it into break mode. You have some control over which run-time errors trigger break mode in the General tab of the Tools⇨Options dialog box.

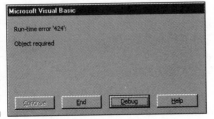

Figure 9-2:
A dialog box showing a run-time error.

Setting breakpoints

If you suspect that a section of code contains a logical error, place a breakpoint just before the miscreant statements. Figure 9-3 shows how the Visual Basic Editor represents a breakpoint on-screen — it's that big dot in the margin of the Code window.

With a breakpoint in place, you can run the program at full speed up to that point, bypassing code that (you hope) works correctly. When VBA gets to the statement that contains the breakpoint, it suspends the program. Once break mode is active, you can examine the variables and then use the Step commands to see how they change as VBA executes each dubious statement one at a time.

To set a breakpoint, all you need to do is click the margin of the Code window next to the target line of code. Alternatively, you can put the insertion point on the correct line and press F9.

You can set breakpoints on as many executable statements as you like. However, you can't set breakpoints on comments, or on statements that VBA doesn't actually execute, such as variable declarations.

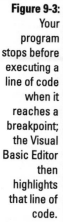

Figure 9-3:
Your
program
stops before
executing a
line of code
when it
reaches a
breakpoint;
the Visual
Basic Editor
then
highlights
that line of
code.

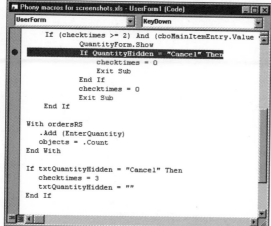

Keep in mind that VBA stops the program and switches into break mode after executing the statement just before the breakpoint. In other words, the statement at the breakpoint hasn't been executed yet and is the next to go after the program continues.

Clearing breakpoints

After you correct the errant code or give up on fixing it for now, you *clear* the breakpoint to remove it. Clearing a breakpoint enables VBA to execute that statement normally the next time that you run the program. The same techniques that you use to set a breakpoint — clicking the Code window's margin or pressing F9 — clear an existing one.

To deep-six all breakpoints, choose Debug⇨Clear All Breakpoints or press Ctrl+Shift+F9. Once you do that, the breakpoints are history; Undo can't restore them.

Knowing where you are in break mode

If a program is running in break mode, the Visual Basic Editor always highlights the statement that is to be executed next. To make sure that you get the message, an arrow in the Code window's margin points to the selfsame next statement. Figure 9-4 shows you what you see (although the black-and-white image leaves much to the imagination).

After you have the next statement on-screen, you can't mistake that highlight. But what happens if you start scrolling to other parts of your code or jump to the Code windows of other modules? You may have trouble finding the next statement again.

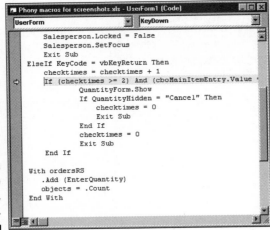

Figure 9-4:
You can't
miss the
statement
that's next in
line for
execution
(as long as
it's visible
on-screen,
anyway).

That's where the suitably named Show Next Statement command comes in. When you choose Debug➪Show Next Statement, the Visual Basic Editor whisks you straight to the statement in question. Another command lets you select a different statement as the next statement, but I cover that topic in the section "Choosing a different next statement," later in this chapter.

Using a breakpoint alternative: The Stop statement

Breakpoints are super-easy to use, but they have one drawback: They're temporary. If you're debugging a complex program, you may not be able to set things right in a single session. Because breakpoints aren't stored with your code, they're gone the next time you open the project in the Visual Basic Editor.

The Stop statement is the solution to this problem. Add this statement to your code wherever you want the program to switch to break mode. Like all code that you type, Stop statements are saved whenever you save the project.

Monsieur or Madame, do you crave an example? Allow me to oblige:

```
. . .
intDataFromMars = GetDataFromMars(1.5454)
Stop
MsgBox "The result is " & intDataFromMars / Z
. . .
```

After inspecting the example code, you can guess that the Stop statement is probing suspect results displayed in the message box. When the Stop statement executes, it forces the program into break mode just after the intDataFromMars function procedure sets the value of a variable. You can now look at the values of both variables involved in the next calculation to see which of them seems to be out of line.

Getting out of break mode

After you're through with break mode, at least for the time being, you can tell VBA to resume normal program execution. Any of the commands that you can use to run a program in the first place work. In break mode, the Run menu item and toolbar button look the same and are in the same places, but their names are changed; both are now called Continue. F5 is still the keyboard shortcut. A Continued program pops back into break mode if it runs into another breakpoint or if any other of the conditions that activate break mode occur.

To stop running the program altogether, use the Reset command. You can find a Reset button and a Reset item on the Run menu. Pressing Alt+F4 stops any running Windows program, including VBA programs. However, you must make sure that you press Alt+F4 only while your VBA program is running, or you'll shut down the Visual Basic Editor, your VBA application, or whatever Windows program is currently active.

Steppin' through code

Like all good debuggers, the Visual Basic Editor allows you to run your program one statement, or step, at a time. Slowing things down in this way is a fantastic trick for catching the very point at which some logic error knocks a critical value out of whack.

To make the best use of this *step-execution* technique, you need a way to see the values of your variables as your program modifies them. The Editor's way-cool Auto Data Tips feature is always available for this purpose, but the Locals and Watch windows give you more details and enable you to change the values if the need arises. I cover all these features a bit later in this chapter.

So now about the three Step commands that you can use in the Visual Basic Editor: Step Into, Step Over, and Step Out. You can access all three commands via the Debug menu, as buttons on the Debug toolbar, or by way of these keyboard shortcuts:

Step Command	Keyboard Shortcut
Step Into	F8
Step Over	Shift+F8
Step Out	Ctrl+Shift+F8

I Stepped Into it this time

The Step Into command is the one to use if you want to execute each and every statement in your program in correct sequence. Each time you invoke this command, VBA runs the next statement in your program and then returns to break mode, where you can see what changes have been wrought. Pressing F8 is the most efficient way to invoke the Step Into command.

This command gets its name because it steps into other procedures that your program calls as it runs. If the next statement calls a Sub or Function procedure, invoking the Step Into command opens the called procedure in the Code window, where you can step through it to see what it's doing.

The Step Into command is available even if you're not already in break mode. If you want to step through the program beginning at the beginning, just give the Step Into command to run the first statement and enter break mode. Used in this way, Step Into runs the procedure containing the insertion point, always starting from the procedure's first line.

Stepping over and out

The Step Over command (Shift+F8 is the keyboard shortcut) works just like Step Into, with the following two exceptions:

- ✔ Most importantly, Step Over doesn't step through the individual statements in a called procedure.
- ✔ You can't start running a program in break mode with Step Over.

If the next statement calls another procedure, Step Over runs the whole procedure in one gulp, going on to the following statement in the current procedure. That's great if you just want to see whether the called procedure as a whole does anything goofy before you bother to check it out in detail. Stepping over a called procedure is also a big time-saver if you're already fairly sure that the procedure works as it's supposed to.

The Step Out command (Ctrl+Shift+F8 is the keyboard shortcut) is a handy complement to Step Into. After you get inside the bowels of a called procedure, you may decide that everything is okay, or you may locate the error and fix it. More embarrassingly, you may just have clicked the Step Into button when you meant to click Step Over (a mistake I make regularly).

In any event, there's no point in hanging around to step through the procedure's remaining statements. Use the Step Out command to run the rest of the procedure at top speed. VBA returns you to the procedure from whence you came, highlighting the statement following the procedure call.

Major manipulations during debugging

In break mode, just because you're running your program doesn't mean that the program's course is fixed in stone. VBA is sophisticated enough to allow midcourse corrections. Specifically, you can edit the existing code and alter the sequence in which statements get executed.

Adding and editing code in break mode

The Code window's editing features are fully operational during break mode. You can type new statements, modify existing ones, or delete them altogether. But what's really special is that most of your changes work immediately, becoming part of the running program. For example, you can declare new variables and use them right away in calculations, perhaps in combination with existing variables. Some edits, such as changing a variable to a different type in its declaration, do bring the program to a halt.

Choosing a different next statement

Suppose that you're stepping through your code in break mode when you realize that the next statement contains a big mistake. Rather than execute the statement and send your program into a tailspin, you can choose to bypass it altogether until you've had a chance to make it right.

Other ways to skip code

You have other options for skipping code that you know is broken. These methods work whether you're step-executing a program in break mode or editing the code before you run it. One approach is to type an apostrophe at the beginning of each line that you want to skip, thereby turning it into a comment. The only real drawback is that commenting — and later "uncommenting" — the code takes time. However, you can comment an entire block of code in a single step by selecting it and clicking the Comment Block button on the Edit toolbar (see Chapter 6).

Sometimes an even better way to skip over code is by using line labels in conjunction with temporary GoTo statements. When the following code runs, VBA completely skips the statements between GoTo AfterTheSkip and the statement following AfterTheSkip: label. When you're ready to run the skipped code again, just remove the GoTo statement or turn it into a comment (type an apostrophe at the start of the line).

```
. . .
GoTo AfterTheSkip
    A = B + C
    D = A + E / F
    G = B + D
AfterTheSkip:
    MsgBox "Today is " &
    Format(Now, "dddd")
. . .
```

The Visual Basic Editor enables you to select a different statement almost anywhere in your code as the next statement, using either the keyboard or the mouse. You can jump forward or backward in the code. In addition to letting you skip over foul code, this also allows you to repeat statements until you're sure you understand how they work.

Just realize that variables retain the values that they have before you make the change. These values may well be very different from what they are when the program reaches the code in the normal sequence. If necessary, you can give the variables any value that you like by using the Immediate, Watch, or Locals windows, which I describe later in this chapter.

If you can keep all that in mind, here's how to select a different next statement:

- ✔ Using the keyboard, move the insertion point to the line containing the statement, and then press Ctrl+F9 or choose Debug⇨Set Next Statement.

- ✔ Using the mouse, drag the yellow arrow pointer in the Code window's margin to the new next statement (see Figure 9-5).

Figure 9-5: Selecting a different next statement enables you to repeat a block of code when you want to study its functioning.

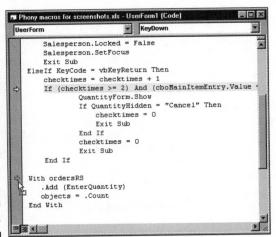

```
Phony macros for screenshots.xls - UserForm1 (Code)

UserForm                            KeyDown

        Salesperson.Locked = False
        Salesperson.SetFocus
        Exit Sub
    ElseIf KeyCode = vbKeyReturn Then
        checktimes = checktimes + 1
        If (checktimes >= 2) And (cboMainItemEntry.Value
            QuantityForm.Show
            If QuantityHidden = "Cancel" Then
                checktimes = 0
                Exit Sub
            End If
            checktimes = 0
            Exit Sub
        End If

    With ordersRS
        .Add (EnterQuantity)
        objects = .Count
    End With
```

Seeing Data Tips

The VBA Auto Data Tips feature enables you to see the current value of any variable wherever it appears in your code. While you're in break mode, hovering the mouse pointer over any variable pops up the Data Tips window — a little box containing the name and current value of that variable. Figure 9-6 shows Auto Data Tips in action.

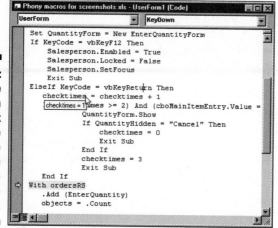

Figure 9-6:
The little
Auto Data
Tips box
shows the
value of the
variable
beneath the
mouse
pointer.

```
Phony macros for screenshots.xls - UserForm1 (Code)
UserForm                           KeyDown

    Set QuantityForm = New EnterQuantityForm
    If KeyCode = vbKeyF12 Then
        Salesperson.Enabled = True
        Salesperson.Locked = False
        Salesperson.SetFocus
        Exit Sub
    ElseIf KeyCode = vbKeyReturn Then
        checktimes = checktimes + 1
        checktimes = 1 imes >= 2) And (cboMainItemEntry.Value =
                QuantityForm.Show
                If QuantityHidden = "Cancel" Then
                    checktimes = 0
                    Exit Sub
                End If
                checktimes = 3
                Exit Sub
        End If
    With ordersRS
        .Add (EnterQuantity)
        objects = .Count
```

In case you don't see the Auto Data Tips box when you should, check to make sure that its box is checked in the Editor tab of the Options dialog box.

You can use a different Editor feature to display the type and scope of a variable, although not so automatically. Place the insertion point in or beside the variable name and then press Ctrl+I to bring up a Quick Info box containing that information. You don't need to be in break mode to use this feature, which is especially helpful if you're working in the middle of a long program whose variables were declared at the top. Figure 9-7 shows the sort of information that you get.

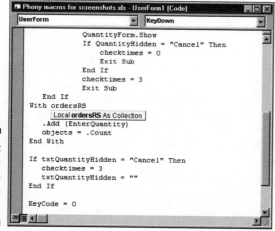

Figure 9-7:
Displaying a
Quick Info
box for a
variable.

```
Phony macros for screenshots.xls - UserForm1 (Code)
UserForm                           KeyDown

                QuantityForm.Show
                If QuantityHidden = "Cancel" Then
                    checktimes = 0
                    Exit Sub
                End If
                checktimes = 3
                Exit Sub
        End If
    With ordersRS
          Local ordersRS As Collection
        .Add (EnterQuantity)
        objects = .Count
    End With

    If txtQuantityHidden = "Cancel" Then
        checktimes = 3
        txtQuantityHidden = ""
    End If

    KeyCode = 0
```

Immediate Gratification

Press Ctrl+G or choose View➪Immediate Window to display the Immediate window, as shown in Figure 9-8. The Immediate window enables you to do the following two things:

✔ See the values of calculations and variables by using the `Debug.Print` method.

✔ Execute individual code statements directly without running them inside a procedure. To execute a statement in the Immediate window, just type the statement and then press Enter.

So what good are these talents, you ask? Allow me to list the benefits:

✔ You can use the Immediate window as a crude calculator. Type an expression such as the following:

```
Print (27 * 398) + 1414
```

Then press Enter and you get the result . . . well, immediately (see Figure 9-8). If you work in the Immediate window, you don't need to specify the `Debug` object.

Figure 9-8:
The
Immediate
window in
action.

✔ You can route intermediate values of variables and expressions at various points in a running program to the Immediate window by placing the `Debug.Print` method in the program's code (not in the Immediate window itself). After the program terminates, you can quickly check to see whether it produced the correct results without displaying a message box for each value. Figure 9-9 shows an example of this technique.

✔ During break mode, you can display the value of any variable or object property by typing a `Print` statement in the Immediate window such as `Print intTotal`. Similarly, you can change the variable or property value by typing a standard assignment such as this:

```
intSomeNumber = 25
```

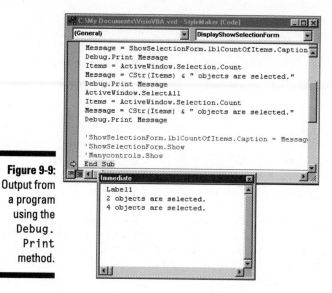

```
C:\My Documents\VisioVBA.vsd - StyleMaker (Code)
(General)                            DisplayShowSelectionForm
    Message = ShowSelectionForm.lblCountOfItems.Caption
    Debug.Print Message
    Items = ActiveWindow.Selection.Count
    Message = CStr(Items) & " objects are selected."
    Debug.Print Message
    ActiveWindow.SelectAll
    Items = ActiveWindow.Selection.Count
    Message = CStr(Items) & " objects are selected."
    Debug.Print Message

    'ShowSelectionForm.lblCountOfItems.Caption = Message
    'ShowSelectionForm.Show
    'Manycontrols.Show
⇨  End Sub

Immediate
    Label1
    2 objects are selected.
    4 objects are selected.
```

Figure 9-9:
Output from
a program
using the
Debug.
Print
method.

You can use the Immediate window in break mode to call Sub and Function procedures just as you normally do — by typing the procedure name and any required arguments. Notice that, during break mode, statements that you execute in the Immediate window can access only those variables, objects, and procedures that are within the scope of the procedure that's currently executing in the program. In other words, executing a statement in the Immediate window produces the same effect as typing it in the running procedure and executing it there.

From the Interesting Facts Department: You can drag selected text from the Code window to the Immediate window, which means that you don't need to retype long expressions or variable names if you want to use them there (warning: you must hold down Ctrl as you drag to *copy* the code to the Immediate window; if you drag without Ctrl, the code is *moved*). The F1 key works in the Immediate window as it does in the Code window, displaying Help on whatever keyword the insertion point lies within. Auto Data Tips do not function there, however.

Keeping an Eye on the Locals (Window)

If you have room to display it, the Locals window should be on-screen at all times when you're debugging a program in break mode. Bring the Locals window into view by clicking its button on the Debug toolbar or by choosing View⇨Locals Window.

As shown in Figure 9-10, the Locals window automatically displays all the variables that are accessible in the current procedure, showing their names, values, and data types. The Visual Basic Editor updates the information each time that you execute a statement, so what you see in the Locals window always reflects the current values.

Local mechanics

As are most Visual Basic Editor windows, the Locals window is dockable by default but you can also display it as a free-floating separate window. Chapter 5 covers the basics of working with Editor windows.

If you can't see all the information in a column, remember that you can re-size the columns. Position the mouse pointer over a column separator in the gray column header just above the main part of the window. After the pointer becomes a double-headed arrow, drag to the left or right to change the widths of the adjacent columns.

Refer to Figure 9-10 to see that some rows list individual variables, while others show items such as arrays, variables of user-defined type, and objects. Such items have no values of their own; instead, they hold variables and other "container" items. After you begin running a procedure, the Locals window lists them in collapsed form; you can't see the subsidiary items that they contain. To expand a collapsed item, click the boxed plus sign to its left. See Figure 9-11 for examples of expanded items.

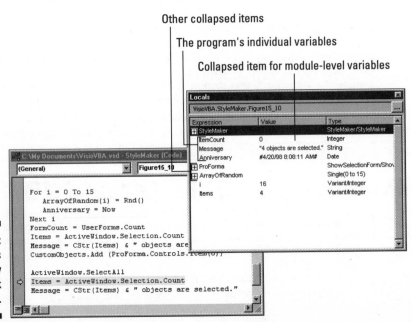

Other collapsed items

The program's individual variables

Collapsed item for module-level variables

Figure 9-10:
The Locals window during break mode.

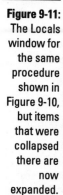

Figure 9-11:
The Locals
window for
the same
procedure
shown in
Figure 9-10,
but items
that were
collapsed
there are
now
expanded.

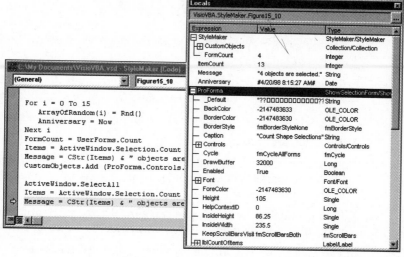

Only variables declared (implicitly or explicitly) in the currently running procedure appear already expanded at the top level of the Locals window's hierarchy. To see module-level variables that are accessible to all procedures in the current module, expand the first item in the Locals window. This item always pertains to the module in which the current procedure is running. You can't work with global variables or with those in other projects in the Locals windows.

Why edit variable values?

Before I tell you how to change a variable's value, you probably should know why you might want to. Here are some good reasons:

✔ A previous line of code contains an error that assigned an incorrect value to the variable. You've caught the mistake, but you want to continue stepping through the program. Before you go on, change the variable's value to what it should have been so that the mistake doesn't affect subsequent statements.

✔ You want to test various alternative values for the variable without changing your code. You can use the Set Next Statement command to repeatedly pass through the same stretch of code, entering different values in the Locals window each time.

✔ The values that the program uses as it runs in real life aren't currently available to it. The program may read information from a database or the Internet, for example. In this case, you can supply simulated values via the Locals window.

How to edit variable values

Okay. To change the value of a variable in the Locals window, follow these steps:

1. **Click twice (but don't double-click) directly over the variable's current value in the window so that only the value is highlighted.**

   Clicking elsewhere in the same row simply selects the entire line.

2. **Type the new value.**

   If you're typing a string value, you must include beginning and ending quotation marks. Similarly, enclose date literals with pound-sign (#) characters.

3. **If you change your mind, you can cancel your entry and restore the preceding one by pressing Esc; otherwise, press Enter to confirm it.**

   The Editor won't accept an invalid value, and you may get an error message telling you what was wrong with your entry.

You can edit any variable's values, including those of individual members of arrays. Just realize that you must expand the array before you can get to its member data elements. With an object variable, you can't change the object that's assigned to it, but you can edit the object's properties (except the read-only ones). Again, you must expand the object to see the editable items. Figure 9-11 shows expanded array and object variables.

The Watch Window: Key Debugging Tool

After you've mastered the Locals window, working with the Watch window is a piece of pie. This window works in essentially the same way, the obvious difference being that *you* get to pick out which values it displays. Figure 9-12 shows the Watch window in action.

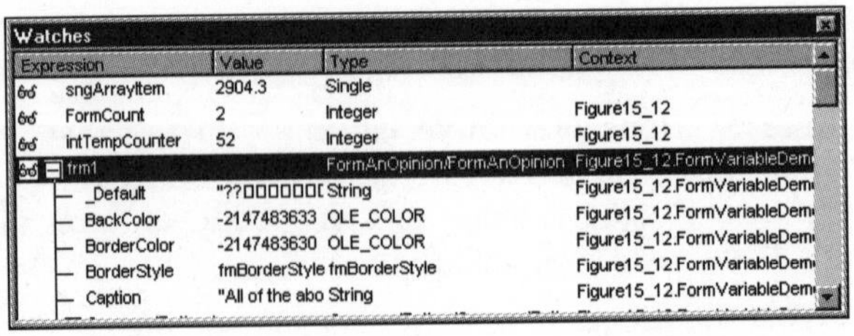

Figure 9-12:
The Visual
Basic Editor
Watch
window.

Use the Watch window when you're debugging large programs in which many different procedures manipulate global variables. By adding these global variables to the Watch window, you can track their current values, no matter what part of the program you're currently stepping through.

The Watch window appears automatically as soon as you define a *watch expression.* (See the sidebar "What else is different compared with the Locals window" for a discussion of watch expressions.) If you want more room on-screen, however, you can put the window away by clicking the close button in the top-right corner.

Adding watch expressions

If you like having options, you'll love the Watch window. Prepare to be overwhelmed by how many ways you can add watch expressions.

No matter which technique you eventually use, you should start in the Code window by selecting the variable or expression that you want to watch. When I say "selecting," I mean selecting the entire item as you would in a word processor, by highlighting it with the mouse or arrow keys.

However, if you want to watch only an independent variable (in other words, an item that's not an object property or an element in an array), you don't actually need to select the whole thing. Putting the insertion point in the variable name will do.

Now for that "overwhelming" list of techniques. You can add a watch based on the selected expression by:

- Dragging the selection to the Watch window. This method creates the watch without any intermediate steps — it's fast, but you give up some control.

- Right-clicking the selection and choosing Add Watch from the shortcut menu to display the Add Watch dialog box, which gives you control over how the watch behaves (see the section "Working with the Add Watch window" later in this chapter).

- Choosing Debug⇨Add Watch, which also displays the Add Watch dialog box.

- Clicking the Quick Watch button in the Debug toolbar, or choosing Debug⇨Quick Watch. The Editor shows you a confirmatory message describing the watch expression that you're about to add, but you can't change anything.

What else is different compared with the Locals window

Besides the fact that what appears in the window is up to you, the Watch window differs from the Locals window in two other important ways:

- Each line in the Watch window lets you track the value of any valid VBA expression, not just an individual variable. Expressions such as (X - Y) > 15, "The color is " & strColor, or even 2 + 2 are perfectly acceptable. That's why entries are called watch *expressions.*
- Because the Watch window can track variables from any module or procedure in the project, it adds a fourth column labeled Context. This column displays the scope in which the window shows a valid value for each variable or expression. If you're executing a procedure outside the defined context, all you see is <Out of context>.

If you're a diehard do-it-yourselfer, you don't actually need to select anything in the Code window. You can just click the Add Watch button and then type the expression of interest from scratch in the Add Watch dialog box.

Working with the Add Watch window

Figure 9-13 shows the Add Watch window, which appears after you choose Debug⇨Add Watch or choose Add Watch from the Code window's shortcut menu. In this window, you define the details of your watch expression.

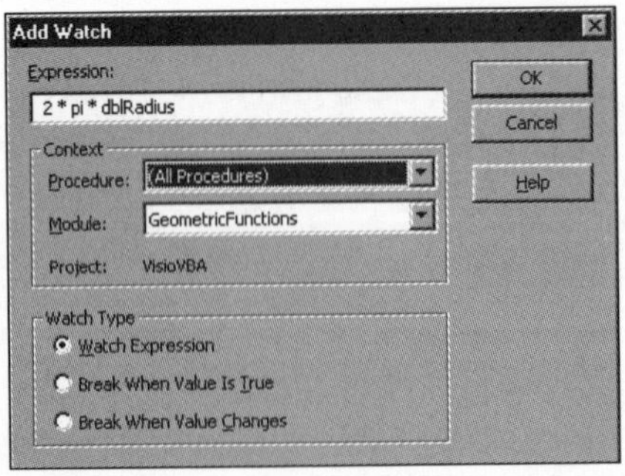

Figure 9-13: The Add Watch dialog box.

The Expression field is, of course, where you specify the expression that you want to watch. If you selected the correct variable or expression before you started, you shouldn't have to change anything, but you can if you want.

The Context section of the dialog box lets you define the procedures in which the Visual Basic Editor actually calculates and displays the value of the watch expression. The values of the Procedure and Module choices are initially set to the procedure in which the variable appeared when you added the watch. If you want to see the value while a different procedure is running, select it by name. If that procedure is in a different module, you must first select its module and then choose the procedure.

If you want the variable value to remain visible no matter which procedure in a given module is executing, choose (All Procedures), the first item on the Procedures list. And if you want to see the value *always* — throughout the entire program — choose (All Modules) from the Modules list. The broader the scope that you choose, the longer VBA takes to calculate and report the value. Still, being able to track a variable wherever you are in the program is often worth the short wait.

For a normal watch expression, leave the Watch Type set to Watch Expression. I explain the other choices a bit in "Using watch expressions to define breakpoints," around the next bend.

Editing watch expressions

The easiest way to modify an existing watch expression is to type changes in the Expression column of the Watch window. Click the line containing the expression to select it; then click the expression itself to highlight it. You can then edit the expression to taste.

As you can in the Locals window, you can change the value of a variable that appears in the Watch window while the program is running. However, you can't change the Context setting for a watch expression in the Watch window. Instead, you must open the Edit Watch dialog box, which is a spittin' image of the Add Watch box. Edit Watch is a choice in the Debug menu and on the shortcut (right-click) menu for the Watch window. After the dialog box opens, you can make changes to the expression's context or type or to the expression itself, just as when you originally defined the watch.

Using watch expressions to define breakpoints

The larger a program gets, the harder it is to keep track of which procedures and statements are changing which variables. Often, you suspect that a variable's final value is incorrect, but you're not sure where to look for the code that caused the problem. In this situation, a breakpoint based on a watch expression can be a lifesaver (or at least a code-saver).

Using the Watch Type option buttons in the Add Watch or Edit Watch dialog box, you can set up the following two types of these automatic breaks:

- ✔ You can have your program automatically enter break mode as soon as it executes any statement that changes an expression to a nonzero value. (In VBA, remember, 0 is False, and everything else is True.) Choose Break When Value Is True for this type of breakpoint.

- ✔ You can automatically enter break mode immediately after the program executes any statement that changes the value of an expression. Choose Break When Value Changes for this type of breakpoint.

Their special talents notwithstanding, these "breaking" watch expressions still function as ordinary watches in the Watch window. You can distinguish watches of different types, however, by the differences in the little icons to the far left of each item. You can sort of see them if you squint real hard at Figure 9-14, but they're easy to pick out on-screen.

After a watch-based breakpoint is triggered by a value change, VBA suspends program execution and enters break mode. In the Code window, the statement that caused the change is the one just before the highlighted "next statement" (the one that will next run). The watch expression that triggered the break is highlighted in the Watch window so that you know which one did it (refer to Figure 9-14).

Figure 9-14:
A "break when value changes" watch expression on variable intItHap pened has just dropped the program into break mode.

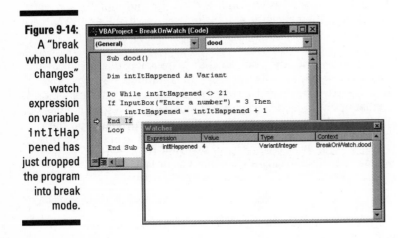

Trapping Wild Bugs with On Error and the Error Object

If something goes unexpectedly wrong while a program is running, the result is often catastrophic. VBA brings the program to a grinding halt, displaying a run-time-error dialog box to give you the bad news about what went wrong — tersely. Refer to Figure 9-2 for a look at this box. Your clickable choices are End (to terminate the program), Debug (to enter break mode), and Help (to display a Help topic about the specific error that you've run into).

None of these options are particularly appealing, especially if you're running the program for real instead of while you're testing it. It would be far less jarring if your program could detect the error and correct it — or at least sidestep it — before VBA muscles in with that ominous run-time-error message. Failing that, you might at least present the user with a more congenial message.

All this is possible but requires you to add your own error-handling code. This section tells you how.

Where run-time errors come from

Run-time errors can occur for the following two reasons:

- ✔ A serious error in your program's logic produces a situation that VBA can't deal with. To haul out the customary example for one more performance, suppose that you've written a statement in which a value gets divided by a variable. If your code assigns a value of zero to that variable, you're sunk; dividing by zero is strictly forbidden, and trying to do so gives your computer a seizure, so VBA stops the program.

- ✔ Some unforeseen circumstance sideswipes your program. A required connection to a database file, network server, or Internet site may be cut off, for example, so your program can't retrieve the values that it needs to do its work.

Either way, the outcome is deadly. Protect your program and your users by writing your own error-handling code.

How error-handling code works

To prevent VBA from dealing with run-time errors and to take care of them yourself, you must adorn each procedure with an *error handler* — a block of code whose sole purpose is to step in if an error occurs. If something goes wrong as the procedure runs, VBA transfers program execution to the error handler. The code in the error handler can figure out what type of error has occurred and take whatever steps you think that the situation warrants.

How to write error-handling code

To add error-handling code to a procedure, you must do three things:

- ✔ Add an `On Error` statement at the beginning of the procedure to tell VBA where the error-handler code is.

- ✔ Type an `Exit Sub` or `Exit Function` statement following the body of the procedure, just before the error-handler code.

- ✔ Write the code for the error handler itself, preceded by an identifying label.

All three steps are vital.

Writing On Error statements

The `On Error` statement enables the error handler by telling VBA where to find the error handler in the procedure code. The full statement has the syntax `On Error GoTo label`, where `label` is a label elsewhere in the procedure identifying the first line of the error handler's code.

Here's how the `On Error` statement looks in a procedure:

```
Sub ErrorHandlerDemo()
On Error GoTo ErrorHandler
 MamaVariable = DoThisFunction (X,Y,Z)
 PapaVariable = DoThatProcedure
 BabyVariable = MamaVariable + PapaVariable
' Stop the procedure here if no error has occurred:
 Exit Sub
ErrorHandler:
(error handling code goes here)
End Sub
```

You should know about two other forms of the On Error statement, which work as follows:

- On Error GoTo 0 disables error handling from this point forward in the procedure and clears the Err object. Use it at a point in your procedure after a previous On Error GoTo label when you want to turn off your own error-handling code in favor of VBA's default screech-to-a-halt system.

- On Error Resume Next causes VBA to ignore the line that caused the error and to continue execution with the following line of code. Obviously, ignoring an error doesn't make it go away. On Error Resume Next is primarily useful when your code uses objects from the host application or other components you didn't create — an advanced VBA skill that I introduce in Chapter 14.

Adding an Exit statement to the procedure

An error handler is part and parcel of the procedure in which it appears, which means that VBA executes the code in the error handler every time the procedure runs. Obviously, this situation isn't right. You want the error handler to run only if an error occurs and at no other time.

To prevent the error handler from running except when it's supposed to, all you need to do is add an Exit statement immediately before the error-handler code, as shown in the example in the section "Writing On Error statements," earlier in this chapter. If you're writing a Sub procedure, the Exit statement should be Exit Sub; for a Function procedure, it should be Exit Function.

Writing the error handler

To minimize coding hassles, always place the code for the error handler itself at the end of the procedure. The error handler requires the following components:

- A label showing where the error handler starts
- Code to determine the type of error that occurred
- Code to deal with the error
- Optionally, a statement to resume execution of the main part of the procedure

Adding a label

To identify the start of your error-handling code, enter a standard VBA label as the first line of the error handler. (Remember that a label is a single word followed by a colon.) The `On Error` statement for the procedure directs execution to this label if an error occurs. In this example, `ThisIsTheErrorHandler` is the required label, as shown in the following code:

```
...
ThisIsTheErrorHandler:
...
  (Error handling statements)
...
End Sub
```

This example shows the error-handling code in its proper place at the very end of a procedure — thus, the `End Sub` statement terminates the error handler.

Getting information about and dealing with the error

The body of your error handler has two main tasks: checking to see what type of error has occurred and doing something about it. Although these chores differ conceptually, they go on almost simultaneously in practice.

The standard method for learning what has gone wrong is using VBA's `Err` object. If you know that a particular variable has a tendency to go haywire, you may want to check that variable directly to see whether its value is out of bounds before you look at the `Err` object. Otherwise, the `Err` object is the ticket.

The `Err` object is always available in every VBA program. You can use it directly, without creating an instance of it first. VBA automatically stores information about the most recent error in the `Err` object. All that your code must do is retrieve the `Err` object's properties, which include `Number` and `Description`.

The `Number` property simply tells you the number of the current error. You can assign this property to a variable or use it directly in a conditional statement, as in the following example:

```
Sub YetAnotherFineMess()
On Error GoTo ImTryinToThinkButNothinHappens
...
(error prone statements)
...
Exit Sub
ImTryinToThinkButNothinHappens:
Select Case Err.Number
 Case 7 ' Out of memory error
 (code for handling error number 7)
 Case 11 ' Division by zero error
 (code for handling error number 11)
 ... (and so on)
 Case Else
 (code for handling all other errors)
End Select
End Sub
```

In the preceding example, the `Select Case` statement checks the `Number` property against a series of values for which you've written specific error-handling statements. Such statements may perform the following tasks:

- Inform the user that something is wrong and ask for instructions via an input box or custom form

- Try again to get valid data from a source that was unavailable earlier or try an alternative source

- Change an errant value to a valid one, recording in a file or via a message box that data had to be changed by brute force to make the thing go

Effective use of the `Number` property requires that you know what each error number means. I don't have space to catalog the possibilities. In some VBA applications — such as those in the Office XP suite — you can find information about the most common errors in the Trappable Errors topic of VBA Help. Locate this topic by typing **trappable errors** in the Help window's Answer Wizard or Index tab. I haven't been able to find this topic in the Office 2000 Help systems.

If your code can't deal with a particular error, or if you don't want to take the trouble, you can still avoid the standard VBA run-time-error message by using the `Err` object's `Description` property. The following example displays a genteel error message based on the text string supplied by the `Description` property:

```
strMyErrMessage = "I'm sorry to inform you that " _
 & "something has gone amiss in this lovely " _
 & "program. According to VBA, the cause of the " _
 & "trouble is "
MsgBox strMyErrMessage & Err.Description
```

Some VBA applications provide additional objects and functions that provide information about application-specific problems. Microsoft Access, for example, offers a separate Error object.

Resuming program execution

After your error handler completes its work, you have a choice: Do you want the procedure to pick up where it left off when the error occurred, or do you want to transfer program execution back to the procedure that called the one where the error occurred?

Place the Resume statement in your error handler if you want to jump back into the current procedure. The Resume statement comes in several flavors:

- ✔ Simply typing **Resume** on its own line transfers control back to the procedure at the statement that caused the error. You should use this version of the statement if your error handler corrected values used in that statement so that you know an error can't occur again.

- ✔ To skip the statement that caused the error, add a Resume Next statement to your error-handling code instead. Execution continues at the statement immediately following the one that caused the error.

- ✔ To jump to a particular point in the procedure, enter a Resume label statement after the error-handling code. Here, label refers to a label somewhere in your procedure but *not* to the label that identifies your error handler. If you use this version, of course, you must also add the label to the procedure.

Chapter 10

Creating Interactive VBA Forms

● ●

In This Chapter

▶ Running and printing forms during the design process

▶ Inserting a new form and filling it with controls

▶ Using the Properties window — the easy VBA way to set properties

▶ Surveying the most important cosmetic and behavioral properties of forms and controls

▶ Working with labels, text boxes, buttons, and frames

▶ Displaying forms in your VBA programs — and shutting them down

▶ Writing event procedures to make your forms interactive

● ●

*V*BA gives you all the tools you need to create fine-looking windows, be they control centers for custom applications or simple subsidiary dialog boxes. This chapter takes you on a quick tour of the skills you need to build working *forms,* the VBA term for custom dialog boxes. You learn how to lay out a form, add controls such as buttons and text boxes, and — most importantly — make the form and controls respond the way you need them to respond.

For expanded coverage of form design and programming, please consult the Bonus Chapter F on the CD-ROM that comes with this book and on the author's Web site dedicated to *VBA For Dummies* at www.seldenhouse. com/VBA. I cover both form design and layout and form and control programming in more depth in this chapter.

Designing Forms

Knowing a few pieces of background information — before you start laying out your forms — is helpful. Knowing this stuff really does help the process go faster and more smoothly.

Running forms

As you lay out a form, you can *run* (display and activate) it whenever you like. Two steps are required:

1. **Select the form window.** Click on the form's window. Alternatively, you can click inside the Code window associated with the form.

2. **Run the form to display it as a working dialog box.** Press F5 or click the Run toolbar button, shown in the margin.

When you run a form, it appears on-screen over your VBA application (that is, the Visual Basic Editor disappears for the moment). You can then test the form by clicking its controls to see what happens. Just keep in mind that if the form is part of a larger program, it may not work right if you run it in isolation.

You must select a form window before the form will run. In the Visual Basic Editor, selection handles around the perimeter of a form remain visible when you click on another Editor window after having selected a form. The form may still appear to be selected, but it won't run automatically when you press F5. If the Macros dialog box unexpectedly pops up, cancel it, and then click any part of the form before you try to run it again.

To stop a running form that you haven't equipped with a Cancel button, you can click the Close button at the far-right end of the form's title bar. Alternatively, press Alt+Tab to get back to the Visual Basic Editor and click the Reset toolbar button.

You must be working in the Visual Basic Editor and use the technique that I describe previously to run a form on its own. However, the goal of creating a form is to run it from your VBA application. To do this, you must trigger the form from other VBA code, as I discuss in the section "Form Programming" later in this chapter. You run *that* code with the techniques that I outline in Chapter 4.

Forms and controls are objects — and they must be programmed

Just to remind you, forms and controls are full-fledged VBA objects, which means that they have properties, methods, and events. Forms are different from other objects in one respect: you can set the properties of forms and controls in dialog boxes, without having to program. Keep in mind, however, that you must write code for every control, with the exception of some label and frame controls. Forms themselves often require code, too. For information on the programming side of the form-design process, see the section "Form Programming" later in this chapter.

A bit of information about forms in Microsoft Access: Although Access uses the standard VBA language for the code you write, and although Access has forms with controls that look and work just like the ones in other VBA applications, Access forms are not standard VBA forms. The properties of Access controls are quite different from those of regular VBA controls, and you can't exchange a form that you design in Access with one that you create in another VBA application.

Planning forms for your program

Laying out forms in VBA is fun and easy, but designing those forms requires some thoughtful planning when you're constructing real programs. Remember that your forms are part of a larger software entity that has a practical mission to accomplish. So before you start fiddling with the forms, spend at least a little time on the following steps:

1. **Define a mission statement for your program.**

   This step applies even if the program has no forms, but you want to hold the overall goal in mind while you plan your forms.

2. **List the specific tasks that the program's forms have to perform in support of that mission.**

   What information does the form have to display for the user to respond to, what information is needed from the user, and what input should the user have in deciding how the program operates? You must translate these tasks into elements of the form.

3. **For each task, decide which type of control makes the most sense.**

   Are you asking the user to make a selection among mutually exclusive options? If so, you need a set of radio buttons (option buttons), but if the options can be set independently, check boxes are the way to go.

4. **Decide where to place each control on the form.**

   Base your decision on the task's importance, how often it needs to be performed, and which tasks are related (so you'll know which other controls this one should be grouped with).

5. **With all these details clarified, you can sketch out your forms, at least mentally.**

   Avoid overloading a single form with too many controls. Judicious use of tab (multipage) controls can help keep the number of forms down, but be ready to add extra forms to the project to avoid clutter and keep them easy to read.

6. **Only after you take care of all this practical stuff can you move on to considering the frills.**

   Will a different font on certain buttons — or special rocket ship spinner controls — really make it easier for the user to get the job done? Carefully used, variety in colors, fonts, or graphics definitely perks up the interest level, but too much variety is a distraction.

I'm not saying that you should spend endless hours in abstract planning. In fact, after you have a rough idea of what you're trying to accomplish, playing around with a tentative form design to test and to see what works and what doesn't is usually helpful. All I'm suggesting is that if you start throwing forms together with no plan at all, you're likely to find yourself making major revisions later.

Printing forms during the design process

As you work on laying out forms for a VBA project, I recommend that you have paper copies that you can carry around as you think about the project. Printed forms are great for scribbling tentative design revisions, and you can pass them around to potential users or other programmers for their reactions.

To print a project's forms in the Visual Basic Editor, follow these steps:

1. **If you want to print only one form, select the form in the Project Explorer; if you want to print all the forms in a project, select any form, module, or other component for that project.**

2. **Choose File⇨Print or press Ctrl+P.**

3. **In the little dialog box that appears, check the Form Image box.**

4. **Uncheck the Code box unless you also want a printout of the form's code.**

5. **Choose Current Module if you want just the current form printed or Current Project if you want to see all the forms on paper.**

6. **Choose OK to start printing.**

Laying out a new form

As Figure 10-1 illustrates, a new form provides a blank canvas for your dabblings in user-interface design. You can alter the form's size and position on-screen, give it a different color, and fill it with the controls that make it do productive tricks.

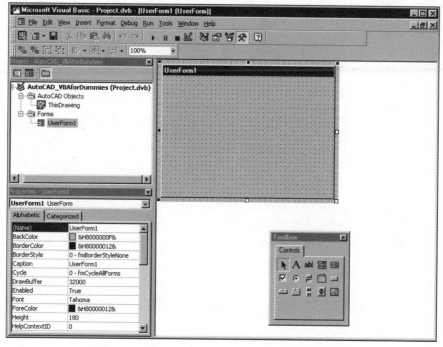

Figure 10-1:
A brand-
new
UserForm;
notice the
Toolbox and
its controls.

Before you create a new form, be sure that the correct project — the one where you want the form to live — is active. Open the project's document in the VBA application, then switch to the Visual Basic Editor. If the application permits you to open more than one document at the same time, or if it uses template documents, use the Project Explorer window to select the correct project. (See Chapter 5 for more about Project Explorer.)

Creating the form

Create a new VBA form by choosing Insert⇨UserForm from the Visual Basic Editor's main menu system or from the Project Explorer's shortcut (right-click) menu. The new UserForm appears in its own window, accompanied by the Toolbox (refer to Figure 10-1), a special toolbar containing the controls to attach to your UserForms.

Adding controls from the Toolbox

When the empty canvas of a new UserForm is on-screen, it's time to start adding *controls* — the little doodads on the form with which people interact. Controls come from the Toolbox.

The Toolbox appears automatically when you create a new UserForm, unless you previously closed it. The Toolbox graciously hides itself when you click any non-form window but pops up again when you click the UserForm window. If the Toolbox isn't visible when you need it, however, choose View⇨Toolbox to call it forth.

To add a control to your form, follow these steps:

1. **Click the Toolbox icon for the control that you want to add.**

2. **Move the mouse pointer over the form.**

   The mouse pointer becomes a cross, showing the icon of the control that you selected.

3. **Click and drag the mouse over the part of the form that you want the control to occupy (see Figure 10-2).**

4. **Release the mouse button.**

   The control appears on the form.

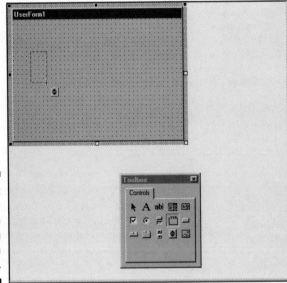

Figure 10-2: Adding a new toggle-button control to a UserForm.

Normally, VBA reverts back to the arrow mouse pointer for selecting objects as soon as you finish adding a new control. If you want to add two or more of the same type of control to a form, double-click the icon for that control in the Toolbox. When you're through, click the arrow icon to stop adding controls.

Working with form and control properties

Because VBA forms and controls are objects, they have *properties* that determine their appearance and behavior. And, as with all object properties, you can examine and change the properties of forms and controls in your code.

For these objects, however, you don't *have* to write code. Instead, the Visual Basic Editor Properties window allows you to easily control many critical characteristics of forms and controls without programming per se. As your programs get more sophisticated, you'll want — in fact, you'll *beg* — to set properties in code. Even then, though, the Properties window is still the easiest way to control the initial settings for form and control properties.

If the Properties window, shown in Figure 10-3, isn't already on-screen, display it by choosing View⇨Properties Window or by pressing F4.

Figure 10-3:
The
Properties
window for
a VBA form.

If you can't figure out what a given property is for or what settings work, just ask for Help. Click the property's field and press F1 to display the relevant topic from the VBA Forms Help file.

Touring the Properties window

The Properties window is especially cool for two reasons:

- ✔ It automatically shows the properties of whatever you selected in the UserForm window (a particular control or the form itself).

- ✔ You can work with the properties for any item on the form by choosing the item from the drop-down list, shown in Figure 10-4, at the top of the Properties window.

Figure 10-4:
The drop-down list at the top of the Properties window lets you see and change properties for any control on a form, or the form itself.

Notice that the display at the top of the window always shows the name and type of the item whose properties you're currently working with.

The bulk of the Properties window is divided into two tabs. Both tabs display exactly the same set of properties, but the Alphabetic tab lists them according to annual income (not really), whereas the Categorized tab divides them into related groups.

Whichever tab you choose, the window works the same way. To the right of the property names, each individual property has a *field* where you can change the property's setting.

Changing property settings

Depending on the individual property, you change the setting in its field in one of three ways:

- ✔ By typing a new setting
- ✔ By choosing the new setting from a drop-down list
- ✔ By choosing the new setting in a dialog box

Some properties allow you to either type a setting or choose it from a list.

You can't tell whether a property has a drop-down list or a dialog box until you click the property field. When you do, a button appears in the field; then you can click this button. (The button has a downward pointing arrow for drop-down lists or three little dots for dialog boxes; refer to Figure 10-3 for an example.)

Don't forget to select the right item

Before you add controls to a form, the form itself is the only item listed in the Properties window. As soon as you add one or more controls, however, you need to start paying attention to which item (the form or one of its controls) is selected. VBA indicates a selection by displaying little square *handles* on the corners and sides of the selected item.

One way to select an item in the first place, of course, is just to click it. But that procedure can be a bit tricky in a crowded form. I suggest that you make it a habit to select form items via the drop-down list at the top of the Properties window. The selection handles appear around the selected item's perimeter just as if you'd clicked it. If you prefer the direct click-it method, at least practice glancing at the display at the top of Properties to make sure that you selected the right item.

Working with key form and control properties

Many properties of forms and controls work identically across different objects and specific properties. For example, you use very similar techniques to change the size of a form and its controls. All of the color-related properties work the same way whether you're setting the color of the form's background or that of a control's text. This section covers the most important format-related properties that are common to forms and controls.

When you create a new form, get in the habit of making the following property settings for the form, before you add any controls:

Step to Take	Property to Set	Comments
Name the form	(Name)	You use the name to refer to the form in your program. Choose a terse name that nevertheless describes its function.
Assign a caption to the form	Caption	The caption is the text that appears in the form's title bar. Choose a caption that helps the user identify the form's purpose.
Specify a default font	Font	
Select a default text color for the form's control	ForeColor	
Specify the form's background color	BackColor	

I discuss these properties in more detail in the following sections.

The name is not the caption

As you may know by now, every object in a VBA program has a name, and forms and controls are no exception. But an object's name doesn't appear anywhere on the form. Instead, you use the name to refer to the object in your code if, for example, your program needs to activate one of the object's methods or to change one of its other properties.

And yes, forms and controls do have a Name property. A form or control name must be a valid VBA name (no spaces or punctuation characters allowed; see Chapter 6). And the name should describe the object's function in your program.

The *caption* of a form or control is something else again. A form's caption specifies the text that appears in its title bar, while a control's caption — if the control has one — specifies the text on the surface of the control. You can change the Caption property by typing a new text string in the corresponding field of the Properties window. In the case of controls, you can click once to select the control and then click again to edit the caption directly on the control. (Don't double-click the control — that action takes you to the Code window.)

Modal versus modeless forms

The classic example of a *modal* form is the typical dialog box: When a modal dialog box is active, you can't work with any other part of the program; you have to close the dialog box in order to work with a different dialog box or directly with a document. Likewise, when a modal form is active, the only parts of your VBA program that can run are the procedures belonging to the form itself. The form can respond to events, but the rest of your program is suspended and the underlying application itself is off limits to the user — until the form is closed. This is a good way to keep users focused on the task at hand, but it prevents them from deciding for themselves what to do in what order.

VBA 6.3 (just like VBA 6 before it) gives you a choice between modal and *modeless* behavior for each form. By default, a form's ShowModal property is True, meaning the form is modal. Change the ShowModal property to False to make the form modeless, which gives users the option of switching back and forth between this form, other open forms, and the underlying VBA application. When a modeless form is on-screen, the user can copy data between two or more open forms, and can scroll the main application window to see other pertinent information — all without having to close and then re-open the form.

Users of your program aren't able to move between forms unless *all* the open forms are designated as modeless. As soon as your program opens a single modal form, the remainder of the program is suspended until the user closes that form. If the program shows other forms before the modal one, those forms remain visible on-screen but can't be activated until the modal form is closed.

While this book covers VBA 6, those of you hanging on to earlier version should note that *all* forms in VBA 5 are modal. VBA 5 forms don't have the `ShowModal` property.

Sizing and positioning forms and controls

Before you do any serious design work on a form, be aware that like any self-respecting graphics program, the Visual Basic Editor has a grid. The *grid* defines imaginary magnetic lines, vertical and horizontal. When you move or resize any item on a form, the edges automatically snap into place along the nearest grid line. I save details on the grid for the section "Working with the grid," later in this chapter.

Okay, now with that out of the way . . . the easiest property to change in a form or control is its size. Although you can set the `Height` and `Width` properties in the Properties window, it's easier to just grab the item by one of its handles — the little boxes that appear on the corners and sides of the item when it's selected. I know — you already know how to resize items; every Windows program that allows you to resize graphical shapes, from Paint on up, uses this system. But here's the drill:

- Drag a bottom or right *side* handle to size the form in one dimension
- Drag the *corner* handle to size the form in both dimensions simultaneously

Sizing forms with the mouse

Notice that only white handles work for sizing — and that most of the handles for a form are black. The black ones don't do anything except set off the form smartly. Forms are always pushed up against the top-left corner of their windows. You can't move a form in its window. But don't worry about this — a form's position in the window doesn't affect its position on-screen.

Sizing by the numbers

You can also size a form or any of its controls by using precise numeric measurements; just change the `Height` and `Width` properties in the Properties dialog box. Key "point": values for these properties are given in points, a point being $\frac{1}{72}$ of an inch.

Controlling a form's position on-screen

You have full control over where the form initially appears on-screen when you run your program (or when you run the form by itself, which you can do to test it). The `StartUpPosition` property is the key.

The default value for this property is 1 - CenterOwner. This specifies that the form should appear in the center of the VBA application's window, regardless of how big it is or where it's located on-screen (well, unless the window is partially off the screen, in which case your form pushes itself all the way to the edge, but never farther than that). If you want your form to appear in the middle of the screen, no matter what the VBA application is doing, set the StartUpPosition property to 2 - CenterScreen instead. To set the position yourself, choose 0 - Manual and then type values for the Left and Top properties, too.

Positioning controls

To change a control's position within a form, just drag the control wherever you want it to go. If you're a stickler for details, you can type numeric position values for the Left and Top properties.

Trés chic with special 3-D effects

If you go in for the faux 3-D look, check out the SpecialEffect property, which is available for forms and some controls. Chosen from a drop-down list, settings other than 0 (for flat) impart a subtle but definite impression of depth to the target object.

Editing controls: The basics

Before you go bananas with the fancier formatting commands for controls, be sure that you know the basics. I discuss how to size and move controls by using the mouse or via their properties in "Sizing and positioning forms and controls" earlier in this chapter. In this section, other simple editing techniques come to light.

Cutting, copying, and pasting controls

As a card-carrying Windows program, the Visual Basic Editor allows you to cut, copy, and paste controls individually or in groups. The standard Windows menu commands and keyboard shortcuts apply. In addition, you can use the Cut, Copy, and Paste buttons in the Editor's Standard toolbar for one-click access to these functions. (These buttons look just like the ones in Microsoft Office.)

The only thing special about these commands has to do with Paste. When you paste a control from the Clipboard, VBA deposits it in the center of the form, even if that part of the form isn't currently visible. If you select a frame or multipage control before pasting, however, the control goes into the center of that item. I discuss frames and multipage controls in Bonus Chapter F on the CD (and on the author's Web site dedicated to *VBA For Dummies* at www.seldenhouse.com/VBA).

Deleting controls

You can delete one or more selected controls without placing them on the Clipboard by pressing the Delete key or choosing Edit➪Delete. Notice that the Backspace key does not work for this purpose, as it does in some other programs.

Selecting multiple controls

You can select a group of controls and then move, resize, cut, or copy them as a unit, or apply other formatting commands as I describe in the section "Formatting controls" later in this chapter. This is also a great way to efficiently set properties they have in common to the same values. To select multiple controls, you can use these methods:

✔ Draw a selection rectangle around the controls that you want to include in the group by clicking the Toolbox arrow pointer and dragging diagonally over the controls. If any part of a control is included in the rectangle, that control is included in the selection.

✔ Click the first control in the group and then Shift+click a control at the other side of the selection area. All controls between the two that you clicked are included in the selection.

✔ Ctrl+click individual controls to add them to or remove them from the selection.

Undoing changes

You usually can reverse the effects of the last formatting change involving controls by using the Undo command (Ctrl+Z). Undo doesn't work after you resize a form, however, nor does it reverse changes that you make in the Properties window.

Working with the grid

The *grid* is an array of horizontal and vertical lines that crisscross your forms. The grid has two functions:

✔ **To visually guide you as you place controls with the mouse.** The visual grid comprises those dotted lines that you've probably seen in your forms.

✔ **To automatically align controls to the grid as you move or resize controls.** No matter how you move the mouse, the edges of your controls always snap into alignment along one of the gridlines. This ensures a reasonable consistency in your form layout, although it limits your flexibility.

The two functions work independently. You can turn off the visible grid and leave automatic alignment on, or vice versa.

Setting grid options

To control the way that the grid works, choose Tools⇨Options. When the Options dialog box appears, click the General tab to reveal the panel of choices that appear in Figure 10-5.

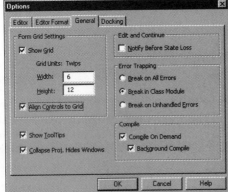

Figure 10-5:
Change grid
settings in
the General
tab of the
Options
dialog box.

Confining your attention to the top-left part of the dialog box, you can see the few simple grid-related options. They are:

- ✔ **Show Grid.** Clear this check box to turn off the visual grid — those dotted lines in your forms. This option doesn't affect automatic alignment to the grid.

- ✔ **Width** and **Height.** These two text boxes allow you to control the size of your grid in the horizontal and vertical dimensions independently. The Width setting controls the distance between each pair of vertical gridlines, which in turn affects the horizontal position of controls. Similarly, the Height setting is for the horizontal gridlines but pertains to vertical position.

- ✔ **Align Controls to Grid.** When this box is checked, the "snap to grid" function is in force. Clear the box to give yourself complete freedom to position and size controls to any measurements that you please. Again, the visual grid can be on when this function is off.

Formatting controls

People notice intangibles such as symmetry, consistency, and general neatness. You want to help users of your forms stay focused on what they're trying to accomplish, rather than distract them with a disorganized jumble of controls.

Fortunately, VBA provides a stable of tools that help you achieve this goal easily. Although laying out a well-organized form still takes some manual labor, the Visual Basic Editor automatic formatting features can handle much of the work.

Using the Format menu

The Visual Basic Editor Format menu (see Figure 10-6) is the control center for commands that affect the layout of controls in a form. Getting on intimate terms with the menu and its multiple submenus serves you well during the process of form design.

Figure 10-6:
The Format menu in the Visual Basic Editor.

Using the UserForm toolbar

When you're working with a form in the Visual Basic Editor, the UserForm toolbar comes in handy. If the toolbar isn't already visible, right-click any toolbar and choose UserForm from the shortcut menu to display it. Figure 10-7 shows how the UserForm toolbar looks in its floating configuration.

Figure 10-7:
The UserForm toolbar offers buttons for common control formatting commands.

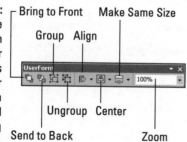

Most of the buttons on the UserForm toolbar correspond to items on the Format menu. Some of them are split buttons — the ones with little down arrows to their right — that provide multiple options. If you click the main part of one of these split buttons, VBA immediately activates the option that was last used. To select a different option, click the little arrow and choose the option from the list.

Grouping multiple controls

Although it's fairly easy to use the mouse to select multiple controls on the fly, this method isn't ideal when you want to work repeatedly with the same set of controls as a unit. By combining all the controls into a *group,* you don't have to reselect the same controls every time you do something to them, and you eliminate the possibility of selection mistakes. Figure 10-8 shows examples of grouped controls.

Figure 10-8:
Several groups of controls; notice that the selection rectangle extends around all controls in each group.

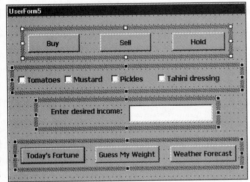

Creating a group is simple. Just follow these steps:

1. **Select all the controls that you want to include in the group.**

2. **Click the Group button in the UserForm toolbar or choose Format⇨Group.**

Grouping lets you apply formatting commands that normally work on single controls to groups as a whole. If you want to even out the spacing between three rows of buttons, for example, you can convert each row into a group, select all three groups simultaneously, and then choose the Horizontal Spacing⇨Make Equal command (see "Adjusting horizontal and vertical spacing" later in this chapter).

Arranging controls on top of one another

Although it's usually best to avoid overlapping controls, such a design can be vital when you need to change the contents of a form while your program runs. If you set each control's Visible property to True or False as necessary, the program can keep all but one of the overlapping controls invisible at any one time. See the Bonus Chapter A on the CD-ROM for more information on this technique.

Inside the Visual Basic Editor, however, every control is always visible — unless, that is, it's buried underneath other controls on the form. When this happens, you can use the Order commands in the Format menu to rearrange the controls.

Here are suggestions for using the Order commands:

✓ If you can get to a tiny piece of a buried control, click there to select the control, and then choose Format⇨Order⇨Bring to Front to place the control on the top of the pile. Have at it.

✓ If the control that you want to work with is completely covered by the ones on top, click the topmost control to select it, and then banish it to the bottom of the pile by choosing Format⇨Order⇨Send to Back. Repeat this process until the control that you want is on top.

✓ If you're arranging controls that will actually overlap while the program runs, you may need to use the Format⇨Order⇨Bring Forward or Send Backward commands to order them just so. These commands move the selected control by one position in the pile.

Formatting multiple controls

Many of the more advanced commands on the Format menu only work on multiple controls, or on selections that include two or more groups. This section describes each of these commands, after an important digression about which selected item has the power in the relationship.

Control and domination

No, this section isn't a sudden kinky detour. In some formatting commands involving multiple controls, one control serves as the reference point for the command. This control is the *dominant control,* in VBA lingo.

When you use the Format⇨Make Same Size command to make uniform a set of selected controls, for example, VBA copies the chosen dimension (height, width, or both) from the dominant control to all the other controls in the set. Likewise for the Align command — the other controls in the set line up with the dominant control, which doesn't move. The effects of the Horizontal and Vertical Spacing commands (also on the Format menu) also depend on which control is dominant.

In Figure 10-9, you see that only one of the selected controls is outlined in white sizing handles. That's the dominant control, whose handles are always white. Other controls in the selection have black handles around their margins.

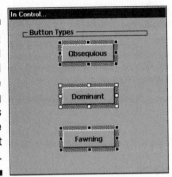

Figure 10-9:
The control
surrounded
by white
sizing
handles
is the
dominant
control.

As you already know, you can select a group of controls in one of two main ways: by dragging a selection rectangle around the entire group by using the Toolbox arrow pointer or by Shift+clicking or Ctrl+clicking each control, one by one. What you haven't seen so far is how to set the dominant control while you're using these techniques. The following table shows how:

Control Selection Strategy	Selection Technique
Choose the dominant control by dragging a selection rectangle	Begin dragging the selection closer to the target control than any other
Choose the first control you click as the dominant control	Shift+click to select each control in the set
Choose the last control you click as the dominant	Ctrl+click to select each control in the set
Choose a different dominant control for an existing selection	Ctrl+click the chosen control twice

Aligning controls

Even with the grid on, it's common to find that controls that ought to be in a straight line or column actually are staggered. Instead of laboriously lining the controls up by hand, enlist the Visual Basic Editor Align commands to do the work for you. You can bring the midline or any edge (top, bottom, left, or right) of each selected control into alignment along either a vertical or horizontal axis.

Follow these steps to align a set of controls:

1. **Select the controls, taking care to choose the one control that should remain in place as the dominant control (refer to the preceding section).**

2. **Choose Format⇨Align and then choose a specific type of alignment from the submenu.**

Alternatively, you can click the Align button in the UserForm toolbar (if it indicates the correct type of alignment) or click just beside the button proper to display the same list of alignment options that appears in the menu.

Making controls the same size

The three Make Same Size commands on the Format menu automatically adjust all selected controls to match the size of the dominant control in the selection. You can bring instant conformity in width, height, or both dimensions. The three commands can also be found on a split button on the UserForm toolbar.

Adjusting horizontal and vertical spacing

The Format menu's Horizontal Spacing and Vertical Spacing commands can each change the space between two or more controls in four different ways. Three of these options are most useful — and one is available only — when the selection includes at least three controls. Here's how the choices work:

- **Make Equal:** Evens out the space between three or more selected controls. The controls at either end of the selection stay in place, while the controls in between move. This command isn't available if only two controls are selected.

- **Increase** and **Decrease:** Add or remove space between the selected controls by an amount equal to one grid unit for the dimension that you're working with. The dominant control stays in place while the others move.

- **Remove:** Moves controls so that no space falls between them, causing their edges to touch. The dominant control doesn't move.

Controls, Behave Yourself!

In this section, the most important VBA controls get individual attention in terms of the functions they play in your programs (the first part of this chapter covers cosmetics). Before the spotlight falls in turn on each control separately, I discuss several important properties governing the behavior of many types of controls. Some of these properties apply to forms themselves, too.

Refer to "Working with form and control properties" earlier in this chapter for instructions on how to use the Properties window to see and change your control and form properties.

Remember that you can test controls visually during the design cycle without doing any programming. When you run a form from within the Visual Basic Editor, the controls react as they should. When you click a button, for example, it looks pressed in. Getting a control to do something useful, however, is another story — I tell that story in the section "Form Programming" later in this chapter.

Using the Enabled and Locked properties

Two properties — Enabled and Locked — govern whether a control or an entire form is accessible to the user. Obviously, you want to give the user access to controls most of the time — otherwise why put them in the form? At times, however, a look-but-don't-touch approach is appropriate. Often, a control should be visible to inform the user that it exists, but it should be *grayed out* or dimmed to show that it can't be used at the moment. When nothing is selected in a word processor, for example, the Cut command can't be used because you have nothing to cut.

The Enabled property determines whether the control or form can receive the focus — the capability to react to mouse and keyboard actions by the user. Only one object at a time ever has the focus in Windows. To keep you in the know about where the focus goes, Windows places a dotted border around the control that currently has the focus.

When Enabled is True, the control appears normally and can receive the focus. When Enabled is False, Windows displays a dimmed version of the control, which can't take the focus (see Figure 10-10).

Figure 10-10:
This dialog box shows examples of enabled and disabled command buttons and option buttons, plus a disabled text box.

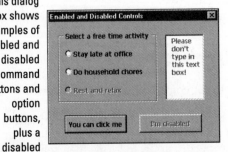

The `Locked` property decides whether the control does anything. If `Locked` is `True`, you can click the control, press its accelerator key, and throw rocks at it, but the control still won't do anything (see "Assigning accelerator keys" later in this chapter). Assuming that `Enabled` is `True`, however, the control can still receive the focus, and it still looks normal on-screen.

Setting the tab order for controls

One of many hallowed Windows conventions is that in a dialog box, pressing the Tab key moves the focus from one control to another. By default, every control that you add to a VBA form takes its proper place in the *tab order* — the sequence in which controls are selected when the Tab key is pressed. (By the way, pressing Shift+Tab walks you through the tab order in reverse.)

You don't need to run a form to check out its tab order. Pressing Tab in the UserForm window selects one control after the next in the same order.

Initially, tab order is based on the sequence in which the controls were originally added to the form. What usually happens is that you add controls as you think of them, not in the proper tab order. But you can take direct control of the tab order — and even remove controls from the sequence if you like.

What you're after is a logical progression from one control to the next. Normally that progression is left-to-right and top-to-bottom, but sometimes skipping controls intended for optional entries makes sense. Anyway, the easiest way to change the tab order for a form is to choose View⇨Tab Order. Figure 10-11 shows the modest dialog box that appears when you choose this command. To reshuffle the controls listed there, click a control you want to move and then click the Move Up or Move Down button as appropriate.

The tab order is actually controlled by each control's `TabIndex` property. The value of `TabIndex` is 0 for the first control in the sequence, 1 for the second control, and so on. If you change one control's `TabIndex` setting, VBA automatically adjusts all the others.

To remove a control from the tab order, set its `TabStop` property to `False`. This doesn't change the control's position in the tab order, so if you set the `TabStop` property to `True` again, the control rejoins the sequence right where it was before.

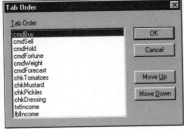

Figure 10-11:
Use the Tab
Order dialog
box to
control how
users
navigate
your VBA
forms
using the
keyboard.

Assigning accelerator keys

Although many people are happy selecting controls with the mouse, some much prefer the keyboard. Be polite — give your users a keyboard shortcut, or *accelerator key,* for each control. When the form is running, pressing Alt followed by the accelerator key moves the focus to the control and may trigger an event (such as the `Click` event).

To make the assignment, type a single character into the Accelerator field in the Properties dialog box. The character should be one found in the control's caption, and should not duplicate the accelerator of any other control on the same form. VBA automatically underlines the accelerator character for you.

To add an accelerator to a control that doesn't have a `Caption` property — such as a text box or scroll bar — follow these steps:

1. **Create a label for the control.**

   I discuss labels in the next section.

2. **Adjust the tab order so that the label comes immediately before the other control.**

3. **Assign an accelerator to the label.**

Now when the user presses the label's accelerator, the focus passes to the control that immediately follows the label in the tab order. Figure 10-12 shows a form that uses this technique.

Figure 10-12:
Pressing
Alt+N when
this form is
active
selects the
text box so
that the user
can type the
pet's name.

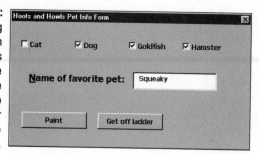

Sending messages with label controls

A *label control* provides a rectangular area on a form where you can display messages. From the viewpoint of a user of your program, a label control isn't much of a control — it doesn't let the user control anything. All it does is display some text or, optionally, a picture. The user can't type over the existing text or even copy it to the Clipboard.

Still, label controls are vital from the programmer's standpoint because they let you communicate messages to your users. Generally, you use labels to identify controls and their functions, as the example form in Figure 10-13 shows. This practice is especially useful for controls that don't have their own captions, such as scroll bars and spinner controls. But if you want to get up on an electronic soapbox, labels accept the most bombastic of messages (see Figure 10-14).

Figure 10-13:
Label
controls at
the top of
this form
identify the
function
of each
scrol bar.

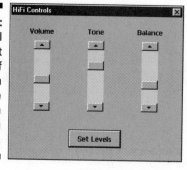

Figure 10-14:
This form
uses a label
control to
display that
long-winded
message in
the center,
and another
label for
the title at
the top.

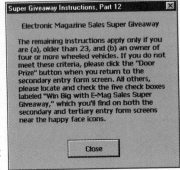

A label can look just like a standard text box and yet still prevent the user from copying its text. Set the label control's `SpecialEffect` property to 2 (for sunken) and its `BackColor` property to white.

Entering label text

A label control displays text known as its *caption*. To place your own text on the label, change the text in the `Caption` property in the Properties window. You can also edit the label text directly, by double-clicking the label so that an insertion point appears. Press Shift+Enter to start a new line. See the section "The name is not the caption" earlier in this chapter for more information.

Making automatic label adjustments

Label controls are capable of adjusting themselves automatically to the text that they contain using settings you set in the Properties window. Figure 10-15 shows examples of these properties in action. For example, you can:

✔ Leave the `WordWrap` property set to `True` (the default) if you want VBA to automatically break the text into separate lines to fit in the available space, much like a word processor does. If you set `WordWrap` to `False`, all the caption text remains on one line even if there isn't enough room to see it all.

✔ Set the `AutoSize` property to `True` if you want the size of the label itself to change automatically to fit all the text. If `WordWrap` is also set to `True`, the label expands vertically. If you change `WordWrap` to `False`, the label widens to accommodate the single line of text.

✔ Use the `TextAlign` property to control how text is justified inside the label: on the left, in the center, or on the right.

Figure 10-15:
The label
controls
shown on
this form
illustrate
different
settings
of the
`WordWrap`
and
`AutoSize`
properties.

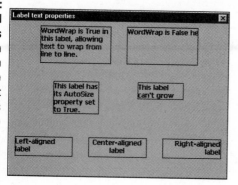

Automatic resizing can be convenient, but it can introduce problems as well. As the label grows, it can start to look out of proportion to the rest of the form. At a certain point, the label may get so big that it covers other controls in the form or runs off the edge. If you use automatic resizing, you have to take special care that the label never has too much text.

Changing label text in code

Although users can't change the text in a label control while your program runs, you can by using the label's `Caption` property. A single line of code is all you need to modify the text to suit what's currently going on in the program. Here's an example of how to do this:

```
lblInspirationalMessage.Caption = "Laugh and be happy!"
```

To place line breaks in label text, use literal strings concatenated with the carriage-return character in the assignment statement. (For more information on stringing text together, see Chapter 11.)

Collecting information with text boxes

Use a text-box control when you want to collect information from the user; your code can retrieve anything that the user types in the text box. Figure 10-16 shows a text box doing its duty.

Figure 10-16:
The large white area in the middle of this form is a text box into which someone has typed a message to the management.

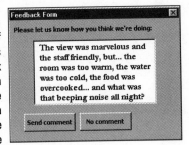

If you're trying to create a dialog box with a single text box for user entry, you probably don't need a form at all. Instead, the VBA InputBox function (which I describe in Chapter 11) may well satisfy your needs. Use text-box controls instead of an InputBox in the following situations:

✔ You want a prettier or uglier dialog box than the standard InputBox function can display.

✔ You need at least one more control besides the text box in the same dialog box.

✔ You want to check entries for validity while a user is typing them.

With a text box, you can program an event procedure that gets triggered each time the user presses a key — and have it show you whether the key that was pressed meets the criteria you set up. With an InputBox, you can only check the entire entry, and only after the user has closed the box.

Placing default text in a text box

You can place a default entry in a text box so that the user doesn't have to type anything if the default is acceptable. To enter the default text, click the text box once to select it and then click it a second time to enter text-entry mode; then you can start typing (don't double-click). Or you can type the text into the Value property field in the Properties window. (*Remember:* Text boxes don't have captions.)

Actually, text-box controls have both a Value property and a Text property. These two properties are equivalent for text boxes, but many other controls, such as option buttons and scroll bars, have the Value property but not the Text property. Because the Value and Text properties function identically for a text box, they're interchangeable. I use Value because I find it easier to remember and because many other controls have that same property. For a discussion and examples of how you can use the `Value` (or `Text`) property, see the sections "Retrieving the user's entry" and "Using a control's default property," both later in this chapter.

Retrieving the user's entry

To find out what text the user has entered in a text box, your program should retrieve the box's `Value` or `Text` property. Typically, you would assign the property to a string variable with a statement such as the following:

```
strTextBoxText = txtMessageFromUser.Value
```

After this code runs, the variable `strTextBoxText` now contains whatever the user types in the text box named `txtMessageFromUser`.

Using a control's default property

Many controls have default properties, and the default property is usually `Value`.

In the case of a text box, you don't need to explicitly name either the `Value` or the `Text` property to set or retrieve the contents of a text box in VBA code. Because `Value` is a text box's *default property,* you can omit it entirely. The following statement places a message into a text box:

```
txtRUListening = "Do as I say!"
```

This example places text the user has typed into a string variable:

```
strWhatIHeard = txtSoundOffTextBox
```

Making automatic text-box adjustments

Text boxes have the same `AutoSize`, `WordWrap`, and `TextAlign` properties that labels do, and they work mostly the same way. See the information on these properties in the "Sending messages with label controls" section earlier in this chapter. However, the `WordWrap` property doesn't do anything except in multiline text boxes, which I describe in Bonus Chapter F on this book's CD.

Getting things done with Command buttons

When you want something done, and you want it done now, nothing gives you the feeling that you're in control like pressing a button and getting an immediate response. *Command buttons* provide that illusion of power in your programs.

The standard-issue command button is just a gray blob with a bit of explanatory text, such as OK, Cancel, or Guess Again, Friend. If plain text is too drab for your taste, you can easily add a little icon graphic to any button. In the button's Picture property field in the Properties window, click the little button with three dots. You get a dialog box that enables you to specify a graphic file. Figure 10-17 demonstrates a variety of command-button controls.

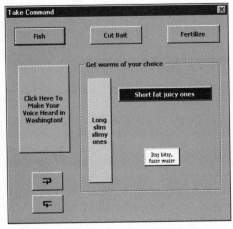

Figure 10-17: Examples of command buttons of different sizes, shapes, and formats; the two buttons at the lower left illustrate graphics used instead of text on command buttons.

Unfortunately, command buttons don't do anything to speak of until you program them. Clicking a command button generates a Click event, but you have to write code to tell VBA what actions to take when the event occurs.

Selecting a default button

In most dialog boxes, pressing Enter triggers a particular button. This is the *default button,* the one that responds when the user presses Enter, unless the focus has been moved to a different control.

To designate a command button as the default button for your form, set the button's Default property to True. Of course, only one button on each form can be the default button.

Creating a Cancel button

If your dialog box can change data or program settings, it's always wise to give users an opportunity to back out before those changes become final. By convention, a button labeled Cancel is this escape hatch. If you're a nonconformist, you might label the button "Never mind" or "Forget it," but concern for the helpless user dictates that you provide a way out, no matter what you call the button.

Also by convention, pressing the Esc key cancels the dialog box, just as if the user had clicked the Cancel button (or whatever you name it) in question. Setting a command button's Cancel property to True means that when the user presses Esc, your program reacts as if a user has clicked the button. It's up to your code to decide what actually happens when this event occurs.

To put it more bluntly, setting the Cancel property to True does *not* automatically mean that when the user clicks the button, the dialog box is cancelled. All it does is connect the Esc key with the button's Click event.

I've been framed!

Frame controls are modest but vital components of VBA forms — and of your tool chest. To the eye, a frame is a simple rectangle with a caption embedded in the top. You place other controls in a frame to group them.

Frames serve the following two purposes:

✔ To set off a group of related controls visually — cueing the user that these controls are in fact related — and lending variety and organization to a large form (see Figure 10-18).

✔ To define a group of option buttons functionally so that a user can select only one of them at a time.

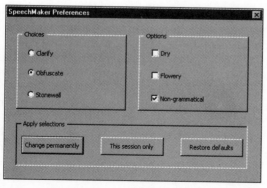

Figure 10-18: The form shown here uses three separate frame controls to organize its groups of buttons.

I take up the details on the latter use of frames in the section " Picking one item from a group with option buttons " later in this chapter. In this section, I stick with the basics: Using frames to organize all types of controls.

Placing controls on frames

Once you've added a frame to a form, placing any other control on the frame binds it and the control together. Now, if you move the frame, the control goes with it, always remaining in the same relative location within the frame.

You can add a control to a frame by

- ✔ Drawing a new control on the frame. Create the new control as you normally would, by clicking the appropriate icon in the Toolbox and then dragging over the target location on your form. In this case, that target location is inside the frame.

- ✔ Moving an existing control into the frame. Drag the control with the mouse until the mouse pointer is within the frame boundary. When you let go of the mouse button, the frame takes ownership.

When you successfully stick a control into a frame, the frame border appears selected whenever you select the control (see Figure 10-19).

Figure 10-19:
When you select a control that's associated with a frame, the frame itself looks selected, too.

Removing controls from frames

Breaking the link between a control and its frame is as simple as dragging the control to another spot on the form. As soon as the mouse pointer is outside the frame's border, releasing the mouse button cuts the connection and drops the control into place. Now the two objects (form and control) can move independently.

Picking one item from a group with option buttons

Many choices in life, and in software, are mutually exclusive. When you order a scoop of ice cream, you can pick spumoni or rum raisin or licorice, but not all three at once. When you buy a dress or a pair of slacks, you specify only one out of all the available sizes. And when you marry Ed, you give up on Fred, Ned, and Ted (Ed sure hopes so!).

In Windows, the most common way to represent mutually exclusive choices like these is with a set of *option buttons,* also known as *radio buttons.* These are the little circular buttons that work like the push buttons on car radios. After all, you can only listen to one radio station at a time (unless you're really radical). Figure 10-20 demonstrates a typical set of option buttons.

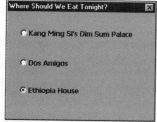

Figure 10-20:
Option buttons at work.

Option buttons should always come in sets — after all, the point is to represent one choice among several. Only one button in a set can ever be selected. Clicking one option button turns off the previously selected button automatically.

Grouping option buttons

Don't worry about straining yourself to create a group of option buttons. All you have to do is plop down the buttons on the same part of the form. VBA automatically treats them as a group, and they behave as expected when the program runs — when one is on, the rest are off.

But what do I mean by "the same part of the form?" Well, this isn't official VBA jargon, but here's the idea: One part of the form is the form itself — the background canvas, if you will. Each frame control you add creates another part. And each page of a multipage control is also a separate part (I cover multipage controls, which produce the notebook-tab that looks so common in Windows dialog boxes, in Bonus Chapter F on the CD). You can even place frames within other frames, or on pages of a multipage control — if you do, each subframe constitutes its own part.

In a form with one or more frames, VBA treats the option buttons that aren't inside any frame as one group, and each frame's buttons as a separate group. See Figure 10-21 to see what I mean.

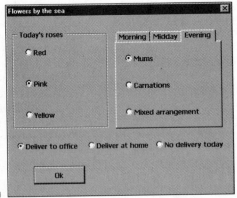

Figure 10-21:
Three
separate
groups of
option
buttons.

Which option button got clicked?

Clicking an option button selects that button but typically causes no other immediate changes. Instead, the dialog box just sits there, allowing the user to think twice and perhaps to pick a different option button. Only when the user clicks the OK button is the selection confirmed.

For you as the programmer, the task is to figure out which option button was selected when the confirming event occurred. To do this, you must check the Value property for each button in the group. Though there are trickier ways to do this, an If...ElseIf statement is a decent solution, as in:

```
If OptionButton1.Value = True Then
    ChosenOption = "Bill"
ElseIf OptionButton2.Value = True Then
    ChosenOption = "Bob"
ElseIf OptionButton3.Value = True Then
    ChosenOption = "Barney"
Else
    ChosenOption = ""
End If
```

Turning options on or off with check boxes and toggle buttons

Option buttons are great when you're working with multiple, mutually exclusive choices. However, when the number of choices collapses to just two, you should use a check box or a toggle button to let the user pick. Check boxes

and toggle buttons are indicated for any choice involving paired opposites
such as Yes or No, On or Off, True or False, and Stay or Leave. In practice, the
big difference between check boxes and toggle buttons is just that they look
different. Here's how:

✔ A *check box* is a little square in which a check appears when the Yes, On,
   or True option is selected. (If the square is empty, the check box is said
   to be *cleared.*)

✔ A *toggle button* looks like a command button, except that when you click
   it, it stays pushed in.

Figure 10-22 shows several check boxes and toggle buttons doing their
chores.

Figure 10-22:
Check
boxes and
toggle
buttons at
work.

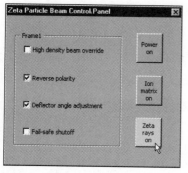

Grouped check boxes

Check boxes are often grouped together to present a list of choices that
aren't mutually exclusive. It's like when you go to the store to buy breakfast
cereal and come home with one box of Toastie-O's, one of Healthy Cardboard
Crunch, and one of Sugar-Coated White Flour Kibbles. Figure 10-23 offers several additional examples. Note that each individual check box still represents
a *yes* or *no* choice for the item that it pertains to.

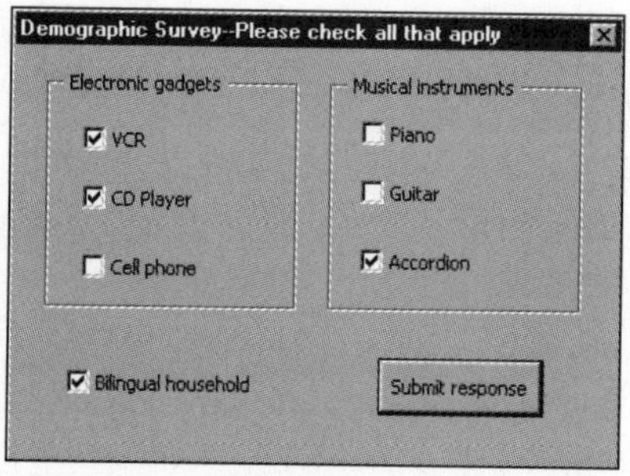

Figure 10-23:
The user
can check
or clear
each
check box
indepen-
dently.

Checked check boxes and toggled toggle buttons

As usual, the `Value` property holds the crucial information concerning the user's interaction with these controls. If a check box is checked, its `Value` property is `True`; if it's cleared, `Value` is `False`. Likewise for toggle buttons: `Value` is `True` if the button is pushed in, `False` if not. So code like this retrieves and acts on the current setting:

```
If tglLightSwitch.Value = True Then
    TurnLightsOn
Else
    TurnLightsOff
End If
```

If you simply want to change the current state of a check box or toggle button to its opposite, the Not operator is the most efficient way to do so. The following code checks a check box if it's currently cleared, but clears it if it's already checked:

```
chkYesOrNo.Value = Not chkYesOrNo.Value
```

Selecting options with list and combo boxes

If you offer more than four or five mutually exclusive choices for an item, your dialog box becomes confusingly cluttered if you present all the choices as option buttons. When the choices *aren't* mutually exclusive, you can get away with maybe 10 or 12 check boxes; the user can consider each check box on its own merits. Beyond that limit, the form becomes too cluttered.

What's a list box?

The *list box* is the Windows solution to such problems. A list box presents a compact list of named options, allowing the user to select them individually in the list. Obvious examples are list boxes for picking a salad dressing or selecting one of the 50 states (see Figure 10-24).

What a list box can't do is accept entries that aren't in the list. Also, you can't present a VBA list box as a drop-down list on a single line. To overcome these limitations, you need a combo box.

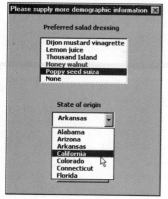

Figure 10-24:
In this form,
the list box
is on the top
and the
combo box
underneath.

Combo boxes

A *combo box* combines the virtues of a list box with those of a text box. The user can pick a supplied item from the list, but if none of these is appropriate, the user can type in an entry from scratch. From a cosmetic standpoint, the main difference between list and combo boxes is that the latter requires the user to click an arrow button to drop down the list of items. Although you certainly have long experience with combo boxes, Figure 10-24 also illustrates one just in case.

From a user's point of view, combo boxes are cool, because the user has free rein to make his or her wishes known. From the programmer's standpoint, however, many situations call for limiting user choices to prevent invalid entries. Because the United States has only 50 states, it wouldn't make sense to allow users to make up their own state entries in an address database. VBA lets you, the programmer, decide whether a combo box can accept an entry typed by the user instead of one chosen from the drop-down list.

Now that you know what list boxes are, don't use 'em

My advice is to use combo box controls for all options you present in lists, whether or not the user is allowed to type in entries that aren't on the list. Forget about list boxes.

Here's why: A VBA list box can't display items in a drop-down list. Instead, it's just a rectangular area on the form where the choices are listed. This doesn't really solve the space-and-clutter problem; if the list contains any significant number of items, it takes up too much room on your form and distracts attention when it's not in use. If the number of choices is few enough to make an unobtrusive list, a set of option buttons or check boxes would work just as well and look more appealing.

In contrast, combo boxes are much more compact because they always display only a single choice from those on the list. And to make a combo box act like a list box — restricting entries to those on the list — all you have to do is set the combo box's `Style` property to 2 (`fmStyleDropDownList`). So why bother with list boxes?

Putting items into a list or combo box

Now for the harder part. You can't use the Properties window to type in the choices that should appear in a list or combo box. Instead, you either have to write code for the control's `AddItem` method or bind the control to a *data source* (meaning a list in an Excel worksheet or an Access database).

To create the list directly in code requires an event procedure for the form's `Activate` event. It should contain a series of statements like the ones in the following example:

```
Private Sub UserForm_Activate()
    cmbOpinionPoll.AddItem "Overpopulation"
    cmbOpinionPoll.AddItem "Global warming"
    cmbOpinionPoll.AddItem "No time to smell the roses"
    cmbOpinionPoll.AddItem "No roses to smell"
    cmbOpinionPoll.AddItem "Taxes on the rich too high"
    cmbOpinionPoll.AddItem "Too many social services"
    cmbOpinionPoll.AddItem "Inadequate social services"
    cmbOpinionPoll.AddItem "HMOs"
End Sub
```

The technicalities of binding a list or combo box to a data source are beyond the scope of this book, but you should know that this technique is available.

So what option did the user pick?

To retrieve the item that the user has selected or typed in a list or combo box, use the object's `Value` property in your code. This works just the way it does in a text box: Assign the property to a suitable variable (string, numeric, or variant), as in

```
strOpinion = cmbOpinionPoll.Value
```

Form Programming

Adding controls, such as command buttons and combo boxes, to a form is a piece of cake, but getting them to do your bidding takes a little more brain power, and some programming. This section cuts through the complexities of the form programming process.

If you've got it, flaunt it!

Once you've decided to include custom forms in a VBA program, the first and most fundamental programming problem is how to get your forms on-screen to begin with. You can construct the most beautiful, elegantly organized form ever, but if nobody gets to see it, so what?

A VBA program can fall back on the user interface of the underlying application, so your programs don't automatically display forms when they run. In this respect, VBA is different from its cousin Visual Basic, in which the program *is* the form, in a sense. At any rate, in a VBA program, you must add code to display a form so that it becomes accessible to users.

Loading and showing forms

Displaying a VBA form involves loading the form into memory and then showing the form on-screen. You can use a single VBA statement to perform both steps; however, you may sometimes find it useful to separate the steps over two distinct statements.

Show-ing windows

The ticket to displaying any form is to execute its Show method. If the form is named FormICa, all you need to type is:

```
FormICa.Show
```

Note that Show is a method of the UserForm object, so you append it to the form name following a period. If the form in question isn't already loaded into memory, the Show method loads it and then displays it. If the form is loaded but hidden, the Show method just makes it visible.

Loading a form without displaying it

Use the Load statement to load the form into memory before you actually display it on-screen. Load is not a method, so the syntax is backwards compared to Show, as in:

```
Load FormAlDeHyde
```

Why load a form without displaying it? Well, if your program uses numerous or complicated forms, this can make your program seem faster to the user. Loading a form takes much longer than displaying it. Because a program of any complexity performs lots of miscellaneous initialization procedures (such as reading data from files, calculating initial variables, and creating objects), a waiting period is typical when the program starts up. If you load your forms at that time too, users won't notice the wait as much as they might later on. The only disadvantage of preloading your forms is that they consume memory that you may need for other purposes.

Making changes in your form before you display it

You can also load a form — without the Load statement — by entering code statements that manipulate a property or method of the form, or of one of its controls. This technique allows your program to make changes in a form before displaying it on-screen. True, the Visual Basic Editor's Properties window allows you to control exactly how the form looks and acts without any programming, but consider this point: You often don't know how the form (or its controls) should look or act until your program is running.

As a simple example, suppose you want the form's caption to display the date and time. You can't predict when someone is going to run your program — and you probably expect it to run more than once — so you need to let VBA figure out the current date and time for you. This simple sample does the trick:

```
Sub DisplayDateCaptionedForm ()
  DateCaptionedForm.Caption = Now
  DateCaptionedForm.Show
End Sub
```

Using a similar approach, you could have the form use a label or text box control to display information about whatever is currently selected in your VBA application. Figure 10-25 shows what you get by running the following VBA procedure in Visio, coupled with an appropriate form:

```
Sub DisplayShowSelectionForm()
  Dim intItemsAs Integer, strMessage As String
  intItems = ActiveWindow.Selection.Count
  strMessage = CStr(intItems) & " objects are selected."
  ShowSelectionForm.lblCountOfItems.Caption = strMessage
  ShowSelectionForm.Show
End Sub
```

Notice the line of sample code that alters the property of a label control in the target form:

```
ShowSelectionForm.lblCountOfItems.Caption = Message
```

Technically, you can't access a form's properties or methods until it has been loaded. You don't need to write an explicit statement to do so, however. VBA automatically loads the form into memory as soon as it encounters a statement that refers to one of the form's properties or methods. Referring to a property or method of one of the form's controls has the same effect.

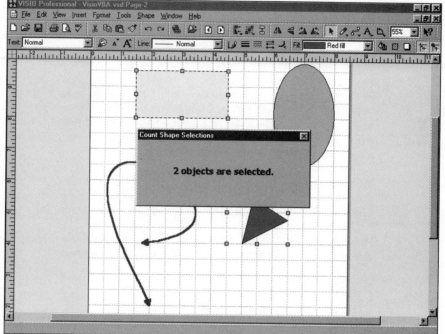

Figure 10-25:
This program figures out what to display in the label control just before you show the form.

Altering a form with the Initialize and Activate events

The example in the preceding section demonstrates one way to make changes in a form before displaying it — from within a standard procedure in a regular module. But there's more than one way to skin a cabbage. In this case, your alternatives are the form's own `Initialize` and `Activate` events. Code that you place in these event procedures runs automatically when the corresponding event occurs. Decide between the two events as follows:

✔ Use the `Initialize` event for code that should run only when VBA first loads the form.

✔ Use the `Activate` event for code that should run every time the form is displayed (including the first time).

For more about writing code for event procedures, see the section "The main events" later in this chapter.

Hiding a visible form

Use a form's `Hide` method to close the form so your program can return to the VBA application's document or activate another form. A statement such as the following does the trick:

```
FormErly.Hide
```

But you can't use the Hide method just anywhere in your program. If the form is modal, you must place the Hide method in an event procedure belonging to the form itself. As I discuss in the section "Modal versus modeless forms" earlier in this chapter, when a modal form is open, the only procedures that can run are those tied to the form.

And by the way, when you do use the Hide method in an event procedure belonging to the form you're hiding, you don't need to use the form's name. VBA is smart enough to know that the Hide method belongs to the form, so when placed within an event procedure belonging to any form, a simple Hide always works to hide that form.

Most often, the Hide statement belongs at the end of the Click event procedure for an OK, Cancel, or Close command button. For examples, see "Adding a Close or Cancel button" and "Programming the OK button" later in this chapter.

Hiding the form doesn't remove it from memory. You can redisplay the form at top speed any time you need it with the Show method.

Removing a form from memory

If you know that your program won't be needing a form again, destroy the form altogether and remove it from memory. In a small VBA program, you have no real need to do this, but when your program becomes large and memory is at a premium, unloading unneeded forms makes sense.

Just as when you load a form, you use a statement, not a method, to unload a form from memory, as in

```
Unload FormAtion
```

Unloading a form also removes it from the screen, if it was visible.

If you know that a form won't be needed again, you can substitute the Unload statement for the Hide method in the form's event procedures that close the form (see the previous section). In that situation, Unload Me is equivalent to Unload formname, since the Me keyword always represents the current form object.

Unlike the Hide method, however, Unload works with modal forms that aren't currently active on-screen. You can unload any form, including a previously hidden modal form via an Unload statement placed in the main part of your program — that is, in a procedure that isn't tied to a form.

The main events

When you activate a Sub procedure that doesn't display forms, your code has full control of what the program does and when it does it. Once a form is on-screen, though, your program enters a much more passive state, watchfully waiting for instructions from the user. As the user presses keys or moves or clicks the mouse, each such action generates a software event. In turn, your program registers each event, checking to see whether the form's code contains an event procedure tied to that event. If not, the event passes through your program without a trace. But if the form does have a corresponding event procedure, the program springs to life, faithfully running the procedure.

An event procedure can do anything that any ordinary procedure can. It can calculate variables, manipulate object properties and methods, and even load and display other forms. After the event procedure finishes running, control returns to the form. The program goes back to waiting for the next event to occur.

Common events

VBA forms and their controls are capable of detecting and recognizing a wide variety of events. (In VBA lingo, when you say that an object "has" events, you mean that the object can detect and recognize those events.) Forms and controls share many events, but each of these objects has a different set of events. Table 10-1 lists the most commonly useful events.

Table 10-1	Selected Events for Form and Control Objects	
Event(s)	*Objects It Applies to*	*When It Occurs*
Activate, Deactivate	Forms	Each time the form is activated (receives the focus) or deactivated (loses the focus)
AfterUpdate	All "action" controls except command buttons (not labels, pictures, frames, or multipage controls)	After VBA has registered a new value for the control, just before exiting the control to move to another one
Change	All action controls except command buttons; also mulitpage and tabstrip controls	When the Value property of the control changes
Click	Forms and all control types	When the user clicks the mouse over the object
DblClick	Forms and all control types	When the user double-clicks the mouse over the object
KeyUp, KeyDown, KeyPress	Forms and all control types	When the user presses or releases a key

Event procedures gotta have code

As Table 10-1 shows, a form or control *can* respond to many events. But when does a form actually respond to a specific event? Only if the form or control in question has an event procedure for that event. Event procedures have to come from somewhere — they come from you. Writing code for an event procedure is called *trapping* the event.

Writing and editing event procedures

Writing an event procedure is just like writing any other VBA code. You just have to know where to put the statements. Code for an event procedure — and any other code associated with a specific form — belongs in that form's Code window in the Visual Basic Editor. Therefore, event procedures for all the controls in the form, as well as for the form itself, go in the form's Code window. So before you start tapping out new statements, follow these three steps:

1. **Display the Code window for the form.**

   Double-clicking the form or control is the quickest way to do so. Alternatively, you can select the form and choose View⇨Code from the shortcut (right-click) menu for the form or control you want to work with. Pressing F7 also works when the form is selected in its UserForm window.

2. **In the Code window, select the object for which you're writing the event procedure.**

   Choose the object from the Object drop-down list in the top-left corner of the form's Code window (see Figure 10-26).

3. **Select the event for which you want to write code.**

   This time, use the Procedure drop-down list in the top-right corner of the Code window.

Figure 10-26:
Selecting a
control in a
form's Code
window in
preparation
for writing
an event
procedure.

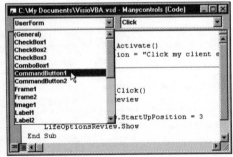

As soon as you choose an event from the Procedure drop-down list, VBA whisks you directly to the event procedure for that event in the Code window. If no code has been written for this event procedure, VBA creates a new procedure skeleton for you, courteously placing the insertion point on a blank line between the opening procedure declaration and the closing statement (see Figure 10-27). If the event procedure already contains code, VBA simply places the insertion point in the top line of the existing code.

Figure 10-27:
A brand-
new event
procedure
skeleton in
the Visual
Basic Editor.

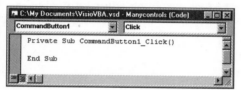

```
C:\My Documents\VisioVBA.vsd - Manycontrols (Code)
CommandButton1                Click

    Private Sub CommandButton1_Click()

    End Sub
```

Event-procedure declarations

You don't have to worry about declaring an event procedure yourself. That's because VBA creates the procedure declaration for you when you select the event in the form's Code window.

As Figure 10-27 shows, the basic syntax for an event procedure is exactly the same as for ordinary Sub procedures that you write in VBA modules. The only thing unique about an event procedure is its name. The name consists of the name of the object (the form or control), followed by an underscore character and the official VBA name for the event. Observe these examples through heavy lenses:

```
Private Sub cmdCalculateSquareRoot_Click()
End Sub

Private Sub UserForm_Activate()
End Sub

Private Sub sclVolumeControl_Change()
End Sub
```

When to change an event procedure's name

The one time you can get into trouble with an event-procedure name is when you change the name of the associated object after you create the event procedure. VBA doesn't change the name of the procedure automatically, so you must go back to the Code window and modify the event procedure name to match the control's new name.

Suppose you've written an event procedure for the `Click` event of a button that VBA automatically named `CommandButton1`. At this point, the procedure name is `CommandButton1_Click`. Now you belatedly give the button a more descriptive name, such as `cmdTakeOutTheTrash`. Unless and until you change the name of the original event procedure to `cmdTakeOutTheTrash_Click`, the button just sits there, mute and unresponsive, when the form runs, no matter how many times you click it.

Because VBA doesn't remove the procedure when you change the button's name, you only have to rename the procedure, not retype it from scratch. Alternatively, you can start a new event procedure for the button, and use the Cut and Paste commands to move the code from the original procedure to the new one.

Click here . . .

In Windows, the `Click` is the quintessential event. You click icons to select them; text documents to position the insertion point; menus to open them; and buttons to trigger them, activating whatever function they perform. Because clicking is so integral an activity in the Windows user interface, you definitely want your VBA forms to respond to mouse clicks. For most types of controls, however, you don't have to write any code to make them do tricks when clicked (I explain why in "When not to write event procedures"). Of course, you *do* have to write code for the most important control of all, the command button.

Every command-button control definitely must have a `Click` event procedure — if you want the button to do anything when someone clicks it. The following event procedure simply counts and displays the number of times the user clicks the button:

```
Private Sub cmdCountClicks_Click()
' Declaring the intCount variable as Static preserves
' its value between calls to the procedure
Static intCount As Integer
intCount = intCount + 1
cmdCountClicks.Caption = "You clicked this button " _
  & intCount & " times."
End Sub
```

This code is fairly straightforward. Each time the event procedure runs — which should occur only when the user clicks the button — the value of the `intCount` variable increases by 1. This value is then used in a string that sets the button's `Caption` property. By the way, declaring the `intCount` variable as `Static` tells VBA to retain the variable's value between passes through the event procedure. If you declared `intCount` with a `Dim` statement, VBA would reinitialize the variable to each time. Here's an event procedure for a button named `cmdMoveThisForm`:

```
Private Sub cmdMoveThisForm_Click()
Move(Left -24), (Top -24)
End Sub
```

In case you're curious, whenever the user clicks the button, this event procedure moves the entire form 24 units up and 24 units to the left. In the procedure's one line of action code, the Move method appears without an object reference; VBA assumes that it refers to the main object of the form, the form itself. If you wanted to move the button instead of the form, you would have used cmdMoveThisForm.Move to specify it as the target object. In the same way, Left and Top are assumed to be properties of the form because no explicit object reference was given.

These two examples are fairly trivial; still, they illustrate the fact that event procedure code looks and acts like any other code.

When not to write Click event procedures

Most VBA controls that you can place in a form have (that is, *recognize*) the Click event. Except in the case of command buttons, however, it's usually neither necessary nor wise to write event-procedure code for the Click event — even when you want the control to respond to mouse clicks. The reason: These controls respond to clicks automatically and in the way that you want them to.

Suppose you place some option buttons in a VBA form. When you run the form, clicking a button selects the one that you clicked; no programming is required to make this happen. In like fashion, VBA handles clicks of a toggle button or check box automatically. VBA knows to alternate the control between its two possible states (out or pushed in for toggle buttons, cleared or checked for check boxes). For its part, a text-box control automatically responds to clicks by positioning the insertion point at the spot where you click.

What VBA can't do — and what you have to do by writing code — is transfer the setting of the control to your program. What text did the user type in the text box? Is the check box checked or cleared? Which option button in the group is selected? Your program won't know unless you write code to collect and use this information.

The key is the control's Value property, which contains the current setting for any control that can assume different states or hold data. You can read the Value property each time it changes by writing an event procedure for the Change event. Alternatively, you can simply read the Value property after you hide the form. See the section "Writing code for the Change event" as well as "Handling common form programming tasks" for more information on these techniques.

Click events in UserForms

Even forms themselves have `Click` events. In practice, of course, most forms are mainly just backdrops on which you place the buttons, text boxes, and other controls with which the user interacts. But if you want it to, an entire form can act as one big button so that clicking it anywhere makes something happen in your program.

Just type the code for the actions you want carried out, inserting it into the `Click` event for the form, as in:

```
Private Sub UserForm_Click()
...(event code goes here)
End Sub
```

Notice that the names of all event procedures for a form as a whole start with `UserForm`, no matter what name you've given to the form. If you do write a `Click` event procedure for a form, be aware that VBA triggers the procedure only if the user clicks the part of the form that isn't covered by any controls. Other mouse-related event procedures work similarly.

Writing code for the Change event

For controls such as scroll bars, spin buttons, option buttons, check boxes, and toggle buttons, `Change` is the main event. These controls do respond to mouse clicks and key presses, but they do so automatically. VBA and Windows handle the dirty details of changing a control's appearance and adjusting its setting according to which key presses or mouse actions occurred.

You may want your program to respond not to the mouse click itself, however, but to the setting change that it caused. In that case, you should write code for the `Change` event. The `Change` event occurs whenever a change occurs in the value of the control (that is, when the control's `Value` property changes). It doesn't matter whether this change results directly from the user's mouse click or typing, or whether it occurs because some other procedure manipulates the control's `Value` property in code statements.

You may also want your program to respond to changes in a control's value when the user finishes working with the control. In this case, write code for the control's `AfterUpdate` event, which is triggered when the focus moves to another control.

An event procedure can do more with a control's new value than just display it, of course. It can also

✔ Check to see whether the value meets certain criteria

✔ Make calculations based on the value, taking other actions depending on the calculated results

✔ Use the control's value to manipulate some other setting, such as the volume of your computer's speaker

Handling common form programming tasks

Once you understand how event procedures work, you can put your knowledge to work in building dialog boxes that work the way you want them to — and the way users expect them to. In this section, I've collected a set of tips covering many of the common scenarios in dialog box construction.

Adding a Close or Cancel button

At a minimum, most dialog boxes have one all-important command button: the one that removes the dialog box from the screen. Depending on the way the rest of the dialog box works, this button is typically captioned Close or Cancel, but captions such as Exit, Finish, All Done, or Give Up would also be appropriate. Every form you make needs such a button.

By convention, both Close and Cancel buttons simply hide or unload the form, without doing much else. Here's how to tell which of them your form should have:

✔ Use a Close button for a form that just displays information or performs tasks immediately, without changing program settings or modifying variables that will be used later in the program.

✔ Use a Cancel button on a form that does change variables or program settings. When the user clicks the Cancel button, the dialog box closes without recording those changes — everything stays the way it was before the dialog box appeared. The form should also have an OK button that confirms any changes that are made.

Easy event procedures for Close and Cancel buttons

Like any other command button, a Close or Cancel button needs a `Click` event procedure to do its job in response to a mouse click. In most situations, this event procedure requires only a single statement, as in these two examples:

```
Private Sub cmdClose_Click()
 Hide ' Object reference to current form implied
End Sub

Private Sub cmdCancel_Click()
 Unload frmOptions
End Sub
```

Either type of button can use either the `Hide` method or the `Unload` statement. To read about the differences between these two ways to close a form, see the "Hiding a visible form" and "Removing a form from memory" sections earlier in this chapter.

Of course, event procedures tied to Close or Cancel buttons can do other tasks before closing the form. One simple example would be a statement displaying a message box asking if the user really wants to close (or cancel) the dialog box:

```
Private Sub cmdCancel_Click()
 Message = "Do you really want to close the " _
 & "dialog box and cancel all the changes " _
 & "you've made?"
 If MsgBox(Message, vbYesNo) = vbYes Then
 Hide ' Hide only if the user clicked Yes
 End If ' Otherwise do nothing
End Sub
```

The keyboard alternative

Remember to tie the Close or Cancel button to the Esc key. People are used to pressing Esc to back out of a dialog box, and you shouldn't disappoint them. You don't need to add a `KeyPress` event procedure — simply setting the button's `Cancel` property to `True` in the Property window does the trick.

Programming the OK button

Imagine you're staring at a typical dialog box. When you click the OK button, you expect the program to accept the current entries in the box as final, making the specified changes in the program's appearance, behavior, or data. The form should then remove itself from the screen.

Gratify these expectations by writing a `Click` event procedure for the OK button. All the code has to do is transfer values from the form's controls to variables in your program, or use the controls' values in conditional statements. The final line in the procedure should be the form's `Hide` method or an `Unload` statement. In the following examples, `txtCName` and `txtCAddress` are text boxes. The first two statements transfer their contents to corresponding program variables. Next, the program checks the status of the `tglSend` toggle button and, if it's on, runs a procedure called `SendBillToCustomer`. Finally, it hides the `Form`.

```
Private Sub cmdOK_Click()
 strCustomerName = txtCName.Value
 strCustomerAddress = txtCAddress.Value
 'check toggle button status
 If tglSend.Value = True Then
 SendBillToCustomer
 End If
 Hide
End Sub
```

Validating Entries

One of the most common tasks performed in event procedures is validation of entries that the user makes by using a control. Often, a program can only accept certain values. However, the user is free to type any text in a text or combo box, and to pick almost any number via a slider or spinner.

The solution is to add validation code to an event procedure for the control. The code looks at the user's entry, evaluating it to see whether it meets your criteria. If so, the code can store the value or pass it along to another part of your program. If not, you can display a message box or another form informing the user of the problem (see Figure 10-28). Alternatively, the code might convert the entry into an acceptable one — say, by capitalizing the lowercase letters.

Figure 10-28: I used a Change event procedure to check the entry in the text box and display this error message to the user.

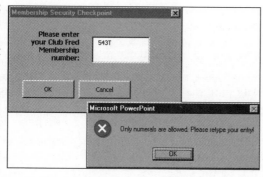

Code for validation routines

Validating the value of a control requires you to write If...Then statements, Select Case statements, or both. This simple example checks a spin button for an unacceptable value:

```
Private Sub spnVolumeControl_Change
  If spnVolumeControl.Value = 13 Then
  MsgBox "13 is not an acceptable setting."
  End If
End Sub
```

Events you can use to validate user entries

Performing validation at any of four points in the cycle of user and form inter-actions can make sense. Each of these validation points corresponds to a dif-ferent event procedure on the current control or the form as a whole, as shown here:

When Validation Takes Place	Event Procedure to Use
Each time a key is pressed	KeyPress event for the control (to evaluate the one key just pressed)
Each time the value of the control changes	Change event (to evaluate the entire value)
When the user finishes working with the control but before moving to another	BeforeUpdate (allows the update to be cancelled, returning the user to the control)
When the user closes the form	Click event for the form's OK or Close button

How to choose a validation event

It's up to you to decide which event procedure to write for validating user entries, based on such factors as:

- ✔ Whether the validation code runs quickly or slowly
- ✔ Whether you want to hassle users at the moment that they create an invalid value or wait until they finish the entry before checking it
- ✔ Whether you base the validation on entries in more than one control

In the simple case in which you want to validate the entire value of a control each time it changes, use a Change event procedure. I discuss the alterna-tives in Bonus Chapter C on the CD.

Part III
Stretching Out

In this part . . .

After you're comfortable with the basics of VBA programming and want to stretch your wings a little, come to Part III. Chapter 11 takes you on a tour through the built-in functions and statements VBA provides — I don't recommend reinventing the can opener, nor should you write a custom procedure when a built-in function or statement can do the job in a single line. Chapter 12 provides a survey of the techniques you need for working with software objects in VBA. In Chapter 13, you find me returning to the subject of data management — but this time to cover advanced storage receptacles, such as arrays and collections.

Chapter 11

Built-in VBA Commands

*B*efore you get rolling on writing your own procedures from scratch, be sure that you're not reinventing the wheel. Out of the box, every version of VBA comes equipped with a little arsenal of built-in commands that can blast through many common tasks. This chapter surveys scads of these ready-made weapons.

Finding Built-In Commands

VBA seems to have a bit of a conflict about its self-image. Oh, how desperately it wants to be seen as a truly *object-oriented* language (I discuss object-oriented languages in Chapter 12). On the other hand, it realizes that some things you may want to do with your program don't fit so naturally into the object-oriented mold.

In a solution worthy of our elected representatives, VBA has shoehorned at least one naturally independent command into an object method, whereas it leaves other actions that seem appropriate for objectifying free, to be used on their own.

Keeping in mind, then, that an action may fall into an unexpected category, you get three types of VBA built-in commands that do useful work.

✔ **Statements.** Although the term *statement* usually encompasses a complete programming directive (see Chapter 7), VBA also refers to individual keywords for specific chores as statements. Some of these statement keywords function as complete statements in themselves. For example, the statement Beep sounds the computer speaker. (Don't go overboard with that one — it may well drive you insane.) Other statement keywords must be used as part of a complete statement. For example, the ChDir (change directory) statement is useless unless you include with it an argument specifying the directory, or folder, to which you want to change:

```
ChDir("\Documents about Dreams")
```

✔ **Functions.** Built-in functions act just like the Function procedures I describe in Chapter 7 — that is, they return a value. Often, you use a function by assigning its value to a variable, as in this example with the Tan (tangent) function:

```
dblTangent = Tan(dblAnyOldAngle)
```

Functions also provide values in more complex expressions or in conditional statements, such as

```
If Tan (dblAcuteAngle) < 45 Then
```

✔ **Methods of built-in objects.** The curious one in this group is the Print method, the Debug object's only one. You use it to direct output to the Immediate window in the Visual Basic Editor, with a statement such as

```
Debug.Print(strMessageFromMars)
```

Although I don't see what benefits come from associating the Print command with an object, this method does perform a very useful role. I cover it further in Chapter 14. Note that although VBA itself does not encapsulate files as objects, you can use a software add-on to manage files and work with their contents using object-oriented techniques (see Chapter 12).

Table 11-1 lists examples of built-in VBA commands drawn from all three categories (statements, functions, and methods). The rest of this chapter explores some of the most generally useful of the built-in commands.

Table 11-1	Examples of Built-In Functions, Statements, and Methods	
Command	*Type*	*What It Does*
Randomize	Statement	Initializes the random number generator
Sqr (number)	Function	Returns the square root of number
Format (string)	Function	Formats string according to your specifications
Date	Statement	Sets the system date
Date	Function	Returns the current system date
Err.Raise	Method of Err object	Generates a run-time error by ID number

Formatting Data

Use the VBA Format function (and its four close relatives FormatNumber, FormatDateTime, FormatCurrency, and FormatPercent) to format any of the built-in data types for display or print purposes according to a pattern you specify. Via these functions, you can easily output a date variable — which VBA actually stores as an unintelligible number — as a short date (12/19/99), as a medium date (19-Dec-99), as a long date (Sunday, December 19, 1999), or in any of several other prefab date and time formats. You can perform similar tricks with numeric values and strings. Format and its cousins convert the values you feed it into new strings, adding any characters necessary to produce the results you want.

Working with the Format function

The original Format function, available in both VBA 5 and VBA 6, is the most versatile. It can handle just about any type of data, and its output is customizable — if none of its 15 or so available prefab formats produces the results you want, you can create your own formats at will.

In simplified form, the syntax for the `Format` function is as follows. The syntax shown here omits two optional and little-used arguments, both related to dates — you can read about them in the Help file:

```
Format(expression,"format")
```

The `expression` argument should contain an expression whose value is the number, date, or string value you want to format (that is, output in a different form). This argument is required, of course.

The `format` argument is the one that does the real work, specifying the way the `expression` data should now appear. This argument must be a string, and as the following example shows, you must surround this string in quotes.

To use the `Format` function, assign it to a variable or to the `Value` or `Caption` property of a control on a UserForm. For example, the statement

```
lblDateMessage.Caption = "The date is " & _
    Format(Now, "Long date")
```

displays the text "The date is Tuesday, March 19, 2002" as the caption of a label control called `lblDateMessage` (assuming that today is Tuesday, March 19, 2002). In this example statement, the `Now` function provides the raw data for the `expression` argument, while the string `"Long date"` that serves as the `format` argument specifies one of the prefab formats discussed in the next section.

Using prefab formats with the Format function

Table 11-2 lists the named, built-in formats available for use with the `Format` function for various VBA data types. You save time if you can find a prefab format that produces the output you want, compared to constructing a custom format yourself. Just plug the appropriate string from the first column of the table into the function as its `format` argument. Remember to enclose the item you select in quotation marks.

I know, it's confusing that I use the same term — format — in three different ways: as the name of a function (the `Format` function); as an argument in the function's argument list (the `format` argument); and, more generally, to mean the ultimate appearance of displayed text with which you're working. If you hit a snag, don't feel bad — just come back here to refresh your memory on the distinctions between these three usages.

Table 11-2	**Named Formats for Use with the Format Function**	
Format Name	*Description of Output*	*Example (Assumes U.S. Settings in Control Panel)*
Numeric		
General Number	Number with no thousand separators	2001.5599
Currency	Number with thousand separators and with two digits to the right of the decimal separator, with currency symbol	$2,001.56
Fixed	At least one digit to the left and exactly two digits to the right of the decimal separator (no thousands separators)	3390.10
Standard	Number with thousand separators, at least one digit to the left and two digits to the right of the decimal separator	1,323.455
Percent	Number multiplied by 100 with two digits to the right of the decimal separator and a percent sign (%) at the right	12.54 %
Scientific	Number in standard scientific notation	1.23E+02
Boolean		
Yes/No	"No" if the value is 0, "Yes" otherwise	Yes
True/False	"False" if the value is 0, "True" otherwise	True
On/Off	"Off" if the value is 0, "On" otherwise	On
Date/Time		
General Date	The date and/or time, formatted as specified in the Control Panel	3/19/02 5:27:45 PM
Long Date	The date formatted according to the Control Panel setting for the long date format	Tuesday, March 19, 2002

(continued)

Table 11-2 *(continued)*

Format Name	Description of Output	Example (Assumes U.S. Settings in Control Panel)
Date/Time		
Medium Date	The date formatted according to the Control Panel setting for the medium date format	19-Mar-02
Short Date	The date formatted according to the Control Panel setting for the short date format	3/19/02
Long Time	The time, including hours, minutes, and seconds, formatted according to the Control Panel setting for the long time format	5:27:45 PM
Medium Time	The time, including hours and minutes, in a 12-hour format with the AM/PM designator	05:27 PM
Short Time	The time, including hours and minutes, in the 24-hour format	17:27

Specifying custom formats

You can create your own custom format by assembling it from a variety of characters that have special meaning as part of the `format` argument. For example, you can use the `Format` function to display strings of text in all upper- or lowercase letters by specifying a `format` argument of `">"` or `"<"`, respectively. I don't have space to list and describe all these special characters — you can find them by looking up the `Format` function in the VBA Help index, clicking See Also, and then looking for User-defined Formats. So as not to leave you completely unsatisfied, the following example shows a couple of custom date formats in action. Plus, it gives me a chance to illustrate another built-in VBA function called `IIf`.

```
MsgBox = "The time is " & Format(Now, _
"h:nn") & ". It's " & IIf(Format(Now, "a/p") = "a", _
"before", "after") & " noon."
```

If it's before noon when you run this code, the statement displays a string such as "The time is 9:07. It's before noon." After noon, you get instead something like the message shown in Figure 11-1, which is the time message produced by the previous example statement. (By the way, I cover the `MsgBox` function in detail in the section "Displaying message boxes" later in this chapter.)

Figure 11-1:
The text in
this
message
box came
from the
expression
shown in
the text.

Now for some explanation. In the first Format function in the example code, the format argument is "h:nn". The h outputs the hour, displayed in military time without a leading zero. After the colon, nn outputs the minute *with* a leading zero for times less than 10 minutes past the hour.

The second time Format is used, it's nested within the IIf function. Here, because "a/p" is the format argument, the function's result is simply "a" or "p" depending on whether the time is before or after 12 noon. Normally, you would use a/p as one component of a longer format argument. In this case, though, no one ever sees the result of the function. Instead, the IIf function uses the result.

Using the IIf function

IIf is a miniature version of an If...Then statement (which I cover in full in Chapter 8). The syntax goes like this:

```
IIf (expression, resultiftrue, resultiffalse)
```

In English, this function works like this: If expression is true, the function's return value is resultiftrue; if, however, expression is false, resultiffalse is the function's return value.

In the previous example, the expression to be evaluated is

```
Format(Now, "a/p") = "a"
```

So here, if the Format function returns a value of a, then this expression is True. If it returns any other value, including p, then the expression is False. VBA in turn determines the result of the IIf function based on whether the expression is True or False. If True, the IIf function returns morning; if False, it returns afternoon instead.

Working with other formatting functions

VBA 6 offers four `Format`-like functions designed for more specific tasks: `FormatNumber`, `FormatDateTime`, `FormatCurrency`, and `FormatPercent`. Like their parent, each of these `Format` offspring returns a string containing the formatted version of an original value. Because they give the results you probably want by default, they can be easier to use than `Format` itself. In brief, they work as follows:

- ✔ `FormatNumber (number, NumDigitsAfterDecimal, IncludeLeadingDigit, UseParensForNegativeNumbers, GroupDigits)`: Returns the original value — the only required argument — as a formatted string. If you omit the optional arguments, `FormatNumber` formats `number` using the defaults specified on the Number tab of the Regional Settings applet in the Windows Control Panel. Assuming your system is set to English (U.S.), you get numbers such as 132,328.55. The `FormatNumber` optional arguments let you override the defaults for the number of decimal places, whether a zero appears to the left of the decimal point for fractional values, whether negative numbers appear in parentheses, and whether groups of digits are separated (for example, with commas).

- ✔ `FormatDateTime(date, format)`: Converts a VBA date value into a formatted string. If you don't supply a `format` argument, the string is formatted according to the system settings for short date and long time on the Date tab of the Control Panel's Regional Settings applet. The `format` argument is a number (not a string as in the `Format` function), but you can specify it using named constants such as `vbLongDate` or `vbShortTime`.

- ✔ `FormatCurrency(number)`: Returns `number` formatted as currency according to your Control Panel settings. Otherwise, `FormatCurrency` works just like `FormatNumber`, and takes the same optional arguments.

- ✔ `FormatPercent(number)`: Multiplies `number` by 100 and adds a percent sign (.05 becomes 5.00%). `FormatPercent` takes the same optional arguments as `FormatNumber`. To drop the digits after the decimal point, use 0 as the `NumDigitsAfterDecimal` argument, as in `FormatNumber (.05,0)`.

Converting Data

As I take pains to point out in Chapter 7, VBA automatically converts between different data types on the fly. The automatic conversions sure are convenient, and the results are usually exactly what you intended. The stress should be on the word *usually,* however.

When the automated conversions leave you unsatisfied, VBA stands ready with a raft of explicit functions for converting data types. Use them to

✔ Ensure that VBA performs the correct conversion.

✔ Perform conversions that VBA doesn't do automatically.

✔ Make your code self-explanatory (okay, *self-documenting*, if you want to sound like a Real Programmer).

The workhorse data conversion commands are a group of functions I refer to as the *C-type* functions. That's C for *convert*, not for the C programming language. VBA has one of these functions for every built-in data type aside from objects — CBool, CByte, CCur, and so on. For example, after execution of the statement boolMaybe = CBool(123), the boolMaybe variable contains the value True (any non-zero number has an existence, I guess, so that makes them all True).

Just realize that, aside from making the type of conversion explicit, these functions don't do anything that VBA automatic conversions can't. (See Chapter 7 for specifics on the CDec function.)

The Fix and Int functions strip off the fractional part of any number you send them, returning a whole number. Unlike the CInt and CLng functions, they don't perform proper rounding — Int (4.989) returns 4, not 5.

These two functions differ only when you use them on negative numbers. With them, Int returns one integer less than the argument value, whereas Fix removes the decimal part of the argument. Int (-9.2) returns –10, for instance.

Working with hex and octal values

The Hex and Oct functions convert standard, base-10 whole number values into strings containing their hexadecimal or octal equivalents. You can't convert in the other direction in your code, but you *can* type in hex or octal literal values, letting the Visual Basic Editor convert them into decimal numbers automatically. The trick is to precede each hex or octal literal with a special code: &H for hex, &O (that's the letter O, not the number 0) for octal. After execution of the statement intBases = 10 + &O12 +&HA, the value of intBases is 30, just as it should be.

Converting between numbers and strings

Several VBA functions convert between numbers and strings. These include:

✔ CStr: CStr turns any non-object data you feed it, including numeric values, into the corresponding string. It adjusts its output according to the number (and date) display formats specified in the Regional Settings applet in the Control Panel. For example, in France, CStr(200.02) gives the string "200,02" as its output. Note that although the output *string* varies according to the regional setting, you must always enter actual numeric values using the format that prevails in the United States.

✔ Str: Converts a number into a string, but it always formats the string according to the U.S. custom, with a period as the decimal separator.

✔ C-type functions for numeric data types: These convert a string to the corresponding numeric value, but only when they recognize all the characters as legitimate within numbers. Again, this determination depends on the Control Panel settings. In France, CDbl ("200 ,02F") gives a result of 200.02; in the U.S., the same statement produces an error, but CDbl ("$200.02") works fine.

✔ Val: Converts the numerals in a string into a numeric value, stopping when it runs into a character that it doesn't recognize as numeric. Regardless of your Control Panel settings, the only characters it recognizes are numerals and the decimal point (period). It ignores spaces, tabs, and line breaks, however. The expression Val("28 190.43 12 by 14") gives 28190.4312 as its result.

✔ Chr: Converts a numeric ANSI value into the corresponding character. Use this function to place characters you can't type in your strings.

✔ Asc: More or less the converse of Chr, this function returns the numeric code of the first character in a string.

Con Text

VBA offers a rich collection of statements and functions for formatting text strings and extracting portions of them that you may find especially mesmerizing. In Table 11-3, I list all the string-related commands I could find.

Table 11-3	String-Related Statements and Functions	
Remember that literal string values (as opposed to variables containing strings) must be enclosed in quotation marks.		
Statement or Function	*Type*	*What It Does (for Statements) or Value It Returns (for Functions)*
Asc(string)	Function	Character code of first character in string
Chr(charactercode)	Function	Character corresponding to charactercode

Statement or Function	Type	What It Does (for Statements) or Value It Returns (for Functions)
Filter(sourcearray, match, include, compare)	Function (VBA 6 only)	An array containing only those strings in sourcearray that contain match as any part of the string. Sourcearray must be an array of string values. If the optional include argument is False, the function returns only those strings that *don't* contain match.
Format(string)	Function	See "Formatting Data" earlier in this chapter
Hex(number)	Function	A string containing a hexadecimal representation of number.
InStr (start, string1, string2)	Function	A number specifying the position of string2 within string1; the search begins at position start, which is an optional argument
InStrRev(string1, string2, start)	Function (VBA 6 only)	A number specifying the position of string2 within string1, counting from the right side of string1; the search begins at position start, an optional argument.
Join(stringarray, delimiter)	Function (VBA 6 only)	One string that combines all the strings in stringarray, which must be an array of string data. By default, Join adds a space between each of the original strings, but you can specify a different delimiter character (surround a literal character in quotes).
Left (string, length)	Function	A string containing length number of characters taken from the left side of string
Len (string)	Function	The number of characters in string
LCase (string)	Function	A copy of string with all its characters converted to lowercase

(continued)

Table 11-3 *(continued)*

Statement or Function	Type	What It Does (for Statements) or Value It Returns (for Functions)
`LSet stringvariable = string`	Statement	Assigns string to `stringvariable` without changing `stringvariable`'s length; aligns string on the left of `stringvariable`
`LTrim(string)`	Function	A new string containing a copy of `string` without any leading spaces
`Mid(string, start, length)`	Function	A new string containing `length` number of characters from string, beginning with the character at position `start`
`Mid(stringvariable, start, length) = string`	Statement	Replaces `length` number of characters in `stringvariable` with characters from `string`
`Oct(number)`	Function	A string containing the octal (base 8) value of `number`
`Replace(string, replace, start, count, compare)`	Function (VBA 6 only)	A new string. Replaces `find`, `find` text with `replace` text within `string`. The arguments `start`, `count`, and `compare` are optional. Use `start` to specify the position where the search begins. Use `count` to specify how many times the `replace` operation is performed, assuming `find` text occurs more than once (by default, all occurrences of `find` get replaced).
`Right(string, length)`	Function	A string containing `length` number of characters from string, reading from the right side
`RSet stringvariable = string`	Statement	Assigns `string` to `string variable` without changing the length of `stringvariable`; aligns `string` on the right of `stringvariable`

Statement or Function	Type	What It Does (for Statements) or Value It Returns (for Functions)
RTrim(string)	Function	A new `string` containing a copy of `string` from which trailing spaces have been stripped
Space(number)	Function	A string containing the specified `number` of spaces
Split (string, delimiter, limit, compare)	Function (VBA 6 only)	An array of strings. This function breaks up the `string` argument into separate, individual strings. By default, it divides the original `string` at spaces, but you can specify a `delimiter` other than the space character (use quotation marks to specify a literal character as the delimiter). The optional `limit` argument specifies the maximum number of strings to return in the array.
StrComp(string1, string2)	Function	0 if the two strings are equal, –1 if `string1` is less than `string2`, 1 if `string1` is greater than `string2` — see Chapter 9 for information on string comparisons
StrConv (string, conversionmethod)	Function	A new string based on `string`, prepared using the specified conversion method
String (number, character)	Function	A string of specified length (`number`) containing a repeating sequence of `character`
StrReverse(string)	Function (VBA 6 only)	A string containing the characters of the `string` argument in reverse
Trim (string)	Function	A new string containing a copy of `string` from which leading and trailing spaces have been stripped
UCase (string)	Function	A copy of `string` with all characters converted to uppercase

Don't be disappointed if you don't find a string function that does exactly what you want. Instead, think of them as building blocks — they often need to be nested to give you the final results you want.

For example, suppose that you have a list of full names stored as strings in this form:

```
"Guess, Helen Ms."
"Tran, Linda Dr."
"Wish, Ferd Mr."
```

The next two sections discuss examples of operations you might want to perform on such a list of names. (By the way, such a list should be stored as an array of strings. I cover arrays in Chapter 13).

Removing characters at the end of a string with Len and Left

Suppose that someone has given you the job of removing the titles at the end of each string. Each name in the list is a different length, so a set formula won't help. However, if the string variable strName contains the original name, the following statement would do the trick:

```
strNoTitle = Left(strName, Len(strName) - 4)
```

If VBA read books instead of code, I could tell it to accomplish the same action by following these steps:

1. **Call the** Len **function to calculate the total length of the original string.**

2. **Subtract 4 from the result of Step 1.**

   Because a total of four characters is taken up by the title at the end of the string (including the space), this action gives the length that the new string should be.

3. **Call the** Left **function, using this calculated new length as the second argument.**

   Left reads the number of characters specified by the second argument, from the string named in the first argument, returning only those characters.

4. **Assign the new, shorter string returned by** Left **to the** strNew **variable.**

Extracting characters from within a string

Working with your new list of names without titles, suppose that you are now asked to extract the first names and place them into a new list. You can accomplish your task with this statement:

```
str1stName = Mid(strNoTitle, InStr(strNoTitle, ",") + 2)
```

The Mid function extracts characters from anywhere in the string that you enter as its first argument. Its second argument tells Mid where in that string to start extracting characters. Here, this argument is an expression consisting of the InStr function plus 2.

For its part, InStr hunts in the specified string (the first argument) for another string (the second argument). In this case, the second argument is that comma that comes after the last name in your list. The value InStr returns is the position number in the first string at which it finds the second string — now you know where the last name ends.

You add 2 to the InStr value to bypass the comma and the space, locating the first character in the first name. Mid extracts the rest of the characters in the string as its result, unless you specify a third (optional) length argument.

Using character codes in string expressions

Suppose that you want to include nicknames — enclosed in quotation marks to indicate that they're aliases — in your list of names. Starting with the original list, you would end up with a new list of strings that looks something like this:

```
"Guess, Helen Ms. ("Scarlet")"
"Tran, Linda Dr. ("Roseola")"
"Wish, Ferd Mr. ("Jocko")"
```

The problem is, you can't enter the quotation marks directly. When you type a quotation mark in your code, VBA interprets it as indicating the beginning or end of a string. Instead, use the VBA Chr function to place quotation marks — and other characters you can't type, or that VBA won't accept — in your strings.

Chr converts a numeric ANSI character code value to the corresponding text character. To place a quotation mark into a string, for example, you use the expression Chr(34), because 34 is the ANSI code for the quotation mark character. After the following code runs, the strName variable contains the string Wish, Ferd Mr. ("Jocko"):

```
strName = "Wish, Ferd Mr. (" & Chr(34) _
    & "Jocko" & Chr(34) & ")"
```

Note that 34 is the code for the typewriter-style quotation mark character. For "curly" quote marks (like the ones around "curly") you need codes 147 and 148 (for left and right curly quote marks, respectively). You can find a complete table of character codes in the main VBA Help system under Visual Basic Language Reference➪Miscellaneous.

VBA also includes named constants for a few non-typeable (and non-visible) "characters" that give you rudimentary control over the format of your strings. The most important of these are as follows:

Constant	Use
vbTab	Aligns text that follows at next tab stop
vbCrLf	Starts a new line

Concatenate these character constants into your strings to achieve the formatting you want. Running the following code gives a string that displays a four-line verse:

```
strQ = "Roses are red" & vbCrLf & "Violets are blue" _
    & vbCrLf & "Sugar is sweet" & vbCrLf "And so are you"
```

Working with Dates and Times

In real-world programming, working with dates and times often assumes a major role. VBA cushions the ride with a panoply of statements and functions for finding out what day or time it is now, making date-related calculations, and extracting from a date variable the component of interest, be it the year, the day of the week, or the hour.

Table 11-4 lists these commands in summary form. I simplified some functions in the table by omitting optional arguments — you can get the dirty details in the VBA Help file. Following the table, a few of the most important date- and time-related commands receive more detailed attention.

To make use of this material, you need a working understanding of how VBA handles date and time data and how date variables work. All that occurs in Chapter 7.

Table 11-4	Date- and Time-Related Statements and Functions	
Remember to enclose literal date values used as arguments within # characters (number signs) and string arguments such as date intervals inside quotation marks.		
Name	**Type**	**What It Does (for Statements) or Value It Returns (for Functions)**
Date	Function	The current system date
Date(datevalue)	Statement	Sets the system date to date-value

Name	Type	What It Does (for Statements) or Value It Returns (for Functions)
DateAdd(interval, number, datevalue)	Function	A new date value equal to date value plus number of the time or date periods represented by interval
DateDiff(interval, date1, date2)	Function	The number of the date or time periods represented by interval between date1 and date2
DatePart(interval, date)	Function	An integer representing the speci fied interval of date
DateSerial(year, month, day)	Function	The date specified by year, month, and day, which must be numeric expressions
DateValue (datestring)	Function	A date value corresponding to datestring
Day(date)	Function	An integer corresponding to the day of the month represented by date
Hour(time)	Function	An integer between 0 and 23, inclusive, representing the hour of the day corresponding to the spec- ified time
Minute(time)	Function	An integer between 0 and 59, inclusive, representing the minute corresponding to the specified time
Month(date)	Function	An integer between 1 and 12, inclusive, representing the month corresponding to the specified date
MonthName(month, abbreviate)	Function (VBA 6 only)	A string containing the name of the month corresponding to the month argument, which must be an integer between 1 and 12. If the optional abbreviate argument is True, the returned string is an abbreviation of the month's name.
Now	Function	A date value representing the cur- rent system date and time

(continued)

Table 11-4 *(continued)*

Name	Type	What It Does (for Statements) or Value It Returns (for Functions)
`Second(time)`	Function	A whole number between 0 and 59, inclusive, representing the second corresponding to the specified `time`
`Time`	Function	A date value representing the current system time
`Time`	Statement	Sets the system time to `timevalue`
`Timer(timevalue)`	Function	The number of seconds since midnight
`TimeSerial(hour, minute, second)`	Function	A date value containing the time specified by `hour`, `minute`, and `second`
`TimeValue (timestring)`	Function	A date value containing the time corresponding to `timestring` (any date information in the string is discarded)
`Weekday (date)`	Function	A whole number representing the day of the week corresponding to `date`
`WeekdayName (weekday, abbreviate, firstdayofweek)`	Function (VBA 6 only)	A string containing the name of the weekday specified by the `weekday` argument, which must be an integer between 1 and 7. If the optional `abbreviate` argument is `True`, the returned string is an abbreviation of the weekday name. You can determine how VBA interprets the `weekday` number by specifying a `firstdayofweek` argument using constants such as `vbMonday`, `vbThursday`, and so on.
`Year (date)`	Function	A whole number representing the year corresponding to `date`

A date with time

A handful of simple statements and functions enable you to work with the date and time stored in your computer's built-in clock, called the *system date and time*.

The Now function returns the current system date and time as a date variable, as in: datSeizeTheMoment = Now.

For work with the system time or the system date separately, VBA provides a pair of commands for each element. These are a bit confusing because each pair contains a statement and a function that have the same name.

For example, to *retrieve* the system time as a VBA date value, you use the Time *function;* but to *set* the time, you use the Time *statement.* In other words, the Time keyword has different actions depending on the context.

```
datItsMyTime = Time ' Time function returns system time
Time (#3:15 AM#) ' Time statement sets the system time
```

The corresponding Date function and Date statement work the same way.

Calculating with dates

Time is a relative thing, right? The whole point of knowing the time or the date is so you can peg it compared to another time or a different date. Sometimes you want to know how far apart two times or two dates are. Or you want to know what the date will be, say, two years and three months from now. Several VBA date-related functions make math with dates and times reasonably simple.

Adding to and subtracting from dates and times

Use the VBA DateAdd function when you want to know what the date will be three years hence or what time it was an hour and 15 minutes ago. These calculations aren't hard for you to do yourself, but they require special handling because dates and times have so many different components and because their units aren't based on a straight decimal system (you have 7 days in a week, 60 seconds in a minute, and so on).

The DateAdd function has this syntax: DateAdd (interval, number, startingdate).

The value it returns is the starting date (or time) to which the specified number of interval(s) has been added. Use a negative number if you want to subtract rather than add. Table 11-5 lists the codes available for the interval argument (remember to enclose them in quotation marks).

Table 11-5	Arguments Available for the DateDiff and DateAdd Functions
Argument (place inside Quotation Marks)	*Interval It Specifies*
yyyy	Year
q	Quarter
m	Month
y	Day of year
d	Day
w	Weekday
ww	Week
h	Hour
n	Minute
s	Second

For example, after the following statement executes, the datWhen variable contains a date value of 90 seconds — a minute and a half — prior to the current time:

```
datWhen = DateAdd ("s", -90, Now)
```

If you then want to output only the time component of that value, you use the Format function with one of the time arguments, as in Format(datWhen,"Medium time"), as I describe in "Formatting Data," earlier in this chapter.

DateAdd doesn't steer you wrong by returning a non-existent date. If you add one month to August 31, you get September 30 as your result. DateAdd is aware of leap years, too.

Note that you can't mix intervals in one pass of the DateAdd function. However, you can figure what the date will be two years and three months from now by using DateAdd twice.

VBA provides two alternative functions for date and time calculations that *do* allow you to mix intervals: `DateSerial` and `TimeSerial`. Each function has three arguments, as shown here:

```
DateSerial (year, month, day)
TimeSerial (hour, minute, second)
```

In each function, you must include all three arguments, and each should be an expression that gives an *integer* value (not a VBA date value). See if you can follow this code fragment, noting the calculation in the third argument:

```
intYear = 1999
intMonth = 12
intDay = 31
datNewMillenium = DateSerial (intYear,intMonth,intDay+1)
```

Of course, any or all of the arguments can be calculated.

Calculating the difference between two dates

Use the `DateDiff` function to figure how many intervals (years, months, weekdays, and so on) exist between two dates or times. Here's a sample:

```
lngHowLong = DateDiff ("m", #2/12/90#, #10/12/01#)
```

After this statement executes, `lngHowLong` — a long integer variable — contains the number of months between the two dates shown. `DateDiff` uses the interval codes for the first argument. In this example, the "m" tells the function to return months rather than years, weekdays, or some other interval.

Calculating a person's age

The following Function procedure uses the `DateDiff` and `DateSerial` functions to calculate a person's age in years. To prevent errors, you can improve the code by testing to be sure that the birth date argument is actually a date value (use the `IsDate` function for this test) and by making sure that the birth date isn't in the future.

```
Function WhatAge(dateDateOfBirth As Date)
Dim intAge As Integer ' use Long if you want ages > 255
IntAge = DateDiff("yyyy", dateDateOfBirth, Date)
' check to see if they've already had their birthday:
If DateSerial(Year(Date), Month(dateDateOfBirth), _
  Day(dateDateOfBirth))> Date Then
  intAge = intAge - 1
End If
WhatAge = intAge
End Function
```

Simple Interactions with the World

Because they more or less act as parasites on larger applications, VBA programs often don't require any user interface elements (dialog boxes, menus, and such). When triggered, a VBA program can swing into action on the document currently active in your application, adjusting what it does according to the contents of that document.

Obviously, though, plenty of programming situations still call for direct interaction with the ultimate user of the VBA program. VBA UserForm tools, which I discuss in Chapter 10, give you the power to create a rich set of interactive windows for your users. But when less will do, less is better.

Two VBA functions, MsgBox and InputBox, provide the basic tools you need to talk to the program's users and let them talk back. Their duties are as follows:

- ✔ MsgBox displays a message, of course, but it also lets you know which of two or more buttons the user clicked.
- ✔ InputBox displays a message and a text box where the user can type a response.

Displaying message boxes

The formal syntax for the MsgBox function is

```
MsgBox(prompt[, buttons] [, title] [, helpfile, context]).
```

As the brackets indicate, only the *prompt* argument — which specifies the message you want to display — is required.

Specifying the prompt

In its simplest form, the MsgBox function acts like a statement. All you do is type it on its own line, supplying the text you want displayed — the prompt — as the single argument, as in:

```
MsgBox "This is a test MsgBox."
```

When this line is executed, VBA displays the message box shown in Figure 11-2, Example A.

You can type parentheses around the prompt, but parentheses aren't required when a function is used as a statement.

Figure 11-2:
Three
simple
message
boxes.

Example A   Example B   Example C

The prompt can be a variable or any expression. As usual, VBA automatically converts numeric values and dates into displayable characters for you. The following code, for example, displays the prompt shown in Figure 11-2, Example B:

```
intWishCount = 3

datWhen = Format(Now, "Short date")
strInfo1 = "As of "
strInfo2 = " wishes left."
MsgBox strInfo1 & datWhen & ", " & intWishCount & strInfo2
```

To display a message on more than one line, separate the lines by adding a carriage return character (ASCII value 13) to your prompt string, using the Chr function (see Example C in Figure 11-2):

```
MsgBox "Here is line one." & Chr(13) & "Here is line two."
```

You can line up text on two or more lines in columns with Tab characters (ASCII value 9).

Creating fancier message boxes

Besides displaying text, a message box can show one of several icons and include buttons of several different types. You wrap up your choices for all these options as a single numeric value: the optional buttons argument.

By adding an icon, your message box can look a little spiffier than the unadorned boxes in Figure 11-2. The example in Figure 11-3 carries the "critical message" icon, which should generate a bit more excitement in the viewer.

The default message box has only an OK button, but you can add buttons labeled Cancel, Yes, No, Abort, Retry, and Ignore in various combinations. You can see a sample of these wares in Figure 11-3.

Figure 11-3:
The icon
and a
couple of
extra
buttons
make this
a spiffier
message
box.

Calculating a value for the buttons argument

As with sundry similar arguments in other functions, you calculate the value
for buttons by adding together constants representing the various available
choices of icons and buttons. You can calculate the number yourself or create
an expression using the named constants VBA has defined for this purpose.
Table 11-6 lists each constant with its numeric value and purpose in life.

Table 11-6	VBA Constants for Message and Input Box Appearance and Behavior	
Constant	*Numeric Value*	*What It Does*
vbOKOnly	0	Displays OK button only
vbOKCancel	1	Displays OK and Cancel buttons
vbAbortRetryIgnore	2	Displays Abort, Retry, and Ignore buttons
vbYesNoCancel	3	Displays Yes, No, and Cancel buttons
vbYesNo	4	Displays Yes and No buttons
vbRetryCancel	5	Displays Retry and Cancel buttons
vbCritical	16	Displays Critical Message icon
vbQuestion	32	Displays Warning Query icon
vbExclamation	48	Displays Warning Message icon
vbInformation	64	Displays Information Message icon

Constant	Numeric Value	What It Does
vbDefaultButton1	0	Specifies the first button as the default
vbDefaultButton2	256	Specifies the second button as the default
vbDefaultButton3	512	Specifies the third button as the default
vbDefaultButton4	768	Specifies the fourth button as the default

Based on the table, the buttons argument in the function call for the Figure 11-3 message box should be 531. But who's counting? Typing the following statement is easier:

```
MsgBox "Pick a button", vbYesNoCancel + vbCritical _
    + vbDefaultButton3
```

Note that VbDefaultButton3, the third of the three constants in the expression for the buttons argument, sets up the third button, counting from left to right, as the default choice. In this case, that third button is Cancel. If you look closely at Figure 11-3, you can see that the Cancel button has the focus — it's highlighted by a dotted line, indicating that if you press the spacebar or Enter, it will be activated.

Who's got the button?

The point of displaying buttons in a message box is to give the user some choice about what action to take. In a message box, the users have nothing to type — they just click one of the buttons. Of course, you need a way to figure out *which* button.

That's easy because the MsgBox function returns an integer value corresponding to the button the user clicks. In the following code, for example, variable intA receives the value returned by the MsgBox function used to display the box shown in Figure 11-3:

```
intA = MsgBox ("Pick a button", vbYesNoCancel + vbCritical _
    + vbDefaultButton3)
```

To minimize the strain on your memory, you can test the returned value against predefined named constants rather than arbitrary numbers. Here are these constants and their actual values:

Constant	Value
vbOK	1
vbCancel	2
vbAbort	3
vbRetry	4
vbIgnore	5
vbYes	6
vbNo	7

An If...Then statement works well to figure out which button was clicked, if your message box has only two buttons, as in this example:

```
If MsgBox ("Go on?", VbYesNo) = VbYes Then
  DoSomething
Else
  DontDoAnything
End If
```

With three buttons to test, you would need an If...Then...Else If statement.

Adding a title

By default, a message box displays the name of the VBA application you're using in its title bar (refer to Figure 11-2). You can substitute any title you like by supplying a string for the title argument when you call the MsgBox function. For example, the complete code for the message box shown in Figure 11-3 is as follows:

```
MsgBox "Pick a button", vbYesNoCancel + vbCritical _
  + vbDefaultButton3, "VBA For Dummies"
```

Obtaining user input

If you need to know more from the user than which of three options to pursue, the InputBox function may be adequate. Here's its formal syntax, minus the more advanced optional arguments:

```
InputBox(prompt [, title] [, default]).
```

As shown in Figure 11-4, this function displays a dialog box that provides a text box, in which the user is asked to type some piece of presumably crucial information. To bring that information into your program, just assign the return value of the `InputBox` function to a string variable:

```
strB = InputBox ("Seat preference?", "NYAir", "Aisle")
```

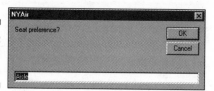

Figure 11-4:
A sample
input box.

Although an input box can collect a much wider range of information than a message box, its basic operations are actually simpler — you have no button and icon options to fiddle with. The *prompt* and *title* arguments work just as they do in the `MsgBox` function. You can make it easier for the users by supplying a *default* response — if they like it, they just press Enter.

Working with Boolean values

The simplest way to toggle the value of a Boolean variable to its opposite is with the logical operator `Not`. All you need do is assign the results of the `Not` operation to the same variable. For example, the following statement makes the `boolBlinking` variable `True` if it started out `False`, and vice versa:

```
boolBlinking = Not boolBlinking
```

Fun with Math and Money

VBA comes chock full of prefab functions for manipulating numbers. These perform chores ranging from the very simple (such as returning an absolute value or a number's sign) to the staple computations of algebra and trigonometry. If the bottom line is sinking, a healthy dose of VBA financial functions may be just what you need to float the business boat again.

With a few exceptions, I don't cover the use of these functions individually. Again, I put them in the book just because they're so hard to dig out of the VBA Help file and you may otherwise miss them. Look over the listings to acquaint yourself with what's available.

Math functions

Table 11-7 catalogs the VBA functions that are specifically math-related. When you're in the mood for math, don't forget to review the data conversion functions that I cover in the section "Converting Data," earlier in this chapter.

Table 11-7	VBA Math Functions
Function	*Value It Returns*
Abs(number)	The absolute value of number
Atn(number)	The arctangent of number
Cos(number)	The cosine of number
Exp(number)	The number e raised to the power of number
Fix(number)	The integer portion of number, similar to the Int function
Int(number)	The integer portion of number. The Int and Fix functions differ in their handling of negative numbers. Int returns the next lower (more negative) integer, whereas Fix simply drops the decimal portion of number.
Log(number)	The natural logarithm of number as a double
Rnd(number)	A random number as a single
Sgn(number)	1 if number is a positive number, 0 if it is 0, and –1 if it's a negative number
Sin(number)	The sine of number
Sqr(number)	The square root of number
Tan(number)	The tangent of number

Deriving other math functions

If VBA doesn't include the math function you seek, don't fret — you can usually put together an expression or Function procedure of your own that can get the job done.

If you're mathematician enough that you're calculating advanced trigonometric functions such as inverse cosecants, you don't need me to tell you how to use them. You may like to know, though, that the VBA Help file comes with a cheat-sheet summary of many such functions, with the expressions needed to calculate them. To see this, search for *derived math functions* in the Help index. The Help topic reminds you that, for example, the logarithm to base N of X can be calculated as = Log(X) / Log(N).

If you think you may ever reuse a math function derived from other functions, make it a permanent part of your VBA arsenal by wrapping it up into a Function procedure. After storing it in a module named something like `MyMathFunctions`, you can put it back to work any time the need for that computation comes up.

Rounding numbers

Rounding off a decimal point number is a common task, especially when you're working with currency values. Curiously, VBA doesn't offer a straight-forward solution. However, the technique discussed here will solve your rounding problems.

VBA has a `Round` function (not available in VBA 5), but it doesn't work reliably. For example, after VBA runs the statement

```
x = Round(2.505, 2)
```

the value of x is 2.5, not 2.51 as it should be. Don't use `Round` unless you're willing to put up with some incorrect answers.

However, a dependable, simple way to round off a number with too many decimal places is to use the `Format` function. Just `Format` the number in question using the custom `format` argument shown in the following example code. (See the section "Specifying prefab and custom formats" earlier in this chapter for details on the `format` argument.)

Here's an example of this technique in practice:

```
sngRoundedNumber = Format(sngUnRounded, "#,##0.00")
```

In VBA 6, you can use the `FormatNumber` function instead to get the same result as in:

```
sngRoundedNumber = FormatNumber(sngUnRounded, 2)
```

Both examples round `sngUnRounded` to two decimal places. To round to a different number of decimal places using `Format`, change the number of zeroes following the decimal point in the `format` argument. For example, the argument `"#,##0.0"` rounds the number to only one decimal place. To change the number of decimal places using `FormatNumber`, just specify the desired number as the second argument.

Note that the variable into which you place the rounded value should be of type string, single, double, decimal, currency, or variant — don't use integers or longs, or you'll lose the fractional part of the result.

Suppose you want to round a value that doesn't have any decimal places to reduce the number of significant digits. The code you need is a bit more involved, but not by much. The following example rounds the original number to two fewer significant digits:

```
sngRounded = Format(sngUnRounded / 100, "#,##0.") * 100
```

Note that the custom `format` argument for this task has no zeroes to the right of the decimal point. In addition, the code divides the unrounded number inside the `Format` function by a power of 10 and then multiplies the function result by that same power of 10. Select the power of 10 equal to the number of significant digits you want to drop. In the preceding example, the 2nd power of 10, or 100, produces the desired answer.

Working with random numbers

If the routine of life has dampened your spirits, liven up your programs by building in some unpredictability. Randomly generated numbers are useful when you're coding programs such as simulations of real-world problems, educational software, and games.

VBA includes two built-in commands specifically designed for generating random numbers. They are:

- ✔ **The** `Randomize` **statement:** Use it to prime the pump of VBA's random number generator. Used with no arguments, `Randomize` seeds the generator with the current system time. That way, you're guaranteed to get a different series of random numbers each time the code runs.

- ✔ **The** `Rnd` **function:** This is the function that actually produces your random numbers. It requires no arguments — you just set `Rnd` equal to a variable or use the function in an expression. `Rnd` returns a floating-point (single) value.

Floating-point numbers like those returned by `Rnd` are commonly used for statistical and scientific purposes. In more mundane situations, however, you usually need integer random values. You may want, for example, to write a procedure that selects the winning raffle ticket number. To convert the value returned by `Rnd` to an integer within a given range, use the following formula:

```
randomint = Int(((high - low + 1) * Rnd) + low)
```

In the formula, the items `high` and `low` refer to the highest and lowest values in your series of numbers — if you specify them correctly, the formula always gives a result within that range.

The Raffle module on the CD-ROM is a complete little program that illustrates the formula and the use of random numbers in general.

Financial functions

VBA offers a load of built-in functions for calculating dollars-and-cents amounts such as payments on a loan (an *annuity,* technically speaking) or the return on an investment. Although I don't have space to cover them all in detail, I do go over the use of the `Pmt` function for figuring out payments on a loan.

Calculating payments on a loan or savings plan

Use the `Pmt` function to compute the payment you have to make (or someone else makes to you) on a fixed-rate mortgage or other loan or to put aside enough to meet a savings goal. Here's the formal syntax of the `Pmt` function's:

```
Pmt(rate, nper, pv[, fv[, type]]).
```

The first argument, `Rate`, defines the interest rate on the loan *per period.* You need to understand that the way you express the rate must correspond to the frequency of payments. If you'll be making monthly payments on an 8 percent mortgage, remember that 8 percent is the yearly rate. In this common situation, `Rate` should be an expression such as .08 / 12 (8 percent divided by 12 months).

The `nper` argument is an integer representing the total number of payments (it stands for *number of periods*) that must be made on the loan. For monthly payments on a 5-year loan, `nper` should be 5 * 12, or 60. Specify the total amount of the loan in the `pv` argument — the *present value.*

The remaining arguments are optional. If you want to calculate how much you should save to hit a financial target, use the `fv` argument to send the target amount as a *negative* number to the `Pmt` function — it stands for *future value.* (The interest rate you expect to earn would be your `rate` argument. If you've already saved something towards your goal, that amount would be the `pv` argument.) The `type` argument lets you specify whether payments are due at the end of each period (in which case, it should be 0, the default) or at the beginning (give type a value of 1).

To use the `Pmt` function in your code, assign it to a variable of the double (floating-point) data type. Here are two examples:

```
dblPay = Pmt (.08/12, 360, 300000) ' Typical mortgage
dblSav = Pmt (.07/12, 120, 12500,-75000) ' Goal = $75,000
```

Putting bread and butter on the table

Table 11-8 summarizes VBA cornucopia of financial functions. To make the table reasonably easy to read, I omitted optional arguments. Look up a function in the Help file for details on its arguments and a salient example.

Table 11-8	VBA Financial Functions
Function	**Value It Returns**
DDB (cost, salvage, period)	The depreciation of an asset over period, based on the double-declining balance method
FV (rate, nper, pmt, pv)	The future value of an annuity of fixed interest rate rate, based on nper number of fixed payments, pmt (the amount of each payment, and present value pv of the annuity (rate and nper must be expressed in the same time interval, such as months)
Ipmt (rate, per, nper, pv)	The interest payment for a given period of an annuity based on periodic, fixed payments and a fixed interest rate
IRR (values())	The internal rate of return for a series of periodic cash flows (values() is an array of payments and receipts)
MIRR (values(), finance_rate, reinvest_rate)	The modified internal rate of return for the series of periodic cash flows (payments and receipts) listed in the values() array
Nper (rate, pmt, pv)	The number of periods for an annuity based on periodic, fixed payments and a fixed interest rate
NPV (rate, values())	The net present value of an investment based on a series of periodic cash flows and a discount rate
Pmt (rate, nper, pv)	The payment for an annuity based on periodic, fixed payments and a fixed interest rate
PPmt (rate, per, nper, pv)	The principal payment for a given period of an annuity based on periodic, fixed payments and a fixed interest rate
PV (rate, nper, pmt)	The present value of an annuity based on periodic, fixed payments to be paid in the future, and a fixed interest rate
Rate (nper, pmt, pv)	The interest rate per period for an annuity
SLN (cost, salvage, life)	The straight-line depreciation of an asset for a single period
SYD (cost, salvage, life, period)	The sum-of-years' digits depreciation of an asset for a specified period

Miscellaneous Built-In Commands

Even with all the tables and discussions presented in this chapter, this review of VBA's built-in commands is far from complete. I discuss some of these commands in later chapters, but I close this chapter with yet another table, Table 11-9, listing sundry commands that you may well find useful.

Table 11-9	Miscellaneous Built-In VBA Commands	
(Remember to enclose literal strings for items such as pathnames in quotation marks.)		
Name	*Function or Statement*	*What It Does (for Statements)/ Value It Returns (for Functions)*
Working with Files on Disk		
`ChDir(pathname)`	Statement	Changes the active directory (folder), but not the active drive
`ChDrive(drivename)`	Statement	Changes the active drive
`CurDir`	Function	Current path (disk and directory name) as a string
`Dir(pathname)`	Function	The name of the first file or directory (folder) matching pathname, which may contain wildcards. Call the `Dir` repeatedly to obtain additional matching items.
`FileCopy source, destination`	Statement	Copies the disk file `source` to `destination`, which may include a path, a filename, or both
`FileDateTime (pathname)`	Function	Date value for the date and time when the file named by `pathname` was created or last modified
`FileLen(pathname)`	Function	Length of the disk file named by `pathname`, in bytes
`GetAttr(pathname)`	Function	An integer representing the attributes of the file or directory (folder) specified by `pathname`
`Kill pathname`	Statement	Deletes one or more disk files (wildcard characters are permissible in pathname)

(continued)

Table 11-9 *(continued)*

Name	Function or Statement	What It Does (for Statements)/ Value It Returns (for Functions)
Working with Files on Disk		
`MkDir pathname`	Statement	Creates (makes) a new directory
`Name oldpathname As newpathname`	Statement	Renames and/or moves a disk file, directory, or folder
`RmDir pathname`	Statement	Removes a directory
`SetAttr pathname, attributes`	Statement	Sets chosen attributes of a disk file. The `attributes` argument represents a numeric value that is the sum of the values for each attribute to be set. VBA provides named constants for each of the available attributes.
Miscellaneous Commands		
`AppActivate title, wait`	Statement	Activates another running application. If the optional `wait` argument is `True`, VBA waits until your program has the focus before activating the application.
`Beep`	Statement	Beeps the computer speaker
`Choose(index, choice1, choice2, ...choicen)`	Function	The value of the item at position `index` (`index` must evaluate to a number) in the list of arguments `choice1, choice2, ...choicen`
`DoEvents`	Function	This function allows Windows to handle other events while in the middle of running your program. In VBA it always returns 0 (zero), so you do not need to assign its value to a variable — use it as a statement.
`Environ(envstring) Environ(number)`	Function	The contents of an operating or system environment variable, specified by name `envstring` or numeric position `number`

Name	Function or Statement	What It Does (for Statements)/ Value It Returns (for Functions)
`RGB(red, green, blue)`	Function	A whole number representing an RGB color value for the `red`, `green`, and `blue` components (you use the RGB value calculated by this function to set color-related object properties)
`Randomize`	Statement	Initializes the random number generator
`Rnd(number)`	Function	A random value; the `number` argument is optional
`SendKeys string, wait`	Statement	Sends the keystrokes specified in `string` to the active window as if typed at the keyboard. If the optional wait argument is `True`, the keystrokes must be processed before your program continues.
Manipulating the Windows Registry		
`Shell(pathname)`	Function	This function attempts to run the program specified by `pathname`. It returns a number representing the program's ID if successful; otherwise, it returns zero.
`DeleteSetting appname, section, key`	Statement	Deletes an entry in the registry
`GetAllSettings (appname, section)`	Function	A variant containing a list of all settings for the specified `section` of application `appname` in the Windows registry (returned as a two-dimensional array)
`GetSetting(appname, section, key)`	Function	A single-key value from the specified `section` of application `appname` in the Windows registry
`SaveSetting appname, section, key, setting`	Statement	Stores a setting in the registry

(continued)

Table 11-9   *(continued)*

Name	Function or Statement	What It Does (for Statements)/ Value It Returns (for Functions)
Manipulating the Windows Registry		
Spc(number)	Function	No useful return value; used to place the specified number of spaces in the output from the Print # statement or the Debug.Print method
Tab(column)	Function	No useful return value; positions output from the Print # statement or the Debug.Print method at column number column (or if column is omitted, at the next print zone)
Working with Variables		
IsDate(variablename) IsNumeric(variablename) IsObject(variablename) IsArray(variablename) IsNull(variablename) IsEmpty(variablename)	Functions	True if variablename is of the indicated type or value (such as Date or Empty); otherwise, False
Len(variablename)	Function	The number of bytes required to store the information contained in variablename
TypeName(variablename)	Function	A string representing the type of variable variablename, which must be a variant
VarType(variablename)	Function	An integer indicating the subtype of variable variablename, which must be a variant

Chapter 12

Object-Oriented Programming

• •

In This Chapter

▶ Conceptualizing objects

▶ Grasping properties, methods, and events — important components of VBA objects

▶ Working with object models

▶ Using forms as objects

▶ Getting and setting object properties

▶ Calling methods

▶ Using object references to identify the object you want to work with

▶ Assigning object references to variables

▶ Creating your own objects with class modules

▶ Using objects efficiently with `For Each...Next` and `With` statements

• •

A core aspect of the VBA identity is its status as an object-oriented software development tool. An understanding of objects is fundamental to
VBA programming, especially when you want to create custom dialog boxes
or put the features of the host application under your control. This chapter
starts by charting the object territory conceptually, and moves on to cover
the nuts and bolts of programming with *objects*.

Objects are vital features of the VBA landscape. Through them, you have
access to the functionality of the underlying VBA application you're working in.
Eventually, you can expand your prowess to the point where you can access
objects from other compatible applications and even build your own objects.

So What's an Object?

Although it's possible to come up with a formal definition of a VBA object,
understanding objects by way of examples and in terms of their functions is a
lot easier.

Objects as components of VBA applications

The easiest way to start thinking about objects is to see them as parts of your VBA application and its documents. A shape in a Visio drawing is an object, as is each *connect* that joins two shapes (see Figure 12-1). So is each layer to which shapes can be assigned, and so is each page where the layers reside. And so is the document itself, to which all the pages, layers, shapes, and connects belong.

Similarly, Excel objects include the cells in which you enter data or formulas, named ranges of cells, the charts that grace many worksheets, individual worksheets, and complete workbooks. And in all Microsoft Office applications — as well as many other VBA applications — the toolbars and menus, and the buttons and menu choices they contain, are objects as well.

VBA objects exist in a hierarchy in which one type of object contains objects of other types. I discuss object hierarchies in the section "What's an Object Model?" later in this chapter. For the time being, though, I concentrate on understanding individual objects.

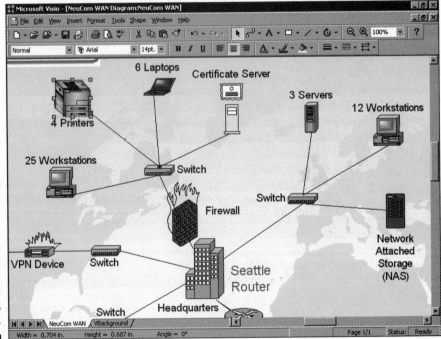

Figure 12-1:
Each graphic and each connecting line is an example of a VBA object.

Objects conceptualized

You may not be able to touch a drawing shape, a worksheet cell, or a toolbar button, but you can fairly easily think of them as *things*. In your imagination, at least, you can cut out a circle shape and paste it on another piece of paper. You can write numbers into that worksheet cell, or you can push that button.

In addition to fairly concrete items like these, however, VBA applications offer up all kinds of more abstract objects. The following are some examples:

- Microsoft Excel has a `CustomView` object, representing a workbook custom view (in Excel, a custom view defines the look of the workbook and its print settings).

- The Microsoft Word `FileSearch` object "represents the functionality of the Open dialog box," to quote the relevant Help topic. Note that this object doesn't represent the dialog box itself, but rather its functionality.

- Visio has a `Style` object, which represents a combination of line, fill, and text attributes for shapes.

- VBA itself has a few objects that are available in all VBA applications. A `Collection` object, for example, represents a grab-bag set of variables or other objects that you want to work with as a unit, regardless of their type.

A practical definition of objects

As you can tell, it's often difficult to imagine a VBA object as a material thing. But that's okay — the more you can let go of such mental models, the more freely you can work with the whole range of available objects. The programmer's pragmatic definition of an object is simple, really. An object is a named item that has

- **Properties:** settings that you can check and change.
- **Methods:** actions the object can perform when your program asks it to.
- **Events:** things that happen to the object, to which it can respond by automatically taking a predetermined action.

If you have any poetic sensibility, the term *objects* may not seem fitting for such richly endowed creatures. Indeed, objects are more like animals than inert lumps. A tiger or a whale has characteristic features such as eyes, limbs, and a tail; an object has properties. A horse or a dog can do tricks on command or run away from danger; an object has methods and events.

Do you still want a technical definition? Try this one: An object is a named unit within a program that possesses both data and the code that acts on that data. An object is said to *encapsulate* the data as well as the related code.

Object classes versus specific objects

Here's yet another technicality to keep in mind: A distinction exists between a given specific object and the pattern on which the object is based.

A particular object represents one specific document, shape, worksheet cell, or what have you. A document object, for example, includes the text of that one document. An *object class,* on the other hand, can be compared to a set of building plans. You can build many houses from one set of plans, but nobody can live in the plans themselves. In the same way, a class determines the types of data that an object can store and defines the object's methods, properties, and events. Based on this description, you construct an *instance* of the class — an object — in which you actually store data. You can create, or *instantiate,* as many objects of a class as you like, each with a separate existence, and each containing different data.

Collection objects

A *collection* is a special type of VBA object. As the name suggests, its role is to simplify working with a set of objects as a group. Typically, all objects in a given collection are of the same type. A Shapes collection in Visio, for example, contains multiple Shape objects, and a Pages collection contains multiple Page objects.

Some collections, however, are less discriminating about which objects they allow in. VBA proper comes with a generic Collection object, which you can use to store objects of any type in any combination. If you're into jumbled hodgepodges, a VBA collection is just the ticket.

The section "Working with Collection objects" later in this chapter describes how to access the individual objects in a collection. In Chapter 13, I show you how to use a collection's properties and methods (a collection is itself an object, remember), and how to create collections of your own based on the VBA generic Collection object.

What's an Object Model?

VBA objects exist in a hierarchical relationship to one another. In addition to having properties, methods, and events of its own, an object at the top of the hierarchy serves as a *container* for one or more other types of objects. These objects in turn each contain other objects, and so on.

For a given VBA application, the specifics of these hierarchical relationships are the application's *object model*. Often presented graphically, the object model specifies which object contains which other objects. Figure 12-2 shows one such representation of an object model.

As you can see in Figure 12-2, the *application object* is at the top of a VBA application's object model. The application object is the container for all the other objects from the application that you can manipulate. Your own VBA programming *project* is also a container object. It contains all the code *modules* (units of code) you write and the forms you design, as well as the project's document. (Chapter 7 defines and discusses VBA projects and their components in more detail.)

Understanding why the object model is important

Because you need to tell VBA which specific object you're working with, fully understanding the object model of your VBA application is critical to efficient work. Following a chart of the object model such as the one shown in Figure 12-2, you can quickly locate the branch that contains the object you're after. In this example you can see that a `Connect` object is a member of the `Connects` collection, which belongs to the `Master` object, which in turn. . . .

Extending the object model

In the programs you write with VBA, you aren't limited to using the objects in only one VBA application. In fact, you're not even limited to VBA applications per se. Other applications and specialized "components" are fair game, as long as they adhere to Microsoft's *Component Object Model* (COM) standard.

COM is the technical specification detailing how objects are defined within applications and other software elements and how those objects are *exposed* so that they can be used by other applications. The jargon word *Automation* refers specifically to the capability of a COM-based application to be controlled by another program. And by the way, COM isn't specific to VBA or even Visual Basic. Many software development tools, such as C++ compilers, understand COM and can access COM objects.

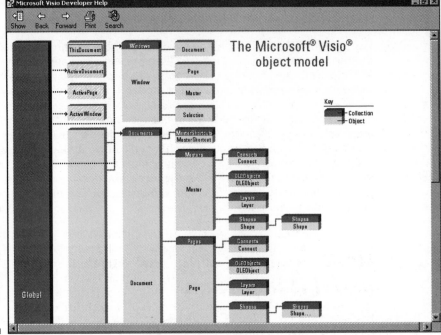

Figure 12-2:
The Visio
object
model,
taken from
the Visio
2000 CD.

Anyway, COM opens up fantastic possibilities for powerful, customized VBA applications. You can readily (I didn't say "easily") build an application that processes information from Word documents, Excel worksheets, Visio diagrams, and so on. Your custom application can show all this information in windows that you've designed but that also use the display capabilities of the individual component `applications.Custom` application development on this scale is decidedly an advanced VBA topic and one that I only briefly touch on in this book (in Chapter 14). Still, I want to stress that VBA is capable of a great deal.

VBA Forms Are Objects, Too

A *form* is any custom window you build with VBA. If your program has its own user interface, the program's main window is a form and so are any additional dialog boxes the program may display (see Figure 12-3).

A key understanding to seal into your brain is that VBA forms are themselves objects. That is, they constitute entities that contain information — representing the layout of the form — and a set of tools for doing things with that information. The official term for a form is `UserForm` *object*.

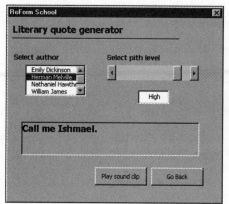

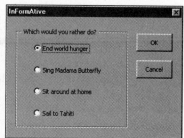

Figure 12-3:
Examples of
VBA forms.

As self-respecting VBA objects, forms fit comfortably into the object model paradigm. Each `UserForm` object belongs simultaneously to two separate collection objects — the VBA project in which the form is stored and the `UserForms` collection, which holds all the forms currently loaded by your program. For its part, a `UserForm` object is a container for a `Controls` collection object, which in turn contains the individual controls you have added to the form.

Likewise, a form's controls — each button, check box, and any other doodad you can see and play with on the form — are also objects. VBA offers a different object type corresponding to each type of control.

The techniques you use in your code to access a particular form or one of its controls, and to use the properties, methods, and events of these objects, are exactly the same as those you use for other objects, as I detail in this chapter. Chapter 10 and Bonus Chapter F both delve into the application of these techniques to forms and controls.

Using Objects in Code: An Introduction

I deal with the theoretical groundwork earlier in this chapter. So in this section, I provide practical directions for programming with VBA objects. I start by exploring the use of object properties, methods, and events in detail. After that, I move on to more fundamental techniques — those for identifying the specific object you want to work with in your code.

The basic rule about object programming

Although the object concept itself can be tough to wrap your mind around, *using* objects is easy. Because objects have names, you always know which one you're working with. In your code, all you need to do to identify one of the object's properties or methods is to type the object name, a period, and then the property or method name.

For example, `MyShape.LineStyle` identifies the `LineStyle` property of a `Visio` object called `MyShape`. Similarly, `MyWorksheet.Calculate` identifies the `Calculate` method of an Excel worksheet object called `MyWorksheet`.

At this point, though, you may be asking yourself, "But how do I know what the object's name is in the first place?" — an excellent question, indeed. The answer takes some explaining, however, so I discuss it in the section "Identifying the Object You Want to Work With," which comes after the discussion of properties, methods, and events. For now, just assume that you can call an object by name.

Using object models

Each VBA application has a different *object model* (hierarchical set of objects), and each of its objects has its own set of properties, methods, and events. You need a working familiarity with the details of the application's object model to put these objects to work in your programs.

In many applications, the VBA Help file has a topic devoted to a map of the application's object model (see Figure 12-4). If you don't see the object model map when you first open the Help system, look for it in the Contents tab where it should be listed as something like, say, Microsoft Excel Object Model. With the object model map as your guide, you can view information on the individual objects by clicking them on the map or by looking them up in the Help index. Typically, the topic for each object has jumps to other topics detailing the object's properties, methods, and events. (I'm talking here about your particular application's VBA Help files, not the general Help system for the application or for VBA. See Chapter 4 for details about working with the VBA Help system.)

The Visual Basic Editor Object Browser is another vital tool for viewing the relationships between the different objects of the application and exploring the objects' properties, methods, and events. Chapter 6 describes the Object Browser in full.

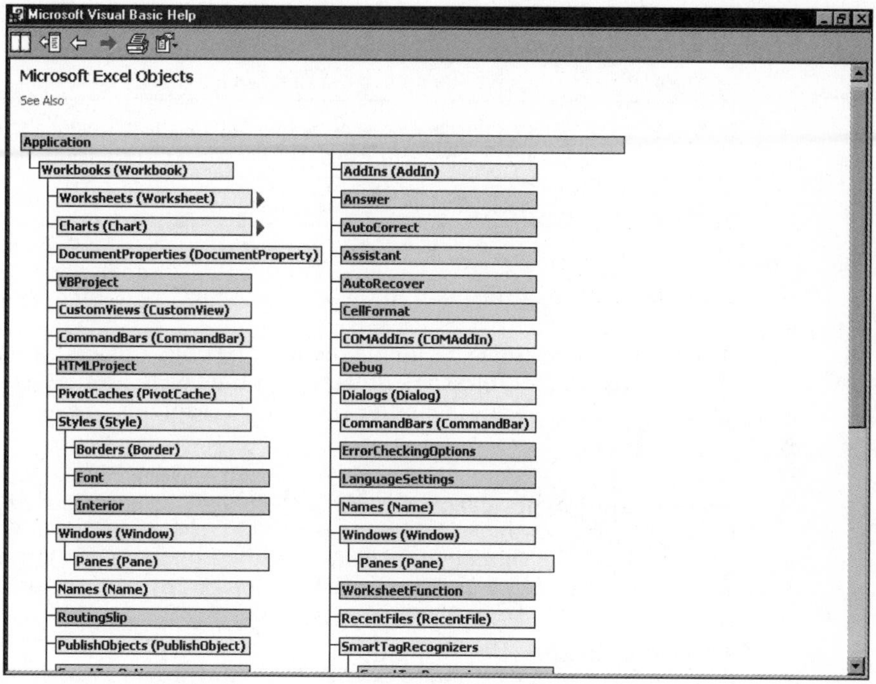

```
Microsoft Visual Basic Help                                    _ 8 X

  []  []  ←  →  []  []

Microsoft Excel Objects

See Also

┌─────────────────────────────────────────────────────────────┐
│ Application                                                    │
└─────────────────────────────────────────────────────────────┘
  ┌──────────────────────────┐      ┌──────────────────────┐
  │ Workbooks (Workbook)     │      │ AddIns (AddIn)       │
  └──────────────────────────┘      └──────────────────────┘
    ┌────────────────────────────┐  ┌──────────────────────┐
    │ Worksheets (Worksheet)    ▶│  │ Answer               │
    └────────────────────────────┘  └──────────────────────┘
    ┌────────────────────────────┐  ┌──────────────────────┐
    │ Charts (Chart)            ▶│  │ AutoCorrect          │
    └────────────────────────────┘  └──────────────────────┘
    ┌──────────────────────────────────────────────┐  ┌──────────────────────┐
    │ DocumentProperties (DocumentProperty)         │  │ Assistant            │
    └──────────────────────────────────────────────┘  └──────────────────────┘
    ┌────────────────────────────┐  ┌──────────────────────┐
    │ VBProject                  │  │ AutoRecover          │
    └────────────────────────────┘  └──────────────────────┘
    ┌────────────────────────────┐  ┌──────────────────────┐
    │ CustomViews (CustomView)   │  │ CellFormat           │
    └────────────────────────────┘  └──────────────────────┘
    ┌────────────────────────────┐  ┌──────────────────────────────┐
    │ CommandBars (CommandBar)   │  │ COMAddIns (COMAddIn)         │
    └────────────────────────────┘  └──────────────────────────────┘
    ┌────────────────────────────┐  ┌──────────────────────┐
    │ HTMLProject                │  │ Debug                │
    └────────────────────────────┘  └──────────────────────┘
    ┌────────────────────────────┐  ┌──────────────────────┐
    │ PivotCaches (PivotCache)   │  │ Dialogs (Dialog)     │
    └────────────────────────────┘  └──────────────────────┘
    ┌────────────────────────────┐  ┌──────────────────────────────┐
    │ Styles (Style)             │  │ CommandBars (CommandBar)     │
    └────────────────────────────┘  └──────────────────────────────┘
      ┌──────────────────────────┐  ┌──────────────────────────────┐
      │ Borders (Border)         │  │ ErrorCheckingOptions         │
      └──────────────────────────┘  └──────────────────────────────┘
      ┌──────────────────────────┐  ┌──────────────────────┐
      │ Font                     │  │ LanguageSettings     │
      └──────────────────────────┘  └──────────────────────┘
      ┌──────────────────────────┐  ┌──────────────────────┐
      │ Interior                 │  │ Names (Name)         │
      └──────────────────────────┘  └──────────────────────┘
    ┌────────────────────────────┐  ┌──────────────────────┐
    │ Windows (Window)           │  │ Windows (Window)     │
    └────────────────────────────┘  └──────────────────────┘
      ┌──────────────────────────┐    ┌──────────────────────┐
      │ Panes (Pane)             │    │ Panes (Pane)         │
      └──────────────────────────┘    └──────────────────────┘
    ┌────────────────────────────┐  ┌──────────────────────┐
    │ Names (Name)               │  │ WorksheetFunction    │
    └────────────────────────────┘  └──────────────────────┘
    ┌────────────────────────────┐  ┌──────────────────────────┐
    │ RoutingSlip                │  │ RecentFiles (RecentFile) │
    └────────────────────────────┘  └──────────────────────────┘
    ┌────────────────────────────┐  ┌──────────────────────┐
    │ PublishObjects (PublishObject)│ │ SmartTagRecognizers  │
    └────────────────────────────┘  └──────────────────────┘
```

Figure 12-4:
The Excel
object
model.

Getting and Changing Object Properties

Properties are probably the easiest object-related concept to grasp. A *property* stores information about some aspect of the object's appearance, behavior, contents, or pedigree, if you will.

A `Document` object may have a `Pages` property that tells how many pages are in the document. A `Shape` object may have a `Fill` property that specifies the shape's color. `CommandButton` objects (representing buttons on dialog boxes) have a `Caption` property that contains the text on the button.

A VBA program can retrieve the current settings stored in most properties. This capability allows the program to decide whether to take some action or to simply display the current setting in a window. Conversely, a program can change a property's setting to alter an object's appearance or behavior — but only if the property permits change (many properties can be retrieved but not modified).

The properties for appearance are the easiest to understand. A `Shape` object in Visio, for example, has the following appearance-related properties, among others.

Property	Description
AreaIU	The area of the shape in internal units
FillStyle	The Visio style describing the shape's color and other fill characteristics
Text	The text displayed on the shape

These properties correspond to the way the object looks in a document.

Behavior-related properties define the way the object reacts to various stimuli. Controls on UserForms are objects, and they have properties such as Enabled, which specifies whether the control responds to events such as mouse clicks.

Some properties, like the AreaIU for a Visio Shape, can take on an infinite range of different values. Others are limited to a list of predefined choices, such as Mauve, Teal, and Chartreuse. Many properties can take only two possible settings, such as True or False, Hot or Cold, or Wet or Dry.

In any case, you can use simple VBA statements to retrieve the current setting of a given property and to change the setting to one you prefer.

What you can't do with some properties

Just knowing *how* to access a property's value doesn't mean that you *can* access them. By design, some properties allow you to retrieve their values but not to change them. These are *read-only* properties. A less common property is *write-only* — you can set its value but can't retrieve the current setting. Most properties are the *read-write* kind — you can both retrieve and change their values.

Property settings are data

Although a property functions metaphorically to describe some characteristic of the object, you should realize that the setting it contains consists of data — no different from the data that you stuff into VBA variables. As such, you can think of a property simply as a more-or-less permanent variable that you don't have to declare. After you understand properties this way, it makes sense that each property stores a particular data type exactly as variables do. A property that can take only two alternative settings (such as True or False, Happy or Sad, or Left or Right) is a *Boolean* property. Some properties are strings, some are integers, some are floating-point or decimal numbers, and so on. Properties can even be objects. (See Chapter 7 for information on the available VBA data types.)

Retrieving a property's current setting

To find out, or *get,* the current setting of a given property, use the property as if it were a function or `Function` procedure — that is, assign the property to a variable in your code. The variable should be of the same or a compatible data type as the property.

In the sample shown here, the object in question represents, say, a question on a computerized test for graduate school admission. The property you're interested in checking is the one that describes how hard the question is on a scale of one to ten.

```
Dim intHowTough As Integer
intHowTough = objTestQuestion.DifficultyLevel
```

The first statement declares a variable to hold the property's current value, while the second statement assigns the property to that variable.

So why bother retrieving a property's current value? Often, you use it in a conditional statement to decide whether to take some other action, based on the value. (In this case, something like "If the question's `DifficultyLevel` is above 8, and if the answer is correct, award double credit" may be in order.) You may also store a property value in a variable so that you can assign the value to the same property of other similar objects.

If you're going to use the property's value only once, you don't need to assign it to a variable — you can access it directly in an expression. The example illustrates this practice:

```
If objTestQuestion.DifficultyLevel > 8 Then
  intTestScore = intTestScore + (intPoints * 2)
End If
```

This practice is convenient, but remember that your program slows down if you repeatedly retrieve a property's value. If you need the value more than once or twice, storing it in a variable is better — VBA can access the value of an ordinary variable more quickly than it can retrieve a property's value.

Changing a property's setting

Remember that properties are just glorified variables. Therefore, you can assign values to them just as you would any other variable — by placing the property name on the left side of an equals sign and the new value on the right. The following statement sets the `objMetalTune`'s `GrungeFactor` property — presumably, a measure of distortion, feedback, and extraneous noise — to 999:

```
objMetalTune.GrungeFactor = 999
```

To make the point excessively, the following two statements set other properties for the same headbanging performance:

```
objMetalTune.Ballad = False
objMetalTune.Title = "I have fleas. Bad."
```

Default properties

Many objects have a default property. You can retrieve or set its value using the object only, without mentioning the property itself by name. Suppose that the default property for the objMetalTune object is Title. In that case, you can simplify the last code statement to read as follows:

```
objMetalTune = "I have fleas. Bad."
```

Default properties are convenient, as long as you're sure that you know which property is the default. If you have any doubt or if you think that you may forget later, I recommend typing out the property name — just to be safe.

Objects as properties

A property of one object can identify another object. This arrangement lets your code access the subsidiary objects that belong to a given *container* object, just as you would the container's other properties. For example, in the following expression, ToolbarItems is a property of the Toolbar object, but its value is a ToolbarItems object:

```
Toolbar.ToolbarItems
```

In fact, using object properties in this way is the critical technique for identifying the specific objects you want to work with. See the section "Identifying the Object You Want to Work With," later in this chapter for details.

Climbing the family tree

Just as an object's properties can identify other objects that belong to it, they can also tell you to which container objects it belongs. In Visio, if you have a Pages object stored in a variable and you want to know which document the Pages object belongs to, the following expression returns a reference to the correct document:

```
Pages.Parent
```

If you need to know which *application* an object belongs to, you can often skip to the top of the object hierarchy by getting an object's Application property, as in:

```
Pages.Application
```

Method Acting

Methods are the named actions an object can perform at your command. Because the code for each method is part and parcel of the object, the object itself knows what to do when you trigger the method.

A graphical shape object, for example, may have a Resize method that changes its size and a Rotate method that rotates it on the document page. A worksheet cell object may have a Calculate method that recalculates the cell value and a Clear method that removes its contents. An object representing an entire document probably has Print and Save methods.

Methods are actually nothing more than procedures that are tied directly to specific objects. To call a method, you type the object's name, a period, and then the method name. Leaving behind metal madness, suppose that an object named objJazzTune represents a digital jazz recording in a multimedia program. Most likely, the object has a method called Play. Here's how to call the method:

```
objJazzTune.Play
```

In more detail, the techniques for calling methods are consistent with the ones that you use to call procedures and VBA functions, as I describe in Chapter 7. To summarize:

- ✔ To call a method that takes arguments, type the argument after the method name. Here, the Play method takes an argument specifying how many times to repeat the tune:

  ```
  objJazzTune.Play 3
  ```

- ✔ If the method takes two or more arguments, separate them with commas (in this example, pretend that Soft is a named constant specifying a quiet playback volume, and intSpeed is a variable representing playback speed):

  ```
  objJazzTune.Play 2, Soft, intSpeed
  ```

✔ To call a method that returns a value, assign the method to a variable or use it in an expression as you would a `Function` procedure. In this situation, any arguments must be enclosed within parentheses:

```
datePlayTime = objJazzTune.Play (2, Soft, intSpeed)
```

As with properties, many different object classes may have methods with the same names. Objects that contain groups of items or other objects typically have an `Add` method, for instance.

Just so it doesn't surprise you, I should mention that a method could change the value of one or more properties. For example, the `objJazzTune` object may have a read-only property called `TimesPlayed` that can be altered only by the Play method, but that you can retrieve via a statement such as `intPlaybacks = objJazzTune.TimesPlayed`. Some objects even have special methods whose sole purpose in life is to set property values.

Comprehending Events

An *event* is something that happens to an object and something to which that object can respond with a predetermined action. Events include:

✔ **A program user's physical actions,** such as clicking with the mouse, moving the mouse, pressing a key, or jumping up and down and screaming. (Okay, so VBA can't recognize "jumping up and down and screaming" events.) The forms you design and the controls on them respond to this type of event, but so may objects in the application itself.

✔ **Things that happen to the object as the application conducts its business.** If you're talking about a document object, events may include the opening or closing of the document or the addition or removal of a page. In Word, the `Application` and `Document` objects recognize such events. In Visio, `Page` objects can respond to nine different events, including `BeforeShapeDelete` and `TextChanged`. See Chapter 4 for more examples of such non-form events.

Your VBA application specifies which events, if any, a given object can recognize. *Your* job is to write the code that determines what the object does when the event occurs. One point may bear clarification: You don't call an event from your own code. Instead, the object automatically takes whatever action you've programmed it to do when the event occurs.

I cover event programming for forms in Chapter 10. The same basic techniques are applicable to non-form events, but details vary from application to application and sometimes even within the same application. Your application's documentation or Help files should provide the specifics.

Identifying the Object You Want to Work With

To do anything useful with an object, you have to tell VBA what object you want to work with by using an *object expression* for this purpose. This is a special kind of VBA expression that uniquely identifies the specific object that interests you. Behind the scenes, the value that VBA calculates based on an object expression is an *object reference,* a value that you can think of as a street address for the object.

Figuring out the correct object expression you need is most of the battle. After you've done that, you can make your life much easier by creating a named variable for the object, using the expression to assign the corresponding object reference to the variable. From then on, you can refer to the object by the variable's name in your code.

Understanding object expressions

An object expression is a *code fragment* (an expression) that "points" at a particular object. You can set the object's properties, activate its methods, or assign the object to a variable by using a valid object expression.

The ideas that I cover here are critical to daily work with VBA, yet they're not easy to grasp at first. Because your program can work with many different objects of the same type, a complete object expression must specify all the objects that contain the one you have in mind. It's something like this: Suppose that you were told to go get "the boy." You'd immediately ask, "Well, which boy?" If you were told instead to get the oldest boy who lives in the third house on Mayflower Street, Arhoolie, Nebraska, United States of America, you wouldn't need to ask that question. (Of course, you might ask "Why?") However, if you're already in the third house on Mayflower Street, and if only one boy lives there, a command such as "feed the boy" is quite adequate. In the same way, if the context is clear, VBA doesn't need the entire list of objects.

Working with properties that are objects

A property of one object can be another object. Objects exist in a hierarchy, with one object, such as a document, serving as a *container* for other subsidiary objects, such as pages, worksheets, or what have you.

The connection between these ideas is probably obvious: If an object contains subsidiary objects, you can identify a subsidiary object via a property of the first object. The expression you use to specify this property *is* the object expression.

For example, consider the following expression, which identifies a specific Range object in a Word document:

```
ThisDocument.Sections(2).Range
```

Notice that this object expression contains two periods, not just one. See, Range is a property of the Section object, which is in turn a property of the ThisDocument object. This idea may make sense to you right away, but if not, the next section, "Getting objects," explains it in detail.

Getting objects

The Application object occupies the very top of the object hierarchy in most VBA object models. However, you usually don't need to include it in object expressions — VBA is smart enough to assume you're working with objects from the current application, unless you specify otherwise.

The typical Application object contains a Documents object, which is a collection representing all the open documents. If you want to work with a specific document, you identify it as a member of this Documents collection object. For example, Documents(5) represents Document object #5 in the Documents collection.

The previous example expression, however, starts with the special keyword: ThisDocument. In many VBA applications, ThisDocument or some similar keyword stands for the particular Document object associated with your project.

In Word, each Document object has a Sections property. This in turn refers to a Sections collection, an object that represents the set of all the pages in the document. So the first part of the previous expression — ThisDocument. Sections — identifies the particular Sections collection that belongs to the ThisDocument object. After you've identified the Sections object, you can select a single member of its collection. Thus Sections(2) refers to the second section in the document.

Now for the final part of the expression. The tricky part here is that, although .Range specifies a *property* of the Section object, the value of that property is a Range *object*. The entire expression, then, supplies an object reference to that Range object. Using an expression that threads its way through the object hierarchy like this to a specific object is called *getting an object* in VBA lingo.

Working with Collection objects

In the following example object expression, the Sections object is a *collection:*

```
ThisDocument.Sections(2).Range
```

A VBA collection is a special type of object that may contain any number of other objects.

Collection objects defined in VBA applications usually store just one type of object. Word's Section collections contain only Section objects. Only Page objects can belong to a Visio Pages collection. (VBA offers a generic Collection object in which you can store objects of any type. Chapter 13 describes how to create and manage your own collections.)

What you need to know about Collection objects is how to access the individual objects they contain. You have two options:

- **Refer to the object by its slot or *index number* in the collection.** That's the method used in the example expression — (2) refers to the second Section object in the Sections collection.

- **Refer to the object by name.** Many objects have names. If you know the name of the object you want to get, you can use it in the object expression instead of a number. Because Page objects in Visio can have names, the following example works:

```
ThisDocument.Pages ("My special page")
```

Creating object variables

Nobody likes to type a long, complex object expression, even a relatively straightforward one, such as ThisDocument.Sections(2).Range. If your program uses the same object more than once, create a named variable to hold a reference to that object. Then, wherever you need to type the complete object expression, you can enter the variable name instead.

Besides being shorter, easier to remember, and easier to type than the original object expression, an *object variable* has two other plusses. First, it makes your code run faster. VBA can locate the object directly, rather than having to look up a series of properties in a series of objects. Second, you can use the same object variable to store references to different objects. That way, you can write flexible code that decides which specific object to store in the variable when the program runs.

In outline, the technique for creating an object variable requires two steps:

1. **Declare a variable that you'll use to refer to the object.**

2. **Assign the object you want to work with to that variable.**

The next two sections cover the details on each of these steps.

Declaring an object variable

You declare object variables just as you do variables of other data types. The standard method is to use a Dim statement (just as with other types of variables, though, you can also use the `Public`, `Private`, or `Static` keyword instead of `Dim` to declare object variables). Here are two examples of object declarations:

```
Dim objGreatBigObject As Object 'A generic object
Dim objShapeObject As Shape 'A Shape object
```

The difference between these two declarations is important. The first statement declares an object variable but doesn't specify the type of object it will contain. You can use this variable to hold different types of objects as the need arises. The second statement declares the particular type, or *class,* of object that you want the variable to store. VBA doesn't allow you to place other object classes in the variable.

These two types of object declarations are referred to as *late binding,* in which no specific class is specified, and *early binding,* in which you do declare the variable as a definite object class.

Whenever possible, you should use early binding and declare the object variable as a specific class. The benefits of early binding include:

- ✔ **Fewer mistakes.** VBA doesn't let you assign incorrect objects to the variable. Just as important, by knowing which class of object you're working with, the compiler can check the rest of your code to make sure that you use properties and methods that are valid for that class. If you use late binding, the compiler can't perform this check. An error occurs while your program is trying to run if it attempts to use invalid properties or methods.

- ✔ **Faster performance.** Because the compiler can determine whether the object has the methods and properties you use in your program, the program doesn't need to pause to check this when it runs.

- ✔ **More understandable code.** You can tell by looking at the declaration what object class the variable is supposed to contain.

In spite of these advantages, using late binding is better in the following two situations:

- ✔ You may *intend* to use the same variable for different classes of objects. This can be a good idea when the different classes share methods or properties that you need to access in your code. With a variable, you don't need to rewrite code that does the same things using different objects.

- ✔ Some objects can't be declared via early binding when they're accessed from another application. Using objects from other applications is an advanced VBA technique — I introduce it in Chapter 10 and Bonus Chapter F — but you should know about this potential limitation.

As you know, a variable of the variant type can hold any type of information, and this includes object references. You can fill any variant with an object reference by using late binding.

Assigning an object reference to a variable

After you've declared an object variable, you must fill it with a reference to a specific object before you can use the variable. To do so, assign an object expression to the variable using the Set keyword, as in this example:

```
Set objShapeObject = ThisDocument.Pages(1).Shapes(4)
```

Note that this syntax differs a bit from the way you assign other types of data to variables (see Chapter 9). As with other data types, you place an equal sign between the variable name and the object to be assigned. However, you must start the statement with the Set keyword.

Emptying an object variable

When you no longer need to access an object, good form requires breaking the tie between the object and the variable with which it's associated. This way, your program can use the memory occupied by the object for other purposes, and you can be sure that your code won't mistakenly make changes to the object.

The technique is simple. Using a Set statement, just assign the Nothing keyword to the variable, as in this example:

```
Set objPriceIsNoObject = Nothing
```

Creating new objects

If the object you want to work with doesn't yet exist, you have to create it. In simple VBA programs, you use the Add method for this purpose. The Add method should work if you're trying to create one of the built-in objects available in your VBA application, that is, the application with which your project is associated. (In some applications, you may need to use a method named something like AddShape or AddDocument — check with the application's VBA Help files to be sure.)

Using the Add method

The trick is to know which object's Add method you should use. What you're looking for is the *container* object in which the object you want to create resides. The container is usually, but not always, a collection object.

For example, say that you want to create a new Layer object in Visio. A Layer object corresponds to a Visio drawing layer, which is a group of shapes that you can manipulate together. Each `Layer` object is contained in a `Layers` object, which represents a collection of (one or more) drawing layers. With this fact in mind, you choose the `Layers.Add` method to create a new individual layer.

Of course, you have to identify the specific `Layers` object in which VBA should create the new `Layer` object. A `Layers` collection object belongs to a particular `Page` object in a given `Document` object. With this in mind, the complete statement required to add a new `Layer` looks something like this:

```
ThisDocument.Pages(2).Layers.Add("NewLayer")
```

The `Layer` object has an `Add` method but you can't use it to create a new layer. The `Add` method of the `Layer` object adds a `Layer` object to an existing layer rather than creating a new `Layer`.

Similarly, if you want to add a new slide to a PowerPoint presentation, a statement like the following would be in order:

```
ActivePresentation.Slides.Add 1, ppLayoutTextAndClipart
```

Again, the new slide is added to the appropriate container object, a `Slides` collection.

Creating a variable for an object you create

Because you've gone to the trouble to type out a long object reference — that's what an `Add` statement amounts to — you may as well create a variable for the new object at the same time. That way, you can use the variable instead of another lengthy object reference whenever you want to access the object in your code. These two statements illustrate this technique:

```
Dim objMyBaby As Slide
Set objMyBaby = ActivePresentation.Slides.Add 1, _
  ppLayoutTextAndClipart
```

Creating objects with New and CreateObject

Other situations require different techniques for creating new objects. These alternatives apply when you're creating

- New copies of an existing form in your own project.
- Objects from a *different* application or ActiveX (COM) component.
- Specific objects based on classes you write in class modules.

Depending on the details of the situation, you may use the `New` keyword in variable declaration or `Set` statements, or the `CreateObject` function to create these objects. I bring up this possibility not to tell you how to do these things here — they're advanced techniques that I cover in Chapter 10 and Bonus Chapter F. Instead, I just want to steer you clear of the New keyword and the CreateObject function when you're trying to create ordinary objects.

What the definition of Is is, really

If you use variables to store object references, a time may come when you want to know whether the object a variable refers to is the same object referred to by another variable, or by an object expression.

Use the Is operator in an expression to check whether two object references refer to the same object. The expression's value is True if they do, or False if they refer to different objects. Here's some sample code to illustrate how Is works:

```
Dim objObject1 As Object, objObject2 As Object
...
If objObject1 Is objObject2 Then
 MsgBox "It's the same object!"
Else
 MsgBox "They're different objects."
End If
```

Of course, you can also compare an object variable against an object expression with the Is operator, as in the expression that I use in the following line:

```
If objObject3 Is ThisDocument.Pages(2).Shapes(3) Then
```

Note that you can't use Is (or any other operator) to compare the *contents* of two different objects.

Efficient Object Coding

VBA includes two multiple-line code structures designed to make your work with objects easier: the With and For Each...Next statements.

Using With statements

Whether you refer to an object with a short, mnemonic variable or with a lengthy, inscrutable object expression, typing it over and over again gets old in a hurry. But you may not have to.

If your program uses the same object in two or more consecutive statements, the With statement allows you to name the object only once. It's easier than retyping the object in each statement and also makes your code easier to understand, and faster, too. Here's an example:

```
With objIHaveNoObjection
  .Name = "The Last Straw" ' Set the Name property
  .DisplayName ' Call the DisplayName method
  sngArea = .Area ' Get the Area property's value
  intStretchFactor = .Rotate (60) ' Call the Rotate
  ' method, assigning its return value to a variable
End With
```

As you can see, within the With...End With structure, you can mix statements that get and set properties with statements that call methods. Note also that the With structure is not a loop — the statements it contains are executed only once.

You can *nest* With structures, that is, place them one inside another. This is perfect when you must perform multiple actions on both an object and one of the objects it contains. The following example illustrates how this works. It performs a series of sundry actions on an AutoCAD Block object. A nested With structure further manipulates one of the drawing objects contained in the Block. The comments in the example should give you a feel for what's going on.

```
With Blocks.Item("Gizmo")
' With the Block named "Gizmo" perform the following:
  ' Rename the Block object via the Name property
  .Name = "Doohickey"
  ' Use the Count property to see how many objects it has
  intNumberOfObjects = .Count
  ' Call AddCircle method with centerpoint = 0,
  ' radius = 5
  .AddCircle (0#, 5#)
  With .Item (1)
  ' This nested With refers to the first
  ' drawing object in the Block object
  ' Use Move method to move the drawing object
  .Move (15, 20)
  ' Change Color property of the drawing object
  .Color = 221
  End With
End With
```

One thing that this example doesn't illustrate is the fact that you can also use values returned by the object's properties or methods in conditions and other expressions. The following statements would be perfectly at home inside the outer With statement of the preceding example:

```
intNewColor = InputBox ("Enter a new color value for " _
 & "the first object in the " & .Name & "block.")
If .Count > 12000 Then
 MsgBox "This is a big Block!"
End If
```

Using For Each...Next structures

Although I devote Chapter 8 to VBA *control structures* (groups of statements designed to direct program flow), I mention one of these structures here since it applies exclusively to objects. A variation on the `For...Next` loop idea, the VBA `For Each...Next` structure performs a set of statements for each object stored in a collection. Although the two statements look much alike, they have some real differences — one of which is that `For Each...Next` is easier to use. Here's the syntax:

```
For Each element In group
(statements to be executed during each pass of the loop)
Next element
```

One key difference between a `For Each...Next` and the standard `For...Next` structure is that you don't have to specify the number of times that the loop should execute — VBA figures that out for you.

For Each...Next in action

The following simple example of a `For Each...Next` statement works in AutoCAD, in which the `Blocks` collection is, of course, a collection of `Block` objects and where each `Block` can hold an unlimited number of individual drawing objects, such as `Cone` and `3DFace` objects. All that this code does is display the name of each `Block` in the `Blocks` collection:

```
Dim objB As Block
For Each objB In Blocks
 Debug.Print objB.Name
Next objB
```

The example may be less than earthshaking, but you should appreciate the potential power. A `For Each...Next` loop can efficiently perform any combination of actions that are available via the methods or properties of each object in a collection.

Hasty escapes from For Each...Next

When you're searching for that particular needle in a boxful, the other needles in the box don't interest you. To perform some action on a specific object in a collection, place a nested `If...Then` statement inside the `For`

Each...Next loop. When the If...Then condition locates the object of your desire, you have no further need to search; an Exit For statement gets you out of the loop quickly.

With the AutoCAD Blocks collection still fresh in your mind, consider the following example:

```
Dim objK As Block
For Each objK In Blocks
  If objK.Name = "WidgetA" Then
  objK.Delete
  Exit For ' here's the escape hatch
  End If
Next objK
```

In this example, the loop uses a nested If...Then structure to hunt for a Block object named "WidgetA" among all the Block objects stored in the Blocks collection. After — and only after — the right Block is found, the statements within the If...Then structure executes. *Execute* is the correct term, for the first of these statements deletes the Block. Mission accomplished. The loop isn't needed anymore, so Exit For terminates it, and the program moves on.

Chapter 13

Baskets for Data Storage: Arrays and Collections

• •

In This Chapter

▶ Using arrays to manage multiple items of the same data type

▶ Understanding multidimensional arrays

▶ Using Collection objects as an alternative to arrays

▶ Defining your own data types to work with related information of different types

• •

*W*ith any luck, you should by this point be comfortable working with variables to represent data of all types, from simple numbers and text strings to sophisticated and powerful objects. But the VBA built-in data types don't meet every need. Frequently, you need to work with similar chunks of information as a group. That situation calls for an *array* — a structured storage compartment for multiple data elements of the same type.

You can work with sets of various types of items in Collection *objects* that you create based on a built-in class supplied with VBA. Within some limitations, collections can have significant advantages over arrays.

Occasionally, you may find it convenient to create your own *user-defined data type*. User-defined data types can be helpful in clarifying your code; they allow you to refer to separate but related items as parts of an entire entity. An array based on a user-defined data type can be a powerful device for working with groups of complex items.

Seeing A-rray of Hope

Suppose that you have a list of numbers representing prices, test scores, or the distances of certain astronomical objects from Earth. Imagine that you type that list on a piece of paper, with each item in a separate row. What you wind up with is a simple array. Here is an example:

Surefire winning lottery numbers

214236

545273

371453

891982

000000

941241

In a list of similar items, like this one, the individual items have unique values but otherwise lack special identifying characteristics. If you want someone else to ponder an item, you say something like, "It's the third item in the lottery-number list." VBA arrays work exactly this way.

Referring to the items in an array

Each VBA array has a name that corresponds to the title of a list kept on paper (like that list of lottery numbers in the previous example). To work with an individual item in the array, you refer to it by the array name and an *index* — a positive-integer number specifying the item's slot in the array. The expression `intLottoArray(3)` refers to the third item (or fourth, depending on the numbering system in effect) in the array called `intLottoArray`. If you're using a variable-naming scheme like the one I suggest in Chapter 6, that `int` at the beginning of the array name indicates that this array is supposed to contain integer values. Therefore, it's a safe bet that the value stored in `intLottoArray(3)` is an integer.

Understanding array data

You should be clear about two key points regarding arrays:

- **You can create arrays of any data type.** VBA happily stores strings, dates, currency values, and all numeric data types in arrays.

- **An array can hold only one data type.** You can't build an array with separate slots for both Date and String data type values.

True as this second limitation may be, you can easily overcome it. As you know, the `Variant` data type can store any kind of VBA data, and arrays of `Variant`s are perfectly okay. Information stored in a `Variant` consumes significantly more memory than it would if it were stored as a more specific data type, however, and this overhead can really add up with arrays of any size. Besides, a random assortment of different kinds of data stuffed into an array rarely makes sense.

On the other hand, working with related items of varying types in organized sets is common. That's the idea behind the typical database. In an address-book database, for example, each record represents a set of information items (such as name and address) about the same general topic (a person in your life). For this kind of data, creating a user-defined data type is the way to go — and you find out how to do so in the section "Defining Your Own Data Types," later in this chapter.

Using arrays of multiple dimensions

Before I get any deeper into working with the individual values stored in an array, I want to back up and consider arrays in general in more detail. One important concept to make room for somewhere is that arrays can have multiple *dimensions*. The simple list of lottery numbers in the example at the beginning of this section is a one-dimensional array. A table or spreadsheet with rows and columns corresponds to a two-dimensional array, as in this example:

Daily sightings of mud hens by three unnamed observers

12	2	21
4	9	3
11	0	0

Imagining arrays of three dimensions isn't much of a strain. Figure 13-1 shows a diagrammatic representation of one such three-dimensional array.

Although forming a mental picture of an array with more than three dimensions is tough, VBA has no trouble with them. VBA arrays can have up to 60 dimensions.

Figure 13-1: This diagram represents a three-dimensional array as a set of cubes, each containing a number.

Declaring arrays

Like ordinary variables, arrays must be declared before you can use them to store data. Fortunately, declaring an array is just like declaring a variable, with one addition to the declaration statement. Here are some examples:

```
' Declare one-dimensional array of Date data:
Dim datTimeOfImpact (cdatMaxObservations) As Date
' Declare array of Currency data, but don't set its size:
Public curPriceQuotes () As Currency
' Declare four-dimensional array of Integer data:
Dim intArrayOfIntegers (34, 13, 29, 4) As Integer
```

As you can see, the obvious difference between declaring an ordinary variable and declaring an array is that you add parentheses following the name. The parentheses can be empty, as in the middle example. Alternatively, the parentheses can contain values specifying the size of each dimension in the array. (Notice that in the first example, a named constant supplies the size of the one dimension in the array.)

Be sure to specify a data type when you declare an array by including the As Type part of the declaration. If you don't, VBA creates an array of Variants, which increases the memory requirements of your program and slows its operation. Arrays of Variants are permitted and may be the way to go in some situations, but you can declare them explicitly when appropriate.

The total number of individual data elements in an array is equal to the product of the sizes of each dimension. You already knew this fact, of course — but this point deserves a brief moment of your fully conscious attention. To figure the total number of integer data elements in the array intArrayOfIntegers (the third example in the set of sample array declarations at the beginning of this section), multiply $35 \times 14 \times 30 \times 5$. That little bitty declaration reserves space for an array consisting of 73,500 elements.

You may wonder why I say that the size of each dimension is one more than its value in the declaration statement (35 instead of 34 and so on). Read on for the answer.

Understanding array element numbering

Unless you specify otherwise, the elements in an array are indexed, or numbered, beginning with 0 — or, to put it slightly differently, element 0 is the first one in the array. For this reason, the value that you enter when sizing an array should be one less than the number of elements that you want to store. If the array is supposed to hold 10 elements, for example, enter 9 as the size.

When you later access the individual data elements in the array, you must keep this numbering system in mind. A reference to intArray (1) is actually a reference to the *second* element in the array.

If you don't like counting from 0, you can start numbering your array from a different number — which usually would be 1. To set things up so that VBA numbers all arrays in the current module starting from 1, place the following statement in the module's declarations section (before any procedures):

```
Option Base 1
```

This statement affects only arrays in the same module, so you must include it in every module if that's how you want to number all your arrays.

You can also specify a numbering scheme for any dimension in an individual array. Here's an example:

```
Dim sngNumbers (55 To 75, 7 To 16, 99)
```

This example declares a three-dimensional array whose first dimension consists of 21 slots numbered from 55 to 75. The second dimension holds 10 slots starting with number 7, whereas the last dimension has 100 slots beginning with 0.

Declaring fixed arrays

If you specify the size of the array when you declare it, its size remains fixed; your program can't make the array smaller or larger later. To declare a *fixed array,* include the size of each of the array's dimensions in the parentheses in the declaration statement. The statement

```
Dim strHappyThoughts (9, 19) As String
```

declares a two-dimensional array that *always* holds 10 rows and 20 columns of string data (of course, the array doesn't actually store the data in rows and columns, but thinking of the array as a tabular list is helpful).

Fixing the size of an array when you declare it can be good practice if you know for sure that the array size won't change. That way, your code can't accidentally make changes in the array size. A potential disadvantage: After the array is declared, the memory that it occupies is reserved for the life of the program and can't be released for other uses.

Declaring dynamic arrays

Declare your array as a *dynamic array* if you

- Don't or can't know the size of your array before your program runs.
- Know that the array's size will change during the course of your program.
- Want to free the memory that it occupies for other variables when you're through using the array. A large array can use a great deal of memory, which you can liberate if the array is dynamic.

To declare a dynamic array, just leave out the array's size when you declare it. The statement prepares VBA for an array of `Date` data elements but doesn't actually create the array:

```
Dim dateBirthdays () As Date
```

ReDim-ming dynamic arrays

A dynamic array can't hold any data until you actually create the array by specifying its size. Use the `ReDim` (re-dimension) statement to do so, as in the following one-dimensional array:

```
ReDim dateBirthdays (intNumberOfBirthdays - 1)
```

Notice that the size of the array created by this statement is based on a variable, presumably one whose value has been determined by a previous sequence in the program. You have to subtract 1 from this value to adjust for the way that VBA starts numbering arrays from 0 — assuming you haven't changed the default numbering system as I describe in the section "Understanding array element numbering," earlier in this chapter.

You must use the `ReDim` statement inside a procedure. You can re-`ReDim` a dynamic array as many times as you like, completely redefining the number of dimensions and their sizes. Just keep in mind that, ordinarily, resizing an array destroys its current contents. Also, you can't change the data type stored in the array except under special circumstances that are too complicated to explain here.

Preserving data when resizing an array

To hold on to some of the data when you resize an array, include the `Preserve` keyword in your `ReDim` statement. The following sequence of statements declares a dynamic array, creates it as a two-dimension array of specific size, and then makes the second dimension larger without destroying its existing contents:

```
Dim dblGalacticMasses () As Double
...
ReDim Preserve dblGalacticMasses (1 To 30, 1 To 50)
...
ReDim Preserve dblGalacticMasses (1 To 30, 1 To 100)
```

Actually, `Preserve` is of limited value — it doesn't allow you to change the number of dimensions in the array, and you can resize only the last dimension (you must still include the sizes of the other dimensions in the `ReDim Preserve` statement, however). Making the array smaller is legal, but if you do so, data in the deleted elements vanishes forever.

Addressing elements in an array

To work with a particular element in an array in your code, list the array name followed by the element's index in parentheses. The *index* contains an integer value for each array dimension. The expression strSayings (4,6), for example, uniquely identifies the string data at row 4, column 6 in a two-dimensional array of strings.

Remember that the numbers or values that you use in an index identify items in an array based on the numbering system that you specified when you declared the array. If you declare an array with the statement Dim strSayings (10, 20) As String, the expression strSayings (4,6) identifies the data at the fifth row and seventh column of the array. If the declaration was Dim strSayings (4 To 10, 6 To 50) As String, the same expression locates the data in the first row and first column.

Using array elements in code

With this system, you can use array data elements just as you would variables. You can

- Assign a value to an array element. The following example assigns a value to a single storage slot in a three-dimensional array of Currency values:

```
curBigDough(5,8,19) = 27.99
```

- Assign a value stored in an array to another variable, as follows:

```
datThatDate = datTheseDates(25,10)
```

- Use the value of an array element in an expression, as follows:

```
intA = 35 * (intB + intCounts(3,2))
```

Using variables in an array index

You're not restricted to literal values in the index, of course. Coding the index with variables is often crucial, as is allowing your program to decide which array element you need at the moment. The last line of the following program shows this method in action:

```
Sub FortuneTeller()
Dim strTodaysFortune(1 To 10)
Dim intUserChoice As Integer
strTodaysFortune(1) = "You become rich and famous."
strTodaysFortune(2) = "You will eat lunch with a stranger."
strTodaysFortune(3) = "Your stocks double in value!"
strTodaysFortune(4) = "You recall where you put your keys."
strTodaysFortune(5) = "A lovely bouquet arrives."
strTodaysFortune(6) = "You will skip lunch."
```

```
strTodaysFortune(7) = "All your dreams come true."
strTodaysFortune(8) = "You return overdue library books."
strTodaysFortune(9) = "No one sees your mismatched socks."
strTodaysFortune(10) = "You meet an old pal at fish market."
intUserChoice = InputBox("To see your fortune, enter a" _
 & " number between 1 and 10")
MsgBox strTodaysFortune(intUserChoice)
```

As an aside, this code would be greatly improved if you added statements to handle invalid entries by the user in the InputBox. Chapter 10 discusses the topic of validating data.

Finding the size of an array

Use the UBound function to discover how many slots are available in a given dimension of an array. UBound is especially useful when you're working with dynamic arrays, because you may not know how many elements an array contains at any given point in your program. The syntax is

```
UBound(arrayname, dimension)
```

The *arrayname* argument, obviously, is the name of the array you're working with, while the *dimension* argument is an integer that tells VBA which array dimension you're inquiring about. If you omit *dimension,* UBound returns the size of the first dimension.

Assigning data to an array . . . in bulk

When you first create an array, the individual elements contain no valid information. At some point in your program, you need to fill those vacancies with some meaningful data. If you're filling multiple values at the same time, the most efficient way to do this is to use nested For...Next loops, one for each dimension in the array. The loop counter is usually a temporary variable declared in the procedure containing the loops.

The following little program illustrates this technique, filling a three-dimensional array with a consecutive series of integers starting with 1. Here's the code:

```
Const Size As Integer = 3
Dim dblMatrix (1 To Size, 1 To Size, 1 To Size) As Double
Sub ArrayFiller ( )
Dim I As Integer, J As Integer, K As Integer, X As Integer
X = 1
For I = 1 To Size
```

```
For J = 1 To Size
    For K = 1 To Size
      dblMatrix(I, J, K) = X
      X = X + 1
    Next K
  Next J
Next I
End Sub
```

The nesting order for the loops determines the order in which data elements get filled. In turn, the order in which elements get filled often matters a great deal in determining their value.

Explaining how all this works in words alone is too complicated, so I'm going to use pictures. Refer to the sample code at the beginning of this section. Imagine the three-dimensional array in the example as a cube, with little cubelets representing the slots for individual data elements. Figure 13-2 illustrates the thought experiment.

Figure 13-2:
In this representation of an array, the arrows correspond to the array's three dimensions; each element has an address based on its position on each of these dimensions.

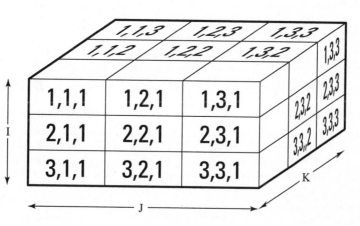

The line of code that actually fills the array elements with their values is `dblMatrix(I,J,K) = X`. In that statement the variables I, J, and K, respectively, represent the first, second, and third dimensions of the array. In Figure 13-2, I arbitrarily labeled the cube's dimensions with these variables.

Now notice how those variables are used in the `For...Next` loops. The counter for the outermost loop is `I`; for the next loop, it's `J`; and for the innermost loop, it's `K`. The key point is that VBA runs through the loops starting from the innermost and working out. The two cubes in Figure 13-3 show two stages early in the filling of the array by the sample code.

What's happening is that while the innermost loop is looping, VBA holds the values of `I` and `J` constant. When the first pass of the innermost loop is complete, the `J` loop — the next one out — has its first chance to loop. This raises the value of `J`; then the innermost loop again runs through an entire cycle. The value of `I` changes only when `J` has looped three times. After `I` is increased, the next row of the array begins to fill (see Figure 13-4).

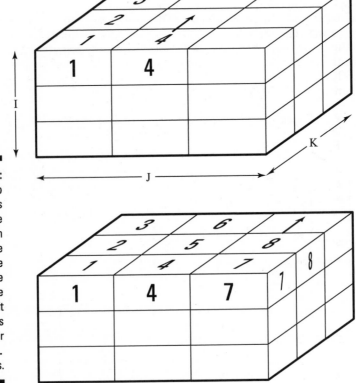

Figure 13-3:
These two diagrams illustrate the sequence in which the example procedure fills the array as it completes the inner `For...Next` loops.

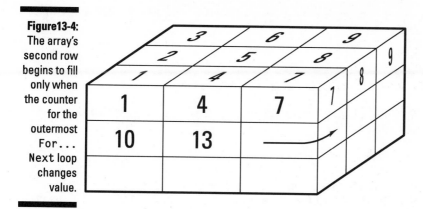

If you understand all this, you can see how changing the loops affects the values assigned to the array. Taking the original code on page xxx as the starting point, suppose that you reverse the nesting order of the loops, with K being the counter for the outermost loop. Here's how the block of code that actually fills the array would now read (notice that the variables are still in the same position in the assignment statement):

```
For K = 1 To Size
For J = 1 To Size
    For I = 1 To Size
       dblMatrix(I, J, K) = X
       X = X + 1
    Next I
   Next J
Next K
```

The resulting array looks like Figure 13-5.

This array contains the same values as the first one, but the values are in different slots.

Copying one array to another

REMEMBER

VBA 6 lets you assign the contents of one array to another with a simple statement such as

```
strCopyOfArray = strOriginalArray
```

The array on the left (the one receiving new contents) must be a dynamic array, but VBA ReDims it for you automatically to match the dimensions of the array on the right. The receiving array must also be able to hold the type of data contained in the original array.

In VBA 5, you have to copy array data element by element, as in

```
' determine the size of the original array and ReDim the
' second array to match
intArraySize = Ubound(strOriginalArray)
ReDim strCopyOfArray(intArraySize)
' perform the copy
For I = 0 to intArraySize
  strCopyOfArray(I) = strOriginalArray(I)
Next I
```

Managing Sets of Data with Collection Objects

When you need to manage sets of related information items, create a `Collection` object for the information. As I discuss in Chapter 12, VBA provides a generic `Collection` class for storage of just about anything. Based on this class, you can create as many `Collection` objects as you like. Although you can certainly use collections to store other objects, they can also hold just about any kind of data that VBA can handle.

A collection can store only a simple list of items, comparable to a one-dimensional array. But because collections are the most common types of arrays, they can do real service.

Weighing the trade-offs in using collections

When you're comfortable working with VBA objects, you may find that Collection objects are easier to use than arrays for handling sets of items. The Add and Remove methods make resizing the collection effortless; they are also much less likely to result in errors than repeatedly using ReDim statements in different parts of your program. (These advantages are especially significant when you must frequently add or remove individual items from the group.)

As a bonus, you can name individual items in the collection so that you can retrieve them by name later. This practice not only gives you an easy-to-remember handle for each element, but also makes accessing the data much quicker when your collection contains more than 100 elements.

One potential downside of using collections is the memory that they can consume. Collections use Variants to store all the information that they contain, and Variants use more memory than most other data types. In a large collection, the increased memory consumption can be significant.

But the most severe limitation of a generic VBA Collection object is that it can't store user-defined data types, which means that it isn't immediately suitable for work with database-type data (see the discussion of such data in "Defining Your Own Data Types" later in this chapter). You can overcome this limitation with some fairly simple programming, however. Besides, if you do serious database programming with VBA, you'll almost certainly be using the predefined database objects such as those provided in the Microsoft ADO and ODBC libraries, instead of creating your own.

Creating Collection objects

Set up a Collection object in your program as you would any other object, using an As clause to specify the type of object. As you do with other objects, you can use either of two variations on the basic technique:

✔ You can declare a variable name for the object and then use a Set statement to create it. Notice that you must use the New keyword in the Set statement to create the new collection, as follows:

```
Dim colMixedBag As Collection
...
Set colMixedBag = New Collection ' Create collection
colMixedBag.Add "Howard, Ethel" ' Add a data element
```

✔ To have VBA create the object automatically the first time that you use the variable in your code, you can declare it with the New keyword, as follows:

```
Dim colSetOfStuff As New Collection
...
' The next statement creates the Collection while
' adding an integer to it.
colSetOfStuff.Add intStuffing
```

Adding data to a collection

After you create your collection, use its Add method to fill it with data, just as you would to add objects to your VBA application's built-in collections (see Chapter 12). The examples in the previous section show the Add method in action.

The complete syntax of the Add method is as follows:

```
Add (item[, key][, before index][, after index])
```

The *item* expression is required. This expression can be a literal value, a variable, an object reference, or a complex expression involving two or more of these components — anything that returns a value that VBA recognizes. The remaining terms in the Add method are optional; I describe them in the next section.

Assigning keys to items

Although you can always refer to an item in a collection by its index or "slot number," giving the item a meaningful name can be helpful. Supply the name as a string when you add the item to the collection, as follows:

```
colFinancials.Add 14323.44, "February sales"
```

The preceding statement adds the value 14323.44 to the colFinancials collection. At the same time, the statement creates a *key* (a name) for the item. String variables work fine, too.

A key isn't just easier to remember than a numeric index; it's the *only* reliable key for quick access to an individual item in a collection. Because of the way that the Add and Remove methods work, the positions of specific data items in a collection can change. If item 63 becomes item 29, you can still pull out its value if you know its *key* name.

The only way to assign a key is with the Add method. To assign a key to an item that doesn't have one or to change the existing key, you must Add the item all over again and Remove the original copy.

Adding an item at a specific location

Sometimes, organizing the items in a collection in a particular order is convenient. But if you can't add the items sequentially in the desired order, no problem — the Add method allows you to insert any item where you want it to go. Use the method's optional before and after terms for this purpose.

Suppose that you want to insert a new item just before the 35th item in an existing collection. Here's the statement that you can use:

```
colAnimals.Add strSpecies, before 35
```

The added item becomes the 35th member of the collection, pushing down all the subsequent members. (Unlike arrays, collections are numbered beginning with 1.) You can also use an existing item's key to tell VBA where to insert the new item, as in

```
colVegetables.Add strVariety, after "Tomato"
```

In this case, VBA searches the collection for an existing item whose key is Tomato, inserting the new item immediately after it.

Paint or get off the ladder — you can include before or after in an Add method statement, but not both.

Adding multiple items efficiently

You can use a For...Next loop to add multiple data items to a collection efficiently, similar to the way that you fill an array, as follows:

```
Dim X As Integer, Y As Integer
Y = 12
For X = 1 To 30
 colHouseOfValues.Add Y * X
Next X
```

Removing items

To state the obvious, the Remove method deletes an item from the collection. You can identify the object that you want to excise by its index number or by its key, as in these examples:

```
colMineral.Remove 2123
colMineral.Remove "Bauxite"
```

Remember that when you remove an item, VBA fills in the gap, so to speak. The index numbers of all the other items farther down in the list decrease by 1.

Count-ing your collection

Losing track of the size of your collection is easy, especially after you Add or Remove a few items. VBA's generic Collection object has only one property — the Count property — but it's vital. You can assign the property to a variable, as follows:

```
intCollectionSize = col20Questions.Count
```

You can also test it in a conditional expression, as follows:

```
If colPrices.Count > 1000 Then
  MsgBox "We have too many entries!"
End If
```

In addition, you can use the Count property in a For...Next loop to perform some action on the entire collection, as follows:

```
Dim Z As Integer
For Z = 1 To colPrices.Count
  MsgBox "The price is " & colPrices(Z)
Next Z
```

A better practice, however, is to use a For Each...Next loop as I describe in Chapter 8.

Accessing items in a collection

To identify the specific item in a collection that you want to work with, you can use the item's index number or key (name), if it has one. For example, you might assign the value of a collection item to another variable, as shown here:

```
datBirthdate = colBirthdays("Sally Tran")
```

Unfortunately, you must keep track of the keys yourself — VBA doesn't provide a way to read the keys of an existing collection. And you can't modify an item's key without deleting the item from the collection and adding it again. Similarly, you can't place a new value in an existing collection item. The following assignment statement does *not* work:

```
colInventory(1465) = 119
```

Again, the only way to change a value in a collection is to remove the existing item and add a new one containing the new value. Dictionary objects, which I discuss in Chapter 14, overcome these limitations of collections.

Using collections for database-type data

Collections based on VBA's generic `Collection` class have limited value because you can't store user-defined types in them. You can work around this limitation by assigning keys very systematically. In the following example, each pass of the `For...Next` loop creates a database record in the collection. The record contains three fields, each of which is added by means of a key formed by concatenating a simple identifier with the current record number. Here's the code:

```
Dim I As Integer, strName As String
Dim strPhone As String, strAddress As String
For I = 1 to Total ' I identifies the record number
  ' Obtain data for this record
  strName = InputBox ("Enter name for this record")
  strPhone = InputBox ("Enter phone for this record")
  strAddress = InputBox ("Enter address for this record")
  ' Add "fields" for this record to collection
  colDatabase.Add strName, "Name" & I
  colDatabase.Add strPhone, "Phone number" & I
  colDatabase.Add strAddress, "Address" & I
Next I
```

You can then retrieve the information stored in a particular record by the identifier and number, as in this obvious example:

```
MsgBox colDatabase ("Name2")
```

If you plan to write a program of any complexity to manage database-style information, don't base it on simple collection objects; they have too many limitations. One alternative is to use plug-in database-access components, examples of which I cover in Chapter 14. If you want to do the work yourself, create your own classes for custom data objects. These classes can contain any combination of data types that you like, which you can access as properties. In addition, you can build in code to ensure that the correct type of information gets stored in each element. I also cover class modules, albeit briefly, in Chapter 14.

Defining Your Own Data Types

Unless you're a mathematician, multidimensional arrays of the same data type are of limited value. On the other hand, bread-and-butter data-management chores often call for working with *different* types of items in sets. A simple way to manage such information in a VBA program is to create a *user-defined data type* to hold it.

The tired filing-card analogy (shown in Figure 13-6) is still the best metaphor for this sort of information, although personal computers have been around for so long now that I don't know whether anybody uses filing cards anymore.

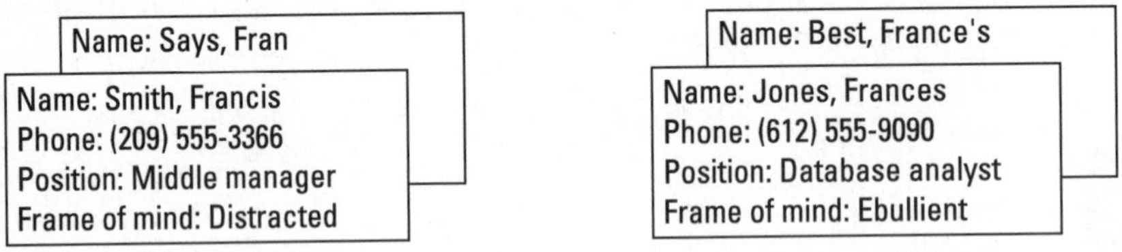

Figure 13-6:
These 3 x 5 cards represent structured information that you can store in VBA user-defined data types.

Name: Says, Fran

Name: Smith, Francis
Phone: (209) 555-3366
Position: Middle manager
Frame of mind: Distracted

Name: Best, France's

Name: Jones, Frances
Phone: (612) 555-9090
Position: Database analyst
Frame of mind: Ebullient

The garden-variety database represents the same arrangement in electronic form. A *database* consists of a set of records, each containing fields for individual items of information. The individual fields can contain different types of data (string, number, date, or what have you). Although the contents of an individual field vary from record to record, the field contains the same data type in every record.

Understanding user-defined data types

In VBA, a user-defined data type simply represents an amalgam of built-in data types of your choice collected under one roof, so to speak. After you define a user-defined type, you can declare variables of that type, just as you would declare variables of the built-in types.

An individual variable based on a user-defined type is comparable to a single filing card or to one record in a database. But to represent an entire set of filing cards or an entire database of records, you simply declare an array of a user-defined type.

Declaring a user-defined data type

Use the Type statement to declare a user-defined data type, as in this conventional example:

```
Type Personnel
   intEmpNumber As Integer 'Employee number
   strLastName As String
```

```
    strFirstName As String
    strAddress As String
    lngPhone As Long
    datDateHired As Date
End Type
```

This block declares a new user-defined type called Personnel. As the indented lines make plain, this type consists of three strings, a long integer value, and a date. (Notice that you must specify names for each of the elements when you declare the type; simply stating the elements' data types won't do.) When you declare a variable of your Personnel type, the variable automatically includes storage space for all five of these elements.

Notice also that a Type statement requires the End Type statement to close the block. If you leave out this last line, the compiler squawks at you.

Another key point: A user-defined type can be declared only at the module level (in the declarations section at the beginning of a module). You can't declare a user-defined type within a procedure.

Declaring variables of a user-defined type

Like the built-in data types, a user-defined type is merely an abstract concept until you actually declare a variable. There's nothing unusual about doing so; the standard syntax for declaring any variable applies. You can use the Public, Private, and Static keywords in declarations of user-defined-type variables. The following example, however, which declares a single variable, is a standard Dim statement:

```
Dim usrOnePerson As Personnel
```

Notice that you don't have to declare the elements within the user-defined type. Although the Dim statement gives your new variable a name, the names of the individual elements are fixed when you declare the type.

To create an entire database of your user-defined type, declare an array with a statement such as

```
Private PersonnelDatabase(1 To 25)As Personnel
```

Working with information in a user-defined type

After you declare a variable of a user-defined type, you can start stuffing it with information. To do so, you must assign a value to each of the elements within the type. And to do *that,* you identify the element by the name of the variable, followed by a period, followed by the name of the element, as follows:

```
usrOnePerson.strLastName = "Smith"
```

If you're filling several elements at the same time, a `With` statement reduces your typing, as in this sample:

```
With usrOnePerson
  .strLastName = "Jones"
  .strFirstName = "Bob"
  .datDateHired = #12/9/48#
End With
```

Use standard array indexing to assign data to the elements in an array of a user-defined type. In the following example, the index is given by a variable:

```
PersonnelDatabase(intENumber).strFirstName = "Sue"
```

Working with variables of a user-defined type as a whole

When a variable of a user-defined type contains a complete set of data, you can assign its contents to another variable of the same type — all at the same time, without messing with the individual elements that each variable contains. To assign the contents of the `usrOnePerson` variable to the second slot in the `PersonnelDatabase` array, use the following statement:

```
PersonnelDatabase(2) = usrOnePerson
```

This trick works great when you're saving or reading information to or from a disk file. You can save a database full of records on disk with code such as the following:

```
Sub WriteData()
Open "C:\Database\People.dat" For Binary As #1
For i = 1 To intDatabaseSize ' Loop for all records
  Put #1, , PersonnelDatabase(i)
Next i
Close #1 ' Close file--required step.
End Sub
```

Bonus Chapter E on the CD covers techniques for reading and writing disk files.

Part IV
The Part of Tens

The 5th Wave   By Rich Tennant

"This isn't a quantitative or a qualitative estimate of the job. This is a wish-upon-a-star estimate of the project."

In this part . . .

This short but succulent dessert section tickles the palate with a host of VBA delights. After nibbling on the samples introduced here, you're sure to want bigger bites.

Chapter 14 introduces a variety of advanced programming techniques that can make your VBA programs really sing. Topics include storing and retrieving information from the Windows registry, tapping the capabilities of other applications and components, reading and writing disk files, and adding more ActiveX controls to the Visual Basic Editor Toolbox. Chapter 15 surveys a flock of other VBA resources you should know about, including magazines, Web sites, and third-party programming tools.

Chapter 14

Ten (Minus Three) Really Cool Things You Can Do with VBA

· ·

In This Chapter

▶ Storing and retrieving program settings in the Windows registry

▶ Accessing objects in other applications

▶ Working with databases in VBA

▶ Storing and retrieving information on disk

▶ Storing tabular information in `Dictionary` objects

▶ Creating your own objects

▶ Installing other ActiveX controls

· ·

*I*f you've already read most of this book, you're a real VBA hotshot. Because you don't need much hand-holding, this chapter introduces a grab bag of potentially crucial skills in a hurry. I can't claim that I cover these rather advanced topics thoroughly, but you should be able to do productive work with the information that I provide here.

Storing Stuff in the Windows Registry

Although you can use little disk files to save and retrieve settings and other variables between times that you run your VBA program, the Windows registry is specifically intended for such housekeeping chores. VBA provides all the tools you need to create registry keys, place data in them, and retrieve that information later.

Use the `SaveSetting` statement to save an entry in the registry. The `SaveSetting` statement automatically creates the key you specify if it doesn't already exist. The syntax is as follows:

```
SaveSetting appname, section, key, setting
```

The *appname, section,* and *key* arguments are names corresponding to levels in the registry hierarchy. All the registry settings for a single VBA program should go in one main registry branch named for the program (use the *app-name* argument to identify this branch). You can divide the settings into sections and keys any way you want, using names for any of these arguments that suit you.

If you call your program "Random quotes" and want to add a registry setting that determines how often to pop up a dialog box containing a random quote, you can use a statement like this:

```
SaveSetting "Random quotes", "Options", "Poptime", "6"
```

The final argument, "6", specifies the actual data you want to store in the registry. Figure 14-1 shows the registry after you run this line.

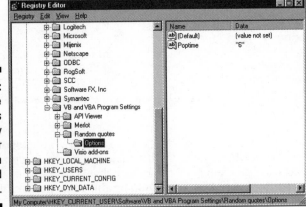

Figure 14-1:
The
Windows
Registry
Editor
showing a
key added
via VBA.

You use a similar function, `GetSetting`, to retrieve values from the registry. In the syntax shown here, the first three arguments are required, but the *default* argument is optional:

```
GetSetting (appname, section, key, default)
```

You can use the `GetSetting` function when you want to answer the question, "What's the current value stored in this registry key?" To use the `GetSetting` function in your code, assign it to an appropriate variable (a string or variant), as in

```
sngTiming = GetSetting ("Random Quotes", "Options", _
    "Poptime")
```

The optional *default* argument enables you to specify the value `GetSetting` should return if it can't find the key that you've specified.

VBA provides two other registry-related commands:

- ✔ The `GetAllSettings` function returns a list of key settings and their respective values in the form of a two-dimensional array of strings.

- ✔ The `DeleteSetting` statement enables you to delete the registry value as well as the key itself.

Exposing Themselves (Accessing the Objects of Other Applications)

A software world of dazzling variety lies just outside the confines of your particular VBA application — and you're free to travel there with VBA. An ever-increasing number of applications incorporate the `COM` object model, brazenly exposing their objects so that you can access them in your own programs (see Chapter 1 for theoretical background on `COM`).

As a relatively simple example, suppose you want to base a Visio organization chart on personnel data stored in your Microsoft Outlook folders. If your VBA skills extend to creating shapes and connections in Visio, your only new challenge is writing code to pull in the information "live" from Outlook. Because Outlook exposes its own objects through `COM`, connecting to Outlook in VBA lets you use those Outlook objects in your program just as if they were native to your "home base" VBA application.

Understanding the basics of cross-application programming

This rule may be obvious: You can use the objects of another application only if that application has been installed on your system. If that requirement is met, working with objects from another `COM`-based application requires three preliminary steps:

1. **In the Visual Basic Editor, add a reference to the external application's object library.**

2. **Declare variables for the objects you plan to use in the program.**

3. **Create the objects using the `CreateObject` function.**

I say more about each of these steps in the next three sections.

Adding a reference to the foreign object model

To inform the Visual Basic Editor about an external application's object model, you add and activate a *reference* to the application's *object library*. In the Visual Basic Editor, choose Tools⇨References to open the References dialog box.

Outlook's object library should already be listed in the dialog box, assuming you've already installed Outlook on your computer. You have to find it in the Available References list, checking its box to activate it and make its objects accessible. If the object library you want to use isn't listed, add the reference to the list yourself by using the Browse button.

Declaring external objects

Use standard VBA syntax to declare variables for objects from external applications. Use the Object Browser or the external application's Help file to learn which objects it makes available. The following statements declare variables for the Outlook objects required in the example program (the CD-ROM that comes with the book includes this code and the related fragments that follow in one complete module).

```
Dim objOutlook As Outlook.Application
         Dim objOLNamespace As Outlook.NameSpace
Dim colFolders As Outlook.Folders ' collection of folders
Dim objPeopleFolder As Outlook.MAPIFolder
Dim colPeople As Outlook.Items ' collection of contacts
Dim objPerson As Object ' one individual contact
Dim strName As String
```

Creating the external object

Declaring the objects announces your intention to use them. You must then actually create the objects you need with `Set` statements inside a VBA procedure.

The key to creating an object belonging to an external application is the `CreateObject` function. `CreateObject` starts the application, which in turn creates the object. The function's return value is a reference to the object, which you can assign to the appropriate variable. To start the application with a specific file or document, use the `GetObject` function instead.

Here's a sample procedure for the Outlook-Visio example — it instantiates the needed objects:

```
Sub PeopleDiagram()
Set objOutlook = CreateObject("Outlook.Application")
Set objOLNamespace = objOutlook.GetNamespace("MAPI")
Set colFolders = objOLNamespace.Folders ' all folders
Set objPeopleFolder = colFolders.Item("Personal Folders")
' redefine variables to drill down into folder hierarchy
Set colFolders = objPeopleFolder.Folders
Set objPeopleFolder = colFolders.Item("Contacts")
Set colPeople = objPeopleFolder.Items
' Call a Sub procedure that puts the Outlook data to work:
ChartAName
End Sub
```

Note that in many situations — including this example — you need the CreateObject function only once. After you create the external application's object, you can access any of its properties and methods. In this case, as is common, those properties include other objects (here, the Folders collection, the Personal Folders and Contacts folders, and the collection of items within the Contacts folders).

Applications you run from within your code via the CreateObject function start up in hidden form — you can't see them on-screen. This is great when you want to use an application's data in your own program without distracting the user. However, sometimes you want to see the application in its usual form. Depending on the application, you may have to activate a Display method or set a Visible property to True. In the case of the previous Outlook example, use the following statement to make the Outlook window appear:

```
objPeopleFolder.Display
```

Using the external objects

At last, you're ready to roll — you can now use the external application's objects in your code, just as if they came from your VBA application. Here's an example of how you might use this technique in Visio to create an organization diagram labeled with the names in the Outlook Contacts folder.

```
Sub ChartAName()
For each objPerson in colPeople
 strName = objPerson.FullName
 ... (code to build Visio diagram from this data)
Next
End Sub
```

The sample code on the CD-ROM doesn't include this procedure because I can't be sure you have Visio. Instead, the `PeopleDiagram` procedure just displays a message box for each contact in the Outlook data. (Of course, you may not have Outlook either, and if that's the case, the example won't work for you at all.)

Managing Database Data with VBA

If you plan to use VBA to work with data stored in "real" databases, such as Microsoft Jet (the database format used by Access), SQL Server, or dBase files, you need help, friend. That help comes in the form of an *object library*. A database object library turns databases and their components — tables, queries, and reports — into proper objects with properties and methods. Because the database is packaged as a set of objects, you don't have to muck around with the details of the database's structure. Additionally, you can use the same set of objects to manipulate many different types of databases. Bonus Chapter D has more information on database programming with VBA, including an introduction to programming with the ADO object library and the SQL database language.

Working with Disk Files

Via an external object library, VBA lets you use object-oriented techniques to manage disk files, performing tasks such as reading directories and copying files. I discuss these techniques in the sections "Working with file properties" and "Copying, moving, and deleting files," both later in this chapter. Alternatively, you can use VBA's older file-handling functions and statements, which I list and briefly describe in Table 11-9.

The time may come when you want your VBA program to store information in a disk file. Maybe you will want to keep track of some settings that the user has selected, or you'll want to keep the values of a few variables on hand for reuse the next time the program runs. Or maybe the program needs to save the results of many different calculations in a disk file or work with information stored in a text document.

Whether you need to access lots of information or just a little, VBA makes working with disk files as painless as you could hope. You don't have to know anything about how Windows keeps track of files. Instead, a few simple VBA objects and their methods handle all the details for you.

By way of clarification, I'm not talking here about reading and writing the disk files of the documents from the host VBA application. Of course, your VBA programs can work with the information those documents contain, and manipulate document files as a whole (typically with `Open` and `Save` methods).

Understanding how VBA handles files

As I point out in Chapter 11, VBA lets you work with files as objects, manipulating these file objects by using their methods and properties. However, this capability isn't part of VBA proper; rather it relies on an external object library. As I detail in the next section, you must add a reference to that library before you can work with files as objects.

VBA has a built-in file-handling scheme that does *not* treat files as objects. You use statements and functions, rather than object methods, to carry out file-related actions. These same techniques still work in VBA, but the file object is preferable for most tasks. However, Table 11-9 lists the relevant statements and functions (and the "Working with Disk Files" chapter on the CD introduces their use).

Referencing the Scripting Runtime library

The Microsoft Scripting Runtime object library supplies the basic tools you need for working with files as objects. Before you write any file-related code, you must reference this library in your VBA project. And before you do that, you must make certain the library is present on your computer.

The Scripting Runtime library lives in a file called SCRRUN.DLL that's located in the Windows\System folder. The library is installed automatically if you're running Windows 98 or Windows NT with the Option Pack, or if you have VBA 6 on your system. If you're working with VBA 5 in Windows 95, or if for any other reason you don't seem to have the Scripting Runtime, you can download it from the Microsoft developer Web site at msdn.microsoft.com/scripting/.

After you've ensured that the Scripting Runtime library is present on your system, you must then add a reference to it in each VBA project in which you intend to use the library. Do so as follows:

1. **Select the target project in the Project Explorer.**

2. **Choose Tools⇔References to open the References dialog box.**

3. **Scroll down to the Microsoft Scripting Runtime item and check its box.**

4. **Close the dialog box.**

   Ta-da! You're done.

Again, you must repeat these steps for each project that uses the Scripting Runtime no matter which version of VBA you're using. (See the "Exposing Themselves (Accessing the Objects of Other Applications)" section, earlier in this chapter, for a detailed discussion about using external object libraries.)

VBA programs that rely on the Scripting Runtime should be distributed only to other users who have the required .DLL file installed on their computers. If you can't be sure, you can distribute the .DLL with your project (include installation instructions).

Accessing files

After you've installed the Scripting Runtime and added a reference to it to your VBA project, you're ready to write object-oriented VBA code that manipulates any file on your disk. Working with an individual file as an object requires three simple coding steps:

1. **Create a** FileSystemObject — **the top-level object for accessing disk files.**

2. **Use a method of the** FileSystemObject **object to open the file in question, or to create the file from scratch.**

3. **Fiddle with the file object by using its methods and properties.**

The following code fragment illustrates these steps. It creates a File object for a file called lacewings.txt, and then copies that file to another location:

```
Dim objFileSystem As FileSystemObject
Dim objFile1 As File
Set objFileSystem = _
  CreateObject("Scripting.FileSystemObject")
Set objFile1 = _
  objFileSystem.GetFile("C:\bugs\lacewings.doc")
objFile1.Copy ("c:\my documents\buggy.doc")
```

Working with file properties

Once you have a File object to work with, you have easy access to all kinds of information about the file via its properties. For example, you can use the Size property to check the file's size on disk:

```
Dim lngFileSize as Long
lngFileSize = objFile1.Size
```

You can also see when the file was last modified using the DateLastModified property:

```
Dim dateFileDate as Date
lngFileSize = objFile1.DateLastModified
```

Copying, moving, and deleting files

File objects can be copied, moved, or deleted using the appropriate method, as in the following:

```
objFile1.Copy "c:\weak efforts\"
objFile1.Move "c:\heroic measures\"
objFile1.Delete
```

Note that unless you're changing the file's name, you don't have to supply a name for the Copy and Move methods, just the destination path. If you don't include the file name, be sure to add a backslash at the end of the path. And by the way, the File object retains its association with the moved file.

To copy, move, or delete *groups* of files, use the CopyFile, MoveFile, and DeleteFile methods on a FileSystemObject object, not on an individual File object. You can use wildcards in the file name specifications of the FileSystemObject methods. The FileSystemObject also provides CopyFolder, MoveFolder, and DeleteFolder methods that act on entire folders, and any subfolders they contain.

Reading and writing data in files

Although it's important to be able to copy, move, and delete entire files, you may also be interested in the data stored within a file. This section introduces the object-oriented techniques you need to read and write that information.

Note that you can use only file-related objects to access file contents as a continuous block of text. Of course, that text can contain numeric data, so you're not limited to storing and retrieving names, poetry, and prose. However, you have to access the data in sequence — you can't just jump to any location in the file.

But File objects don't provide a means for working with data in a structured format as you might with simple databases. In structured files, each record occupies a predetermined amount of space, allowing you to read or write any record by specifying its number. You can work with these random access files in VBA, but not via objects. Instead, use VBA's Open, Put, and Get statements.

Opening text stream objects

To read or write data in a file, you must first open the file as a *text stream*. As you might expect, you work with a text stream in your code as a TextStream object. You can accomplish this in one of the three following ways:

- ✔ Open an existing `File` object as a text stream.

- ✔ Create a new file and open it as a text stream in one step.

- ✔ Directly open an existing disk file as a text stream.

The following procedure opens three separate `TextStream` objects (using each of these techniques, in the order presented in preceding list), writes data to one of them, and then closes them:

```
Sub TextStreamDemo()
Dim objFileSystem As FileSystemObject
Dim objFile1 As File
Dim objTextStream1 As TextStream
Dim objTextStream2 As TextStream
Dim objTextStream3 As TextStream
Set objFileSystem = _
 CreateObject("Scripting.FileSystemObject")
' Create a File object, then use it to create a
' text stream object
Set objFile1 = _
 objFileSystem.GetFile ("C:\ExistingFile.txt")
Set objTextStream1 = _
 objFile1.OpenAsTextStream (ForReading)
' Create new file and open as text stream object
Set objTextStream2 = _
 objFileSystem.CreateTextFile ("C:\NewFile.txt")
' Open an existing file as a text stream
Set objTextStream3 = _
 objFileSystem.OpenTextFile ("C:\OldFile.txt")
' Write 2 lines of text to one of the streams
objTextStream2.WriteLine "In a cavern, in a canyon"
objTextStream2.WriteLine "Excavating for a mine"
' Close all 3 text streams
objTextStream1.Close
objTextStream2.Close
objTextStream3.Close
End Sub
```

Although all three techniques create `TextStream` objects, they aren't interchangeable. The particular technique you use determines how you access data in the underlying file. See the next section for more on this subject.

Choosing and using data access modes

A given `TextStream` object can enable you to read data from a file, write data to it, or both. Actually, a `TextStream` object allows one or more of *three* distinct *IO modes* (IO stands for "input-output"). One mode is *reading*, and the other two modes are for writing — *ordinary writing* (which starts writing characters at the beginning of the text stream) and *appending* (which starts writing at the end).

The IO mode, or modes, available for a particular TextStream object depend on which technique you use to create the text stream (of the three that I describe in the previous section) and, in the case of the File object's OpenAsTextStream method, which mode you specify. Here's a breakdown:

Method (Object)	IO Modes Available in Resulting Text Stream
CreateTextFile	read and write (FileSystemObject object)
OpenTextFile	read and append (FileSystemObject object)
OpenAsTextStream	read, write, or append (one IO mode only) (File object)

When you create a TextStream object from a File object, you specify the IO mode as an argument to the OpenAsTextStream method using one of three appropriately named constants: ForReading, ForWriting, and ForAppending. For example, if you wanted to add more text to the end of an existing file, you might open a text stream with the following statement:

```
Set objTS = _
  objFile.OpenAsTextStream (ForAppending)
```

Reading and writing file data

After you create a TextStream object with the IO mode or modes that suit your purposes, you can get down to business and start working with the file's contents. Several simple methods are at your disposal.

You can read and write data as individual characters or in lines. Unless each item of data occupies the same number of characters, I recommend the line-oriented technique. When you need to read a line of data, you don't have to know how long the line is, just which line number it occupies. And a "line" can consist of any number of data characters, from zero on up.

Anyway, to read data from a text stream, assign to a variable the value returned by one of the TextStream object's read methods. This sample code should give you the idea:

```
' reads the next line from the file into the variable
strSomeText = objTextStream.ReadLine
```

The available read methods are as follows:

Method	What It Does (of TextStream Object)
Read(characters)	Reads the specified number of characters starting from the current file position
ReadLine	Reads all the characters from the current file position up to the next newline character
ReadAll	Reads the entire file
Skip(characters)	Skips the specified number of characters when reading a file. The next read begins with the first character after the skip.
SkipLine	Skips the entire next line in the file. The next read begins with the first character after the skipped line.

To write data to a text stream, you simply supply the characters to be written as a string to the Write or WriteLine method, as in

```
' write a literal string
objTextStream.Write "Hello, Central."
' write a variable, followed by a newline character
objTextStream.WriteLine strMyTwoBits
```

Method	What It Does (of TextStream Object)
Write(string)	Writes the specified string to the text stream
WriteLine(string)	Writes the string plus a newline character to the text stream
WriteBlankLines(lines)	Writes the specified number of newline characters to the text stream

Closing text streams

After reading from or writing to a text stream, always close the TextStream object to free up system resources and memory, so other programs or users can access the file. The Close method is simplicity itself:

```
objSomeTextStream.Close
```

Understanding text stream limitations

Text streams are fine for recording and retrieving relatively small amounts of data. The main problem is that you can't move freely around in them. The read methods start reading data from the beginning of the file and continue toward the end of the file. Although you can use the Skip and SkipLines methods while reading to jump ahead a specified number of characters or lines, respectively, you can't skip in reverse — a statement such as `objTextStream.Skip(-10)` causes an error.

Unfortunately, `TextStream` objects don't have a method or property for specifying the starting position for the next read directly. However, you can accomplish more or less the same thing. You must first close and reopen the text stream, and then `Skip` one fewer characters than the desired location. For example, if you want to start reading from the 5th character in the file, the following statements do the trick:

```
objTextStream.Close
Set objTextStream = objFile.OpenAsTextStream(ForWriting)
objTextStream.Skip(4)
objTextStream.Read(25)
```

You're even more limited when you write data to text streams because you can't skip around at all in the file. Each write action starts where the previous one left off, overwriting any text that might already be present in the file.

If you need a way to alter some data somewhere within a file without changing the information that comes before it, you must read in the entire file, make the changes in the resulting string variable or variables, and then rewrite all the data to the file.

Using Dictionary Objects

`Dictionary` objects are useful for storing simple 2-column tabular information. For each entry in the table, one column contains the item's name, or *key,* the other column the value you're interested in. Think of a dictionary — the words would be the keys, and the definitions their values. But `Dictionary` objects can store values of any data type.

You can work with `Dictionary` objects in both VBA 5 and VBA 6. However, they aren't a built-in feature of VBA itself. Instead, they're available through the Microsoft Scripting Runtime library, which I discuss in detail in the section "Working with Disk Files" earlier in this chapter. To use `Dictionary` objects in a VBA program, you must follow the directions in the section "Referencing the Scripting Runtime library," earlier in this chapter.

Dictionary object basics

Use the techniques that I describe in the "Exposing Themselves (Accessing the Objects of Other Applications)" section, earlier in this chapter, to declare a variable for your dictionary and then to create the dictionary, as shown in this example:

```
Dim dictBigCats As Scripting.Dictionary
Set dictBigCats = CreateObject("Scripting.Dictionary")
```

Next add keys and values to the dictionary by using the Add method, as in:

```
dictBigCats.Add "Cheetah", "Fast and lean"
dictBigCats.Add "Lion", "Roaring and maned"
dictBigCats.Add "Panther", "Black, not pink"
```

Better than collections

Dictionary objects improve on VBA's similar Collection objects, which I cover in Chapter 12, in several simple but important ways:

- ✔ You don't need to know the keys to get at them, and the associated values. Instead, you can access the keys *en masse* with a For Each...Next loop as in:

  ```
  For Each airplane in dictBiplanes
    MsgBox dictBiplanes(airplane)
  Next
  ```

- ✔ You can change the value of an entry by directly assigning a new value using the key. In the following example

  ```
  dictVacationDestinations("Number1") = "Fresno"
  ```

  In collections, you have to delete the original entry, and then add a new one.

- ✔ You can delete all the entries in a dictionary by using the RemoveAll method. To accomplish the same task with a collection, you must use a For Each...Next loop.

I don't have room to detail techniques for sorting dictionaries and selecting subsets of items that match your criteria. However, such basic database functionality is relatively simple to implement. You can find guidance and code samples in Bruce McKinney's article "Understanding the Dictionary Class" in the July, 1999, issue of *Visual Basic Programmer's Journal* (Fawcette Technical Publications), also available online at www.vbpj.com.

Do-It-Yourself Objects

After you become comfortable using the built-in objects available in VBA and other object libraries, you may want to try your hand at building your own. Although you can perform great feats of legerdemain using standard Sub and Function procedures, compartmentalizing your code into objects can have real advantages, to wit:

- ✔ By keeping all the code that manipulates a set of data inside a single object, you reduce the opportunities for bugs to creep into your program when you make modifications.

- ✔ Your programs are easier to read and understand.

- ✔ You can create as many independent copies of an object as you want by writing two quick statements for each copy.

- ✔ Mentioning the benefits of *polymorphism* will probably get me into trouble, but . . . using the same properties and methods with different object classes can be handy. That's what polymorphism is all about. I don't have room to cover this topic here, but you should know that this powerful programming technique exists. Books on advanced VBA topics cover polymorphism.

As you know by now (especially if you read Chapter 12), an object consists of some data (the object's properties) and code that alters that data (its methods). Because properties are just variables and methods are just procedures, writing the actual code that defines an object is no big deal. But you do have to follow some rules so that VBA can figure out what you're trying to do. The next few sections describe these rules.

Creating class modules

In VBA, a *class* is the pattern upon which an object is based. The class determines which properties, methods, and events the object has, and how each of those components behaves.

To create a class, you start by inserting a new class module in your VBA project (choose Insert⇨Class Module). A class module window looks and works exactly like a code window. Before going any further, name the new class using the (Name) item at the top of the Properties window.

Understanding the components of a class definition

The typical class has three main components:

- ✔ Private declarations for the variables used internally by the object

- ✔ Public property procedures that allow procedures in your standard modules to retrieve or alter current property settings

- ✔ Public method procedures that define actions that the object's methods will perform

The simple class definition shown here for a make-believe `Thermostat` class has all three of these elements. This example does nothing useful, but it does work and it's on the CD-ROM in case you want to try it out. If you want to enter the code yourself, name the class module `Thermostat` in the Properties window, and then type the following in its Code window:

```
Private sngDegrees As Single ' property variable
' Code for the Let Temperature property procedure:
Public Property Let Temperature(ByVal sngInput As Single)
  sngDegrees = sngInput
End Property
' Code for the Get Temperature property procedure:
Public Property Get Temperature() As Single
  Temperature = sngDegrees
End Property
' Code for the CalculateEnergyUse method:
Public Sub CalculateEnergyUse()
  Const cstConversionFactor = 2.45
  Dim dblResult
  dblResult = sngDegrees * 365 * cstConversionFactor
  MsgBox "Annual energy use for this thermostat" & _
  " setting is estimated at " & dblResult & " watts."
End Sub
```

Declaring class variables

Use the Declarations section at the top of the class module to declare any variables that you plan to access in more than one property or method. Always declare them as `Private`. After all, the whole point of using objects is to ensure that your program can't access the data directly. Variables that you use only in one property or method should be declared there.

At a minimum, you need to declare a variable for each of the object's properties. The variable name should *not* be the name as the property (I show you how to define the property's name in a moment). But you can also declare other data that the object uses internally and that won't be accessible to other parts of your program.

Writing property procedures

The secret to endowing an object with a property is to write a pair of special procedures, the `Let` and `Get` *property procedures*. Both procedures in each pair should have the same name.

The name of a property is the name you choose for the property's `Let` and `Get` procedures. The name should describe the content or function of the property, of course.

Oh, one other point: If you're creating a property representing an object reference, you substitute a `Property Set` procedure for a `Property Let` procedure as half of the property procedure pair. Otherwise, such properties work the same as properties of other data types.

Setting object properties with Property Let procedures

A `Property Let` procedure sets the value of a property. In its simplest form, a `Property Let` procedure takes a value supplied as an argument, assigning that value to a variable that represents the property. To repeat the previous example:

```
Public Property Let Temperature (ByVal sngInput As Single)
  sngTemp = sngInput
End Property
```

When in the main part of your program you write a statement that sets the property, such as the following, VBA calls the `Let Temperature` procedure with 75 as the argument:

```
Thermostat.Temperature = 75
```

Of course, your property procedures aren't limited to one line of code. You can add statements that check the argument to ensure that it falls in a valid range before you assign it to the property. You can also perform other actions, depending on the particular argument.

Retrieving object properties with Property Get procedures

A `Property Get` procedure works like a `Function` procedure in that it returns a value — the value of the property, of course. As in a `Function` procedure, you assign the value you want it to return to the procedure name — which also happens to be the property name. Here's the example code again:

```
Public Property Get Temperature() As Single
  Temperature = sngTemp
End Property
```

Other parts of your program can call the `Get Temperature` procedure to assign its return value to a variable, or test the return value in conditional statements, as in these examples:

```
sngCurrentSetting = Thermostat.Temperature
```

```
If Thermostat.Temperature > 80 Then
  MsgBox "Consider turning down the heater!"
EndIf
```

Writing methods

Methods are simply ordinary `Sub` and `Function` procedures that you happen to store in a class module. In most cases, of course, a method should do something directly related to the object itself, by manipulating the data stored in the object. But if you want, you can add a method that calculates the price of tofu in Tennessee to any class.

VBA automatically associates methods you write with the class you add them to. You can call your own methods from other parts of the program just as you would the methods of built-in objects.

Using your custom objects

You use an object based on one of your own classes in the same way you would work with the built-in objects of VBA and your application. The steps are:

1. **Declare a variable for the object, as in:**

```
Dim objCustomThermostat As Thermostat
```

2. **Use a** `Set` **statement to create the actual object you'll be working with.**

For example:

```
Set objCustomThermostat = New Thermostat
```

3. **Access the object's properties or trigger its methods as you would with any other object.**

For example:

```
objCustomThermostat.Setting = 65
objCustomThermostat.CalculateEnergyUse
```

Adding ActiveX Controls

Despite its reputation for software imperialism, Microsoft has taken pains to make its development tools "open." Based on the ActiveX spec, anyone can create new controls that work with just about every Windows-based programming language — including C++, HTML, Visual Basic — and VBA. Of course, Microsoft defines the standards that govern how these plug-in software components work, so it hasn't actually given up any power.

Anyway, the benefit to you is that you can add new features by plugging in additional ActiveX controls that don't come in the standard VBA set. You can freely mix controls from any source to meet the needs of your programming projects. And all ActiveX controls work in fundamentally the same way as the built-in controls — which, by the way, are ActiveX controls, too (see Chapter 10).

Chapter 15 covers a smattering of the hundreds of commercial and shareware ActiveX controls you might find useful in your own work. In this chapter, I stick with the general techniques for using ActiveX controls and tips on accessing the common dialog box control that comes with Windows.

Some ActiveX controls don't work properly in every programming environment. Before you plunk down money for a control, be sure to verify that it actually performs as promised in your version of VBA. Also, be aware that ActiveX controls written in Visual Basic may work in your VBA program, but are likely to require the large (approximately 2MB) Visual Basic runtime files.

Adding new controls to the Toolbox

Before you can use an ActiveX control in your VBA programs, you must do three things:

1. **Install the control software on your computer's hard disk.**

   I guess that makes sense.

2. **Register it as an available control in Windows.**

   You can register controls in various ways. The installation process may have done it for you, but if you have to do it yourself, the easiest way for VBA programmers is in the Visual Basic Editor.

3. **Select the control to activate it for use in VBA.**

Registering a control

To register a new control, make sure that you know the name of the disk file that contains the control and where it's located on your hard disk. Then follow these steps:

1. **Choose Tools⇨References to display the ActiveX references available to your project.**

2. **Click Browse to display a standard-issue Windows dialog box for opening files.**

   In the Files of Type combo box, select ActiveX controls.

3. **Locate the file for the control and double-click it to open it.**

   Opening the file returns you to the References dialog box.

4. **Scroll to the item for the control in the list and make sure that its little check box is checked.**

5. **Close the dialog box.**

Putting the tool in your Toolbox

After you've registered a new control, your next step is to activate it by placing its icon on the Toolbox. Here's how:

1. **Select any** UserForm **window active in the Visual Basic Editor so that the Toolbox is visible.**

2. **Either right-click the Toolbox and select Additional Controls or choose Tools⇨Additional Controls.**

3. **Scroll through the list of available controls to locate the one that you want to activate; when you find it, check its little check box.**

4. **Close the dialog box.**

   The icon for the newly activated control appears on the Toolbox. Figure 14-2 shows the Toolbox with a bunch of new controls.

Figure 14-2:
The VBA
Toolbox
sporting
a bunch
of new
ActiveX
controls.

If you use lots of third-party controls, you can organize them on separate pages of the Toolbox. To add new pages to the Toolbox, right-click over the tabbed area at the top and choose New Page. The page that's showing when you activate a control is the one that receives the control's icon.

Using ActiveX controls in your programs

As soon as you have an ActiveX control on the Toolbox, you can add it to your forms just like the stock controls that come with VBA. However, to make the control do something useful, you need to know how its properties and methods work. For that, you need the documentation and Help files that come with the control. If the control was properly designed and installed, you should be able to get Help on any of its properties by pressing F1 when that property is selected in the VBA Properties window.

Chapter 15

Ten (Times Three) VBA Resources

● ●

In This Chapter

▶ Getting VBA information from software publishers

▶ Finding the prime printed periodicals pertaining to VBA

▶ Looking for VBA resources on the Web

▶ Getting cool ActiveX controls and add-on software tools

● ●

*A*fter you can tread water comfortably at the deep end of the VBA pool, you're ready to start flailing around in style. This chapter points you in the direction of further information and key software tools that together help make you an accomplished swimmer. (Disclaimer: The number mentioned in the chapter title may not agree with the actual count of VBA resources that I mention in this chapter — I never actually added them up.)

Your First Stop for More VBA Info

VBA programming is actually pretty simple, at least when it comes to working with variables, controlling program flow, and displaying forms. You're more likely to hit a sandbar with your VBA application's object model. You need to know which objects you need in your program, how to refer to them correctly, and which of their properties and methods to access, or you'll find yourself on frustrating bounces through the Help system. When you need guidance with a VBA application's objects, the first place to turn is the publisher who created the application in the first place.

Steal that source code

The maker of every VBA application offers help of one kind or another when it comes to using that application's features and object model in your programs. Remember to check the Help files supplied with your application for source code examples as well as more formal reference information. Beyond that, you can often find entire sample programs on the publisher's Web site. All of this material is fair game as a starting point for your own procedures and programs.

Look at what's available from Microsoft

What? After reading this book, you need *more* information on VBA? Well, consider buying a copy of the Microsoft Visual Basic documentation. Essentially, the documentation is simply a printed copy of the Help files, but many people find the information easier to refer to on paper rather than in electronic form.

You can find lots of other resources for VBA programmers on the Microsoft Developer Network Web site. The main VBA site is:

```
www.msdn.microsoft.com/vba/
```

For developers, the most relevant page is the Corporate Developer Home. You should also look at the Visual Basic site:

```
www.msdn.microsoft.com/vbasic/
```

Microsoft also has a special page for VBA development in Office. The address is:

```
www.msdn.microsoft.com/office/
```

The areas for the individual Office applications and the Microsoft Knowledge Base offer articles with programming tips and traps for the individual Microsoft VBA applications.

Magazines and Newsletters

The forests suffer for it, but the printed page is still the most convenient way to gain access to reference information. Visual Basic magazines and newsletters abound. The typical issue includes reviews of ActiveX controls and other software tools, tips, and secrets for handling difficult programming situations, and loads of source code. Most of these topics are directly applicable to VBA, and often, they even include VBA-specific articles.

Check out the following printed journals:

- *Microsoft Office & Visual Basic for Applications Developer* (Informant Communications Group, Inc., 10519 E. Stockton Blvd., Suite 100, Elk Grove, CA 95624-9703; phone 916-686-6610)

  ```
  www.officevba.com
  ```

✔ *Visual Basic Programmer's Journal* (Fawcette Technical Publications, 209 Hamilton Ave., Palo Alto, CA 94301; phone 650-833-7100)

```
www.windx.com
```

✔ *Inside Visual Basic* (Element K Journals, 800-223-8720)

```
www.elementkjournals.com/ivb/
```

Public VBA Web Sites

One way to convince your boss that you're working extremely hard without really straining is to spend hours of prep time on the Web. Tons of sites devote themselves to Visual Basic, and you can consume weeks tracking down obscure programming secrets and collecting ActiveX controls. You can assure the boss that eventually, when you finally get down to writing code, all your research will boost your productivity dramatically.

Programming pages on the Web are usually well endowed with links to other relevant sites. Starting with the following addresses, you should have no trouble finding enough to keep you busy:

✔ `www.vbapro.com/`

✔ `www.mvps.org/vbnet/`

✔ `www.vbcity.com/`

✔ `download.cnet.com` (choose the Software development link)

✔ `www.geocities.com/WallStreet/9245/`

✔ `odyssey.apana.org.au/~abrowne/homepage.html` (Access development)

✔ `www.slipstick.com/dev` (Outlook development)

✔ `www.outlookexchange.com` (Outlook and Exchange development)

Of course, you may also want to check out the Web sites maintained by the software tool vendors that I mention elsewhere in this chapter.

A Galaxy of ActiveX Controls

At last count, the number of ActiveX controls had already surpassed the count of stars in the known universe. If you can think of something you want your VBA program to do, chances are that somebody has already designed an ActiveX control to do it for you. You can choose from boatloads of ActiveX controls — and I've managed to round up a boatload or two of some of the best of these (in trial version form) for the *VBA For Dummies* 3rd Edition CD. And if you really can't find just the right control, maybe you've hit on a business opportunity — consider creating your own controls and marketing them to the masses.

Tool mania

Before you spend days assembling a collection of individual controls, consider buying a package deal. Many software publishers offer collections of ActiveX controls that cover the waterfront, or at least a few piers. Many such toolkits start with enhanced versions of the standard controls, with more formatting options and more control over data display. These are often supplemented with new kinds of controls, such as gas gauges, meters, and knobs. You may also get grid controls for working with spreadsheet and database data, "tree" controls that let you display information in a Windows Explorer-like window, controls for faxing or printing, and invisible controls that perform timing or let you fiddle with the Windows registry.

As a starting point, consider the offerings of the following companies:

Infragistics Corp.

www.protoview.com

ComponentOne LLC.

www.shersoft.com

Picturesque programming

Unaided, VBA does a pretty good job of importing pictures in various file formats and displaying them on your forms. But, if your VBA program needs to work with a format that VBA doesn't recognize or especially if you want to jazz up the images with special effects, you need an ActiveX graphics control set. One such product is:

Lead Tools

Available from: Lead Technologies Inc.

www.leadtools.com

Charts a la carte

Although it takes a sharp-thinking individual to comprehend the trends lying hidden in endless rows of numbers, anyone can understand a bar graph or pie chart, or at least claim to. VBA doesn't come with charting features, but you can add them easily with ActiveX controls such as:

ProEssentials
Available from: Gigasoft

```
www.gigasoft.com
```

teeChartPro
Available from: Steema Software

```
www.stema.com
```

3D Charting Toolkit
Available from: Nevron LLC

```
www.nevron.com
```

Word processing controls and spreadsheet grids

Text boxes are fine when you only need to collect a line or two of the user's input. If you expect your program to turn out complete, formatted documents, however, a text box obviously doesn't cut the mustard.

When it comes to presenting numbers and allowing the user to manipulate them, VBA is even more limited. You would have to be a card-carrying masochist — and have lots of time on your hands — to attempt building a spreadsheet-like grid for rows and columns of numbers using the VBA stock set of controls.

One very viable solution, if you have Word and Excel on your system, is to tap into their objects with VBA. No matter which VBA application your program runs inside, it can activate Word or Excel documents and extract their data using COM (see Chapter 14 for an overview of how this works).

Loading Word or Excel takes time though, and you don't have full control over the way they look on-screen. ActiveX controls offer nimbler, more customizable alternatives that you can integrate directly into your own forms. Try the following:

Spreadsheet control

Spread

Available from: FarPoint Technologies Inc.

```
www.fpoint.com
```

Formula One

Available from: Tidestone Technologies Inc.

```
www.tidestone.com
```

Word processing controls

TX Text Control

Available from: The Imaging Source America

```
www.theimagingsource.com
```

TE Developer's Kit

Available from: Sub Systems Inc.

```
www.subsystems.com
```

Take the money and run

Yet another of the many strangely wonderful things you can do with ActiveX controls is authorize credit card purchases via your modem or via direct Internet connections. If you're designing a custom system for order entry or retail point of sale, just plop the control on a form. You can then use its methods and properties to send the bank the credit card information from your customers and retrieve the bank's verdict on their creditworthiness. Of course, using a custom form to process credit card orders only makes sense if you're developing a full-scale database system. If you're working in VBA instead of Visual Basic, you're most likely using Access.

PCCharge DevKit

Network Commerce Inc.

```
www.gosoftinc.com
```

Design your own controls

Microsoft isn't just allowing third-party developers to create ActiveX controls — they're actively fomenting such efforts. Visual Basic 5 and 6 come with the tools you need to create your own controls. Be aware that you may need to include the Visual Basic run-time files when you distribute programs containing controls built using Visual Basic. Don't forget to include installation instructions with the files.

Miscellaneous Stuff

Aside from ActiveX controls, a variety of other alluring software tools beckon the harried VBA programmer, sweetly promising to make the development cycle speedier and less painful — for a fee, of course.

Industrial strength calculations

The strengths of VBA lie in the areas of object-oriented programming and visual forms design. When it comes to raw calculation speed, however, VBA falls behind other programming languages. If you're writing programs for NASA or the Census Bureau, consider the PowerBasic compiler. PowerBasic calculations run 4 to 20 times faster than the same code running in Visual Basic, according to one extremely unbiased source (PowerBasic's publisher).

PowerBasic isn't a replacement for VBA but rather an add-on to it. You still use VBA to get the program started, to communicate with objects in your application, and to display forms. However, you compile the code for your hard-core calculations with PowerBasic, which turns it into special DLL programs that VBA can activate when the time is right. Although it doesn't have VBA's object-oriented features, the core of the PowerBasic language is virtually identical to VBA, so you won't have much to learn.

PowerBASIC Inc.

www.powerbasic.com

Help, help!

You won't have any trouble getting your VBA programs to display custom Help screens, but creating the Help files in the first place isn't so easy — unless *you* get help.

The official way to construct a Help file involves tiresome labor and lots of trial and error with a boring, inscrutable, non-visual programming language. Nobody does it that way. Instead, follow the crowd and get yourself a program that converts the output of your word processor into a Help file automatically. That way, you can set up your Help file visually, much like you create forms in VBA. Up-to-date tools that support both "classic" Windows Help and the newer HTML Help format include:

RoboHelp

eHelp Corp.

```
www.ehelp.com
```

EasyHelp/Web and EasyHTML/Help

Eon Solutions Ltd.

```
www.eon-solutions.com
```

Appendix

About the CD

*H*ere's some of what you can find on the *VBA For Dummies*, 3rd Edition CD-ROM:

- ✔ Six bonus chapters on the CD (fully indexed and listed in the Table of Contents at the beginning of the book).

- ✔ Source code files containing sample code from the book — for anyone who hates to type.

- ✔ A wide variety of shareware and demo versions of ActiveX controls that you can use to dress up your VBA forms.

- ✔ Utilities for managing ActiveX controls and the Windows Registry, and for adding macro and AutoCorrect capabilities to the VBA development environment.

- ✔ A trial version of ClipMate, an indispensable Windows Clipboard enhancement utility — great for programming VBA code, and for general use in Windows, too.

- ✔ Trial versions of EasyHTML/Help and EasyHelp/Web (user-friendly tools that convert Microsoft Word documents into Windows Help files), which are perfect for creating online documentation for your custom VBA programs.

System requirements

Make sure that your computer meets the minimum system requirements in the following list. If your computer doesn't match up to most of these requirements, you may have problems in using the contents of the CD — but then, you probably wouldn't be able to run your VBA application either.

- ✔ A PC with a 486 or faster processor.

- ✔ Microsoft Windows 95 or later, or Microsoft NT 4 or later.

- ✔ At least 32MB of total RAM installed on your computer.

- ✔ At least enough available hard drive space to install software from this CD — you need less space if you don't install every program.

- ✔ A CD-ROM drive.

If you need more information on the basics, check out these books published by Hungry Minds, Inc.: *PCs For Dummies,* by Dan Gookin; *Windows 95 For Dummies, Windows 98 For Dummies, Windows 2000 Professional For Dummies, Microsoft Windows ME For Dummies,* all by Andy Rathbone.

How to use the CD

To install items from the CD to your hard drive, follow these steps:

1. **Insert the CD into your computer's CD-ROM drive.**

2. **Click the Start button and choose Run from the menu.**

3. **In the dialog box that appears, type** d:\start.htm.

    Replace *d* with the proper drive letter for your CD-ROM if it uses a different letter. (If you don't know the letter, double-click the My Computer icon on your desktop and see what letter is listed for your CD-ROM drive.)

    Your browser opens, and the license agreement is displayed.

4. **Read through the license agreement, nod your head, and click the Accept button if you want to use the CD.**

    After you click Accept, you're taken to the Main menu. This is where you can browse through the contents of the CD.

5. **To navigate within the interface, click any topic of interest to take you to an explanation of the files on the CD and how to use or install them.**

6. **To install software from the CD, simply click the software name.**

    You'll see two options: to run or open the file from the current location or to save the file to your hard drive. Choose to run or open the file from its current location, and the installation procedure continues. When you finish using the interface, close your browser as usual.

Note: We have included an "easy install" in these HTML pages. If your browser supports installations from within it, go ahead and click on the links of the program names you see. You'll see two options: "Run the file from the current location" or "Save the file to your hard drive." Choose to "Run the file from the current location" and the installation procedure will continue. A Security Warning dialog box appears. Click Yes to continue the installation.

To run some of the programs on the CD, you may need to keep the disc inside your CD-ROM drive. This is a good thing. Otherwise, a very large chunk of the program would be installed to your hard drive, consuming valuable hard drive space and possibly keeping you from installing other software.

What you'll find

The following sections summarize software that's included on the *VBA For Dummies,* 3rd Edition CD.

Bonus VBA For Dummies chapters

Since VBA programming is big topic, I simply didn't have room for everything I wanted to cover in the printed book. In the six bonus chapters we've provided on the CD, I expanded on topics that are vital to many VBA programmers, with an emphasis on Microsoft Office-specific issues. The chapters are fully formatted and illustrated, just like the chapters in the book, and come in PDF format for viewing and printing with the Adobe Acrobat Reader, also included on the CD-ROM. Better, the content of the chapters is even indexed and included in the book's Table of Contents.

The CD chapters are as follows:

- **Bonus Chapter A, "VBA Programming in Office":** Provides programming tips that are applicable to all Microsoft Office applications, covering such topics as customizing toolbars, taking control of the Office Assistant ("Clippy"), and storing program information with specific documents.

- **Bonus Chapter B, "VBA Programming in Word":** Shows you how to handle common Word-specific programming tasks such as manipulating windows, selecting and inserting text, and searching for and replacing content or formatting.

- **Bonus Chapter C, "VBA Programming in Excel":** Gives you the skinny on working with cells, ranges, and worksheets in your code, creating custom functions for use in worksheets, using Excel's built-in functions in your VBA code, and tapping Excel events so your programs can respond dynamically to worksheet changes.

- **Bonus Chapter D, "Database Programming":** A meaty chapter that serves as a solid yet compact introduction to the techniques you need to access and modify information stored in databases on your own hard drive or the network server. Using these techniques, you can endow your VBA programs with database prowess whether you're working in Access, Word, CorelDraw, or any other VBA application.

- **Bonus Chapter E, "Working with Disk Files":** Covers VBA's built-in system for reading and writing disk files, an alternative to the object-based method covered in Chapter 14.

- **Bonus Chapter F, "More on VBA Forms":** This chapter is packed with ideas for enhancing the custom dialog boxes you build with VBA. I describe how to add (and remove) graphics, customize the mouse pointer, use the VBA MultiPage control for tabbed dialog boxes, and much more.

VBA For Dummies source code

In the *VBA For Dummies* source code folder on the CD-ROM, you'll find lots of VBA source code and UserForm files from the text. Because getting "real" results from VBA depends so much on the application you're using, these little programs don't do much of practical value. However, they do illustrate basic techniques of VBA programming, and you may prefer to use them in this pre-fab form instead of retyping the code from the book. When necessary, I enclose code fragments in real procedures so that they'll run correctly without additional work on your part.

The source code and UserForm files are organized by book chapter into subfolders. You can access these files from the CD as needed or use our "easy install" to copy them to your hard drive for later use. To use a source code module or UserForm, fire up the Visual Basic Editor, open the VBA project in which you want to use it, and then choose File⇨Import. In the resulting dialog box, navigate to the folder on the CD or your hard drive where the item is stored, select the module, form file, or class module you want to import, and then choose Open. The imported item appears in your project, where you can run it by pressing F5.

You're welcome to communicate questions or suggestions to me at VBA@ seldenhouse.com. I'll post any corrections or additions to the sample code to the following address:

http://www.seldonhouse.com/vba

Word macros

I've also included on the CD a set of custom Word macros that supply missing features or improve on existing ones. Each procedure is stored as a separate module in its own file so you can install them in any combination that suits you. I describe the function of each macro in the comments you can find in the code at the beginning of each module. Again, you can leave these files from the CD or use the "easy install" page to copy them to your hard drive for faster access.

Follow these steps to install a macro in Word:

1. **Open the Word template or document where the macro is to reside.**

2. **Switch to the Visual Basic Editor.**

3. **Choose File⇨Import.**

4. **In the dialog box that appears, navigate to the folder on the CD or your hard drive where the macro is stored.**

5. **Select the module file that you want to import choose and Open.**

   The imported item appears in your Word project. You can then use the techniques described in Chapter 4 to run it.

CodeCrafter_2000 from Code Craft Corp.

30-day Trial version. CodeCrafter 2000 is specifically designed as an add-in to the Visual Basic Editor in Microsoft Office and provides automated error-handling, commenting, and new code insertion. It formats your code for you, helps you build text and SQL strings, and can locate variables that you've declared but have never used in your code. For more information see: `http://www.codecrafter.com/TrialReg.htm`.

PrettyCode.Print from vbCity.Com

Shareware version. Use the freeware utility PrettyCode.Print to print out your source code on neatly formatted pages so that the code is easy to read. Select a separate font for various code items, such as procedure declarations, comments, and the body of the code, and print headers and footers that identify the source program. If you ask it to, PrettyCode.Print prints brackets around structures, such as `If...Then` statements and loops. See `http://www.vbcity.com` for more information.

Software from Eon Solutions, Ltd.

Shareware. EasyHelp/Web and EasyHTML/Help are excellent shareware Help development tools that let you use Microsoft Word to build custom Help files for your own VBA programs. EasyHelp/Web generates both WinHELP format and standard HTML files, and EasyHTML/Help produces Help files for Microsoft's HTML Help viewer. Also included on the CD is EasyCrypt, a simple file encryption program that password protects any file or folder — which may be a good idea when you're working on source code that you don't want others to see or play with. See `http://www.eon-solutions.com` for more info.

RoboHelp Office from eHelp Corp.

15-Day Trial version. RoboHelp is the acknowledged Cadillac of Help authoring tools. You can use it to build complete Help systems in any of several widely used formats (WinHelp, HTML, Microsoft HTML Help), with special features for adding Help to Web sites. RoboHelp comes with a comprehensive set of utilities for analyzing and streamlining your Help system. For more information, see `http://www.ehelp.com`.

Tools from GravityBox Software

Demo version. If you ever decide you need Outlook-like functionality in a program you plan to distribute to others, take a look at these cool packages of Active X controls:

- **GbSchedule**: Includes three ActiveX controls which together provide a complete set of programmable features for building sophisticated appointment scheduling applications.

- **GbDials**: Features five visually-interesting readout controls, including a thermometer and a faux-LED dial.

- **GbListBar:** A control for building vertical, graphical icon-based selection bars with the look of Microsoft's Outlook.

- **GbControlPack:** A set of six cool controls including a calendar, a text-based date input box with drop-down calendar, a toolbar with pushbuttons, and more.

- **GbColorCombo:** A control that lets users select colors from a dropdown palette.

- **GbGraphs:** Add simple charts and graphs to your forms.

See `http://www.gravitybox.com` for more info.

ProEssentials from GigaSoft

Evaluation version. ProEssentials are complete sets of ActiveX charting components for us VBA-heads. You can place the controls in ASP-based Web pages that you build in Access for dynamic charts that don't require the user to download the chart control. For more information, see `http://www.gigasoft.com`.

teeChartPro from Steema Software

Demo version. Another full set of ActiveX controls for use on your VBA forms and ASP pages. For more information, see `http://www.steema.com`.

3DCharting Toolkit from Nevron LLC

Consisting of 5 ActiveX controls, this package enables you to add very cool, graphically sophisticated 3D charts and text to your programs. For more information, see `http://www.nevron.com`.

CodeBase from Sequiter Software

Trial version. CodeBase is a complete database system for programmers based on the tried-and-true dBase/FoxPro file format. For us VBA-heads, CodeBase comes with ActiveX controls that tie your data to your on-screen forms; an object-based interface to the data through ADO is also available. For more information, see `http://www.sequiter.com`.

COM Explorer, Registry Crawler, and SimpleRegistry Control from 4Developers

Trial versions. The 4Developers tools found on the CD include

- **COM Explorer:** A powerful utility for exploring, managing, and fixing ActiveX Controls and other components.

- **Registry Crawler:** A quick, robust search tool for the Windows registry with bookmarks that enable you to access any Registry key directly from the system tray.

✔ **SimpleRegistry:** An ActiveX control that lets your VBA programs store and retrieve information from the Windows Registry with more control than you get in VBA.

For more info, see `http://www.4developers.com`.

VBToolBox and SafeCard from Massinissa Software

Trial versions. VBToolBox is an ActiveX control that packages 30 Windows API functions into a single control to add advanced functionality to your VBA programs with little codings.

SafeCard is a plug-in component for validating credit and debit cards. Use it in point-of-sale and Web-based business programs you write in Access or other VBA applications.

See `http://www.massinissa.com` for more info.

TX Text Control from The Imaging Source

Trial version. TX Text Control is a full-featured word processor encapsulated into an ActiveX control. As an Office VBA programmer, you can tap Word for word processing chores. This approach, however, has its drawbacks: All users of your program must have Word on their systems, and Word, because it's such a big application and uses so much memory and system resources, can slow down your program. See `http://www.theimagingsource.com` for more information.

Tools from Polar Software

Trial versions. Polar Software offers a cool set of powerful ActiveX controls including

✔ **Polar Draw:** Provides powerful features for creating line-art (vector) graphics. Flow-charting and text-editing features are included.

✔ **Polar Crypto:** Lets you password-encrypt and -decrypt confidential files from your VBA programs by using high-level security (using encryption keys up to 256 bits in length).

✔ **Polar Zip:** Gives your VBA programs the ability to save and open industry standard ZIP-format compressed files. Encryption features are also included.

For more information, see `http://www.polarsoftware.com`.

Jetpack from Chisel Software

Evaluation version. If you're planning to add database features to your VBA program and don't want to use Access, Jetpack may be the ticket. It's a collection of ActiveX controls that let you create, modify, search, query, and report on Microsoft Jet databases (see the online Chapter "Database Programming" for details on your options when it comes to writing database programs in VBA). See `http://www.chiselsoftware.com` for more information.

Access 2000 to Visual Basic 6 Converter from Irie Software

Shareware versions. Access is a great database development tool, but Visual Basic is better for distributing applications to other users. But if you've developed an Access database and want to convert it to Visual Basic, you've got some serious labor ahead to consider. Consider the Access 2000 to Visual Basic 6 Converter, which handles much of the grunt work for you. See http://www.iriesoftware.com for more info.

Tools from Blue Squirrel Software

Demo versions. Some of the demos from Blue Squirrel on the CD include

- **ClickBook:** A printing utility that works within Windows to allow printing customized day planner pages, wallet booklets, brochures, greeting cards, catalogs, microfiche, and more from Internet, Windows, or CD-ROM files! ClickBook helps you scale, rotate, and duplex your digital photos, favorite on-line content, or other critical information into more than 40 mobile and convenient layouts. You can even design your own custom layouts and save up to 70 percent in paper costs!

- **ASP Charge:** An ActiveX control that lets you add automated credit card processing to your point-of-sale or e-commerce VBA programs.

- **Grab-a-Site:** This utility downloads complete Web sites to your hard drive, retaining the original names and directory structure and making the Web pages themselves accessible offline.

See `http://www.bluesquirrel.com` for more info.

List & Label from combit GMBH

Trial version. List & Label is an ActiveX control that encapsulates a complete form and label design, mail merge, and reporting application into a drop-in component There are almost unlimited options for creating reports, sub-reports and combinations of lists and other objects. See `http://www.combit.net/us` for more information.

Tools from Developer Express, Inc.

15-day trial versions (excepting XpressSideBar, which is freeware). Developer Express' ActiveX components cover the waterfront with the following individual tools:

- **XpressEditors Library:** A set of 15 individual edit controls for displaying, entering, and modifying information on your VBA forms.

- **XpressInspector:** A very flexible vertical grid for editing data.

- ✔ **XpressPrinting System:** A control that adds printing functions to your programs.

- ✔ **XpressQuantumGrid:** An all-in-one control for displaying data in tree format or in lists or grids.

- ✔ **XpressQuantumTreeList:** A control for presenting data in lists and hierarchical tree formats.

- ✔ **XpressSideBar:** An Outlook-style navigation bar.

See http://www.devexpress.com for more information.

ClipMate from ThornSoft Development

Shareware version. ClipMate dramatically enhances the Windows clipboard. This great shareware utility is a necessity for anyone doing serious editing, whether you're working with code, text, or graphics. See http://www.thornsoft.com for more info.

Macro Magic from Iolo Technologies

Trial version. Macro Magic is an award-winning utility for automating repetitive tasks in Windows applications — including the Visual Basic Editor — that lack their own macro recorders. It records and plays back keyboard and mouse actions and enables you to enter sequences of actions, such as opening a file or pausing until a specified window appears. See http://www.iolo.com/download/default1.htm for more information.

Tools from Insight Software Solutions

Shareware versions. Insight offers a passel of little programs that may well find a place in your software toolkit. The utilities found on the CD include

- ✔ **Macro Express,** a high-end keyboard-and-mouse macro programs.

- ✔ **Keyboard Express**, a more economical and more basic macro utility

- ✔ **ShortKeys**, which turns short abbreviations into complete text entries-much like Word's AutoCorrect feature – which means you won't have to repeatedly retype those long variable and procedure names in your code.

- ✔ **Capture Express**, a straightforward screen capture utility.

- ✔ **SmartBoard**, which competes with ClipMate as a powerful enhancement to the Windows Clipboard.

- ✔ **Web Compiler**, which converts HTML Web pages into standalone hypertext applications that users can view without firing up their browser.

See http://www.wintools.com for more information.

Acrobat Reader from Adobe Systems

Freeware version. Adobe's ever-popular PDF viewer software is available on the CD if you don't already have it (you'll need a PDF viewer to read the bonus chapters on the CD). See `http://www.adobe.com` for more information.

If you have problems (of the CD kind)

When you're working with complex software, you always face the possibility of glitches. If you can't get the items on the CD-ROM to work properly, the two likeliest problems are that you don't have enough memory (RAM) for the programs you want to use, or you have other programs running that are affecting installation or running of a program. If you get error messages, such as `Not enough memory` or `Setup cannot continue`, try one or more of the following methods and then try using the software again:

- **Turn off any antivirus software that you have on your computer.** Installers sometimes mimic virus activity and may make your computer incorrectly believe that a virus is infecting it.

- **Close all running programs.** The more programs you're running, the less memory is available to other programs. Installers also typically update files and programs. If you keep other programs running, installation may not work properly.

- **Add more RAM to your computer.** This is, admittedly, a drastic and somewhat expensive step. However, adding more memory can really help the speed of your computer and allow more programs to run at the same time.

- **Reference the ReadMe.txt:** Please refer to the ReadMe file located at the root of the CD-ROM for the latest product information at the time of publication.

If you still have trouble with installing the items from the CD, please call the Hungry Minds Customer Service phone number: 800-762-2974 (outside the U.S.: 317-572-3993). If the installation process goes all right but the software itself doesn't seem to run, contact the manufacturers at the Web sites that I listed throughout this appendix, or via the phone numbers shown in the accompanying electronic documentation.

Index

Hungry Minds, Inc.
End-User License Agreement

5. **Limited Warranty.**

   (a) HMI warrants that the Software and Software Media are free from defects in materials and workmanship under normal use for a period of sixty (60) days from the date of purchase of this Book. If HMI receives notification within the warranty period of defects in materials or workmanship, HMI will replace the defective Software Media.

   (b) **HMI AND THE AUTHOR OF THE BOOK DISCLAIM ALL OTHER WARRANTIES, EXPRESS OR IMPLIED, INCLUDING WITHOUT LIMITATION IMPLIED WARRANTIES OF MERCHANTABILITY AND FITNESS FOR A PARTICULAR PURPOSE, WITH RESPECT TO THE SOFTWARE, THE PROGRAMS, THE SOURCE CODE CONTAINED THEREIN, AND/OR THE TECHNIQUES DESCRIBED IN THIS BOOK. HMI DOES NOT WARRANT THAT THE FUNCTIONS CONTAINED IN THE SOFTWARE WILL MEET YOUR REQUIREMENTS OR THAT THE OPERATION OF THE SOFTWARE WILL BE ERROR FREE.**

   (c) This limited warranty gives you specific legal rights, and you may have other rights that vary from jurisdiction to jurisdiction.

6. **Remedies.**

   (a) HMI's entire liability and your exclusive remedy for defects in materials and workmanship shall be limited to replacement of the Software Media, which may be returned to HMI with a copy of your receipt at the following address: Software Media Fulfillment Department, Attn.: *VBA For Dummies,* 3rd Edition, Hungry Minds, Inc., 10475 Crosspoint Blvd., Indianapolis, IN 46256, or call 1-800-762-2974. Please allow four to six weeks for delivery. This Limited Warranty is void if failure of the Software Media has resulted from accident, abuse, or misapplication. Any replacement Software Media will be warranted for the remainder of the original warranty period or thirty (30) days, whichever is longer.

   (b) In no event shall HMI or the author be liable for any damages whatsoever (including without limitation damages for loss of business profits, business interruption, loss of business information, or any other pecuniary loss) arising from the use of or inability to use the Book or the Software, even if HMI has been advised of the possibility of such damages.

   (c) Because some jurisdictions do not allow the exclusion or limitation of liability for consequential or incidental damages, the above limitation or exclusion may not apply to you.

7. **U.S. Government Restricted Rights.** Use, duplication, or disclosure of the Software for or on behalf of the United States of America, its agencies and/or instrumentalities (the "U.S. Government") is subject to restrictions as stated in paragraph (c)(1)(ii) of the Rights in Technical Data and Computer Software clause of DFARS 252.227-7013, or subparagraphs (c) (1) and (2) of the Commercial Computer Software - Restricted Rights clause at FAR 52.227-19, and in similar clauses in the NASA FAR supplement, as applicable.

8. **General.** This Agreement constitutes the entire understanding of the parties and revokes and supersedes all prior agreements, oral or written, between them and may not be modified or amended except in a writing signed by both parties hereto that specifically refers to this Agreement. This Agreement shall take precedence over any other documents that may be in conflict herewith. If any one or more provisions contained in this Agreement are held by any court or tribunal to be invalid, illegal, or otherwise unenforceable, each and every other provision shall remain in full force and effect.

Installation Instructions

To install items from the CD to your hard drive, follow these steps:

1. **Insert the CD into your computer's CD-ROM drive.**

2. **Click the Start button and choose Run from the menu.**

3. **In the dialog box that appears, type** d:\start.htm.

   Replace *d* with the proper drive letter for your CD-ROM if it uses a different letter. (If you don't know the letter, double-click the My Computer icon on your desktop and see what letter is listed for your CD-ROM drive.)

   Your browser opens, and the license agreement is displayed.

4. **Read through the license agreement, nod your head, and click the Accept button if you want to use the CD.**

   After you click Accept, you're taken to the Main menu. This is where you can browse through the contents of the CD.

5. **To navigate within the interface, click any topic of interest to take you to an explanation of the files on the CD and how to use or install them.**

6. **To install software from the CD, simply click the software name.**

   You'll see two options: to run or open the file from the current location or to save the file to your hard drive. Choose to run or open the file from its current location, and the installation procedure continues. When you finish using the interface, close your browser as usual.

   Note: An "easy install" is included in these HTML pages. If your browser supports installations from within it, go ahead and click on the links of the program names you see. You'll see two options: "Run the file from the current location" or "Save the file to your hard drive." Choose to "Run the file from the current location" and the installation procedure will continue. A Security Warning dialog box appears. Click Yes to continue the installation.

To run some of the programs on the CD, you may need to keep the disc inside your CD-ROM drive. This is a good thing. Otherwise, a very large chunk of the program would be installed to your hard drive, consuming valuable hard drive space and possibly keeping you from installing other software.